ZAMBIA
STRUGGLES OF MY PEOPLE,
2nd EDITION

I0039523

VOLUME ONE

Charles Mwewa

Africa in Canada Press
Toronto
2017

ZAMBIA

Struggles of My People, 2nd Edition
Volume One

In text: Author, 2017
In published edition: Africa in Canada Press, 2017.

Second edition published in 2017 by:

AFRICA IN CANADA PRESS

www.africaincanadapress.com

All rights reserved. No part of this may be reproduced, stored in a retrieval system of transmitted, in any form or by any means, electronic, mechanical, photocopying or otherwise, without the prior written permission of the publisher/author.

© In text: Charles Mwewa
© In published edition: Second published 2017

Author: Charles Mwewa, www.charlesmwewa.com
Typesetting and design by: Charles Mwewa
Cover design by: PowerBrain, South Africa
Printing: Africa in Canada Press

ISBN: 978-1-988251-12-7 (Canada)
ISBN-10: 1988251125

The publishers have made every effort to trace and acknowledge copyright holders, but if any have inadvertently been overlooked, they will be pleased to make the necessary arrangements at the first opportunity.

DEDICATION

For

Cuteravieve,

With all my love!

PREFACE

This book was originally published by Maiden Publishing House in Lusaka, Zambia in 2011. There are three reasons why I undertook to update the original manuscript from one book into a second edition comprising three volumes. First, it is due to changes both at home and globally which warranted the update. And second, the first edition was published as a one stop-shop for all themes and topics on Zambia. It captured Zambian history, economy, law, politics, culture, and so on. This framework was initially necessary because it unified a singular Zambian story within one book. However, the bulkiness of the first edition, which totaled 1,100 pages, made it a big challenge for the readership. Three relatively smaller chunks of the same book were required to enable quick and accessible readership as well as the use in, not just the academia, but for social consumption. Third, the recommendations made by the Ministry of General Education (Zambia) – Curriculum Development Center – were invaluable in the reconstruction of the book.

The result, therefore, has been a restructuring of the book into three volumes, following closely the pattern divide of the original manuscript. There is, in addition, minor variations in terms of chapter-count. Where possible, grammar has been polished and minor typos have been fixed. This book is volume one of the second edition. Each of the three volumes begins from Chapter 1, respectively, and omits the sequestration into parts from the original manuscript.

A companion Test Bank (ISBN: 978-1-988251-18-9) has accompanied this volume, providing ready answers to suggested multiple-choice questions. Key words used in each chapter and a set of review challenge questions have been included in the Test Bank. This companion is designed for instructors and professors using this volume as an academic textbook. In limited situations, however, students may find this companion useful only as a test of understanding of the chapter after independently completing the assessment.

Indexing, footnoting and stylistic changes are prominent in these volumes and have been adjusted to respective page counts. The speech given by Professor Dickson Mwansa, founder of the Zambian Open University, has been upgraded to a foreword in all the three volumes. The reordering is deliberate, to impress upon the reader, the uniqueness of the book and the political-neutral tone under which it has been written. The three volumes transform the original manuscript from a self-serve, interest-based magnum opus into an academic-specific textbook for Zambian colleges and universities, especially those participating in a Zambianization 101 Course.

The entire Selected Bibliography from the original manuscript has been retained as well, with the addition of selected new Zambian titles in the marketplace. The strategic inclusion of the entire over-fifty-page worth of reference resource is designed to provide a source for further research on issues and themes covered in these volumes.

The Story of Zambia's Struggle

The story of Zambia's struggles is one that affects every Zambian, past, present and future. It is the story of Zambia's journey towards true independence. When they gained that sweet independence, it was not envisaged that with it would come with enormous challenges, challenges of not their making, challenges, sometimes artificial and machined. Every former colony of the imperial powers has had to go through similar challenges as Zambia has done.

Nevertheless, Zambia's story is different. Unlike most newly independent African countries which had been left with sufficient numbers of educated personnel to man industries, burn power, and run governments, Zambia was poorly inherited, with only a very few educated men and women. For a few years after independence, a honeymoon period of relative prosperity, Zambian fathers drove the economic and political machine with fewer troubles.

However, like a volcano that brews underground, the resource-depletion of the Central African Federation, the inadequacy of educated and skilled manpower, and the novice management skills of the first leaders began to erupt slowly but steadily. Molten magma of political and economic fusion would not stop even for a minute after that. It continued to spread like a malignant cancer, wiping out health cells and obliterating newly grown ones.

This cancer continues to give Zambia no breathing space. It continues to defy all odds. But there is hope, because Zambia is not a destination. Zambia is a journey. It was conceived between 1911 and 1952 in the ecclesiastical haciendas by the first African devoted men in Northern Rhodesia who passed the torch to the freedom fighters during the Federation from 1953 to 1963. The Republic of Zambia was born on October 24th, 1964 as a unitary state, as opposed to a federal state, with a president, a unicameral National Assembly, and a constitutionally independent Judiciary. This Sub-Saharan Republic was born landlocked, surrounded by eight strong neighbors: Angola to the west; the Democratic Republic of Congo (Congo DR) to the north-west; Tanzania to the north-east; Malawi to the east; Mozambique to the south-east; Zimbabwe to the south; and Botswana and Namibia to the south-west.

Post-colonial Zambia, comprising a population demographic of 99.5 percent Africans and 0.5 percent others, is a habitat of four Republics. The First Republic spanned from 1964 to 1972. This was followed by the Second Republic from 1973 to 1990. The MMD government under Frederick Chiluba (also known as FTJ) ushered in the Third Republic in 1991. A Fourth Republic is said to have been triggered by the Patriotic Front (PF) in 2011 under the administration of Michael Sata.

The land of Zambia lies on a great African plateau chunking an area of about 752,614 square kilometers. At its widest point, Zambia is about 1,167 kilometers from East to West, and about 1,046 kilometers from North to South. Known as the *air-conditioner* state in Africa, Zambia boasts of the cool and dry, hot and dry, and hot and wet seasons. From as low as eight degrees Celsius to as high as 35 degrees Celsius, the land attracts as little as 700 milliliters of rains in its drier parts to as much as 1,400 milliliters in the northern rainfall areas.

A unique nation, Zambia owes its peculiar shape to the colonial process which carved Africa into many pieces. Peter Burnell of the University of Warwick calls this peculiar shape, "The butterfly-shaped country of Zambia." The mighty Zambezi River lends the name to the nation, is flanked by three others, and is the longest in the country.

The beginning of Zambia is, thus, known, but the end is elusive. What is clear, however, is the resilience of the Zambian people to face every challenge with grace. Its leaders, past and present, though sometimes with grand errors which all human beings are prone to, have worked very hard and under difficult circumstances to create for the Zambian people a good future.

The *struggles of my people*, however, are older than Zambia itself. From as early as 1889 when Litunga Lewanika realized he had been tricked into signing a bogus treaty; to the early 1900s when Donald Siwale and his colleagues decided to discuss why it was that Africans were being called "boys" by Europeans although they were grown up men; to the shooting to death of six Black Africans by the White Northern Rhodesian police in 1935; to the passing of the Federation of Rhodesia and Nyasaland Order-in-Council of 1953 which discriminated against the interests of the territorial governments with those of the federal government; to two years before Zambian independence when in 1962 the colonial government designed a constitution which granted electoral advantage in the Legislative Council to the Whites at the expense of the Africans; to the signing of the Barotseland Agreement in 1964; to independence; our people have braced struggles far-reaching and vexatious.

The dream of the Zambian fathers and mothers was, and has always been, the creation of a nation with democratic means of governance which exerts the general will, guards against the emergence of any form of dictatorship, entrenches and protects human rights, embraces the Rule of Law and provides avenues for good governance. This dream is awake in every Zambian at home and abroad. It may diminish due to marauding circumstances and deprived occurrences that have relegated the nation to oblivion, but deep down the national psyche, this dream lives on.

Themes in the Book

There are five major themes in this book. Each chapter is the elucidation of any one of these themes or a combination of them. Whatever the case may be, these themes are designed to bring to light the political, economic and personal struggles of the Zambian people from pre-colonial to post-Third Republic Zambia. The themes illustrate:

First, that democracy and development in Zambia cannot be adequately defined without taking into consideration Zambia's uniqueness and historical factors that impact upon its culture, society and future well-being;

Second, that a definite change of mind-set is essential if Zambia is to manipulate its people, natural and financial resources into productivity;

Third, that generational disparity exists in Zambian leadership formation that affects the choice of developmental models and for the most part, limits its investment, innovativeness and technological proficiency;

Fourth, that a combination of, or hybrid, ideological and pragmatic approach is necessary to unlocking Zambia's economic potential; and

Fifth, that a belligerent approach espoused by the International Financial Institutions, Cooperating Partners and the donor governments pre-empts Zambia's most coveted inventiveness, sophistication and free experimentation.

Beyond the Themes

For Zambia to emerge as a key player and an equal partner in terms of the economy, politics and technology, it must vigorously analyze past events, and hopefully learn from them, and insist that it has what it takes to transform its people and means of production into a viable resource and to proactively exert its place in the community of nations.

Zambia is rich, diverse and relatively well-resourced country. One can brag about its land and peoples. Specifically, of its great reservoir of information that can positively impact on its *Collective Political Conscience* (CPC); its rich nature, teeming with beautiful natural wildlife; its long winding rivers inundated with healthy, sumptuous fishes and reptiles; its dams, man-made and natural; its valleys and mountains falling and rising like the waves of the magnificent Mosi-oa-Tunya Falls (Victoria Falls); its flora, green and lashing with nutrients; its fauna, indeed, an exploration into African animal diversity; its culture, rich, sundry and emblematic of its sense of order, respect and deference; its languages, seventy and over, and yet, Zambia remains united and flourishing in inter-tribal amity; its mineral wealth, precious and the envy of the world; its people, mostly Black (with a diversity of other colors), industrious and deeply friendly; its politics, democratic, elections fair and free, and peaceful conduct of elections for over fifty years.

To that list, we can add the potency of its intellectuality, the brilliance of its professors, the beauty of its environs, the virility of its traditions, the forte of its resolve, the stability of its CPC, the endurance of its progeny, and the hope of a continued free, democratic and prosperous society.

The Uniqueness of the Book

This book is a comprehensive documentation in significant details, yet in an easy-to-understand format, of the struggles of the Zambian people. It is significant in five substantial ways: First, many books written about Zambia tackle a specific topic, for example on politics, economics or gender. This book deals with most of the aspects which are a subject of the struggles of the Zambian people, including political, economic and social issues.

Second, most books written about Zambia draw upon outside sources researched by non-Zambian authors and scholars. This book, while relying on outside sources to some extent, for the most part, draws upon the works done by Zambians and augments them with stories and experiences of the real Zambians. It is a documentation of the experiences and struggles of the Zambians.

Third, this is one of the few books which give greater weight on the issue of corruption in Zambia. The chapters on the *Universality of Corruption* and the *Chiluba Matrix* covered in Volume Two add an aura of balance to the fight against corruption in Zambia. Many books on Zambia give only anecdotal reference to corruption. This book argues in context, and proffers a local and international framework under which corruption thrives and must be addressed.

This is one of the first books to give a comprehensive review of economic policies which have come to define Zambia, and offers suggestions for economic recovery. In this vein, and considered together, this is the first book which offers a comprehensive economic recovery theory on Zambia. This is a huge move away from simply documenting economic factors or simply re-stating economic and political challenges affecting Zambia. The chapters on sexual-orientation, on Dual Citizenship and the discussion on the Diaspora, give a holistic view of human rights in Zambia, and the economic and practical benefit of the Dual Citizenship and the Diaspora to Zambia, respectively.

Fourth, in its three volume sets, this book is a one-stop-shop and shifts towards a global approach to discussing issues pertinent to Zambia. The book is adequate and does not need supplementary material for the complete understanding of the struggles of the Zambian people. Although topic-specific books may give additional resources for the clear articulation of many issues affecting Zambians, this book alone is enough for the most part.

Fifth and last, the style employed in this book meets the needs of both lay and expert readership. The personal approach employed to the social aspects of the struggle such as poverty (see chapters 2, 3 and 4), for example, grants a human element to the struggles of the people of Zambia while the objective approach in discussing economic, political and democratic aspects lend an intellectual nudge to the struggle.

Comprehensive Digest

This book has been written from a comprehensive research perspective on issues pertinent to the struggles for self-assertiveness of the people of Zambia, their quest for true freedom, and the prospects of the future for a free, democratic and prosperous Zambia. Special notice of the contributions of many Zambians and other authors on Zambia to the struggles affecting Zambians has been taken. Consequently, as much space as possible has been devoted to Zambian authors, researchers and scholars to return a flavor that is truly Zambian.

Each chapter in the book has been comprehensively researched and written. However, for a complete understanding of political, economic, media or social issues, the following resources are recommended:

On colonialism and the struggles for Zambia's independence, Sophena Chisembele, *Zambia: The Freedom Struggle and the Aftermath*; Henry S. Mebeelo, *Reaction to Colonialism*; Bizeck Jube Phiri, *A Political History of Zambia: From the Colonial Period to the Third Republic;* William D. Grant, *Zambia: Then and Now;* Alexander Grey Zulu, *Memoirs of Alexander Grey Zulu;* Kapasa Makasa, *Zambia's March to Political Freedom*; Simon Mwansa Kapwepwe, *We Can Forgive But We Cannot Forget;* Wittington Sikalumbi, *Before UNIP*; G. Mwangilwa, *Harry M. Nkumbula: A Biography of the Old Lion of Zambia*.

On poverty and poverty reduction strategies, *Africa Social Research* by the University of Zambia's Institute of Economic and Social Research; *Assessment of Poverty Reduction Strategies (PRSP) in Sub-Saharan Africa: Case of Zambia* by OSSREA; *Poverty Reduction in a Political Trap: The PRS Process and Neo-Patrimonialism in Zambia* by Walter Eberlei, Peter Meyns, and Fred Mutesa; and *Cassava is the Root* by Rhoda Namwalizi Lester.

On civil war, the military and peace and order in Zambia, Patrick Wele, *Zambia's Most Famous Dissidents*; William Simukwasa, *Coup! or Civil Military Relations (CMR) in Zambia: A Review of Zambia's Contemporary CMR History and Challenges of Disarmament, Demobilization and Reintegration* edited by Gilbert Chileshe, Margaret Chimanse, Naison Ngoma and Paul Lwando.

On Zambian politics, Beatwell S. Chisala, *The Downfall of President Kaunda;* John Mwanakatwe, *End of Kaunda Era* and *Teacher, Politician, Lawyer;* Kirbey Lockhart, Zambia *Shall Be Saved*; Frederick T.J. Chiluba, *Democracy: The Challenge of Change*; Amos Malupenga, *Levy Patrick Mwanawasa: An Incentive for Posterity*; Billy Sichilongo Sichone, *Mwanawasa;* Akashambatwa Mbikusita Lewanika, *Hour for Reunion*; Mwelwa N. Chibesakunda, *Parliament of Zambia;* Kenneth Kaunda, *A Humanist in Africa* and *Zambia Shall Be Free;* Sikota Wina, *A Night Without a President*; Malama Sokoni and Temple, M., *Kaunda of Zambia*; and Vernon J. Mwaanga, *An Extraordinary Life.*

On foreign aid, the donors and development, *Aid and Poverty in Zambia: Mission Unaccomplished* by Oliver Saasa and Jerker Carlson; *Foreign Aid, Debt and Growth in Zambia* by Per-Ake Anderson, Arne Bigsten, and Hakan Parson; and *Dead Aid* by Dambisa Moyo.

On education in Zambia, Henry F. Mukulu, *Education, Development and National Building: A Study of New Trends and Philosophy of Education*; Dan O'Brien, *The Struggle for Control of Education in Zambia: From the Colonial Period to the Present;* and John Mwanakatwe, *Growth of Education in Zambia since Independence.*

On culture and traditions, the following books by Mwizenge S. Tembo are relevant: *The Bridge; Satisfying Zambian Hunger for Culture: Social Change in the Global World; Zambian Traditional Names: The Meaning of Tumbuka, Chewa, Ngoni, Nsenga, and Tonga Names; Afrikaanse Mythen en Lengenden;* and *Legends of Africa.*

On Zambian economy, *Difficult Decisions: Changing a Nation* by Richard Sakala; *Political and Economic Liberalization in Zambia* by Lise Rakner; *Zambia's Stock Exchange and Privatization Program* by Kenneth K. Mwenda; *Promoting and Sustaining Economic Reform in Zambia*, edited by Catharine Hill and Malcolm McPherson; *Israeli Settlement Assistance to Zambia, Nigeria and Nepal* by Moshe Schwartz; and *Social Welfare in Zambia* by Ndangwa Noyoo.

On Zambian mines, mineworkers, class struggles and urban development, *The Management of Urban Development in Zambia* by Emmanuel Mutale; *Mineworkers in Zambia: Labor and Political Change in Post-Colonial Africa* by Miles Larmer; and *Class Struggles in Zambia 1889-1989 & The Fall of Kenneth Kaunda 1990-1991* by Munyonzwe Hamalengwa.

On gender issues in Zambia *Africa's Troubled Political Disorder: A Case on Zambia; Aging in Zambian Cities,* by Ann Schlyter; and *Beyond Inequalities 2005: Women in Zambia* by Nakatiwa Mulikita.

On Zambian criminal justice, state of prisons and repression, Munyonzwe Hamalengwa's *Thoughts are Free*; Richard Sakala's *A Mockery of Justice*; Vernon J. Mwaanga's *A Detainee's Diary* and *The Other Society;* Simon Zukas' *Into Exile and Back*; and Miles Larmer's *The Musakanya Papers.* A gem on criminal justice and law in general in Zambia is Muna Ndulo, whose books include *The Law of Evidence in Zambia* (with John Hatchard); *A Case Book on Criminal Law* (with John Hatchard); and *Civil Liberties Cases in Zambia* (with T. Turner), among others.

Hamalengwa has written other books related to Zambian, Canadian, and international law, including: *The Book on Judges; Political Halley's Comet: The Death Penalty in Global Comparative Perspective; African-Canadians under Legal, Judicial, Political and Media Attack; The Case against Tribalism in Zambia; Getting Away with Impunity: International Criminal Law and the Prosecution of Apartheid Criminals; The Politics of Judicial Diversity and Transformation: Canada, USA, UK, Australia, South Africa, Israel, Colonial and Post-Colonial*

xiii

World and International Tribunals; and *The International Law of Human Rights in Africa.*

On media and press in Zambia, *The Worst of Kalaki and the Best of Yuss* by Roy Clarke; *Newspapers and Magazines in Zambia: A Question of Sustainability* by Fackson Banda; and *Community Radio: Its Management and Organization in Zambia* by Francis Kasoma P.

On medicine and health-related issues, *Green Medicines: Pharmacy of Natural Products for HIV and Five AIDS-related Infections* by Kazhila Chinsembu.

On Zambian law, from Kenneth K. Mwenda (alone, as an editor or in contribution to other authors' works): *Contemporary Issues in Zambian and English Company Law: A Comparative Study; Legal Aspects of Banking Regulation: Common Law Perspectives from Zambia; Public International Law and the Regulation of Diplomatic Immunity in the Fight against Corruption; German Hyperinflation 1922/1923 – A Law and Economics Approach; The Challenge of Change in Africa's Higher Education in the 21ˢᵗ Century; Comparing American and British Legal Education Systems: Lessons for Commonwealth African Law Schools; Country of Origin – A Law and Economics Approach to the Concept of 'Made in Australia'; Legal Aspects of Combating Corruption: the Case of Zambia; Legal Aspects of Financial Services Regulation and the Concept of a Unified Regulator; Combating Financial Crime: Legal, Regulatory and Institutional Frameworks; The Legal Administration of Financial Services in Common Law Jurisdictions: with special attention to the dual regulation system in Zambia; Contemporary Issues in International Economic Law; Economic Integration and Development in Africa; Anti-Money Laundering Law and Practice: Lessons from Zambia; Frontiers of Legal Knowledge: Business and Economic Law in Context; Principles of Arbitration Law; Banking and Micro-finance Regulation and Supervision: Lessons from Zambia; Zambia's Stock Exchange and Privatization Program: Corporate Finance Law in Emerging Markets; Banking Supervision and Systemic Bank Restructuring: An International and Comparative Legal Perspective; The Dynamics of Market Integration: African Stock*

Exchanges in the New Millennium; Contemporary Issues in Corporate Finance and Investment Law; Legal Aspects of Corporate Capital and Finance.

Kenneth Mwenda has also written four other volumes on public intellectualism and sociopolitical musing and inquiry titled *Public Intellectualism and Sociopolitical Inquiry through Metaphor and Musing.*

Organization of Volume One

This volume is organized *per* the following format. There are fourteen (14) chapters of related themes and topics. However, the five themes in the book may be found in any of these chapters provided they contribute to a unified and complete understanding of the political, economic and personal struggles of the Zambian people.

Chapter One relives the author's memories of Zambia's 19th independence celebrations as a child at Mibenge Primary School in Mibenge's village in Samfya-Mansa district of Luapula Province. It introduces the major theme of independence, the founding parents of the independent Republic of Zambia, and the promise of a prosperous, democratic and free nation. In Chapter Two, the author recounts his childhood experiences in Zambia. This chapter details the struggles of the Zambians at a personal level and the experiences of the author as a youth in the Second Republic. In Chapter Three, the author explores his contributions to the Zambian political process as a community organizer. Special regard is given to the University of Zambia (UNZA) and its place in Zambia's socio-political development. Chapter Four brings the theme of poverty to the fore. It discusses the events and actions that have relegated Zambia to a poorest and highly indebted nation. In addition, and this is one of the improvements made to the second edition, this chapter discusses shanty-towns in Zambia, drawing from the author's well-received articles which appeared in various online media between January 2015 and July 2016.

In Chapter Five the story of pre-independent Zambia is told, with implications on the political and economic future of the nation. The creation of Northern Rhodesia is discussed and the first four of the *five significant events* that laid the foundation of the difficulties and challenges Zambia would face after independence. Chapter Six discusses the last of the *five significant events* that laid the foundation for Zambia's struggles. It also discusses the struggles for independence in greater details, including the genesis of political organization in Zambia. In Chapter Seven, the author offers a theoretical basis for Zambia's independence and ascertains that independence was inevitable for the Black people of Zambia.

Chapter Eight discusses the Second Republic and the reign and downfall of President Kaunda. Chapter Nine explores coup attempts in Zambia and the factors that have led to their failure. In view of the future of Zambia, this chapter investigates the political implications of coup attempts to the nation's young democracy.

Chapter Ten focuses on the presidency of Zambia. As an institution called the presidency, and as a person who occupies that office, the presidency in Zambia has been pivotal to the very ethos of national politics. The presidency is discussed in relation to the military. The historical interaction between the presidency and the military in Zambia explains why even under extreme national distress, a coup has never materialized. Qualities that will define the president of Zambia in the 21st Century are discussed here, too. A special addition is made to this chapter on the suitability of women as presidents.

Chapter Eleven introduces the Rule of Law in Zambia and answers the question of whether law rules in Zambia in relation to the presidency of Levy Mwanawasa. Excerpts from the author's wildly-read column in the *Zambian Eye* dubbed "Law and Development" have been imported into this chapter to give a comprehensive understanding of the rule of law concept and its implication on presidential powers.

In Chapter Twelve, human rights are discussed. The chapter reminisces on what has historically been considered human wrongs and why they have ascended to human rights in the 21st

Century. The AU is brought to bear on the effectiveness or lack of it in protecting human rights violations in Africa in regards to regime change engineered by Western powers. The case of Libya is discussed as well.

Chapter Thirteen lays bare the issue of repression in Zambia. Real victims can retell their ordeals and from their account lessons are learned that future Zambian leaders should take to heart in their quest to create a just, strong, free and democratic nation.

Chapter Fourteen discusses criminal justice in Zambia and the state of Zambian prisons from the historical perspective.

Style Used in this Book

The book (in all three volumes) is written in American English, with appropriate British or Canadian English equivalent where required. Depending on purpose, whether for personal struggles or to highlight the personal experiences of the author, the first-person pronoun is employed. However, where an objective assessment is required, the third person is used accordingly. This variation is necessary to capture the personal, political and economic struggles of the Zambian people.

Charles Mwewa
April 2017
Toronto, Canada

ACKNOWLEDGMENTS

Three people deserve to be acknowledged. Dr. Munyonzwe Hamalengwa, professor of law and at the time of revising this book, Acting Dean of the School of Law, at the Zambian Open University has worked tirelessly and hard to ensuring that this book becomes a source material for Zambian colleges and universities.

My brother, Mr. Charles Chibwe, is another person I would like to acknowledge. The promotion and distribution of the first edition of this book in Zambia has been hugely due to his tenacity and inexorable solicitations.

Mr. Isaac Chandangoma was instrumental in bringing the first edition to the Zambian population in 2011. For his enthusiasm and hard work, I am deeply grateful.

Last and not least, the following members of my family – Clarice, Emmerance, Tashany-Idyllia and Cutravieve – who give me tremendous motivation, encouragement and love. This book has always been a family project, and I am forever indebted.

TABLE OF CONTENTS

ABBREVIATIONS

AAC	Anglo-American Corporation
ACC	Anti-Corruption Commission
ADD	Alliance for Democracy and Development
AFC	Agriculture Financial Corporation
AG	Attorney-General
AG	Auditor-General
AGOA	Africa Growth Opportunity Act
AIDS	Acquired Immunodeficiency Syndrome
AMEC	African Methodist Episcopal Church
AMWU	African Mine Workers Union
ANC	African National Congress
ANIP	African National Independence Party
APA	American Psychological Association
APRM	African Peer Review Mechanism
ARASA	AIDS and Rights Alliance for Southern Africa
ARC	African Representative Council
AU	African Union
AWEP	African Women Entrepreneurship Program
BBC	British Broadcasting Corporation
BFM	Barotseland Freedom Movement
BND	German Federal Intelligence Service
BOZ	Bank of Zambia
BRE	Barotse Royal Establishment
BRICS	Brazil, Russia, India, China and South Africa
BSAC	British South Africa Company
BTR	BlogTalkRadio
CAF	Central African Federation
CBC	Canadian Broadcasting Corporation
CBE	Order of the British Empire
CBU	Copperbelt University
CC	Constitutional Council
CCMG	Christian Churches Monitoring Group
CCNR	Christian Council of Northern Rhodesia

CCZ	Christian Council of Zambia
CD	Campaign for Democracy
CDC	Commonwealth Development Corporation
CDF	Constituency Development Fund
CEEC	Citizens Economic Empowerment Commission
CEI	Independent Electoral Commission (of Ivory Coast)
CENTO	Central Treaty Organization
CFAN	Christ for All Nations
CFF	Compensatory Finance Facility
CGS	Credit Guarantee Scheme
CHAKA	Christian Alliance for the Kingdom of Africa
CIA	Central Intelligence Agency
CJA	Commonwealth Journalists Association
CMR	Civil Military Relations
CNMC	China Non-ferrous Metals Mining Company
CNN	Cable News Network
CNU	Caucus for National Unity
CNU	Congress for National Unity
COMESA	Common Market for Eastern and Southern Africa
CONCACAF	Confederation of North, Central American and Caribbean Association Football (Soccer)
COZ	Credit Organization of Zambia
CPA	Commonwealth Parliamentarians Association
CPC	Collective Political Conscience
CPI	Corruption Perception Index
CRTC	Canadian Radio-TV and Telecommunication Commission
CSBZ	Cold Storage Board of Zambia
CSO	Central Statistical Office
CSR	Corporate Social Responsibility
CUP	Committee for Unity and Progress
CUSA	Credit Unions Savings Association
CV	Curriculum Vitae
DBE	Dame Commander
DBZ	Development Bank of Zambia
DEC	Drug Enforcement Commission
DFID	(British) Department for International Development

DNC	Democratic National Congress
DOC	District Officer Cadet
DP	Democratic Process
DPBZ	Dairy Produced Board of Zambia
DPP	Director of Public Prosecution
DRC	Democratic Republic of Congo
DSEA	Department of Social and Economic Affairs [UN]
DWB	Driving While Black
ECA	Economic Commission for Africa
ECZ	Electoral Commission of Zambia
EFZ	Evangelical Fellowship of Zambia
EI	Employment Insurance (Canada)
ENRC	Euroasia Natural Resources Corporation
ESAF	Enhanced Structural Adjustment Facility
EU	European Union
EVI	Economic Vulnerability Index
EZLs	Emerging Zambian Leaders
FDD	Forum for Democracy and Development
FDI	Foreign Direct Investment
FIFA	International Federation of Soccer Associations
FIMACO	Financial Management Company
FINDECO	Finance Development Corporation
FNDP	Fifth National Development Plan
FNDP	Fourth National Development Plan
FOCAC	Forum on China-Africa Corporation
FODEP	Forum for Democratic Process
FoI	Freedom of Information Bill
FORD	Forum for Restoration of Democracy
FRA	Food Reserve Agency
G-20	Group of 20 Countries
GBE	Dame Grand Cross
GDP	Gross Domestic Product
GNI	Gross National Income
GNP	Gross National Product
GRZ	Government of the Republic of Zambia
HAI	Human Assets Index
HCF	Hillcrest Christian Fellowship

HIPC	Highly Indebted Poor Countries
HIRC	Highly Indebted Rich Countries
HIV	Human Immunodeficiency Virus
HMRC	Her Majesty's Revenue and Customs
IACs	Indigenous African Churches
IAEA	International Atomic Energy Agency
IBRD	International Bank for Reconstruction and Development
ICT	Information and Communication Technology
IDA	International Development Association
IELTS	International English Language Testing System
IFC	International Finance Corporation
IFIs	International Financial Institutions
IFMIS	Integrated Financial Management Information System
INDECO	Industrial Development Corporation
INDP	Interim National Development Plan
INTERPOL	International Police
IOT	International Observer Team
IPPA	Investment Promotion and Protection Agreement
IT	Information Technology
JASZ	Joint Assistance Strategy for Zambia
JCTR	Jesuit Center for Theological Reflections
KBE	Knight Commander
KCMG	Order of St. Michael and St. George
KONNOCO	Konkola North Copper Mine
LAD	Language Acquisition Device
LAZ	Law Association of Zambia
LDCs	Least Developed Countries
LCM	Luanshya Copper Mines
LCMS	Living Conditions Monitoring Survey
LEAs	Local Education Authorities
LGBTI	Anti-Lesbian, Gay, Bisexual, Transgender and Intersex
LMS	London Missionary Society
LP	Labor Party
LTTI	Livingstone Trades Training Institute
MCC	Member of Central Committee

MCM	Mopani Copper Mines
MDGs	Millennium Development Goals
MDP	Movement for Democratic Process
MFEZs	Multi-Facility Economic Zones
MFIs	Microfinance Institutions
MI6	British Secret Intelligent Service (SIS)
MINDECO	Mining Development Corporation
MMD	Movement for Multiparty Democracy
MNA	Ministry of Native Affairs
MO	Method of Operation
MOREBA	Movement for the Restoration of Barotseland Agreement
MUZ	Mineworkers Union of Zambia
NADA	National Democratic Alliance
NAFTA	North American Free Trade Agreement
NAMBOARD	National Agricultural Marketing Board
NAMECO	National Media Corporation
NAP	National Anti-Corruption Policy
NATO	North Atlantic Treaty Organization
NCC	National Citizens' Coalition
NCC	National Constitutional Conference
NCCM	Nchanga Consolidated Copper Mines
NCPPIS	National Correctional Prevention Policy and Implementation Strategy
NDPs	National Development Plans
NEPAD	New Partnership for Africa's Development
NERP	National Economic and Recovery Programs
NGO	Non-Governmental Organization
NGOCC	Non-Governmental Organization Coordinating Committee
NHC	National Heritage Council
NIDO	Nigerians in Diaspora Organization
NIEC	National Import and Export Corporation
NIV	New International Version (Bible)
NPD	National Party for Democracy
NPT	Non-proliferation of Nuclear Weapons
NPV	Net Present Value

NRANC	Northern Rhodesia African National Congress
NRDC	Natural Resources Development College
NRNA	Northern Rhodesia Native Association
NS	Natural Sciences (UNZA School of)
NUPTW	National Union of Postal and Telecommunication Workers
O.P	Office of the President
OAU	Organization of African Unity
OECD	Organization for Economic Cooperation and Development
OLIZAWA	Organization of Zambians Living in Western Australia
OMOs	Open Market Operations
OPEC	Organization of Petroleum Exporting Countries
OPV	Oral Polio Vaccine
OYV	Operation Young Vote
OZAFO	Our Zambian Forum
PA	Provincial Administrator (Colonial)
PAC	Public Accounts Committee
PANA	Pan-African News Agency
PEM	Paris Evangelical Missions
PEMFAR	Public Expenditure Management and Financial Accountability Reform
PF	Patriotic Front
PHI	Presidential Housing Initiative
PIG	Party and Its Government (UNIP)
PM	Primitive Methodists
PNT	Privatization Negotiation Team
POGG	Peace, Order and Good Government
PPP	Purchasing Power Parity
PRGF	Poverty Reduction and Growth Facility
PRICCA	Prisons Care and Counseling Association
PRSP	Poverty Reduction Strategy Papers
PUDD	Party of Unity for Democracy and Development
R&D	Research and Development
RAI	Rural Action International
RCM	Roan Consolidated Mines
RDC	Rural Development Corporation

RSK	Republic of South Korea
RST	Rhodesia Selection Trust
RWUZ	Railway Workers Union of Zambia
S&P	Standard and Poor's
SADC	Southern African Development Community
SADC-PC	SADC Protocol against Corruption
SAP	Structural Adjustment Program
SCN	Suprachiasmatic Nucleus
SCVP	Special Cancer Virus Program
SEATO	Southeast Asia Treaty Organization (Defunct)
SEP	Small-Scale Enterprise Development Program
SIDO	Small Industry Development Organization
SITET	Special Investigations Team on Drug Enforcement
SMEs	Small and Medium Enterprises
SNA	System of National Accounts
SNDP	Sixth National Development Plan
SPL	Scottish Premier League
SQUAM	Standardization, Quality Assurance, Accreditation and Metrology
SSIAZ	Small-Scale Industries Association of Zambia
SU	Scripture Union
SUV	Sports Utility Vehicle
TAZ	Theology Association of Zambia
TAZARA	Tanzania Zambia Railway Authority
TB	Tuberculosis
TBZ	Tobacco Board of Zambia
TFC	Task Force on Corruption
TFP	Total Factor Productivity
TIZ	Transparency International Zambia
TSPP	Theoretical Spiritual Political Party
TUC	Trade Union Congress
UCZ	United Church of Zambia
UDI	Unilateral Declaration of Independence
UFCS	United Free Church of Scotland
UFP	United Federal Party
UK	United Kingdom
UMCA	Universities' Mission to Central Africa

UN	United Nations
UNCAC	United Nations Convention against Corruption
UNESC	United Nations Economic and Social Council
UNICEF	United Nations Children's Fund (formerly United Nations International Children's Emergency Fund)
UNIDO	United Nations Industrial Development Organization
UNIP	United National Independence Party
UNITA	National Union for the Total Independence of Angola
UNP	United National Party
UNZAIFEC	UNZA Inter-Fellowships Committee
UNZASU	University of Zambia Student Union
UP	United Party
UPND	United Party for National Development
UPP	United Progressive Party
US	United States (of America)
USAID	United States Agency for International Development
USSR	United Soviet Socialist Republics
UTH	University Teaching Hospital
VIS	Village Industry Services
WCED	World Commission on Environment and Development
WEF	World Economic Forum
WMDs	Weapons of Mass Destruction
WTO	World Trade Organization
WVI	World Vision International
WWW	World Wide Web
ZACAFA	Zambian Canadian Friendship Association
ZaCoMeF	Zambia Community Media Forum
ZADECO	Zambia Development Conference
ZAF	Zambia Air Force
ZAMCAN	Zambian Canadian Association (Foundation)
ZAMSIF	Zambia Social Investment Fund
ZAMTEL	Zambia Telecommunications Corporation
ZANA	Zambia News Agency
ZANACO	Zambia National Commercial Bank

ZCBC	Zambia Consumer Buying Corporation
ZCCM	Zambia Consolidated Copper Mines
ZCCM-IH	ZCCM Investment Holdings Plc.
ZCFFS	Zambia Cooperatives Federation Finance Services
ZCTU	Zambia Congress of Trade Unions
ZDA	Zambia Development Agency
ZDC	Zambia Diaspora Connect
ZEMEC	Zambia Elections Monitoring Coordinating Committee
ZENA	Zambia Enrolled Nurses Association
ZEWU	Zambia Electricity Workers Union
ZFE	Zambia Federation of Employers
ZIMCO	Zambia Industrial and Mining Corporation
ZIMT	Zambia Independent Monitoring Team
ZISS	Zambia Intelligence Security Service
ZMK	Zambian Kwacha
ZNBC	Zambia National Broadcasting Corporation
ZNFU	Zambia National Farmers Union
ZNOC	Zambian National Oil Corporation
ZNS	Zambia National Service
ZNUT	Zambia National Union of Teachers
ZOFRO	Zambia Opposition Front
ZRA	Zambia Revenue Agency
ZSIS	Zambia Security and Intelligence Services
ZUFIAW	Zambia Union of Financial Institutions and Allied Workers

LIST OF LATIN TERMS USED IN THE BOOK

Ad hoc	For this special purpose
Ad infinitum	"To infinity," or "continue forever, without limit"
Agenda	Things to be done
Alabi	Literally, "Somewhere else," - It is an explanation offered to avoid blame or justify action; it is an excuse. It is often used as a defence in criminal law
Alma mater	One's old school or university
Anno domini (AD)	In the year of the Lord
Audi alteram partem	Hear the other side
Bona fide	In good faith
Casus belli	The circumstances justifying war
Ceteris paribus	Other things being equal or unchanged
Corrumpere	Means to pervert, corrupt, deprave or spoil
De facto	In fact (in contradistinction to *de jure*)
De jure	By right (in contradistinction to *de facto*)
Dramatis personae	The list of characters in a play
Erectus	Uprightness
Et alii (*et. al.*)	And others
Et cetera (etc.)	And so on
Ex gratia	Purely as a favor
Ex nihilo	Out of nothing
Ex officio	By virtue of office
Facta, non verba	"Deeds, not words"
Fiat	Let it be done
Fiat Justitia ruat Caelum	Let justice be done though the heavens fall
Honoris Causa	For the sake of honor
Ibidem (*ibid.*)	In the same place
Id est (i.e.)	That is
Imprimatur	"Let it be printed"

In absentia	While absent
Infra	Below
In toto	Entirely
Inter alia	Among other things
Magna Carta	Great Charter
Modus operandi	The manner of working
Nemo iudex in causa sua	No person is permitted to be judge in their own cause
Per capita	By the head
Per se	Taken alone
Prima facie	On the face of it
Priori	From what was before
Quasi	As if
Sic	Thus (indicates an error deliberately reproduced)
Sine qua non	An indispensable condition
Stare decisis et non quieta movere	"To stand by decisions and not disturb the undisturbed" or simply, "Let the decision stand."
Status quo	The existing condition
Supra	On an earlier page
Terra nullius	Empty land
Vice versa	The order being reversed
Vice	In place of
Videlicet (viz.)	Namely
Vis et voluntas	Force and will
Volenti non-fit injuria	That to which a man consents cannot be considered an injury
Vox populi	Voice of the people

FOREWORD

I [felt] very highly privilege...to launch the book *Zambia - Struggles of My People* by Charles Mwewa. It was only later afternoon Friday last week [July 22nd, 2011] that Dr. Hamalengwa Munyonzwe, a colleague who is fully established as a lawyer in Toronto, invited me through a telephone call to come and play this role. I first met Hamalengwa in 1980 when I went to do my Master's degree at the University of Toronto and stayed longer with him when I returned to do my Doctorate in 1990 after a lapse of about eight years before finally coming back in 1994. I obliged to come here [Makumbi Hall, Hotel Intercontinental, Lusaka] and I asked for a copy of the book so that I could read it over the weekend for me to formulate some ideas on what to say.

The combination of the [three volumes] makes this book about the biggest book of our time written and focusing on Zambia. It is encyclopedic in coverage but lucidly and coherently held together. It is written with passion and concern, hence its title *Struggles of My People*.

I skimmed through the...volumes and what I can say from the outset is that the reading of the book is compelling, stimulating and provoking with the intention to leveraging change in each one of the citizens, particularly those privileged to lead to advance social and economic development of Zambia; promote the rule of law and human rights; banish corruption from our midst; adopt and embrace a liberal attitude to others including those with different sexual orientations; and nurture young people to play an upfront leadership role while the old guards take the back role. It is a critique of the Zambian people of which the author is one.

As he says while he is in Canada no day passes without him thinking about Zambia and how it could be advanced to be like all developed countries. The book is also about the author's intellectual growth through time and space and revelation of influences from primary school to UNZA and in the Diaspora which provides from whose vantage point the book is written.

Prof. Dickson Mwansa
Vice-Chancellor,
Zambian Open University,
Lusaka, Zambia

July 24th, 2011

1 | Zambian Independence

In thy cozy loamy soils deeply flowed mine young blood
In thy sun-scorched patches birth-ed thee a patriotic lad
How this thought of hilarity mine psyche partly flood
Thy progeny in hope mine entrails thou maketh glad
Thy black visage daily mine heart gladly beholdeth
For thine good, whence mine desire dryly flourisheth
Oh Zambia, kind Mother to me thou may be more
Oh land, thy toil, the oil that boileth our common soul!

Chapter Focus

At the end of reading this chapter, you should be able to:

- Understand the meaning of colonialists (foreigners or new-comers)
- Identify events and peoples that made Zambia's independence possible
- Define the concepts of "struggle" and "struggles for independence"
- Explain what and why the Africans desired political independence

BRIEF INTRODUCTION

In this chapter, the author relives the memories of Zambia's 19th independence celebrations as a child at Mibenge Primary School in Mibenge's village in Samfya-Mansa district of Luapula Province. It introduces the major theme of independence, the founding fathers of the independent Republic of Zambia, and the promise of a prosperous, democratic and free nation.

§1.1 Mibenge

My parents came from Mibenge Village in the Mansa-Samfya area of Luapula Province, Zambia. Mibenge comprised several smaller villages each headed and called by the name of the headman. Within Mibenge there was also a village by the same name, which was headed by Chief Mibenge himself. In addition, Chief Mibenge presided over several group of villages including Kombaniya, Kolwe, Kafula, Chilema, Sendapu, Mwanda, Shitini, and many others.

My father was born at Chilema village to Kalubeya Mwewa[1] and Rosaliya Chibesa. My father belonged to the *Bena-Ngulube* (or the Warthog-clan). My mother, on the other hand, was born at Kombaniya village to Chinama Chibwe and Ndaliya Mukomango. My mother's clan was the *Mbeba* (or the Mouse-clan).

I hurled from Kolwe's village, about 30 to 40 kilometers from Chief Mibenge's palace in Mibenge village.[2] Mibenge Primary School was situated near Chief Mibenge's palace. At the time, Mibenge Primary School consisted of only three blocks of about three classrooms each with about two offices. There were also other unfinished classrooms being built. The school, the teachers' houses, the clinic and the palace were built from modern bricks and tin-roof. Most the houses and huts in the villages had thatched roofs.[3]

---

[1] Kalubeya Mwewa was from the Lion's clan or the *Bena-Nkalamo*

[2] Kolwe was not a village *per se;* it was a stream. However, because Kombaniya and Chilema where my mother and father were born, respectively, were along the banks of the Kolwe Stream, all the villages adjacent became known collectively as Kolwe's village.

[3] In the 1980s, there were other individuals who were richer than Chief Mibenge, like Sendapu and his brother Mulonga, who owned large farms and had vehicles and several workers. Mulonga's mansion was elegant with most of the features of modern building facilities.

§1.2 October 24th, 1983

It was here at Mibenge that I first heard about Zambia's Independence Day. It was October 24th, 1983. The school had set up a large round thatched arena. Several goats were slaughtered. There were dancing and feasting. All I could remember was that everyone who made a speech talked about *Bamwisa.*[4] I later came to learn that the term referred to foreigners, and the colonialists. In Zambia, all White foreigners are collectively referred to as *Abasungu* (singular: *Musungu*), which is a transliteration of the Swahili, *Wazungu*, which literally means, "People who move around."[5]

Children sang and danced.[6] In their songs and dances they were talking about the domination of the person they called foreigner. He had yoked them like animals, they said. He had taken away their humanity. He had subjected them to slavery conditions in their own land. He had called them "ka-boys"[7] when they were supposed to be grown-up men and women. He had reduced them to second-class citizens. He had spoiled their will to exist as free and independent people. Now he was gone. They were finally free. They sang. They danced. They ululated!

These songs, and particularly the message they oozed, would impact me for many years to come. I still remember them very vividly. I can see children dancing in the dust without shoes on

---

[4] In Aushi language, a Bemba dialect spoken in Luapula Province of Zambia, this term loosely refers to economic plunderers, as in when the British imperialists colonized Northern Rhodesia, for so Zambia was called, they also plundered Zambia economically.
[5] Peter Firstbrook, *The Obamas* (New York: Crown Publishers, 2010), p. 84
[6] Dancing and singing was not peculiar to Mibenge. Children danced away with girls in the evenings to *Nsale-nsale chinkamba*. Children did even more; they played all day to "Game and Touch," to "Eagle and Rounders," to *Sojo and Digo*, to *Kalambe*, to *Kankuluwale*, to *Chidunu* and to *Tela*!
[7] Colonial masters called Zambian men working for them as servants, boys. The prefix "ka" in Bemba language denotes a belittling epithet associated with people of the lowest rank.

3

them. Some of these kids were wearing the school khaki uniforms, torn and dirty. But they were happy. They had a reason to celebrate. They were free. As they sang, they repeatedly praised Kenneth David Kaunda[8] (known as "KK" by the people of Zambia), Mathew Mainza Chona,[9] Harry Mwaanga Nkumbula,[10] Simon Mwansa Kapwepwe,[11] Reuben Kamanga,[12]

---

[8] Kenneth Kaunda was Zambia's first Republican president. He ruled Zambia for over 27 years before he was defeated in an election in 1991 by Frederick Chiluba.

[9] Mathew Mainza Chona was born in Monze town in Southern Province of Zambia in 1930. His brilliance as a young student awarded him a scholarship to Munali Secondary School. He later got a scholarship from the British colonial government to study law at Gray's Inn in England. He was the first Zambian to qualify as a barrister in 1958. He became President of UNIP in 1959, the party that paved the way to Zambia's independence. He was Vice-president and later the first Prime Minister of Zambia. He died in 2001. <http://www.mainzachona.com/index.htm> (Retrieved: January 20th, 2010)

[10] Born in January 1916, Harry Mwaanga Nkumbula is among the founding fathers of Zambia's independence from British colonial rule. Nkumbula and his "A Team," define Zambia's present day identity. He is also among the founding fathers of Zambia's first native political party, the Northern Rhodesia African National Congress (NRANC). Founded in 1948, the party was first led by the late Godwin Mbikusita Lewanika. In 1951, Nkumbula was elected president of NRANC. The party was later renamed African National Congress (ANC), as a link to the African National Congress in South Africa. The party leadership team, the so-called "Zambian A Team," included Harry Nkumbula himself, Simon Mwansa Kapwepwe, Kenneth Kaunda, Mainza Chona, Grey Zulu, Dixon Konkola, Robinson Nabulyato, Paul Kalichini, Raphael Kombe, Nalumino Mundia, Reuben Kamanga, among others. <http://www.zambian.com/zambia/directory/people/last-name-nn/html/harry-nkumbula-zambian.html> (Retrieved: January 22nd, 2010)

[11] Simon Mwansa Kapwepwe was born on April 12th, 1922 in Chinsali. He was former and second Zambian Vice-president (1967-1970) and UNIP's deputy leader until he left UNIP to form the United Progressive Party (UPP) in 1971. In February 1972, UPP was banned. It is believed that Kapwepwe was the one who coined the name "Zambia," a derivative of "Zambe" or "Zambe" literally "God." So, Zambia may also mean that which belongs to God! He died on January 26th, 1980 after suffering from a stroke.

[12] Reuben Kamanga was Zambia's first Vice-president after independence. Other persons who have held that position are Simon Kapwepwe (1967-

Alexander Grey Zulu,[13] and so many others. I already knew that Kenneth Kaunda was the President of Zambia at the time. I did not need to look any further to realize that Kaunda's name was on everyone's lips in the village. His presence on the Zambian currency, the Kwacha,[14] was a constant reminder of his dominance and power. I knew nothing else about the rest. Later I would read history books and learn that they were prominent Zambian founding fathers.[15] They had together fought for

---

1970), Mainza Chona (1970-1973), Levy Mwanawasa, (1991-1994), Gen. Godfrey Miyanda (1994-1997), Gen. Christon Tembo (1997-2001). Enoch Kavindele, Nevers Mumba, Lupando Mwape and Rupiah Banda have been Vice-presidents between 2006 and 2008. George Kunda was Vice-president from 2008 up to 2011. Guy Lindsay Scott, born on June 1st, 1944, was the first White Zambian Acting-president from October 2014 to January 2015. Scott served as Vice-president of Zambia from 2011 to 2014. Inonge Wina was the first female Vice-president of Zambia appointed by President Edgar Lungu on January 26th, 2015. In 1973, after the adoption of the Chona Commission which launched the Second Republic, the Vice-presidential office was vacated and was replaced by UNIP's Secretary-General as the second highest ranking official in Kaunda's government.

[13] Grey Zulu was UNIP Secretary-General, the second highest ranking official in the UNIP government. UNIP had abolished the office of the Vice-president and was replaced with one of the Secretary-General in 1973.

[14] According to Grotpeter et. al. in Historical Dictionary of Zambia, Kwacha is a "word meaning either dawning or the 'dawn is here.' It was used by the African nationalists as a rally cry in the period prior to independence. It was chosen for the name of the standard currency note when Zambia replaced its pound in January 1968." Moreover, "Kwacha-Ngwee" was "used either separately or together as a nationalist slogan during the several years before Zambian independence. 'Ngwee' is an intensifying expletive; the root of it is derived from a word meaning 'light' or 'bright.'" Kwacha-Ngwee, thus, means, "Cheer up and have faith, for a great new day is almost here" (p. 193).

[15] The use of the term "father" in this book does not connote the Leader Principle of infallibility reminiscent of hero-worship of the Zambian presidents. It does not also strike a religious connotation as is usually the case in religious circles. This book maintains the view that there is only One God and Father of all. However, the term "father" or "mother" may be used, from time to time, in a political sense, to denote the founders of the Republic of Zambia.

Charles Mwewa

Zambia's independence. They had made tremendous sacrifices. Some even died in what is called the struggle for Zambia's independence.[16] Those who lived were immortalized in song and dance. Some of them were in the ruling United National Independence Party (UNIP).[17] Others were silenced, while others

---

[16] In early 1960s, most countries in Africa campaigned vigorously to end the rule of the colonialists on their people. The first country to gain political independence in Africa was Liberia in 1847. Egypt became independent in 1951 and was followed by Morocco, Sudan and Tunisia in 1956. Ghana became independent in 1957 and Guinea in 1958. A slew of countries got independence in 1960 and they were: Chad, Benin, Nigeria, Ivory Coast, Madagascar, Central African Republic, Mali, Niger, Senegal, Burkina Faso, Mauritania, Togo, Zaire, Somalia, Congo, Gabon and Cameroon. These were immediately followed by Sierra Leone in 1961. In 1961, South Africa was recognized as the Republic of South Africa, although the Black people continued to suffer under the policy of apartheid. In 1962, Algeria, Burundi, Rwanda and Uganda became independent with Kenya and Tanzania gaining theirs in 1963. Zambia and Malawi became independent and sovereign states in 1964. Gambia followed in 1965. Botswana and Lesotho became independent in 1966 and they were followed by Equatorial Guinea, Mauritius and Swaziland in 1968. Guinea-Bissau and Libya got theirs in 1969 while Angola, Cape Verde, Comoros, Mozambique and Sao Tome became independent in 1975. For Seychelles, it was in 1976; for Djibouti, 1977; and for Zimbabwe, in 1980. Namibia and the Republic of South Africa gained independence in 1990 and 1994, respectively, with the latter breaking free from the apartheid saga with the election of Nelson Mandela as its first Black president. The latest country to gain independence in Africa is South Sudan on Saturday, July 9th, 2011 at 12:01am with Juba as Capital City.
[17] UNIP governed Zambia from 1964 to 1991 under the presidency of Kenneth Kaunda. The party was founded in October 1959. After Kaunda was released from prison in January 1960, he assumed leadership over the party. The new constitution promulgated on August 25th, 1973 and the national elections that followed in December 1973, were the final steps in achieving what was called a "One-Party Participatory Democracy." National policy was formulated by the Central Committee of UNIP. UNIP had become the only party in Zambia. The president of UNIP was the sole candidate in elections for the office of president and was selected to be the president of UNIP by the party's General Conference. UNIP's Secretary-General was the second-ranking person in the Zambian political hierarchy after the president.

were side-lined.[18] But all of them had one vision for Zambia when they fought: To make Zambia a free, prosperous and democratic state.[19] To achieve that, they first had to win political independence. So, they fought. They were fighting for Zambia's self-determination. They were fighting for freedom – to exist as a sovereign nation. However, as will be established in this book, independence alone was not enough to solve the many challenges pummeling the copper-producing African nation.

§1.3 October 23rd, 1964

Just before they gained that sweet independence, they had gathered together on tenterhooks at the newly-built Independence Stadium along the Lusaka-Kabwe Road on October 23rd, 1964. Kaunda was Prime Minister of Northern Rhodesia.[20] Dressed in a *kente* cloth toga, given to him by Kwame Nkrumah[21] for that occasion, and flanked by his fellow freedom fighter and Minister of Foreign Affairs at the time, Simon Kapwepwe, who was also clad in a similar toga, Kaunda was poised to become the first president of the Republic of Zambia in minutes' time. Then it happened.[22] As the British

---

[18] See §6.9

[19] In Volume Three, arguments have been made that the immediate goal of the *Pro-independence Zambian Leaders* was to gain political independence. They needed to shape economic development as a natural consequence of political independence, but it was not their immediate concern.

[20] Zambia

[21] Kwame Nkrumah was the first president of Ghana, a Western African state, and a freedom fighter for the liberation struggles of that country.

[22] Grotpeter *et. al.* report that, "The Republic of Zambia was officially born on October 24th, 1964 when the British flag was lowered and the multicolor [green, red, black and orange] flag of Zambia was raised," (*Historical Dictionary of Zambia*, p. 1); See also *Times of Zambia*, "Zambia's Independence: 1964 Celebrations,"

Union Jack[23] was being lowered, and so was the new flag of Zambia being raised. The Zambian new National Anthem accompanied.[24] Standing on the podium and cheering were Kaunda, Her Royal Highness Princess Royal,[25] Queen Elizabeth's auntie who represented the Queen,[26] and Sir Evelyn Hone.[27] Then the floodgates of the Independence Stadium opened, women and girls ululated, men and boys whistled and fireworks sparked the sky. Once the last loop of the Zambian flag was hoisted to the flag post, on October 24th, 1964, Zambia was born![28]

<

http://www.times.co.zm.news/viewnews.cgi?category=8&id=1004123512> (Retrieved: April 21st, 2010)

[23] British flag

[24] The Zambian National Anthem sings to the tune of *Nkosi Sikelele Africa* (God Bless Africa) which was composed by Enoch Mankayi Sontonga (1860-1904). Sontonga was a teacher from South Africa. In 1897, he composed the words of *Nkosi Sikelele Africa* for his pupils, but the song grew in popularity and was made a hymn. It became known as the Bantu National Anthem. In 1925, the South African Africa National Congress (ANC) party adopted it as its national anthem. In 1961, Tanzania similarly adopted it as its national anthem upon the attainment of its independence. In Zambia, there was a competition and words were derived from six leading contestants, one of them is believed to be a Briton, but the music and tune were those of *Nkosi Sikelele Africa*. On October 24th, 1964, a school headmaster from Chingola by the name of Chamululu conducted the choir of young Zambians who sang the national anthem as the flag was being raised.

[25] Her Royal Highness Princess Royal presided as the Special Guest of Honor on behalf of Queen Elizabeth II.

[26] Queen Elizabeth gave Kaunda a brand-new Rolls-Royce for use during the independence ceremony and the US government gave him a new Chrysler convertible.

[27] Evelyn Dennison Hone (1911-1964) was the last Governor of Northern Rhodesia and a keen sympathizer of Kaunda. In the 1964 election, UNIP won 35 percent of the total European votes. Sir Evelyn Hone invited Kaunda to form the first Black government and Kaunda became the first Black Prime Minister of Northern Rhodesia on January 22nd, 1964. The Evelyn Hone College in Lusaka is named after Sir Evelyn Hone.

[28] According to Grotpeter *et. al.*, the flag of Zambia "was introduced to Zambians in June 1964 by Kenneth Kaunda; its base color is green,

By the Instruments of Independence signed and sealed by Her Majesty the Queen, Kaunda had become the new president of Zambia early on October 24th, 1964.[29] Kaunda was sworn in by the Chief Justice as the first president of Zambia around Ten O'clock on independence morning.

A *Times of Zambia* reporter describes the mood at independence as one of jubilation, happiness and celebration: "The mood in Lusaka, in particular was one of jubilation, happiness and celebration. In the evening, the whole city center was lit up in colorful electric bulbs."[30] Independence celebrations continued throughout Zambia.

This was the mood that greeted me on that Independence Day of 1983 at Mibenge Primary School. Those who were older and who had experienced the actual independence seemed to have been taken aback to 1964.

Despite Kaunda's assiduous leadership and vision, the struggle for Zambia's independence was an African community effort. At the Lancaster House[31] constitutional talks meeting in London, England, where Kaunda and his entourage subsequently chose October 24th as Zambia's Independence Day, to be "on the same date and month on which the United Nations (UN) was created,"[32] Kaunda was flanked by political party leaders from the United Federal Party (UFP), Labor Party (LP) and many other

---

representing the grassland of the country and its agricultural products. The eagle in flight represents Zambian freedom. The orange stripe symbolizes the country's (copper) mineral resources. Black represents the color of most of the population, and the red stripe is symbolic of the blood shed for freedom," (*Historical Dictionary of Zambia, supra.,* p. 116)

[29] Instruments of Independence consisted of the constitution and other legal documents which declared Zambia an independent and sovereign state.

[30] *Times of Zambia,* "Zambia's Independence: 1964 Celebrations Relieved," http://www.times.co.zm.news/viewnews.cgi?category=8&id=1004123512> (Retrieved: April 28th, 2009)

[31] On May 2nd, 1964

[32] *Times of Zambia, supra.* The other probable reason for choosing October 24th could have been to rhyme with Kaunda's *United National* Independence Party (UNIP) which was first formed in 1959.

stakeholders in Zambia's struggle for independence. Among them was Aaron Milner,[33] a freedom fighter who had "hosted several freedom fighters from the region including the late Mozambique President, Samorah Machel, South Africa's Oliver Tambo, and the late Zimbabwe Vice-president Joshua Nkomo, among others."[34] These men and women, collectively, sacrificed their lives for the political independence of Zambia. Many of them will never be sung in our heroes' hymnaries, and yet they were indispensable to our freedom. They were indefatigable in their quest for our political emancipation. The struggle of the Zambian people cannot be adequately narrated without their contribution.

§1.4 Struggles of the Zambians

As Zambia comes of age and passes its golden jubilee, it is a witness to the sacrifices of our fathers and mothers. They were motivated by something deeper than a military reveille,[35] and as Guevara notes, by a "soldier's response: 'Until death, if

---

[33] Aaron Milner had his Zambian citizenship revoked in 1980 for his alleged role in the late lawyer Edward Shamwana's coup attempt. At the formation of UNIP, Milner was elected UNIP's Deputy Secretary-General, the post that also saw him co-ordinate the movement of all arms from the neighboring Tanzania. In the first African government, Milner served as Parliamentary Secretary in the Office of the Prime Minister before becoming Minister of State for Presidential Affairs and much later Secretary-General to the Government and Head of Cabinet Civil Service. During the construction of the Tanzania Zambia Railway Authority (TAZARA), he was serving as Minister of Power Transport and Works, before moving on to Defence in the same capacity and finally Home Affairs, the last ministerial position he held before his citizenship was revoked.

[34] Nerbet Mulenga, "Freedom Fighter Aaron Milner Predicts a Better Zambia, Preaches Community Dedication," *Times of Zambia*, <http://www.times.co.zm> (Retrieved: April 29th, 2009)

[35] *Kwacha* literally means wake-up-call, dawn or daybreak. Reveille is a military term meaning a wake-up-call!

necessary!' It carries the solution to serious problems involved in creating our [world] of tomorrow.'"[36] They were deterred neither by the whip of prison nor the sting of death. They stood and sang of their faith in Zambia with pride; they believed they were free. They promised they would work the land with great joy while remaining united.[37]

Indeed, independence has accrued us supreme authority over our land. Political authority has been attained, but are we economically or intellectually free? Are our laws strong enough to save us from ourselves? Do we see in every human being potential for a dignified and right-based existence?

For Zambia, independence has always been an elephant in the room. This book is the detailing of the political, economic and personal struggles of the Zambian people. Every time the word struggle is used in this book, it will connote the idea of striving, laboring hard, pain and anguish, and the exertion of relatively forcible effort to obtain an objective.

My approach in this book is based on that eternal Latin maxim of *Fiat Justitia ruat Caelum* or "Let justice be done though the heavens fall." I have labored to detail the story of the struggles of my people with the deportment of a cogent observer and the diligence of a linear historian.

Struggle can be the stringboard to progress, prosperity and democracy. It has been said that, "The probability that we may fail in the struggle ought not to deter us from the support of a cause we believe to be just."[38] Struggle can be a catalyst for change: "Change does not roll in on the wheels of inevitability,

---

[36] Ernesto "Che" Guevara, *The African Dream: The Diaries of the Revolutionary War in the Congo* (New York: Grove Press, 1999), pp. 58-59
[37] Zambian National Anthem, Stanza One
[38] Abraham Lincoln

but comes through continuous struggle. And so, we must straighten our backs and work for our freedom."[39] Struggle is, thus, a process, not only an experience. Like Barack Obama once said, "Today we are engaged in a deadly global struggle.... If we are to win this struggle and spread those freedoms, we must keep our own moral compass pointed in a true direction." And indeed, that compass in the true direction, should continue to lead Zambia towards true liberation, because the attainment of independence was merely stage one in our common journey called ZAMBIA!

---

[39] Martin Luther King, Jr.

2 | My Zambia

Here my people, I write, from over the seas, I write
To a people black and lovely, let me be right
I am yours from abroad; I am a patriot and a child
Your own blood, a product of your need and pride
To my Motherland, in the fair land tilled with nature
A place of splendid civilization, of a seasoned culture

Chapter Focus

At the end of reading this chapter, you should be able to:

- Appreciate the experience of the Second Republic
- Understand the drive for Zambia-specific themes
- Identify the entrenchment of economic disparity in the Zambian structural formation
- Sequester the deleterious effects of shanty-town poverty
- Appreciate the meritorious effects of a good education

BRIEF INTRODUCTION

In this chapter, the author recounts his childhood experience in Zambia. He relates the struggles of the Zambians at the personal level to his experiences as a youth in the Second Republic.

§2.1 Luano Primary School

Although I began my Grade One Primary School education at Mibenge in the Samfya-Mansa district, I would not remain there longer than Grade Two Term One. Shortly after the death of my

Charles Mwewa

father in 1983, my elder sister, Mary Kalaba, took me to Chingola
where I would spend eight years of my teenage life. I was
immediately enlisted at Luano Primary School in Grade Two
Term Two in Kapisha Compound. Luano was the least of all
primary schools in Chingola.

The school was in the poor compound of Kapisha where the
only thing we prided in was the Kapisha Hotspring.[40] Most
children who attended Luano were from very poor families.
Some of them did not wear shoes. The majority did not even have
a meal before coming to school. Most people in Zambia are
aware of the corollary of poverty. However, you cannot
understand the stinging power of poverty until you have a chance
to live in a shanty-town like Kapisha.[41]

The harsh and hustle of the Second Republic were
experienced here. For me, Kapisha constituted Zambia, the
Zambia in which I was raised, or should I say, in which I raised
myself! I will never forget the hardships of the Second Republic.
If ever there was a time when I thought of life as meaningless, it
was during my primary school days. Before my father passed
away, he shielded us from poverty. He had worked hard both to
provide and create a good life for me and my siblings. Now he
was gone, I was there learning how to survive under very
despicable economic conditions.

Each time I went to buy paraffin from Kapisha to downtown
Chingola, I passed by the residence of Edward Shamutete[42] near
Chingola Civic Center. I sold paraffin in the nights to raise some
money to pay for my school fees and buy school necessities. It
was embarrassing. Yes, even though Kapisha was predominantly
a poor area, there were some economic activities and some jobs

---

[40] The Kapisha Hotspring is a natural phenomenon which spills out hot
water. It lies about 15 kilometers east of Chingola. You could place an egg
there and have it cooked perfectly within no time. As a child, I visited the
spring several times and could only wonder on the beautiful creation of God
right near where I lived.
[41] Shanty-towns are discussed in §4.8 in Chapter 4
[42] Former CEO and Chairman of ZCCM

14

that were considered disgraceful. Selling paraffin was one such activity.

Shamutete's residence was huge and elegant. I would wonder every time I passed there what it was like to live in such a mansion. A lot of questions would run through my mind. Although I had once experienced a relatively good life, all that was swallowed up in the poor economic condition I found myself. Shamutete was implicated in a national plundering scheme between 2007 and 2009. While some people own mansions through ingenuity and hard work, some, like Shamutete, did so at the expense of the governed poor masses.

Chingola was a microcosm of Zambia in miniature. The rich and powerful lived in the areas like Riverside, Nchanga South and Chingola downtown. The middle-income families lived in areas like Lulamba, Kabundi East, Chikola, Chiwempala and etcetera. The majority poor were squeezed in shanty-towns like Kapisha, Soweto, and so forth.

By Zambian standards, Kapisha was the cleanest shanty-town in Zambia following Chingola itself which was voted the cleanest of all Zambian towns. Most people in Kapisha were self-employed in vocational-related trades like carpentry, brick-laying, black-smith, and etcetera. Others were marketeers and small-scale traders in perishable farm-produce, second-hand clothes commonly called *kombo*, and so on.

Although when people retired or were fired from the lucrative mining or maid-servant jobs they relocated to Kapisha, most were self-made people, and eventually rising within the compound ranks to fend for themselves a life of reasonable existence. The rich ones by the Kapisha standards included bar-and-tavern owners like the proprietors of the Buseko Bar and Tavern, Chilemba Bar, and etcetera.

Social life in my Kapisha revolved around three activities. On Saturdays and Sundays people attended church. In the evenings, most men visited bars and taverns and pubs. Most boys and girls played soccer and netball, respectively, especially during after-school hours. I studied hard for school and played soccer with the same passion.

In Kapisha sexual encounters were the order of the day. Kapisha, like Mibenge village, was a society where boys became men before their time and girls celebrated their puberty before most girls did in other towns. I have recaptured the elaborate rites of passage ceremonies in a narrative poem titled *Ode to Aushi Women*.[43]

§2.2 Kapisha at a Glance

I have mentioned that people did different activities to survive in Kapisha. For my sister, Mary, she was a small businesswoman. She sold cassava, *chikanda*,[44] roasted groundnuts, and so on, near our local bars. Buseko Bar and Tavern was her favorite bar. Here she would set her table every day from seven in the evening until midnight. Moreover, it was here where she met her late husband, Henry Mangisha.

Meanwhile, I did all the other household chores, from fetching for water at the only pump in the vicinity which only dropped water from 4:00 am to 6:00 am. I was there early in the morning every day with two to three huge basins and buckets lined up to have a chance. Then I swept the house, the yard and sometimes cooked before going to school. I lived with Mary like that until she was married and relocated to Lulamba. I was in Grade Four or Five.

I had very few good childhood friends in Kapisha. Friends like Rodgers Katema, Saxon Vwalika, Yotam Sinkamba, and

---

[43] See Charles Mwewa, *Song of an Alien* (New York: iUniverse, 2009), p. 114

[44] *Chikanda* is a certain root found along river banks in Zambia. It is pounded into mortar with a pestle into powder, and then mixed with pounded groundnuts. It is then made into a hard-brown tasty ball. I remember growing up and singing a song about the colonial masters that they did have their sausages but we also had our *chikandas*!

Masautso Phiri naturally come to my mind. Charles Chama, famously called "Palos," though older than me, was a very reliable friend, who from time to time, lent me his bedroom for studies and social cavorts.

§2.3 Struggling to Survive

For the most part growing up in Kapisha Compound, I lived with my uncle and auntie, the Bwalyas. Life was harsh and hard at the Bwalyas. My uncle was a charcoal burner. Even by the Kapisha standards, that was the lowest level of poverty in Chingola. In Kapisha at that time, you worked very hard to hide the profession of your parents, especially if they burned charcoal for a living. For us, however, it was common knowledge. Our house was House Number One Luswishi Street. House Number Three Luswishi Street was the residence of the Kapisha Catholic Parish priests.

It was a strike in contrasts. Our house was unfinished, and leaked sporadically during the rainy season. In fact, we had to stand the whole time it was raining. If it rained in the night, we were not going to sleep that night. If they say survival is of the fittest, there to survive was a matter of smartness! The priestly residence was the envy of the compound which made our house look even poorer.

In the 1980s, former president, Kaunda, gave a coupon subsidy for mealie meal to the Zambian poor. My uncle was in the bush at the time, and so he missed the opportunity. I would later regret why he did not register for coupons. In the late 1980s, there were rampant food and mealie meal shortages in Zambia.

People lined up for hours to buy just a half liter of cooking oil and a 25 kilograms' bag of mealie meal.[45]

We sometimes went for days without *Nshima*.[46] Other times my guardians would take days in the bush burning charcoal before coming back to Kapisha. Where they burned the charcoal was so far that I loafed the idea of accompanying them there. Every Saturday, they would insist that Mwamba, their late son, and I accompany them. We would bring up all kinds of excuses. I usually claimed that I had homework and Mwamba faked sickness.

Despite all this, however, the bush was the best experience I always cherished. There, food was plentiful. We kicked out of the ground a sour-tasty fruit called *Intungulu*. We dug out bush mice and roasted sumptuously tasting fresh maize (cone). Despite the distance, the bush was a paradise.

I remember that at some point growing up in Kapisha I had only one pair of shorts, no underwear and frequently getting embarrassing moments. In fact, what I called my only clothes was a torn-out pair of a *khaki* school uniforms which had also become my regular attire after school. Breakfast was a luxury, and we made use of mangoes when they were available. Sometimes we mixed mealie meal, wet it with a few drops of water, and fry it into some minces we called *Amashola*. That, sometimes, was all that we had for lunch or dinner.

Night-time was drama. We usually did without beds, or even mattresses. We had to use empty sacks. We hardly had any blankets and my auntie provided us with her *Chitenge* wrappers for beddings. This did not matter whether it was in the coldest month of June or in hottest October.

For the most part of that time, I had no concept of money; it was non-existent. I thought that it was meant for the affluent in Riverside, Kabundi South and Town-center. I walked along the

---

[45] Mealie meal is Zambia's staple food. It is prepared into a hard ball-like porridge called *Nshima*. It is served with vegetables and meats, collectively known as relish.

[46] See *Nshima, ibid.*

town walkways and admired the rich who were mostly White folks. I kept wondering why even after several years of independence, foreigners still possessed the best and the wealth of Zambia. We wallowed in poverty like chickens while they lived in luxury and plenty.

Meat was another luxury in Kapisha. Some families boasted of having meat at Christmas, we sometimes had vegetables even at Christmas. I do not have any idea how I survived all that. But I had good friends. Goodson Sanga was my best friend. His father owned a small but successful bread selling business at the market. Goodson would take me to his home and have his portion of the *Nshima* with me. Robinson Sakala (Robby) also did the same. He was another one of my trusted friends. I always wonder where these two are. In the lowliest moments of my life, they stood with me. Robby's mother was like a real mother to me. She would inquire if I had eaten, and she provided me with food.

From a life of plenty with my father to one of emptiness and hunger, I quickly knew only one thing remained. I decided to place all my hope in education. I studied hard; I postpone all lustful desires and committed to self-control. I was very determined. And it paid dividends.

§2.4 Long Parades

At Luano Primary School, I had a rare privilege of learning the art of classroom leadership from Grade Two to Grade Seven. It did not matter which teacher took over our class, I was always chosen as captain (or monitor as he or she was known), of my class. Each time I was sent to collect books from the headmaster's office I saw the portrait of former president Kaunda on the wall. Each Monday we had a parade and sang the National Anthem, there would be the mention of Kaunda.

In primary school, most social studies books, and in Grades Eight and Nine, all the civics books, had former president

Kaunda from cover to cover. For me, and those who grew up in my Kapisha, we had no knowledge of other Zambians who had fought and won our political independence. That was the same thing I observed at Mibenge.

My chance came. Once when former president Kaunda came to Chingola, Luano Primary School was among all the schools lining up to welcome him. We had lined up for over six hours before the president finally arrived. Even when he did, some of us who were shorter and tiny did not have any chance of seeing him.

For some reasons, I got lucky. Because we did not know in which car he was, we only banked on chance. Then suddenly, just near where I was standing, I saw a hand with a white handkerchief pop out of the Volvo. It was him. My intestines moved; it was like I was seeing God himself. But he was human, plain and simple. With all the pomp and splendor that preceded him, he was not a super human. I wondered why the entire nation regarded a fellow human being as *Wamuyayaya!*[47]

As we were going home that day, I began to think very hard. I was tired and hungry. And even if I was going back home, there was nothing there in terms of food. I was frustrated. Why would one-man so-called president be so protected, so honored, so venerated when the millions of us were living lives that were less than humans? Why would a few people in government continue to enjoy the labor of the poor hard working citizens while the majority was wallowing in abject poverty?[48] Why should others,

---

[47] Kaunda had proclaimed himself as life president or at least through his UNIP cadres. *Wamuyayaya* means "forever." Some of his cadres would shout, "KK!" and others would respond, "*Wamuyayaya!*"

[48] In 1906, Joseph M. Juran suggested that 80 percent of land in Italy was owned by 20 percent of the population. He coined the principle called the *Pareto*, named after an Italian economist Vilfredo Pareto, who made the initial observation. The *Pareto Principle* is known as the 80-20 rule or the law of the vital few because for many events, roughly 80 percent of the effects come from 20 percent of the causes. I observed in Zambia that this principle happened to the detriment of the majority poor, who accessed only

very few in numbers, be so lofty and rich when myriads were basking in indecency, poverty and premature and uncouth deaths?

§2.5 Academic Genius

Luano Primary School was just a walking distance from Number One Luswishi Street where I lived. And there was no question that I was the most intelligent pupil (student) at Luano Primary School during my time. I broke all academic records imaginable. I was focused and determined. I had a few trusted friends at Luano Primary School. Christine Nachula was my desk-mate from Grade Two to Grade Seven. She was a very shy, but serious girl and we always treated each other with respect. My most important friend at Luano was called Theresa Mushibwe. She had a kind heart and was a very pretty girl. Mary Namukonda Chimaramafundo was another of my close friends at Luano.

Luano Primary School was an object of ridicule. At sports competitions, we performed poorly, in academics, we were last, and in extra-curricular activities we were at the bottom of the list. No-one, as far as I can remember wanted to either enlist at Luano or be associated with Luano.

But Luano would be my prize and reward for the five years of my primary school life there. When I went to Luano in Grade Two, I purposed to change Luano's academic history and outlook. I began to work hard. I joined every club imaginable at Luano. I even played in the soccer senior squad. In academics, I was the cream of the class. I came out first from Grade Two Term Two until I completed my Grade Seven. I can only remember coming out number 14 once, because I had missed two subjects

---

about 20 percent of the national wealth, even when they constituted about 80 percent of the population!

21

in Mr. Silungwe's examination. That term, I believe it was in Grade Four Term Three, Beatrice Chansa came out number one. I remember because this was significant; I had never known any other number except number one. From then on with Mr. Japhet Mbewe as my new teacher, I cruised on to Kabundi Secondary School with flying colors. At the time, Kabundi was one of the three leading secondary schools in Chingola; the other two were Chingola and Chikola secondary schools. There were other prestigious private secondary schools in Chingola as well.

§2.6 The Bemba Proverb

In Bemba, they say, *Umwana ashenda atasha nyina ukunaya.*[49] The Bemba people of Zambia believe in mobility. They believe that exposure to a wider world is necessary in opening people's worldviews. I did better in academic subjects because I had access to books and class notes. However, I had no access to television or radio from which most of the current affairs questions in the general knowledge category of the knowledge tests emanated.

In Kapisha Compound, radio was another luxury. Only a few households owned radios. During soccer matches we would be glued to a small radio listening to commentaries by Dennis Liwewe or his son Ponga. Television was not even heard of; I knew televisions existed, but my family did not own one.

I was missing on a great deal of what went on in Zambia. That is why I read anything my eyes gazed upon. I sometimes imagined if I had the exposure some students had at Kabundi! I always came first in my class, but not without great sacrifice. Lack of access to information is a challenge. Information is necessary for development. I struggled to know what was going

---

[49] This proverb literally means that a less traveled child only appreciates his mother's cooking. The Bembas believe that exposure to other civilizations, cultures and information in general gives a person an upper hand in terms of personal development and competence.

on in the country. Lack of a radio or television impacted negatively on my perception of life. The only place I was familiar with was Kapisha and anything outside of it was unknown to me.

When children grow up without proper information, they fail to innovate and this has devastative consequences on the overall development of a nation. For example, in Kapisha where we had no access to information, our only window to the world was rumors. Whether those rumors were true or not, we believed them. In other words, lack of information leads to lack of innovation and independent rational thinking. In societies where access to information is limited or non-existent, poverty and ignorance rank high.

§2.7 By the Maple Tree

As I moved to Canada later in life, I realized that Zambian children and Canadians or children from the developed nations are all the same except that the latter have early access to information. This disparity explains why kids from the rich and developed nations grow up with the capacity and nurtured inclination towards technological, scientific and artistic development. Moreover, children from rich nations have a rare privilege to have necessary resources available to experiment and invent.

§2.8 Zero to Hero

In the 1990 Grade Eight Term One test at Kabundi in English Composition, I got a zero out of 40. I wrote that English test with no knowledge of how a Composition should be written. In fact, I had written everything in one paragraph: No introduction, no content body, and no conclusion. Mr. Musonda, our teacher in the English subject, had no pleasant words for me. I deserved a zero.

I failed the test because I had no access to information. I knew what to say, but not how to say it. Like most children from the poor shanty-towns without libraries and community educational facilities, the only means of information we had was a teacher. If the teacher also hailed from a poor educational system, you can only imagine how impoverished the quality of learning. With all the challenges I faced in Grade Eight Term One, I decided to move heaven and earth and do better in the Mock Examination.[50]

The following term, and importantly because it counted in the scheme of competition, especially with Edward Chembeya,[51] I enlisted the help of Kenneth Chenga.[52] Kenneth loved to study. He taught me the fundamentals of a good Composition. True to his lecture, I went ahead and came out top of all four Grade Eight classes at Kabundi Secondary School that year. Later, during the Mock Examinations in Grade Nine, I was number one, leaving everyone far behind, including Edward. However, Edward settled the scores in the final examinations; I was second.

Both Edward and I were accepted at Hillcrest Technical Secondary School, at that time, one of the schools for the cream of Zambia's secondary education system.[53] At Hillcrest, Edward and I found ourselves in the same class. We were mature enough to know that school was not all about competition. Besides, at Hillcrest we had found those who matched our wits and even exceeded them, like Sweathen Mwenefumbo; a true born genius!

---

[50] At Kabundi Secondary School, like in most secondary schools in Zambia, just before the final Grade Nine Examinations going into Grade Ten, the school prepares what it believes is a mockery of the final exams. From this Mock Exam, one can measure how prepared they are for the final.
[51] Edward was an astute student who worked very hard and competed tenaciously with me.
[52] Kenneth is now a Christian pastor and he and I have maintained our communication.
[53] Located in the town of Livingstone, Zambia's tourism Capital, Hillcrest was the school for the children of the Zambian politicians and reputable personalities. One of the pupils in my class at Hillcrest was Musaku Mwenechanya (now Dr. Mwenechanya). Later when I went to UNZA I learned that Musaku's father was Professor Mwenechanya who was the deputy vice-chancellor of UNZA in the late 1990s.

§2.9 Philosophical Basis

Shortly before going to Hillcrest in Grade Nine Term Three, two events had taken place which would shape my philosophy of life and my conviction of a democratic society, respectively. First, I had become a Born-Again Christian. The circumstances leading to my conversion were purely by accident. I had asked my then best friend, Elijah Sinyinza, if I could stay with him during the days leading up to the examinations.[54] I did so for two reasons: I wanted to be near to Kabundi Secondary School; and I wanted to take advantage of electricity which we did not have in Kapisha Compound. Elijah lived with his brother in the Nchanga mine area. In Volume Two, I write about my conversion experience.

§2.10 Witness to Multipartism

The second event that shaped my philosophy of life happened at Buyantanshi Park where I had a rare opportunity to witness the excitement of the masses and hope of a return to multipartism. On that innocently looking day, the month and date of which I cannot remember, but it was towards the end of the year in 1991. At Buyantanshi Park were gathered a throng of people waiting for Frederick Chiluba to give a speech.[55] Lloyd Sinyinza, Elijah's nephew, came with exciting news that Zambia had a new hero. He said his name was Chiluba and he spoke with a "nice accent." Then Lloyd said that Chiluba would use words like "harass" and "embarrass" in the same sentence. Later I came to learn that what

---

[54] Elijah, a very successful entrepreneur, and I are like true blood brothers. In Lusaka, we visited each other frequently and our families have remained true to each other. In 2003, Elijah acting as my Best Man, contributed K10 million towards my wedding.

[55] Buyantanshi means "Progressing" or "Moving Forward" or "Development."

Lloyd was alluding to was a poetic technique of rhyming.[56]

The atmosphere was hilariously charged. People had such a sense of expectation I had never seen before. I still remember a blind singer with a banjo who sang *Tukekalakenge.*[57] He sang about how under Chiluba and Mwanawasa Zambia would be better again.

Chiluba carried an aura of dignity with him. Perhaps it was because of the excitement of the time. But whatever he was, people liked it. In fact, he did not even say much. He only said that he had delayed coming because some of Kenneth Kaunda's stooges were bent on destabilizing the meeting. And the people cheered and hailed, "Shame, shame, shame!" This was my first time to see and hear Chiluba.

§2.11 Life at Hillcrest

When I arrived at Hillcrest Secondary Technical School in 1992, for so it was called until it was changed to Hillcrest High School in 1994 with the introduction of co-education, I had these two experiences on my back. I was a Born-Again Christian and a witness to multiparty democracy in Zambia. I quickly found a Scripture Union (SU) there which was led by Christian Bwalya, and I joined the Hillcrest Christian Fellowship (HCF). Shortly after, I became a school librarian.

---

[56] Later, I read that Chiluba was not the first to string together the "harass-embarrass" coinage; Kaunda had used the same structure on January 17th, 1963 when he gave a maiden speech. Kaunda said, "We intend to create in this, our mother country, conditions that will attract investors to it.... But I am afraid to say that we have two things here that may continue to *harass and embarrass* us...." (Colin Legum, *Zambia, Independence and Beyond: The Speeches of Kenneth Kaunda*, p. 4)

[57] Literally, we shall live better. It is in the Bemba language.

3| Political Activism

Open your mouth for the mute,
For the rights of all the unfortunate;
Open your mouth, judge justly,
And defend the rights of the afflicted and
needy! - Proverbs 31:8 and 9

Chapter Focus

At the end of reading this chapter, you should be able to:

- Ascertain that students have been the first among the pre-independence throng of pressure groups to agitate for the end to colonialism
- Understand the meaning of political activism in institutions of learning
- Link the conditions of Zambia's economic posture to the state of violence or lack of it at the highest learning institutions in Zambia
- Identify factors that have led to UNZA closures
- Discern the idea of a "Nation within a Nation"

BRIEF INTRODUCTION

In this chapter, the author explores his contributions to the Zambian political process as a community organizer. Special regard is given to the University of Zambia (UNZA) and its place in Zambia's socio-political development. The contribution of the author as leader of the community of Zambians in Canada is also canvassed.

§3.1 UNZA – Political by Design

UNZA is political by design.[58] No matter from where one looks at it, UNZA is wired to protest, and sometimes, protesting for nothing at all. Tembo admits, "Before I went to the University of Zambia...I heard that it was too politicized."[59] She heard right.

UNZA is a world, a nation within a nation. To all those who have had a rare privilege of passing along, as Elliot Phiri describes it, "The still waters of the Goma Lakes," the old ways pass away, for better or for worse, and a new way of thinking, and even of doing things, emerge.

There are three things that happen to anyone who has ever stepped a foot at UNZA. First, they are introduced to the true meaning of independence. UNZA is the hub of the liberal dogma, freedom rings loud and clear at UNZA. UNZA is Zambia's center for intellectualism, defined by Mazrui as "an engagement in the realm of ideas, rational discourse and independent inquiry."[60] Thus, UNZA has helped to shape democracy in Zambia both through intellectualism, and where it has been appropriate, through activism.

Second, UNZA teaches balance. UNZA students learn early that it does not pay to "wash books in water" or to "study in darkness."[61] During the so-called *Gold Rush* period, usually in first-year before students learn the color and taper of the institution, many sad experiences are usual. Many naïve first-

---

[58] The University of Zambia or UNZA was founded in 1965 but it opened its doors to the first students in March 1966.

[59] Tabitha Mvula and Thomas Nsama, "Juliet Tembo – Life at UNZA," *Post Lifestyle*, Sunday, December 4th, 2003

[60] Ali Mazrui, "Pan-Africanism and the Intellectuals: Rise, Decline and Revival," in Thandika Mkandawire (ed.) *African Intellectuals* (Dakar: Codesria Books, 2005), p. 58

[61] See my poem, "Idle Mind" in Charles Mwewa, *Song of an Alien* (New York: iUniverse, 2009), pp. 144-145

year females are lured to the balconies of solidarity to taste the flavor of the most venerated *Monk Sausage*.[62] They may as well know, if they pay attention to the speech of the Vice-Chancellor, the only time he or she ever encountered the student body directly in their student life at UNZA, that life at UNZA is not linear.

It is, therefore, not a secret that many girls in the *Gold Rush* period are either deeply enchanted or are plainly promiscuous and open for abuse. The term *UNZA Open* is attributed to girls who have had a love affair with at least second-, third- or fourth-year male students at UNZA. It is ironic that future intellectuals are first fried in the pots of "broken virginities"[63] before they are cloaked into attires of borrowed brains.

From the *Gold Rush*, students emerge with different poses. Some become either reckless or ingratiate themselves as *UNZA Rumpens,* which is an oxymoron. These are usually very bright students who simply love to make others pay, that is in peaceful times. They are dead-low drunkards who throw verbal sobriquets on sane campers. However, they become an asset during demonstrations, commonly referred to as *Vivas*. They constitute the frontline of vandals, rabble-rousers and political agitators during *Vivas* at UNZA.

Some emerge with unfinished business. If they are ladies, they may acquire *Landlords.*[64] They are *Momas* and may exchange men like under garments. They are partnered with *Mojos* who go around stroking women like selecting ripe mangoes from a bunch of greens!

The rest may fall in any of the two categories. They may have been strict Christians when they came to UNZA. These usually join such religious groups at campus as *Chi-Alpha*, Bread of Life, the Catholics, the Jehovah's Witnesses, the Seventh Day

---

[62] Small dried fish commonly called *Kapenta* in Zambia. It is sometimes shortened to *Monk Sauce! Kapenta* is part of a staple of the Zambian diet.
[63] Song of an Alien, *supra*.
[64] This describes a relationship between a UNZA female student and a man outside the campus. These are usually prominent persons in the Zambian society.

Adventists and so on. These only know how to *pound* the Bible and are collectively known as *BAs!*[65]

The other category generally comprises self-defined *Monks*. They are cromulently known as *Inshimbi* or metal, because they have a reputation of cramming for sciences and mathematics. They usually enlist in the School of Natural Sciences (NS). Special types of *Monks*, called *Bungwes*, have vowed never to come near the "scent of a woman."

Third, UNZA teaches cooperation. The life of a *Monk*,[66] *Mojo*,[67] *Moma*[68] or *BA*[69] at UNZA revolves around studies, sex and feeding. Students may come together in groups and form a *Kambis* or Kambilombilo for the purposes of economizing on spending. They are graced by young girls and boys who bring fruits and vegetables right to the *rezs*[70] for sale. These boys and girls hail from the nearby shanty-towns like Kalingalinga. They are known as *UNZA Veg*. A common meal for most students, especially *Monks*, is *Nshima* with *Monk Sausage* or *Monk Chicken*[71] from well-pummelled *dust* or *powder* made on red-hot *Stone-age*[72] on the balcony.[73] After a successful *diving*,[74] some students, usually *UNZA-Diz*,[75] those who have learned the

---

[65] Born-Agains

[66] Guys who chose to remain celibate

[67] Guys who indulged in highlife of girls and beers

[68] Ladies who indulge with men and love wild-parties

[69] Born-Again Christians, usually very strict on morals and dedicated to religion

[70] These are student residences or hostels. They include International, President, Kwacha, October, Vet, and so on.

[71] Common eggs are referred to as *Monk Chicken*.

[72] These are makeshift plate cookers from stoves.

[73] *Monks* call mealie meal dust or powder.

[74] Some students, especially those who are already broke, may from time to time *dive* or strategically visit other *Kambis* just at meal time to have a chance of feeding with the group.

[75] *UNZA-Diz* are those students who are routine drunkards.

ropes,[76] may wonder out of campus to wash away the meal with a pint of Sheki-Sheki![77]

§3.2 Mulenga Endorsement

There is no better way of beginning to narrate this author's shadowy political activism than what Chisala Mulenga wrote to him. Mulenga reminded him of how he had influenced a young organization called Operation Young Vote (OYV):

Dear Charles,

My name is Chisala Mulenga currently living in Boston, MA. I first heard of your name when I worked for Operation Young Vote (OYV) right after I graduated from high school about eight years ago. I also learned that you were the consultant on the creation of OYV and everyone there spoke very highly of you.[78]

In the year 2000, Nkhuruma Chama Kalalula came to the author's room which was President 6 Room 10 (President 6-10) at UNZA, Great East Road Campus, to consult with him on the formation of OYV.[79] Kalaluka was flanked by Garth Mambwe Chenda.[80] They believed this author could help in the launch of their vision. They needed his input to avoid some common pitfalls of most new initiatives.

It was late in the evening when they arrived at President 6-10. He sat with them, listened to their intentions and then gave his input. They put to work theirs plus his ideas and the result was the formation of the first organization in Zambia advocating for youth vote. Before the elections in 2001, Kelly Salati and this author presented together at Radio Phoenix a phone-in radio

---

[76] Survival mechanisms
[77] Sheki-Sheki is a form of a locally-brewed Zambian beer.
[78] From the Facebook email of July 1st, 2009
[79] Nkhuruma Chama Kalalula was the first president of OYV and before then had been an active leader in UNIP's youth wing.
[80] Garth Chenda succeeded Nkhuruma Chama Kalalula as OYV president in 2002.

program for the youth vote.[81] There were many people calling in and asking for information on voter registration and the voting process.

In 1999, Salati had run for UNZASU president against Simambo Banda. What Salati did not know was that this author had advised Banda on how to defeat Salati in those elections. Banda, who became UNZASU president that year, had consulted with this author on the best strategy to defeating Salati in the election. In fact, Banda had used the leverage of people-power this author had at UNZA to gain voter momentum.

After the Banda-Salati UNZASU race, this author was also responsible for Kelvin Hambwezya's ascendance to the UNZASU presidency in 2001. Hambwenzya sought his help in winning the UNZASU elections. Hambwenzya and him had become close friends just prior to Hambwenzya's nomination as the UNZASU presidential candidate. Hambwenzya knew one thing his opponent did not know. He knew how to harness the support of masses through this author's help.

In addition, Hambwenzya knew that this author had the people-power, an advantage his predecessor had so successfully exploited. This author was leader of UNZA Inter-Fellowships Executive Committee (UNZA-IFEC), co-chair of the UNZA Poetry Club,[82] and author.

§3.3 Student Violence

Students have both moral and political rights to agitate against government. But during this author's time as a student at UNZA, he found student behavior of stoning and vandalizing the public's cars and property unacceptable. There is no justification for

---

[81] In 2000, Kelly was UNZASU presidential candidate. His chief opponent was Simambo Banda. Simambo went on to winning that election.

[82] Elliot Phiri and this author founded the UNZA Poetry Club at UNZA

student rabblerousing whenever there is demand for action from government.

In oppressive regimes, such as existed during apartheid in South Africa, although illegal, there is a moral justification for the oppressed masses to resort to violence to register their grievances in defiance to bad laws. The situation in Zambia, especially in the Third Republic, did not warrant such behavior. In August 2009, Copperbelt University (CBU) students rioted and burned a vehicle belonging to a local businessman whom they also robbed of K200 million. Students at both UNZA and CBU continue to engage in similar behaviors to the detriment of the Zambian infrastructural mishmash.

§3.4 Life at UNZA

In the 1990s, Zambia had only two universities, UNZA and CBU. The educational, political and legal, among others, were all located at UNZA Great East Road Campus. The Medical School is located at UNZA Ridgeway Campus. By its design, UNZA was and has always been the center of political activism. Once one was accepted to UNZA, in one form or the other, they acquired a political deportment.

First, nothing came easily at UNZA. From registration, to scrumming for a few recommended available books at the library, to securing meal allowances, everything demanded a fight.

Second, being one of the only two universities in a country of over twelve million people then, UNZA was the headquarters of free thinking and philosophical agitation.

At UNZA, everything took a political twist: Religion, culture, leisure, and everything in between were overtly politicized. In 2000 when this author was canvassing the support of the Catholic community at UNZA to be a part of UNZA-IFEC, the Catholic Chaplain, an astute Jesuit priest and lawyer, accused him of "trying to win the Catholics to his side."

Charles Mwewa

UNZA was and has always been a distinct form of socialization. Girls came whole and graduated broken; boys came quiet and graduated vocal. Two places at UNZA determined students' destiny: The rooftops and the Goma Lakes. At both places plans were hatched, names changed, ideas born, and virginities broken.

During peaceful times, nobody cared what another did or said. But during disturbances *mojos, monks, momas,* and *BAs* joined forces in protest. And there is a history to this. Since its inception, UNZA students have shaped Zambia's political landscape. UNIP's landslide electoral victory in 1964 was partly premised on the people of Zambia's desire to advance themselves in terms of education.

Two factors necessitated the establishment of UNZA in 1966.[83] Out of a population of roughly three and a half million people, only about a hundred were graduates. UNZA would serve to increase that number. Another, and probably more pressing factor, was that Kaunda needed to "honor his pledge over an accelerated expansion of educational facilities at all educational levels."[84] The establishment of UNZA would prove to be just an election campaign promise fulfilled or an improvement in educational delivery in Zambia; it would signify an essential force in forging Zambia's political temerity.

Mwanakatwe has informed that students were among the pre-independence throng of pressure groups that joined forces with the political class to agitate for the end of colonialism:

---

[83] Officially, UNZA was established in 1965. Lecturers and tutorials were first provided at Ridgeway Campus (former Oppenheimer College) near the University Teaching Hospital (UTH). Construction of permanent buildings for lecturer and accommodation began in 1966 at what is now known as the Great East Road Campus. UNZA Great East Road Campus was completed in 1968.

[84] Patrick Motondo Wele, *Zambia's Most Famous Dissidents* (Solwezi: PMW, 1995), p. 42

In pre-independence days, practically all effective pressure groups among Africans recognized the urgent task of political and economic development. The African civil servants, the trade unions, church leaders and even students in government-owned and mission schools joined forces from time to time with the political class in the fight against colonialism.[85]

UNZA students did not wait long after independence to carry on the tradition. Per Wele, the first form of student agitation at UNZA began in 1965 at the British High Commission to Zambia in Lusaka, "when the British flag was threaded by the first students."[86] This happened after a rumor had circulated that four freedom fighters had been hanged in Southern Rhodesia without due process. This rumor was later disproved but not before the student agitators had tasted the bitter corners of the Lusaka Remand Prison.

§3.5 UNZA Closures

This author was accepted at UNZA in 1996 to do a four-year Bachelor of Arts degree. He was expected to complete it and graduate in 1999. But instead, he graduated in 2002. It took him six years to do a four-year undergraduate degree at UNZA all due to the disturbances at the institution. Usually, a nation's educational standards are judged by the state and the quality of its highest institutions of learning. For Zambia, UNZA said it all in plain language.

Wele has cited about five UNZA closures between the First and Second Republics. The first closure took place on Thursday, July 15th, 1971. The reason cited for the closure was that government had received and considered "reports of discipline and lawlessness among students at university campus of UNZA."[87] The UNZASU Executive and other students who

---

[85] John M. Mwanakatwe, *End of Kaunda Era* (Lusaka: Multimedia Publication, 1994), p. 218
[86] Wele, *supra.,* p. 43
[87] *Ibid.,* p. 51

signed a letter in which the students were alleged to have insulted the president on July 11th, 1971 were Ronald Penza, Cosmas Chola, Gerry Chabwera, Jonathan Momba, John Chileshe and Enerst Kasula.

On July 7th, 1971, UNZA students demonstrated and on July 15th, 1971, President Kaunda closed UNZA claiming that the students' behavior was "highly insulting to the Head of State and quite irresponsible."[88] The students had demanded a say in the events happening in Zimbabwe. This was UNZA's first closure.

The second UNZA closure happened on February 10th, 1976 after "200 students...staged a demonstration in support of MPLA."[89] The Minister of Education cited provocation, intimidation and violence as having necessitated the closure.[90]

After six years, UNZA closed again for the third time. The student union leaders were agitated by the launching of the Institute of Human Relations.[91] The students did not see anything relevant in such an institute other than it would put the workers and peasants to sleep. The underlying objective of the Institute, which also had received the anointing of John Mwanakatwe,[92] was to promulgate the philosophy of Humanism. The students were averse to this which they considered as the first stage in the creation of a "man-centered society." On April 21st, 1982, UNZA was closed.

The fourth UNZA closure was caused by hikes in tuition fees. Prompted by the IMF and the World Bank, UNZA had raised the fees by over 30 percent sending students into campus

---

[88] *Ibid.*, p. 47

[89] Wele, *supra.,* p. 57

[90] Fwanyanga Mulikita; for a more comprehensive coverage of the second closure of UNZA, see Hamalengwa's *Thoughts are Free.*

[91] Or the School of Human Relations. It had to have two objectives: to conduct research in the sphere of human relations; and to be able to publish the *Zambia Journal of Human Relations.*

[92] Former Minister of Education

histrionics.[93] On May 18th, 1986, the UNZA administration[94] closed the campus because students were accused of "insulting the leadership of the Party and Its Government (or PIG)."[95] On June 30th, 1990, UNZA closed for the fifth time. It is this closure which was material to the downfall of former president Kaunda.

In the late 1980s, the IMF and the World Bank had introduced SAPs[96] to Zambia. The students felt that the conditions attached to these stabilization programs ignored the structural problems of Zambia. Coupled with the gradual withdrawal of the subsidy[97] on maize announced on June 19th, 1990 by the then Prime Minister, Malimba Masheke, "Dissension over the increase reached such a feverish peak that the writing was evidently seen on the wall for the government."[98]

In Zambia, SAPs were partly the underlying cause of the 1991 pro-multiparty democracy. Previously, Kaunda and UNIP had shown a lack of commitment in the implementation of stabilization and SAP policies between 1973 and 1991. On many occasions, the UNIP government failed to fulfill the agreed targets and had the agreements suspended or canceled. However, as the economic situation worsened, government was perceived as having been responsible for the economic crisis. Thus, the demand for democracy in Zambia was also an expression of opposition to the effects of structural adjustment.[99]

[93] Boarding fees rose from K1200 to K1900
[94] Under the Vice- chancellorship of Dr. Jacob Mwanza
[95] Wele, *supra.*, p.73
[96] SAPs or Structural Adjustment Programs refer to the austerity measures that the IMF imposes as prerequisites for further foreign aid, see Grotpeter *et. al, Historical Dictionary of Zambia,* p. 415.
[97] Subsidy on mealie meal was gradually withdrawn from K114.50 to K269.00 for "Breakfast meal" and from K82.30 to K198.00 for "Roller meal."
[98] Wele, *supra.*, p. 74
[99] See Simutanyi, "The Politics of Structural Adjustment in Zambia," p. 825

On June 26th, 1990,[100] the students marched on Cairo Road in demonstration against the food shortages and price increases. Through the student incitement, the mob grew and widened its tentacles to include cigarette sellers,[101] marketeers and unruly youth. This mob transformed itself into a demolisher of supermarkets, shops and government buildings. Looting and rioting married and gave birth to a *Dark Tuesday*.[102]

While events in the country, and specifically the closure of UNZA, were simmering, a pressure cooker was seething at ZNBC. It began with the surprise announcement: "Due to the escalating cost of living followed by the food riots, the Zambia Army has decided to take over the government. This is Lt. Mwamba Luchembe."[103] The event was too much for Alexander Grey Zulu who announced that the coup attempt had been foiled by the commandos under the command of Brigadier General Weston Chanda.[104] President Kaunda, who was opening a Trade Fair in Ndola, was awakened to the "Lord is My Shepherd."[105]

The events surrounding UNZA demonstrations and closures, and the riots that rocked the City of Lusaka leading to the Luchembe coup attempt and the shaking up of the UNIP regime under Kaunda have been well captured in Chiluba's book, *Democracy: The Challenge of Change*: "The University of Zambia has always been a center of political agitation. By the end

---

[100] Frederick Chiluba, in *Democracy: The Challenge of Change* (1995) on page 64, places this date on June 25th, 1990

[101] Also known as *Mishanga-Sellers* in vernacular

[102] Tuesday, June 27th, 1990, prompted by an erroneous revelation that Kaunda had a stack of US$5 billion in foreign banks insinuated by Gen. Christon Tembo, from UNZA to Chilenje, the mob ransacked and looted Kabulonga Supermarket, mistaken to have been owned by the Kaunda family. In fact, the supermarket was owned by Lendor Burton.

[103] Wele, *supra.*, p. 171

[104] As Secretary-General of UNIP, Grey Zulu was the second most important politician in Zambia, and at ZNBC he announced that the coup was the work of one undisciplined soldier.

[105] Psalms 23

of 1980s students and academic staff alike were predisposed to be dissatisfied with the government, which on several occasions had closed the university and disrupted the academic program, sometimes in retaliation against their political outspokenness."[106]

UNZA is, and has always been, a partner in the Zambian democratic process. Despite that, UNZA has also been a place where dreams have been shuttered, minds deranged and public infrastructure destroyed.

§3.6 ZAMCAN President

In 2005, this author met Chasaya Sichilima at the wedding ceremony of Naomi Chiwala in Toronto. Sichilima was asked to sing a song in Bemba from his musical album, *Walasa*. When this author listened to Sichilima's music, he just fell in love with it. Sichilima is a widely known Zambian musician and recorder. Sichilima and the author met again on the subway train in Toronto. Sichilima introduced the author to the Zambian Canadian Association (Foundation) or ZAMCAN.

In 2007, Sichilima and the author served together in the ZAMCAN Board with him as Secretary and the author as vice-chairman (for before ZAMCAN became a foundation on June 12th, 2009, the president carried the title of chairperson and the deputy president was vice-chairperson). In that year, Musaba Chailunga was voted *in absentia* as chairman, taking over from Kaluba Chilaisha.[107]

On April 24th, 2010, at the AGM held in Toronto, the author was elected president of ZAMCAN.[108] The author felt it was a

---

[106] Chiluba, *supra.,* pp. 64-65

[107] Chailunga holds a degree in Business Administration and a Post-Graduate Diploma in Information Technology. In 2006-2007, Chailunga served as president of the Zambian Canadian Association (ZAMCAN). In 2008, Chailunga served as chairman of the ZAMCAN Diaspora Dual Citizenship Sub-Committee with me as his vice. In 2009, Chailunga was elected the first chairman of the Zambia Diaspora.

[108] I became the ninth ZAMCAN president since inception after Dr. Sam Sikaneta, Dr. Grace Mchaina, Mr. CK Kasapu, Dr. Cephas Masikini, Ms.

ripe time for to serve his community in that capacity. Except for a brief resignation in 2015, this author has served the Zambian community in Canada ever since.

§3.7 ZAMCAN's 10th Anniversary

This author was motivated to serve the Zambians in Canada as ZAMCAN president for two reasons. First - because he wanted to contribute to the continued relationship between Canada and Zambia. Ken Coates has described Canada and Zambia relations as "long-standing partners."[109] In fact, Canada was one of the first countries to come to Zambia's help shortly after independence. Former president, Rupiah Banda, acknowledged: "Our bilateral relations with Canada date back to 1966, barely two years after we attained our independence in 1964. The first effort that Canada made was to support our young government in the development of the educational sector. Canada, through Carlton University in Ottawa, provided the first Vice-chancellor of the University of Zambia, Professor Douglas Anglin."[110]

Professor Anglin has written extensively about Zambia including, *Zambia Crisis Behavior*. This author had a rare pleasure of honoring Professor Anglin *in absentia* at the celebration of ZAMCAN's 10th Anniversary as the first patron of the organization.[111] Two other persons honored at this event were

---

Mary Mutuna, Mr. Kaluba Chilaisha, Mr. Musaba Chailunga, and Mr. Chasaya Sichilima.

[109] *Discover Zambia,* "The First Canada-Zambia Trade Mission," 2010/2011, Volume 5, p. 34.

[110] *Ibid.*, p. 5; On January 7th, 1990, another Canadian was appointed as Governor of the Bank of Zambia; his name was Jacques Bussieres.

[111] On October 23rd, 2010 during the 46th Independence Party celebrations, and also marking ZAMCAN's 10th Anniversary, I presented certificates of outstanding leadership to the ZAMCAN founders who included: Dr. Sam Sikaneta, Ms. Mbonélla Phiri, Mr. Chisanga Puta-Chekwe, Dr. Grace

Mabel Opoku, for continued support, and Alan Wadham, for having served the longest on the ZAMCAN Board. Canada, indeed, has continued to enhance the flavor of Zambia's human rights record, spearheading good governance and democracy.[112]

The contribution of Zambians to the progress and strength of Zambia-Canada relations at community level began as early as 1958. Many Zambians who passed by the falling leaves of the maple trees either made some attempts or laid the foundation of ZAMCAN. Among them was Dickson Mwansa and Kaela Mulenga. Mulenga was "encouraged by [his] experience from Sweden (Scandinavia) where [he] had founded the African-Scandinavian Association – on the premise that without such an organization the interests of African immigrants would not be looked after well."[113] This noble cause continues to define ZAMCAN's mandate and community organization.

In the words of Chisanga Puta-Chekwe, "The idea of forming a Zambian Canadian group first arose around 1991."[114] Puta-Chekwe met with Sam Sikaneta at Toronto "to discuss several matters including the establishment of the Zambian Canadian Association." They were joined at the Metropolitan Hotel by the late Chinkangala Fostino Lombe.[115]

To continue with the momentum, the founders met at the Sikaneta's residence in Cambridge, Ontario, to formalize the formation of ZAMCAN. It was at that meeting where the provisional by-laws and other formation mappings took place. To sum up, the following account of the formation of ZAMCAN is commonly adopted:

> In the summer of 2000, Samuel Sikaneta and Chisanga Puta-Chekwe made contact with a number of like-minded Zambians in

---

Mchaina, Dr. David Mchaina, Dr. Lowesha Kapijimpanga, Mr. Zamanga Chulu, Mr. Kaluba Chilaisha, Mr. Michael Moyo, Dr. Promil Paul, Dr. Marcia Barron, Mr. Viktor Mubili, and Ms. Chavuka Saviye.

[112] *Ibid.*

[113] Email exchange of October 16th, 2010 with Kaela Mulenga.

[114] ZAMCAN files, October 29th, 2008.

[115] See §13.2

and around Toronto and Ottawa to plan a party to celebrate Zambian Independence Day on a grand scale. These like-minded individuals included Jean Puta-Chekwe, Julie Tembo, Ruth Chikosa, Zamanga Chulu, Kirkwood Achiume, Lowesha Kapijimpanga, Marcia Barron, Grace Mchaina, David Mchaina, Kaela Mulenga, Mbonélla Phiri and Joan Sikaneta. The First Secretary at the Zambian Embassy in Washington DC, John Mulutula, and his wife were invited to the function. This defining event was held at the First Ethiopian Place on Yonge Street, Toronto, on October 29th, 2000. Chinkangala Fostino Lombe helped to find support for sponsorship of [the] organization. On December 16th, 2000 with about forty members from the community, at the Metro Community Hall, 55 John Street, Toronto, Ontario, ZAMCAN was officially launched.[116]

At the 10th Anniversary of ZAMCAN, this author's message was the same he has promulgated since he became active in the community: To love ZAMCAN and the people of Zambia. And this forms his second reason why he was motivated to become president of ZAMCAN: "As I have always said, 'Love ZAMCAN.' Embrace it as a treasure. Through it our children have a rare chance to exert their national spirit and pride."[117] This continues to be this author's philosophy for community service and organization.

§3.8 Community Organizer

During the US 2008 primaries, Senator Hilary Clinton kept hammering on candidate Barack Obama's supposedly lack political administration experience. She mocked his community organization skills. She campaigned that as a community organizer, Obama was ill-prepared to lead the US. President Obama went on to be elected as the first Black president of the

---

[116] *Ibid.*

[117] Charles Mwewa, Speech for the 10th Anniversary of ZAMCAN held at Sapphire Banquet and Conference Center in Mississauga, Canada, on October 23rd, 2010.

US. He was re-elected in 2012. President Obama began as a community organizer. During the primaries, this was made an election issue and some even saw it as a political liability. Competing candidates like Sarah Palin farced over administrative experiences. First, she was former Mayor of Wasilla, and second, she was Governor of Alaska. Obama, Clinton and John McCain were all US senators.

Does community organizing matter in the political leadership matrix? This author's experience as a community organizer informs him so. The true evidence, however, can be proffered from the first two years of President Obama's presidency. The community-organizer-president did in his first two years of presidency more than what many so-called great American presidents had failed to do in their entire tenures. President Obama passed the Healthcare Bill into law on March 21st, 2010.[118]

This was "A watershed moment for America, a defining victory for its president. The core element of change upon which Barack Obama was elected came to pass Sunday night in the form of sweeping health-care reform."[119] And on May 1st, 2011, Obama triumphed where his predecessors, Bill Clinton and George W. Bush, had failed: He killed Osama bin Laden. In addition, President Obama went on to enact the financial reform, small business loans, ACTA, unemployment legislations, and many others.

As hinted by Potter, "The core element of change upon which Barack Obama was elected" was the Health-Care reform. It does not matter whether President Obama served two terms or three terms, he had been permanently etched into history as one of the greatest presidents of America.[120]

---

[118] The famous Obamacare, which President Trump vowed to repeal and replace.
[119] Mitch Potter, "Obama Wins Epic Health-care Battle," *The Toronto Star*, (Monday, March 22nd, 2010)
[120] In the mid-term elections of November 2nd, 2010, the Republicans won big especially in the House of Representatives. Many thought this was

There are three reasons why this author believes presidents or leaders with community organization background succeed in the art of presidency. First, they understand human nature. Many people think that all that matters is administrative or political experience. While that is true, it is not always necessary. Community organizers do understand the nature of the people they serve.

Second, administration is usually done in the offices, away from the harsh realities of the day-to-day struggles of the people. The community organizer delves into the very belly of society, negotiating all the hassle and tussle of poverty, hunger, lack, and many ills grizzly buffeting the community.

Third, community organization is government on wheels or government in action. It accords the organizers an opportunity to provide practical leadership in the day-to-day affairs of the people. It teaches, "How to develop leadership potential and respond to the needs of the people."[121] Community organization defines leadership which is of the people, for the people, and by the people, which is democracy.

As a community leader, one of the commonest experiences one can have with the Zambian community is beginning meetings and functions on time. Zambians rarely turn up for meetings and functions on time. It has become increasingly practicable for the Zambian Canadian leadership to schedule events with the

---

judgment on President Barack Obama. The economy of US at that time was still performing badly and unemployment rates ranged in the 9th to 10th percentage points. However, for many years to come, the achievements of President Obama will match, and even exceed those of many great US presidents. Americans seemed to have forgotten that the whole world was in a global recession. It would take longer than normal for their economic policies to begin to bear fruits. Any president in the place of Barack Obama would face the same challenges.

[121] Cynthia Gordy, "The Community Organizers Who Discovered Obama," *Essence.Com*, (Wednesday, March 17th, 2010)

"Zambian Time"[122] in mind. This means that a thirty minute to one-hour time contingency is budgeted for to capture a reasonable attendance before meetings or events could commence. This habit is costly in terms of time and money. In Zambia, this weakness can be tolerated without deleterious repercussions. However, in Western formations where "Time is money,"[123] it impacts very negatively on organizational success. A community that has a reputation of diligence and magnanimity like the Zambia's can erase all its successes with a simple stroke of time mismanagement.

The very nature of community organizing is that it is a democratic arrangement. Consensus must be sought to reach any decision that the community may consider their own. Fortunately for ZAMCAN, there is a formidable email communication system that works very well for the community. Although many of the people may not respond there and then to announcements or requests, the email system has proven to be very effective in informing the community on events such as weddings, funerals, birthdays or any news that the Board deems relevant to the people.

---

[122] An event that is slated to begin at 12:00 noon, for example, is presumed, according to "Zambian Time," to begin at least thirty minutes to one-hour later. Thus, a 12:00 noon event is, in fact, a 1:00PM event in "Zambian Time," and so on. Elias Chipimo, Jr., has lamented this tendency by Zambians to mismanage time in his book, *Unequal to the Task?*

[123] This has been conveniently captured this mantra in a poem called "Time", see Charles Mwewa, *Song of an Alien*, p. 146

4| Rural Poverty in Zambia

Poverty and war can aggravate the evil in human-beings to commit atrocities unimaginable in human relationships. Poverty is evil.

Chapter Focus

At the end of reading this chapter, you should be able to:

- Understand the genesis, expansion and impact of rural poverty in Zambia
- Examine how poverty affects life expectancy, innovation and productivity
- Debunk the myth of poverty despite independence
- Examine the Quebec poverty elimination model and ascertain ways in which it can positively impact Zambia
- Review Zambia's development plans
- Examine Shanty-Towns in terms of problems, analysis and proposed solutions

BRIEF INTRODUCTION

In this chapter, the theme of rural poverty is brought to the fore. It discusses the historical events and actions that have relegated Zambia to a poorest and highly indebted nation. It exposes the impact of poverty on the productive demography of the nation.

§4.1 Aura of Poverty

Poverty affects people's will to survive. And where most of the citizenry is concerned, poverty damages the very soul of the nation. In Zambia, where poverty levels are in their highest percentiles, the nation is barely on a resuscitation machine. Where poverty dominates like in Zambia, the good is swallowed in the bad. It is very easy to forget that something developmental is going on in such a nation. For example, there could be enormous efforts being made to development, but all such efforts will be dwindled by data that support poverty and by media images and stories that even strengthen poverty further.

Influenced by his childhood experience, this author has vowed to fight poverty to his death and to strengthen democracy with all he has in him. On March 13th, 2010, an organization called Rural Action International founded by Rodah Namwalizi Lester[124] invited this author to officiate as Guest of Honor representing ZAMCAN.[125] He was flanked by Rachel Bezner Kerr who gave a keynote speech on her research work among the rural communities in Malawi.[126]

---

[124] Rodah Namwalizi Lester is a Zambian and author of *Cassava is the Root*. She is married to Brad Lester, a Canadian who has had an extensive work among the rural populations of Zambia since the 1980s. In *Cassava is the Root*, Lester describes her development work with the Mozambican communities between 1989 and 2001. These development works took place in three areas of Nampula, Lago and Inhambane. She addresses issues of poverty affecting rural women and provides insights into the factors influencing them. The book is also loaded with traditional African recipes.

[125] ZAMCAN is an association responsible for the Zambian Canadian affairs in Canada. See also §3.7

[126] Rachel Bezner Kerr is a Professor of Geography at the University of Western Ontario. She is Research Coordinator for the Soils, Food and Health Communities Project in Malawi.
<http://geography.uwo.ca/faculty/beznerkerr/>

This author spoke about the experiences of a rural and shanty-town child in the Zambian context. He gave what most of the people present described as an emotional speech. Part of that speech is reproduced below:

> In 2007 and 2008 I had a rare pleasure of meeting Mrs. Rhoda Lester, author of *Cassava is the Root*. In this book, Mrs. Lester's heart goes to the poor of our beloved continent, Africa. Like most African mothers, she both lived and worked among the rural African women and children. Her story is not an anecdotal retelling of what someone else has experienced. It is, rather, a first-hand appeal, from a mother, sister and African stateswoman who has had both the passion and courage to do something about what she believes in.
>
> Rural Action International (RAI) is a dream we all carry. All of us who have had the chance to be in Africa or work with African women and children can attest to the legitimacy of RAI.
>
> A village is portent with untapped potential. It is a mine of underused reservoir. All a village needs are hearts and hands that can give some form of support, materially as well as financially. With that help, there are countless projects that can be created, projects which will make our villages self-sufficient. And this is what RAI is all about.
>
> Poverty in Zambia is real and growing at a faster rate and we need concerted efforts to curb it. There is no-one who suffers more than the rural woman and her child. I believe empowerment is the best weapon against poverty.
>
> And let me add, of organizations like RAI, there are many women and children who are working very hard to improve the quality of their lives. There are also many government programs aimed at improving the lives of our women and children. This is the hope we still have for the Zambian woman and child. It is that despite what they have gone through, they have come out strong and determined.

On April 5th, 2010, in an email addressed to family and friends of RAI, Secretary/Treasurer of the organization highlighted the salient features of this author's speech which implored everyone present to contribute to ideas such as RAI:

The event would not have been possible without the support of many volunteers who contributed in a variety of ways as well as the spirit of goodwill of all the participants. The Special Guest, Charles Mwewa, Vice-president [president from April 24th, 2010] of the Zambian Canadian Foundation, gave a moving address highlighting his own personal experience of growing up in, and overcoming African poverty. He reminded us of the role of African women and he urged Rural Action International, and all those gathered, to adopt the passion and commitment to community development as described in the book, *Cassava is the Root*. His memorable contribution was a reminder that we can all make a difference.[127]

For Africa, in general, and Zambia, living above poverty is a struggle, what Lester calls, "The struggle for well-being and economic empowerment."[128] In 1964, Zambia gained political independence. But the battle for economic independence is far from over. The challenge is, whereas for political independence one would blame the colonialists, for poverty, however, pinpointing a definite cause is very difficult indeed.

In Zambia, as in Africa in general, poverty has a multi-causal and historical genesis. Focus, however, is on the practical ways of alleviating, and even wiping out poverty completely.

Poverty is not a problem that can be defeated by Zambia alone. Poverty can be defeated if a partnership is forged among the local communities, government, NGOs, charitable organizations and the international community. Lester, who has worked extensively among the African rural communities, nods this fact when she acknowledges that, "The international community, particularly non-governmental organizations (NGOs) ... have worked with communities in Africa to try and overcome the deep wounds of slavery, colonialism, war, and

[127] Rhoda N. Lester, "Launch of Action Rural International," email of April 5th, 2010
[128] Rodah Namwilizi Lester, *Cassava is the Root* (Toronto: Rhoda Lester, 2010), p.4.

natural disasters."[129] Indeed, this has been the better way forward.

§4.2 Rural Poverty

One cannot look at the poverty situation in Zambia and fail to see its historical genesis. Most people in Zambia are hard working. This author's sister, Mary Kalaba, is a good example. She was a single mother when the author lived at her home. She worked very hard under very harsh conditions to ensure that her children and the author had food, clothing and attended school.

In Zambia, a woman usually has to sacrifice her own pleasure, leisure and dignity in order to provide a much more decent level of living for her family. She has, most of the time, assumed the role of a bread-winner when the husband dies or is absent. She goes out of her way to fend for her family.

When Europe scrambled for Africa, the colonial governments were not interested in empowering the Africans to be self-sufficient. Rather, the colonial powers were interested in plundering the Zambian resources to build Southern Rhodesia, for so was Zimbabwe called, and South Africa. Zambia was only used as a resource base, especially for copper reserves.

With the disruptions in the village setting brought about by able-bodied men and boys leaving for cash-for-work in the urban areas, most villages were depleted of sedulous men to develop the rural areas. This left the villages with woman and unfit men, and essentially giving impetus to rural poverty.

Lester has bemoaned thus: "How low can Black women sink while other races raise themselves up at their expense? They have worked plantations of cotton yet they have no clothes to wear. They have coconut plantations yet they don't have soap to wash their children or themselves. They have to care for cashew trees and process fruit yet their children are dying with malnutrition."[130]

---

[129] *Ibid*, p. 4
[130] Lester, *supra.*, p. 6

This charge is from a Zambian woman, a mother who has lived most of her life for the struggling women and children of Africa. She writes about what she has seen and known. No-one better than Lester, can bring out this impassioned charge. Her burden is the collective wish of all Zambian people.

Coupled with the indignities of the profit-motivated appeals of some organizations which solicit donations for charitable work in Africa, contemptible, and overtly despicable images of the sufferings of the Zambian women and children are used as marketing tools. For most people, especially in the Western Hemisphere, sadly, those images are the only window they have of the Zambian villages and rural areas. While these images are used intentionally to wool would be donors, their unintentional negative impact on the sanity and dignity of the Zambian women and children cannot be overlooked.

Again, Lester agrees. She observes that media portrayals of people in Zambia render a defeatist illusion in the minds of those who watch the images. She notes that such propaganda eventually dilutes the genuine efforts women organizations and other groups are making in Zambia:

> The media portrayal of crisis situations inevitably gives a negative picture of African women. All the children see are orphans. Most of the pictures circulating show naked children with mucus running from their noses. You see the mother waiting as her child dies in the makeshift clinic or on the long march from danger. Then you see other races or better-off classes of women representing the suffering of these women and children because these are the ones with education and privilege. Someone with power, wealth and education is asking for money on behalf of the children. Of course, you and I know that there are millions of capable women in Africa who feed these children. Just because they're being kept behind closed doors does not mean they've all died.[131]

---

[131] *Ibid.,* p. 8.

In Lester's voice one hears the urgency and responsibility with which she speaks. In Chapter Two, the author discussed how his auntie sacrificed her own *Chitenge* wrapper for his blankets. He hinted how his uncle trekked deep into the bush to fetch for their food. Lester's tone subscribes to the challenges most people in rural and shanty-towns of Zambia go through every day.

Zambian women and children, especially in rural areas, do not need to accept to be down on the stairs of poverty. Zambian women and children are humans who deserve a decent living and improved hygiene and a long life. When poverty is talked about in Zambia, it almost inevitably centers on rural and shanty-women and children. These feel the sharp edges of hunger and lack on a constant basis.

The Living Conditions Monitoring Survey (LCMS) IV,[132] of 2004, estimated that as much as 68 percent of the Zambian population fell below the national poverty-line, earning less than K111,747 (US$25). LCMS VI (2010) reduced that rate to 64 percent. However, almost 50 percent of people of Zambia live in poverty. In Zambia, like in Africa in general, "more than 70 percent of the continent's poor live in rural areas and depend on agriculture for food and livelihood."[133]

Most people in villages are subsistence farmers. People grow crops to sustain themselves throughout the year. Through *Chitemene System*, crops like maize (cone), sorghum, finger millet and groundnuts are grown.[134] These crops provide the

---

[132] The main objectives of the LCMS include; monitoring the effects of the various government policies on the wellbeing of households and individuals, monitoring poverty levels and the severity of poverty, to highlight vulnerable groups in society who can be targeted using policy action by government, and to monitor changes in the living conditions of the population over time. A method used to measure shanty-compound poverty in Zambia is the JCTR's monthly Basic Needs Basket (BNB), an effort to measure the cost of living for a family of six in ten of Zambia's towns.
[133] Rural Action International website
[134] Under the *Chitemene* System, the branches of trees are cut and burned under a tree to provide ashes which are used as manure. *Chitemene* in the local Aushi dialect literally means "to cut by yourself." *Chitemene*, however,

entire necessary food requirements of a healthy meal such as carbohydrates, proteins, and vitamins. Some people return to their villages to till the land when they retire from their industrial, factory or office work in urban areas.

The solution to poverty for the most part is in the very backyard of the poor's daily routines. Seventy percent of Africa's poor people live in rural areas where they depend on agriculture to survive. The best way to curb poverty, is to empower the Zambian rural poor through agriculture. Most of them cannot produce crops because they lack implements and fertilizers. And when they produce crops they usually fail to sell those crops.

A two-pronged approach, ensuring that the rural farmer produces the crops they want and in the quantity they want, and a means of storing and marketing the excess, is preferred. This two-pronged approach will ensure that food production is sustainable and progressive in Zambia. The result will be self-empowerment and rural prosperity.

§4.3 Economic Apathy

In Zambia, like in most African states, a few people live better at the expense of the majority. In fact, if the Western media captured, without prejudice or bias, the lives of the powerful and affluent in Zambia, the average person in those countries would be mesmerized. For long they have watched one-sided documentaries made specially to woo donor support.

In early 1980s, this author lived at Mibenge village. Within the village there were other mini-villages called *Imyundas*. These *Imyundas* were very distant villages-within-villages. It took this author's family the whole day to reach the *Inyundas*. The paths to the *Imyundas* were inundated with impassable streams, incredible valleys and poisonous snakes.

---

leads to soil erosion and deforestation. *Chitemene* may be a threat to global warning.

The author remembers every school holiday going there for any number of weeks until school resumed. There, life was simple. People there lived in simple huts, slept on simple mats and used basic utensils to dine. No-one there cared how or what they wore. Nature and human life overlapped. People spent the whole day either cultivating the fields, fishing or collecting wild fruits. They also dug for mice and hunted for game.

Afterwards, the author left for the real villages at Mibenge comprising Chilema, Kombaniya, Ndoba, and many more. People usually stocked food-stuffs, such as millet, sorghum, groundnuts, and etcetera, into a special mud-constructed silo called *Ubutala*. *Amatala* (plural) were especially made to withstand horrific weather and to keep the produce free of mice and other rodents. It was always a pleasure returning to the main villages at Mibenge.

The first time the author saw the *Imyunda*-type of huts and lifestyles showing on television in Canada, he was shocked. This time they were being used to raise sympathy and attract donations. These captions would show a young child, naked, thin and destitute doing adult-rated chores. The excuse is usually that the parents are dead due to HIV/AIDS. The voice, usually of a celebrated Western narrator, would recite a sympathetic story about this innocent child. The viewers would then be invited to donate a specific amount of money meant to help alleviate the suffering of this child.

Suffering is real in many parts of Africa. That is the truth. But not all African children and women just like not all Westerners live in prosperity. By parity of argument, however, the numbers of orphaned children in Zambia is alarming. The Zambian Government lacks both the resources and enough personnel to successfully deal with this challenge. In this regard, the work of charities with a mandate to empowering such children is a welcome investment.

While the mission of organizations soliciting for donations using African images is well understood, the approach is devastating to the already-marred image of Africa. What such presentations do to the image of Zambia is unimaginable. The extent to which these organizations go to bring out these images is impressive. It took the author the whole day to reach the *Imyundas*, and this explains the extent to which such charities go to taint the great image of Africa. It would be diplomatic suicide, for example, to capture the desperate images of the ghettoes or squalors in New York and use them for charitable reasons!

Grant, who spent four years working as a District Officer in the then Northern Rhodesia, and who went back to Zambia in 2006, has this to say about the television commercials: "The Western image, fostered by TV coverage of famine victims and advertisements for charity organizations, of sadness and despair, may have been true in *extreme* instances, but my experience of every class and types of Africans was that, everywhere and always, they would laugh and see the humor of life (Emphasis added)."[135] Western television propaganda on Africa has diminished Africa's capacity to compete favorably in the world economy.

When people hear, and see these images, they make up biased conclusions about life and experience in Zambia. Having lived in North America, and in Africa, this author sees very little difference in terms of happiness in life. Those who own property or have good jobs in Africa should not even dream of relocating to the West. There is just so much to live for in Zambia!

It cannot, however, be disputed that charitable organizations have done a commendable job in bringing to the fore the sufferings of the Zambian rural poor. The problem is in the methodology. This practice has brought many a common African great anguish. In Toronto, there are many homeless people on the street, despite Canada having one of the best social services on the globe. This scenario has been captured from a humane

---

[135] William D. Grant, *Zambia: Then and Now – Colonial Rulers and Their African Successors* (London: Routledge Taylor & Francis Group, 2009), p. 92

viewpoint in *The Seven Laws of Influence* regarding a Snack Sunday initiative this author developed for a period of twelve months between 2007 and 2008 where the homeless and street people in downtown Toronto were provided with free food.

What is shocking is that all the bad images of sufferings and poverty shown on television are of Africans or Asians. There is no organization which shows the poor people of the Western countries. The reason is simple, because most donor funding comes from the West, it would be a self-defeatism strategy to show that in these countries some people are suffering as well. If Zambia is to move from dependence to self-sufficiency, these issues need serious debate.

§4.4 Poverty and Life Expectancy[136]

Poverty has a direct co-relationship with the number of years that an individual is expected to live. In Zambia, the official average length of life of persons in the population of approximately close to 14 million people is 52.36 years.[137] The implications are enormous for Zambia. This means that most Zambians may not be able to value investment because life is deemed short.

---

[136] According to *Index Mundi*: Zambia Demographics Profile 2011: The population stood at 13,881,336 (0-14 years: 46.7 percent - male 3,253,125 and female 3,228,844; 15-64 years: 50.8 percent - male 3,544,640 and female 3,508,344; 65 years and over: 2.5 percent - male 148,531and female 197,852); Median age stood at 16.5 years (male: 16.5 years and female: 16.6 years); Population growth rate was 3.062 percent; Birth rate was 44.08 births/1,000 population; Death rate was 12.61 deaths/1,000 population; Life expectancy at birth of the total population was 52.36 years (male: 51.13 years and female 53.63 years: and HIV/AIDS prevalence: adult prevalence rate was 13.5 percent (2009), people living with HIV/AIDS was 980,000 (2009) and HIV/AIDS deaths were 45,000 (2009).

[137] This figure was 38.63 years in 2009 in a population then of 13 million people according to the US Department of State, Bureau of African Affairs' 2009 Estimate of Life Expectancy in Zambia. Clearly, this shows that Zambia is making tremendous progress.

The direct impact on productivity cannot be overemphasized. The loss of productive workforce may lead to deepening levels of poverty, loss of tax revenue, high dependency ratios and to worsening international debt. But indirectly, investor confidence erodes where such investors cannot see plausible reasons to invest.[138] It may exacerbate the crisis in education and impose heavy government spending in healthcare. All these factors have tremendous negative impact on economic growth and could jeopardize further efforts at alleviating poverty in Zambia.

§4.5 Poverty despite Independence

In Chapter Seven, reference is made to the question of whether Zambia was ready to embrace independence in 1964. It is posited that Zambia was and the subsequent poverty condition does not controvert that position. The economy of Zambia, from the First to the Second Republics, is explored in Volume 2.

Despite political independence, Zambia faced an economic challenge. That challenge was inherent in four aspects of the Zambian economy: The mixed blessing of copper; the disorientation of the transport sector; the reliance on the capitalist economies; and the negligence of the manufacturing and agricultural capabilities, and of rural development.[139] Zambia had inherited political structures without economic resources.

---

[138] However, according to the World Bank and the International Finance Corporation's report dubbed *Doing Business 2011: Making a Difference for Entrepreneurs* of November 5th, 2010, Zambia was one of the ten most-improved economies in the world for doing business.

[139] See Timothy M. Shaw, "Zambia: Development and Underdevelopment," (1976) *Canadian Journal of African Studies*, Vol. 10, No. 1, p. 7; Alistair Young, *Industrial Diversification in Zambia*; Douglas G. Anglin, "The Politics of Transit Routes in Land-locked Southern Africa," in Zdenek Cervenka (ed.), *Land-locked Countries of Africa* (Uppsala: Scandinavian Institute of African Studies, 1973); Charles Elliot, "Growth, Development or Independence?" in Heide and Udo Ernst Simonis (eds.), *Socio-Economic Development in Dual Economies: The Example of Zambia* (Munich:

Here is what justifies the genius of the founding leaders of Zambia – they were ready to take the bull by its horns. Since Godwin Lewanika,[140] the Africans had been subjected to a game of cat and mouse. During all this period, the resources of Northern Rhodesia went to develop other territories. When the Colonial Office knew that it had quite left nothing in Northern Rhodesia, it then decided to grant the so-called independence to Zambia.

Zambia, at independence, would have to depend on foreign expatriates to operate its major sectors including government services. Specifically, Zambia lacked capable educated people to run its government. At independence, Zambia's educated people could be counted. One of Zambia's notable, and the first Zambian university graduate was John Mwanakatwe. On November 1st, 2009, this author had a rare privilege of moderating the Mwanakatwe Memorial Service in Toronto, Canada. At the service Chisanga Puta-Chekwe[141] gave the following eulogy, reproduced below in part:

> John Mupanga Mwanakatwe (JMM) achieved many firsts. He was Northern Rhodesia's first university graduate. He had a distinguished career as a teacher at Munali where he taught Bemba, English and Latin. He then scored another first by becoming the first African to serve as Principal of a secondary school. Another first

---

Weltform Verlag for African Studies Institute, 1971); and Charles Elliot, *King Copper: The Extraction of Copper and Its Impact on Zambian Society* (London: Europe/Africa Research Report, 1971)

[140] Godwin Lewanika was the first leader of the Northern Rhodesia Congress, which was shortly changed to Northern Rhodesia African National Congress (ANC)

[141] Puta-Chekwe is one of the sons of Robinson Puta, a nationalist political figure of the 1950s who was active in trade union movements. Puta-Chekwe studied law at the University of Birmingham in England. A Rhodes Scholar, he received a Master of Law degree from the University of London, and B.A. and M.A. degrees in philosophy, politics and economics from the University of Oxford. On March 9th, 2009, Puta-Chekwe was appointed as Deputy Minister of Citizenship and Immigration and Deputy Minister Responsible for Women's Issues by Premier Dalton McGuinty, former Premier of Ontario Province.

came when late JMM was asked to serve as Assistant Commissioner at the Northern Rhodesia Commission in London. After the 1964 one person one vote election in Zambia, Mwanakatwe became the Minister of Education and presided over the desegregation of schools in the country. He later held other portfolios such as Minister of Finance.[142]

Compounding Zambia's rural poverty and poverty in general after independence were external factors. Principal among these was political instability in the central-southern African region because of the struggles for freedom: "Conflicts with Rhodesia resulted in the closing of Zambia's borders with that country and severe problems with international transport and power supply."[143] Despite the constructions of the Kariba Dam[144] and the Tanzania-Zambia Railways Authority (TAZARA),[145] respectively, Zambia's problems were still not solved.

Zambia continued to face the challenge of an increasing number of refugees pouring in from the neighboring countries. Zambia's strong support for South Africa's African National Congress (ANC) party, which had its headquarters in Zambia's Capital City Lusaka, further created security problems with South Africa.

The twin most significant events in the history of Zambia after independence, as far as the national economic situation is concerned, were the Mulungushi Reforms of 1968 and the severe worldwide decline in the price of copper in the mid-1970s.[146]

---

[142] Kaela Mulenga, "Memorial for Zambian Heroes" (2009)
[143] *Ibid.*
[144] The Kariba Hydroelectric Station on the Zambezi River provided sufficient capacity to satisfy the country's requirements for electricity.
[145] A railroad to the Tanzanian port of Dar-es-Salaam, built with Chinese assistance, reduced Zambian dependence on railroad lines south to South Africa and west through an increasingly troubled Angola.
[146] In April 1968, Kaunda announced the Mulungushi Reforms to restructure the Zambian economy. The government would acquire over 51 percent equity shares in the number of foreign-owned companies. The new structural

This was also the beginning of huge Zambia's foreign debt accumulation. For Zambia to compensate for this fall-out, the nation borrowed extensively from the international donors. However, "In 2005, Zambia qualified for debt relief under the Heavily Indebted Poor Countries (HIPC) initiative, consisting of approximately US$6 billion in debt relief."[147] Some bilateral debt was eventually cancelled, but this was excluding commercial debt. It was expected that the resources which went to serving external debt would be used to finance rural projects.

§4.6 "Strong and Free"

In the light of the forgone, few facts demand attention. Kaunda showed exceptional genius in salvaging the country amidst very challenging, and lack of qualified manpower, circumstances. For example, the birth of Zambia was against a backdrop of extreme criticism of the "methods of British expansion...loss of life...[and] there was scarcely a single educated African of *note*."[148] Emphasis is on "African of note," although only about 100 Africans could be categorized as educated at independence. Moreover, Zambia's behavior during the Unilateral Declaration of Independence (UDI) crisis was

---

arrangements would be controlled by the Industrial Development Corporation (INDECO). Two major foreign mining corporations were targeted: The Anglo-American Corporation and the Rhodesia Selection Trust (RST). The former became the Nchanga Consolidated Copper Mines (NCCM) and the later, Roan Consolidated Mines (RCM). The Mining Development Corporation (MINDECO) was quickly created as the mother-body of all parastatals in Zambia. This was followed by the Finance and Development Corporation (FINDECO), which allowed Kaunda to gain control of insurance firms and building societies. INDECO, MINDECO, and FINDECO came under an omnibus parastatal, the Zambia Industrial and Mining Corporation (ZIMCO) in 1972 with Kaunda as Board Chairman. In 1982, NCCM and RCM were merged into the Zambia Consolidated Copper Mines Ltd (ZCCM). This completed the process of nationalization.

[147] Kaela Mulenga, "Memorial for Zambian Heroes," *supra*.
[148] Gann & Duignan, *Colonialism in Africa: 1870-1960*, p. 224

highly commendable.[149] If Zambia lacked political leaders, lack of quality leadership was not one of it. Under the circumstances, and mostly augmented by external factors, Kaunda's Zambia made very important headways.

As discussed above, raw materials in the form of copper left Zambia for Zimbabwe, and real infrastructure development was neglected in Zambia. Zambia, then known as Northern Rhodesia, "was as yet regarded as a native country, a reservoir of labor, a speculative investment for the future, but not as a major area of White settlement."[150] Kaunda, within a short space of time, managed to build key infrastructures in the nation. In 1966, just two years into his presidency, he built UNZA and on July 12th in the same year, he was installed as UNZA's chancellor.

In January 1969, former president Kaunda launched the Kwacha as the official unit of currency, and subsequently, nationalized the copper mines. Between 1970 and 1975, he built the TAZARA and major roads in Zambia. Kaunda is, indeed, Zambia's *pioneer extraordinaire*, a fact he acknowledged in the speech he delivered at the opening of UNZA on March 18th in 1966: "We are *pioneers* and, in a way, we are faced with more problems than a pathfinder who has no beaten track before him."[151]

Kaunda's successor, Frederick Chiluba, liberalized the economy and Zambia's private industry, and "by the mid-1990s, despite limited debt relief, Zambia's *per capita* foreign debt remained among the highest in the world."[152] Moreover, Chiluba's efforts necessitated home ownership to sitting tenants; resurgence of private sector investment; the emergence of

---

[149] See Douglas G. Anglin, *Zambian Crisis Behavior,* p. 17

[150] L.H. Gann, *A History of Northern Rhodesia: Early Days to 1953* (London: Chatto and Windus, 1964), p. 149

[151] *Modern History Sourcebook,* "President Kenneth Kaunda of Zambia: African Development and Foreign Aid," (March 18th, 1966)

[152] Kaela Mulenga, "Memorial for Zambian Heroes" (2009).

commercial activities in Zambia; and on February 21st, 1994, he launched the Lusaka Stock Exchange into operation.

From the inception of multiparty politics in Zambia, and to the subsequent liberalization of the national economy,[153] Zambia, especially under the Mwanawasa regime, slowly began to see stability in the economy.[154] The IMF praised then President Banda for the way he managed the economy during the global financial crisis which resulted in the country recording growth. Former IMF Managing Director Dominique Strauss-Kahn was impressed with the measures that Zambia put in place to manage the crisis.[155] Much of this growth was due to determined Zambian leadership. It is important to note that the leadership of Zambia for the most part has made tremendous strides in reducing the levels of poverty. It has been augmented by foreign investment, especially in the mining sector. Relatively higher copper prices on the world market between 2005 and 2010 contributed to this growth.[156]

However, growth is not the same thing as development. Per Chumbow,[157] "Development is not synonymous with growth, for

---

[153] O'Donnell and Schmitter (1986) differentiate between liberalization and democratization. In a purely political sense, liberalization means the "disassembling of authoritarian regimes," while democratization involves the "construction of democratic institutions of governance." See also Peter VonDoepp, "Political Transition and Civil Society: The Cases of Kenya and Zambia," (Spring 1996) *Studies in Comparative and International Development*, Vol. 31, No. 1, p. 25; and Samuel Huntington, *The Third Wave: Democratization in the Late C20th* (Norman, OK: Oklahoma University Press, 1993)

[154] Zambia's economy has stabilized, attaining single-digit inflation in 2006-2007, real GDP growth, decreasing interest rates, and increasing levels of trade.

[155] *Times of Zambia*, "Country's Done Well – IMF," March 12th, 2010

[156] See *Toronto Star*, "TSX Catches Up to Surging Copper Price," (Thursday, December 30th, 2010), p. B7

[157] B.S Chumbow, "The Place of the Mother Tongue in the (Nigerian) National Policy in Education," in N. Emenanjo (ed.), *Multilingualism, Minority Languages and Language Policy in Nigeria* (Agbor: Central Books, 1990)

there can be growth without development as, for instance, in a situation of population explosion without concomitant economic growth or a rapid increase in the indicators of human development without a consumerate eradication of poverty."[158]

Chumbow's observation of decades ago resonates with the experiences of many Zambians today. Indeed, statistics, figures and projections point to growth in economic indicators. Between 2003 and 2008, the price of copper surged on the international market, a big chunk of foreign debt was forgiven through the HIPC initiative, and inflation was brought to single digits. Although despite all these plusses, national development[159] has not been moving in tandem with poverty eradication or the positive change in the citizens' standard of living. There is, however, informed hope brewing in the hearts of the Zambians that this growth will translate into better living for all. The aura of poverty is not a permanent shadow, but a temporary silhouette that will one day be lifted with the resilience of the Zambian people, good economic policies and sound political principles.

§4.7 Zambia without Poverty

As noted above, poverty has been a persistent issue in Zambia since independence. It is Zambia's enemy number one, and it should not just be killed, it must be murdered. It is a manifest reality of over 80 percent of the population. In the ensuing segment, an attempt to highlight a legal strategy, drawing from Quebec's shining example, and the political will that is essential

---

[158] *Ibid.*, p. 169

[159] Chumbow, *ibid.*, defines National Development as the "nation's human resources acting on its natural resources to produce goods (tangible and intangible) in order to improve the condition of the average citizen of the nation state."

to ending poverty in Zambia and provide a framework for future adjustment is made.

From the outset, it must be restated that poverty is not only an exclusive government problem. Poverty requires leadership from all levels of society: The community, the civil society and churches, government ministries and agencies, the private sector and the business world as well as the persons themselves who live with and experience poverty daily.

The Quebec Model

What sets Quebec (one of the ten provinces of Canada) apart is the decision its government made in 2002. In that year, Quebec unanimously passed an *Act to Combat Poverty and Social Exclusion* (the "Act").[160] The preamble to this Act is telling, and states, in part: "WHEREAS poverty and social exclusion may constitute obstacles to the protection of and respect for human dignity…the effects of poverty and social exclusion impede the economic and social development…the fight against poverty and social exclusion is a national imperative…." The objective of this Act is well-spelled out in Chapter 1, namely, "To guide the Government and Québec society as a whole towards a process of planning and implementing actions to combat poverty, prevent its causes, reduce its effects on individuals and families, counter social exclusion and strive towards a poverty-free Québec."

The emphasis of this Act is to combat poverty; prevent its causes; and reduce its effects. It is a comprehensive law that defines poverty as low income, lack of means, inability to make informed choices and absence of power by the victims of poverty. In other words, Quebec has in place an official poverty measurement tool. It has established targets and timelines, identifiable measurement tools, a community engagement process, mechanisms for accountability and reporting, as well as

---

[160] (R.S.Q., c. L-7)

adequate investment, all set within a human-rights framework of the Act.

In Quebec, it is an abuse of human rights to be poor. In other words, it is "illegal" to be poor in Quebec. This came so eloquently when Quebec set to reduce poverty in the province by half over a 10-year period; Quebec intends to achieve the lowest levels of poverty in the industrialized world. Quebec experiences one of the lowest rates of poverty despite relatively equal income distribution comparable to Canada or the US. In 2002, for example, employment in Québec grew by 3.4 percent, exceeding Canada's rate of 2.2 percent at that time and the zero average rates for the Organization for Economic Co-operation and Development (OECD) countries. By 2015, Quebec's unemployment rate stood at only 8 percent; Canada's was at 6.8 percent.

Zambia's Efforts and Development Plans

In Zambia, President Kenneth Kaunda (KK) had an economic vision. Shortly after independence, he embarked on a program of national development planning which was called the Transitional Development Plan before implementing the very First National Development Plan (NDP) of 1966–71. This plan provided for major investment in infrastructure and manufacturing and was generally very successful. The heart of this and subsequent NDPs was self-reliance. By the time of the 4th NDP in 1989, it was clear that Zambia needed a bigger vision of reducing dependence on mining.

In 2006, Levy Mwanawasa articulated the 5th NDP (2006 – 2010) aiming at making Zambia "A prosperous middle-income country by 2030 [Vision 2030]." In 2011, Rupiah Banda kept the promise and articulated the 6th NDP dubbed, "Sustained economic growth and poverty reduction." At the heart of the later development plans have been emphasis on government's calls to set an enabling environment for growth by the inclusion of the private sector as a key player.

At independence, Zambia's economy was mainly dependent on copper mining that accounted for 90 percent of its export earnings. The UNIP government commenced rapid nationalization of the economy shortly after independence, paving the way for state-led development. State intervention in the economy was set in motion with the 1968 Mulungushi Economic Reforms that allowed the party and its government to acquire 51 percent shares from private retail, transportation, and manufacturing firms. Nationalization enabled the State to control 80 percent of the economy through parastatals. Under UNIP, the model for economic growth had become one in which the State became the engine of growth. There was a political will, but no sweeping legislative regime to cement a poverty combating plan.

In 1991, the MMD government of Frederick Chiluba came to power. The MMD adopted fully-fledged Structural Adjustment Programs (or SAPs). It implemented economic reforms more rapidly than its predecessor and earned the reputation of a model liberalizing economy. It borrowed heavily from the donor community to offset deficient export earnings and to finance development. However, SAPs did not promote sustainable development in Zambia. By 2004, Zambia's gaping debt had started to stiffen development leading to Zambia becoming one of the highly indebted poor countries of the world (HIPC). SAPs lay stress on exports of primary products (copper) as well as on heavy and unsustainable borrowings, and overlooked the export of manufactured goods. It obliterated domestic demand in Zambia.

That is when Mwanawasa came in. He saw sense in Kaunda's simple but effective style of economic management. He embarked on the 5th NDP, basically continuing from where KK left. But Mwanawasa died. His predecessor was defeated in an election. And this is one of the reasons Quebec legislated for the Act because a political decision has limitation on the implementation of development or poverty reduction plans. Fortunately for Zambia, the late Michael Sata also saw sense in the 6th NDP. However, Sata died in 2014 and was succeeded by Edgar Lungu.

By October 2014, the Patriotic Front (PF) government had revitalized the plan and christened it the Revised Sixth National Development Plan 2013-2016 (R-SNDP). It revised the 6th NDP while taking into consideration the priorities of the PF government. It aimed at achieving the objectives of Vision 2030. But despite those efforts, why did the Zambian poverty situation not change? Quebec, again, may offer an answer for Zambia.

What Poverty Legislation Can Do

What makes Quebec a model is not that it is the only nation with a heart for the poor. Zambia is, as well. What makes the Quebec Model an envy of the world is partly in its legislative apparatus. By enacting a law that guarantees prosperity and designates poverty as a human-rights issue, Quebec tackled the problem of poverty in a framework that safeguarded continuity, assured implementation and ensured accountability. The same could not be said of many other countries, including Zambia.

In the Quebec case, for example, the regime set for maintenance of social assistance, investment in training and supporting access to employment, the improvement in the low-income disposable income, the support of local social initiatives, and increased access to social housing. This then became the vision of each successive government in Quebec. If the Quebec Model was transposed to Zambia, over 60 percent below the poverty datum-line would claim to have their human rights violated.

The other issue that requires urgent attention in the fight against poverty in Zambia is the prevalence of shanty-towns. These are death-traps; Zambia's most deadly killers.

§4.8 Shanty-Towns

There are no official statistics on how many of shanty-towns[161] there are in Zambia because every year, more and more keep mushrooming around cities and towns. However, one of Zambia's shanty-towns called Misisi Compound has been identified as one of the five worst slums in Sub-Saharan Africa. Misisi, from best estimates, could have between 90 and 120,000 people living in there with an average life expectancy of less than 32 years. Lusaka, the Capital City of Zambia, has over 50 percent of its population living in adjacent shanty-towns.

Living in the developing formations has not been easy for many residents. The standards of living have generally been low. Even for those who have the means of good living such as good jobs, money and power, the future is usually bleak or fickle and uncertainties loom large in terms of the politics and economies of these nations. The gaping disparity between the haves and have-nots is so large that some people are basically economic prisoners in their own nations. Majority of people in Zambia live in these shanty-towns with some of the worst conditions in the world. These shanty-towns tend to be unplanned and are often illegal. Houses are self-built using basic materials and the towns have fewer basic services such as running water, electricity, health facilities or sewage systems. These settlements developed because of chronic housing shortage especially for the urban poor. Most shanty-towns have developed on the outskirts of large urban centers.

People's lack of basic needs usually leads them to living a communal life sharing limited facilities like toilets, salt,

---

[161] Also-known as Shanty Compounds or Shanty-Compounds

cigarettes and space. That's the reason why when there's an outbreak of a disease like cholera, it spreads fast. Local brews like *Umunkoyo, Tobwa, Katata, Katubi* or *Chibuku* are usually imbibed from the same straw, thereby spreading ailments and communicable diseases all year-round.

Every year more and more people leave the Zambian villages to settle in the shanty-towns. This has a historical nuance to it as discussed below. Thus, the shanty-towns are some of the most over-populated areas in Zambia. With this increased over-population comes the problem of service delivery, access to basic needs of life and early deaths for the majority who cannot survive. More than one-third of Zambians live in urban areas, many crowded into these shanty-towns. The cities themselves leave much to be desired; they are usually an extension of the shanty-towns only that some of them have limited access to scarce amenities and electricity. The cities and shanty-towns exist in a symbiotic relationship – one feeding on the other as the other draws its survival blood from the other.

A common feature of the shanty-towns is the prevalent of garbage (rubbish) heaps just adjacent to, and sometimes right at the heart of the compound. The market places are harbingers of germs and diseases as people, animals and microbes mingle to jam through openly-cast and uncovered food and water. And there is no housing plan: Slum-huts are used as homes, streets are erratically structured and women and children can be seen selling maize (or cone) on the streets. All along the roads and even in the commercial centers people sell all types of merchandise, unplanned.

The largest impact of HIV/AIDS has happened in shanty-towns and there are few facilities for orphaned children there. Those children who are not looked after within their extended families and communities end up living rough as street children in the cities. Over-population creates conditions necessary for famine, disease or war.

As explained in Chapter 2, the author lived in Kapisha Compound. Even by the Zambian standards, shanty-towns are a pathetic sight. Kapisha was no different.

Shanty-towns can only compare to pigsties of the Bible's Prodigal Son.[162] For Zambia, colonialism had everything to do with the genesis of shanty compounds but it should not be blamed for everything. Before colonialism, Zambians lived in large village enclosures with plenty of space with relatively good sanitation. But the colonialists needed the Africans as cheap labor. A policy was adopted requiring each employer to provide housing to their employees. Movements were restricted. And when labor was no longer required, the Africans were repatriated back to their villages.

Fast forward to Zambia's independence in 1964, the new government abolished the population moving restrictions. But soon this only attracted rural-urban migrations as the rural population hunted for employment and an affluent lifestyle in the urban areas.

Ironically, during the colonial days, the colonial government had put strict restrictions on town planning. It controlled town management to ensure quality housing across the board. With the relaxing of these restrictions after independence, town management started to become erratic or unplanned. In addition, political caderism in the Second Republic (1972 – 1990) allowed UNIP ward chairpersons to dictate town planning. This uncouth trend continued even up to the modern times where councilors can allocate plots indiscriminately.

However, the biggest problem began with the new rural migrants who came to urban areas in search of employment. When they could not find housing there, they began to construct temporary housing units "because the tenure of housing available in rural areas was not easily available in urban areas."[163]

---

[162] See Luke 15:11-32
[163] See Charles Mwewa, "Zambian shanty towns: Death-traps or developmental opportunity, "Zambian *Eye*, September 15th, 2015

Since independence, one can identify three trends in housing tenure in Zambia: First, unemployed renters who cannot afford to pay rent may occupy any space available for survival. This is mostly common in shanty-towns. Second, owners or occupiers may construct houses for personal or family occupation. This is mostly common in rural areas. And third, those with access to housing may offer accommodation to relatives and friends.

In 1991, the MMD under Chiluba ushered in a Third Republic. It came up with a new housing policy. Whereas the UNIP government before it had built houses to be rented out to people in formal employment, the new MMD government emphasized home-ownership. It sold local and central government homes to occupiers. This did not curb the shortage of houses; those who bought these houses were already occupying them.

The colonial government which had begun the problem of urban-labor migration had done a good job to avoid housing shortage by creating pool houses meant for rotational occupation. But the MMD government, while empowering sitting-tenants with home-ownership, had worsened housing shortages by the sale of local authority and government houses without replacing them.

The factors that attracted the rural population to migrate to urban areas have been allowed to persist. These factors are mainly four: A concentration of developmental projects (industrial, services or manufacturing) in urban areas; biased developmental agendas by the successive governments; a view that Lusaka and major urban towns are suitable places to live in; and lack of a cogent resettlement policy or program in place.

For example, in 2007, the Mwanawasa administration endorsed the plan to destroy illegal shanty-towns that had mushroomed in Lusaka and other urban areas. But they had no resettlement plan in place. A similar program by the Zimbabwean government in 2005 had backfired.

There is a solution to this quagmire. And that solution cannot be a quick fix. It should be a multi-layered and comprehensive proposal involving all stake-holders – renters, home-less people, shanty-town dwellers, government, private sector, businesses, and to some extent, international community – and should be carried out in the interest of the state. And just like in every problem-solving matrix, the best place to begin is at the problem issue.

The Problem

As discussed above, the shanty compounds usually have little access to electricity, running water and sewage systems. They were developed because of the chronic housing shortage in the urban areas. They can be found mostly on the outskirts of large metropolis. In shanty compounds, available services are incapable of affording a basic standard of living. Thus, the risk of contagious and water borne diseases looms large.

However, the biggest problem the Zambian shanty compounds face is the rate at which they grow. Due to this rapid growth, no government is ready or equipped enough to deal with them. The Zambian Government does not have enough money to maintain the existing facilities or to improve them. Ancillary to this is the problem of creating further complications with an informal system existing in the shanty compounds which fends for itself.

Most people in the shanty compounds lack education, are informally employed and may not have the necessary skills needed in the formal sector. Therefore, government may not have the requisite resources both to relocate them and to create the necessary jobs required for resettlement. The Zambian Government has opted to do one of the two things: During the Mwanawasa regime, it attempted to demolish the shanty-towns, and in all other regimes, have done little or nothing. Both actions are inadequate.

The Analysis

In the first place, doing little or nothing is not a solution. And demolition of the shanty compounds comes with its own challenges. And some of which are: It exacerbates unemployment and may endanger social solidarity, impels riots and creates disruptions.

Relocating the people to their original villages is not an intelligent solution, either. It looks attractive, but it is not workable. Most people in the Zambian shanty compounds come from a certain village. They or their ancestors migrated to the towns because of any number of reasons. These reasons include looking for low cost housing but being not able to find any, they resort to finding patches of ground that no-one else wants, usually on the outskirts of the cities, and there they build a shelter with whatever is available. Some come to shanty compounds because they want access to services such as clean water, electricity or sewage disposal. Others still come to the shanty compounds because they are in search of good health-care.

There are usually insufficient doctors and clinics in the villages and these immigrants may wish to be closer to the major cities. But the majority immigrates to the towns and end up in the shanty compounds because they are in hunt for employment. The belief that life is better in the city is immediately dwindled when these immigrants begin to learn that there are more people than jobs in the formal economy. Thus, they are forced to make a living from whatever chances they can find in the informal economy, for example, shoe-shiners, street vendors selling snacks or even picking over rubbish from the piles to see what they can recycle. Lack of good paying jobs immediately relegates these new dwellers to lives of crimes, drugs and extreme poverty.

But for whatever reason, these communities have acquired an identity that is peculiar. They are inadaptable to the village life anymore. The villages must be developed in their own rights as discussed earlier. There is an unsubstantiated myth that the villages offer a better life than the shanty compounds. Villages may, in relativity. However, this myth is tramped by the reality. In fact, most young and able-bodied young people are leaving the villages for the shanty compounds in droves. What is required is to develop the areas where the migrants are coming from, and not to demolish the existing ones. The thinking is that if the would-be immigrants can have access to vital services, access to good education, availability of employment and sound health-care, right in their villages, they would stay and develop the villages. This is a sound statement of fact.

The Zambian shanty compound must be respected. Some of them have become middle class suburbs. Development or lack of it there has occurred over a long period. In Zambia, the reality, sadly, is that the informal sector in shanty compounds pays more money than being a landless peasant farmer in the villages does. Yet, still, the newer towns in shanty compounds still lack basic services.

Improvements have been gradual – usually because of the dwellers' own diligence, and not of government. What comes to mind is the thought of replacing these shanty compounds with gated communities constructed over their ruins. But as observed, this is almost always stalemated by lack of resources.

The Paradigm for a Solution

Any solution that is designed to solve the shanty compound problem in Zambia must take into consideration the tripartite existence of a city, the shanty compound and the village. One cannot be undertaken without the other two. What happens to the city affects the shanty compound and which in turn affects the village. Growth of urban cities eases the pressure on the rural villages so that there are more jobs available and less people to feed. And yet, all (city-dwellers, the villagers and the shanty compound residents) have one thing in common: They are all in need of employment, they want access to quality education and sound health-care, they want ready and accessible services and they want sustainable development.

This tripartite solution must involve the key stakeholders – the government;[164] the people themselves;[165] and the cooperating partners, local as well as international.[166]

On November 27th, 2015, Pope Francis strode into Kenyan Kangemi shanty-town and lashed out at the nation's elite for neglecting the poor. The pontiff said, referring to the pathetic picture portrayed by the shanty-towns and perpetuated by the elites of the African governments: "These are wounds inflicted by minorities who cling to power and wealth, who selfishly squander while a growing majority is forced to flee to abandoned, filthy and run-down peripheries.... To deny a family water, under any bureaucratic pretext whatsoever, is a great injustice, especially when one profits from this need."[167]

The pontiff warned of "new forms of colonialism."[168] In colonial days, the invading nation plundered the dominated nations without having regard to the dominated's plight and wellbeing. But colonialism is now dead, except now a worse form of colonialism may be among us. It is worse because Africans are subjecting themselves to housing that is only fit for dogs and pigs. This internal colonialism in Africa, manifested in the sprawling shanty-towns filled with tin-roofed homes must be stopped.

---

[164] Which will provide the legislative scheme necessary to enable development to bloom within the ambit of the law.

[165] Who, in fact, are the custodian of development!

[166] Which shall supply the resources required to sustain the initiative.

[167] *The Daily Monitor*, "Pope slams rich over 'dreadful injustice' to poor," http://www.monitor.co.ug/News/National/Pope-slams-rich--dreadful-injustice--poor/688334-2974370-1cwugoz/index.html (Retrieved: September 28th, 2016)

[168] *Ibid.*

The pontiff also bemoaned what he termed as "the dreadful injustice of social exclusion."[169] It must be reiterated here that pure Capitalism cannot be advocated for Africa in the context of housing, either. Africa does not have mature institutions and the discipline necessary to implement pure capitalistic practices. In Africa, there is still room for social-democracy where the equitable (not equality) sharing and distribution of land, access to infrastructure and to minimum basic services should be made available to every citizen. This is, especially, applicable to Zambia.

When the pontiff challenged, "Our world has a grave social debt toward the poor who lack access to drinking water because they are denied a life consistent with their inalienable dignity,"[170] he was on point. And his call must be taken as an urgent clarion. In a world where 70 percent of the earth is surrounded by water, why should people still be going without clean water?

The pontiff was calling upon the African governments to consider developing the three "Ls" — land, labor and lodging. Kangemi compound in Kenya which is one of eleven shanty-towns dotting around Nairobi, East Africa's largest city, with 50,000 residents living there without basic sanitation, is not different from Zambia's Kapoto, Kalingalinga, Mtendere, Kapisha-Soweto, Chaisa, Chibolwa, to mention but a few shanty-towns, dotted all along Zambian towns.

Zambia does not have a comprehensive legal framework aiming at housing. Under Part III of the *Zambian Constitution*, i.e. "Protection of fundamental rights and freedom of the individual", articles 11 and 22 come much closer to protecting people's lodging rights, but not necessarily. Let us review.

In article 11(d), an individual is provided for the "protection for the privacy of his home and other property and from deprivation of property without compensation." And under 22(b), there is provided for "The right to reside in any part of Zambia." Thus, Zambians have the rights and freedoms to reside

---

[169] *Ibid.*
[170] *Ibid.*

anywhere they want, and to own property and to be guaranteed freedom from intrusion into their privacy. However, there should also be guarantees for the protection of decent housing.

Equality of opportunities is guaranteed, but not equality of results. Granted. But this will be inimical to the developing nations where ownership of decent housing is still a struggle. The shanty-towns illustrate this precarious situation for Africa. Africa in general and Zambia, must constitutionalize housing as a basic human right. Zambia should amend the provisions above to make it a violation of human rights where housing standards do not meet the minimum requirement for human decency. Government should have the overarching right to enforce these standards. This can be done in two ways.

One way of doing this is to create standards for housing in which the current shanty-town standards will be censured. The other way, is to privatize housing so that competent developers can provide decent housing to the poor at subsidized cost.

Under this proposed model, the priority is a right, and then decency, safety and the health of the citizens. And this is meant, as written earlier, namely, that shanty-towns, in the context of Zambia, need to be *modernized,* not demolished without a plan in place.

Demolition of the shanty-town-like housing is expensive. The people themselves who live in these death-traps may welcome this program, with some inconveniences here and there, of course. To create a win-win situation and to ensure that the program is self-supporting, with a minimal government and other aid, shanty-town owners whose housing is being demolished should be employed in the demolition process (and in some cases, in the construction phase). Directly or indirectly, mild inconveniences will occur but these could be offset by effective planning and by the utilization of the right approach. However, as mentioned, demolition should not be the plan, unless it is part of an effective plan.

5| Pre-Independence Zambia

Thou art depraved, O thinking man
And thy good to thy nature tied;
Born free, yet everywhere in chains,
And in forced freedom thine trust earns

Chapter Focus

At the end of reading this chapter, you should be able to:

- Understand that historical colonialism is a key factor in the discussions of Zambia's political and economic freedom
- Understand that thriving African kingdoms existed in the territory now known as Zambia before the advent of colonialism
- Define the concept of *Terra Nullius* and its implication on the future of Zambia
- Understand the genesis and future of the 1964 Barotseland Agreement
- Identify the first four significant pre-independence events that would impact Zambia at independence and beyond

BRIEF INTRODUCTION

In this chapter, the story of pre-independence Zambia is told, with implications on the political and economic future of the nation. The creation of Northern Rhodesia is discussed and the first four of five significant events that laid the foundation of the difficulties and challenges Zambia would face after independence. The 1964 Barotseland Agreement is discussed in the context of competing traditional or customary and state or legal demands.

§5.1 Colonialism: Not an Excuse

There is a dodgy, uncontested but popularized view that colonialism should not be factored in discussions of the precarious economic, cultural and political conditions in which most African nations are found. Parag Khanna, a Senior Research Fellow at the New America Foundation, and author of *How to Run the World*,[171] appeared Monday, February 21st, 2011 on CNN's *Parker Spitzer* and alluded to this interpretation. There is, downrightly, no excuse for dictatorial regimes such as existed in Libya, Egypt, Tunisia, or indeed, in Zimbabwe, which used colonialism as an ante for their autocratic harangues. But colonialism remains a key factor in the discussion about Zambia's quest for true freedom. Colonialism laid the querulous foundation upon which the conflicts and economic and political problems Africa presently countenances are based. Discussing colonialism is inevitable for Zambia. If not for lessons to be learned, it should be for future resource and wealth preservation.

Colonialism sold Africa to the West.[172] For example, in Namibia, "White Namibians make up just six percent of the population but control over 90 percent of the land."[173] Perhaps the Mugabe land reforms were too ambitious, but the truth remains that developed formations have always been custodians

---

[171] Parag Khanna, *How to Run the World: Charting a Course to the Next Renaissance* (New York: Random House Publishing Group, 2011)
[172] See Baffour Ankomah, "The Trouble with Namibia," *New African*, June 2011, p. 41
[173] *Ibid.*

of their own resources; Africa has not.[174] Talib Ray has, indeed, educated: "Today Africa is plagued with leaders who are confused by the thought that [other] countries are going to show them the way to economic independence. History has shown otherwise."[175]

It is, therefore, the position of this author that history must be brought to bear on events that have consigned Africa to a poor and diminished continent. In stating that, however, this author does not intend to demean the fact that Africans themselves have contributed to this state of affairs. Indeed, Marcus Garvey has correctly observed that, partly, "The...stumbling block in the way of progress in the race [Black race] has invariably come from within race itself."[176] However, that has been only in dealing with the symptoms of the disease rather than the cause of it.

In a controversial article dubbed, "African Solutions to African Problems."[177] Musiitwa argues that (sic), "African's failure to accept some responsibility for about 50 years of substandard leadership forces conversation to revert to the source of 'all' Africa's development problems: colonialism."[178] Despite being written from an Afropolitan[179] perspective, the article offers two irrefutable facts and one canard, a grave misconstruction about colonialism.

First, and undeniably so, colonialism is the source of, if not all, then most of Africa's developmental problems. And this is clarified in the ensuing pages. Second, there is something like

---

[174] *Ibid.*, p. 4
[175] *Ibid.*
[176] Randal Robinson, *The Debt: What America Owes to Blacks* (New York: A Button Book, 2000), p. 81
[177] Jacqueline Muna Musiitwa, "African Solutions to African Problems," *Mail and Guardian,* (May 30th, 2011)
[178] *Ibid.*
[179] Musiitwa, *ibid.*, defines Afropolitan as, "A cosmopolitan African, with global exposure and viewpoints, who retains a commitment to, knowledge of and passion for Africa."

African solutions to African problems.[180] Third, admittedly, African leaders are partly responsible for the underdevelopment of Africa, but African leadership is not sub-standard, and this author has demonstrated likewise.[181]

§5.2 Interesting History

To think of the history of Zambia, is to think of that of Africa at large. Correctly, Zambia has been called the *Real Africa*.[182]

---

[180] However, this is not the reversion to, as Chailunga puts it, "build[ing] better thatched houses, and maybe deeper wells and encourage women to stay home, any suggestion for anything technically advanced is unAfrican" (Email of June 2nd, 2011). In Møller, Bjørn, *The African Union as a Security Actor: African Solutions to African Problems?* (London: Crisis States Research Center, 2009), the research cites, "shared values and norms," as necessary catalysts to African peace or development. (Also see Chrysantus Ayangafac, "African Solutions to African Problems," *African Files*, July 9th, 2009; Samuel Wonwi Thompson, "African Solutions for African Problems? National and International Responsibility for Conflict Resolution," *The Perspective*, July 31st, 2004; and Alieu Jabang, "Africa's Problems Require African Solution," *The Point*, Tuesday, May 4th, 2010). "African Solutions to African Problems" became part of parlance as a matter of necessity, following the 1994 genocide in Rwanda when African countries watched the international community stand by as over 800,000 Tutsis and moderate Hutus were massacred by Hutu extremists. (See Chris Fomunyoh, "African Solutions to African Problems: A Slogan Whose Time Has Passed," National Democratic Institute for International Affairs, February 9th, 2005). There is also an organization calling itself, "African Solutions to African Problems (ASAP)" in South Africa which mobilizes small groups of women to harness scarce local resources to address the needs of orphans and vulnerable children.

[181] See Volume 2

[182] The phrase, "Zambia: The Real Africa" was used in relation to Zambia's tourism potential. That motto has now been replaced with, "Zambia, Let's Explore." The nature of Zambia is barely unspoiled attracting thousands of tourists from all over the world. Zambia is unarguably very rich in both scenery and wildlife, making Zambia the tourist heart of Africa. Experts

The nature and environment of Zambia has changed from what Sir Charles Dundas, a colonial administrator of the old days described as, "Flat, featureless bush and low forest land,"[183] to constituting now some of the most attractive landscapes of the world. Despite this, however, as Grant has painfully acknowledged, Zambia hugely remains forgotten.[184] Grant laments, "Zambia is the forgotten country of Africa. Celebrities don't go there, nor, it seems, do foreign journalists or world leaders. This is a pity, because Zambia is both a beautiful and an interesting country."[185]

Beautiful, that is common knowledge, however, *interesting*, that is where the story begins. It is interesting because although Zambia has been in existence for decades, it seems that its history has been unfairly written from the 1900s for those who care, and from 1924, for historical records. There is, thus, an urgent need to accurately record history because it repeats itself, as the French say, "plus ça change, plus ça reste la meme,"[186] or indeed, as George Santayana has truthfully presaged, "Those who ignore history are doomed to repeat it."

The rude reality is that Zambia is barely known outside its eight-bound borders. Its talents remain untapped, its resources

---

agree that Zambia's environment has remained unchanged since the very beginning of time.

[183] See Richard Hall, *Zambia* (London: Frederick A. Praeger Inc., 1965), p. 1

[184] William Grant was one of the last generations of British Colonial Service Officers in Northern Rhodesia (Zambia). He served there at the apex of the Federation of Rhodesia and Nyasaland from 1958 to 1961. In his book, *Zambia, Then and Now: Colonial Rulers and their African Successors*, Grant makes a hearty comparative analysis of the Northern Rhodesia (Zambia) under which he served as a Colonial Service Officer under the African successor. He calculates that Zambia was under British Government colonial rule for 40 years (1924 – 1964) and under self-government for 42 years (1964 – 2006). He charges that both have had almost equal time to make their mark.

[185] Grant, *Zambia, Then and Now: Colonial Rulers and their African Successors* (London: Routledge, Taylor & Francis Group, 2009), p. xi

[186] This may be translated into English as, "The more things change, the more they remain the same."

undermanaged, and its image, if not mired in media reportages, is hardly known. "We have found that a staggering 60 percent of the wealthy highly educated people in North America, Europe and Asia either had never heard of Zambia or knew nothing at all about the country."[187] What is unknown, or what has blatantly been ignored about Zambia, is the focal point of this chapter.

§5.3 Early Inhabitants

The discovery of the fossils of the so-called Kabwe Man[188] or Broken Hill Man at Broken Hill or Kabwe in 1921 provides more details as to who could have occupied Zambia in the far away past. Kabwe Hill Man could have been living in this area between 123,000 and 107,000 B.C or possibly as early as 248,000 B.C.[189] Archaeologists have long established that *Homo Habilis* who lived about 1.8 million years ago, and is considered the earliest human being known to the world, "lived also in Zambia."[190] In fact, *Zinjanthropus* bones have been found in Zambia "not far from Lusaka."[191]

Nonetheless, the original inhabitants of modern day Zambia could have been the Bushmen (also called Sans), who were hunters and gatherers and who also lived a nomadic life with Stone Age technology. They mainly gathered fruits and nuts, but they also hunted antelopes.

The Bushmen were the only inhabitants of the region until

---

[187] Mark O'Donnell, Tourist Council of Zambia chairman, *The Post* (July 25th, 2010)

[188] *Homo Rhodesiansis*: Rhodesian Man was one of the first names for Kabwe Man

[189] John J. Grotpeter; Brian V. Siegel; and James R. Pletcher, *Historical Dictionary of Zambia, Second Edition* (London: The Scarecrow Press, Inc., 1998), p. xi

[190] Richard Hall, *Zambia* (North York: Frederick A. Praeger Inc., 1965), p. 5

[191] *Ibid.*

the 4th Century,[192] when the Bantu people started to migrate from the north. Historical records show that Iron Age began in Zambia in A.D 50.[193] The earliest Bantu speaking people who inhabited the territory could have been the "Ila who came into the country during the first century and introduced the Iron Age."[194] By A.D 1200, the Tonga had settled at Sebanji Hill in Zambia.[195] The Bantu people had a far more developed technology. They were farmers and had iron and copper tools and weapons, as well as knowledge about pottery.[196]

Even today the Ila and Tonga people are knowledgeable and good farmers in food production and cattle farming. They were sedentary and lived in small self-sufficient villages with a few houses, growing sorghum and beans, as well as keeping cattle and goats.

These early migrations were joined by the Bisa, Lala, Chewa, Lenje, Lozi, Lunda and Bemba by the 12th Century. The Mbunda, Luvale and Kaonde joined later. They "co-existed or integrated with people that were already there before them."[197] These all collectively speak a Bantu language which is linguistically similar. The similarities themselves could have arisen because of contiguous tribal proximity.

The early farmers practiced *Chitemene*[198] agriculture and they had to constantly move further south when the soil was

---

[192] In early years, the territory that is called Zambia had no recorded history. People moved around freely in a nomadic fashion, establishing settlements where they could under the rule of African chiefs.

[193] Grotpeter *et. al, supra.*

[194] Government of the Republic of Zambia, *Interim Report of the Constitutional Review Commission*, Lusaka, June 29th, 2005, p. 13

[195] Grotpeter *et. al, supra.*

[196] The Bantu people of Central Africa had used copper tools as back as the fourth century. When the representative of the British South Africa Company (BSAC) under John Cecil Rhodes came, and signed mineral concessions with Chief Lewanika, and their subsequent claim to have discovered copper deposits in the area presently known as Zambia, the natives had been using copper for generations.

[197] *Interim Report of the Constitutional Review Commission, supra.,* p. 14

[198] Slash and burn agriculture

exhausted. The indigenous Bushmen were either assimilated into the new culture or pushed aside into areas not suitable for agriculture. Agriculture led to the growth in population. By the 11th and 12th centuries a more advanced society was beginning to emerge. Even though most villages were still self-sufficient, long distance trade was developing. Copper mining was intensified. Copper crosses were probably used as a currency. Ivory carvings and cotton textiles were other export commodities. One of the most famous archaeological sites for this period is *Ing'ombe Ilede.*[199] The increase in trade resulted in larger political units and more complex social structures.

The period between the 16th and 19th centuries saw the emergence of organized Iron-Age kingdoms as well as widespread immigration. Four kingdoms were established in this period – and these were the Kazembe-Lunda in the north which centered around the lower Luapula River, the Bemba in the north-east, the Ngoni[200] in the east and the Lozi in the west on the upper Zambezi River.

The territory of the present-day Zambia, being far inland,[201] did not have direct contact with non-Africans until relatively recently in its history. Arab and Portuguese traders were visiting by the 18th Century. The first recorded visits by Europeans to the

---

[199] At *Ing'ombe Ilede*, trade in the form of batter system boomed. Batter system is the exchange of goods for goods.

[200] The Ngoni under Zwangendaba crossed the Zambezi River in 1835 and moved north. It is believed that they crossed the Zambezi River under the Eclipse of the Sun. "The Ngoni in the Eastern Province of Zambia fought many wars before the arrival of the White man. However, the Ngoni warriors did not constitute a standing army in the sense of the modern armies of today. Albeit, they had drawn lessons from Shaka Zulu's approach to warfare, and that partly explains their success as they moved from South Africa to the north. They were eventually halted by European armed forces with their superior weapons in 1898." (Bizeck J. Phiri, "Civil Control of the Zambian Military since Independence and Its Implication for Democracy.")

[201] Zambia is a landlocked country; it does not have a seaport or coastline.

area we presently call Zambia were the Portuguese.[202] Manoel Caetano Pereira[203] and Dr. Francisco Jose Maria de Lacerda[204] visited Zambia in 1796 and 1798, respectively. Both came via Tete in Mozambique to Mwata Kazembe's Capital to try and get the chief's agreement to a Portuguese trade route between their territories of Mozambique and Angola. Lacerda died within a few weeks of arriving at Kazembe's Kingdom but left a valuable journal which was carried back to Tete by his priest and which was later translated into English by the explorer Sir Richard Burton.

It is believed, however, that the Portuguese first settled in Zumbo, Mozambique, in 1720, which is just across the Luangwa River from Zambia, at the confluence with the Zambezi River. Around 1820, they had settled on the Zambian side at Feira.[205] So it is very likely they were visiting the Zambian territory between 1720 and 1820.

§5.4 *Terra Nullius*

It is posited from the outset that the history[206] of Africa in general, and then of Zambia as written by European historians is highly misleading.[207] Africa teemed with thriving civilizations as

---

[202] The Arabs came in as traders and merchants, while the Europeans were missionaries, civil servants, commercial farmers, miners, adventurers, and entrepreneurs.

[203] He was a mixed person of Goanese and Portuguese blood; he was a trader.

[204] Francisco Jose Maria de Lacerda was an explorer.

[205] Modern day Luangwa

[206] In his *Society Must be Defended*, Michel Foucault posits that the victors of a social struggle use their political dominance to suppress a defeated adversary's version of historical events in favor of their own propaganda, which may go so far as historical revisionism.

[207] Zambia is as large as France, Switzerland, Austria and Hungary combined, covering 750,000 square kilometers and lying in the tropical belt on South Central Africa. Zambia is about 10 to 18 degrees south of the Equator. Zambia is located on a high plateau, averaging 1,300m above sea

far back as the 13th Century. Ancient states such as Ghana, Mali, Bornu, Axum, Kivu, Benin, and the Bantu kingdoms in central-southern Africa were hives of political, economic and cultural hegemonies.

The colonial doctrine of *terra nullius*,[208] which dominated the 1884-5 Berlin Congress in the quest to acquire land in Sub-Saharan Africa, was a suppressive thesis which postulated that colonized land was empty of human inhabitants and, therefore, could be claimed and settled in by colonists. The Berlin Congress, ironically, declared *terra nullius* the very land in which gigantic ancient states and empires thrived to be shared among the major European powers for occupation and colonization.

The very idea of congressing to share Africa with "no single African representative at Berlin,"[209] by ambassadors, who had not set foot in Africa,[210] is grossly exploitive. Britain, France, Germany, the US, Belgium, Italy, Japan, and many nations in Europe in their imperial quest deemed Africa "unclaimed space,"[211] culminating in the "biggest land grab in history."[212] A prominent statesman has noted this irony in the context of the relationship between the public law of Europe and African law:

---

level. Zambia lies within the tropical latitude with the general plateau height giving it a moderate climate which has earned Zambia the nickname, the "air conditioned state." The climate is very temperate with little humidity (only in wet season). The country, although landlocked, has many lakes and rivers with beaches and water spots. There are three distinct seasons: cool and dry from May to August; hot and dry from September to November; and warm and wet from December to April. Only in the valleys of the Zambezi and Luangwa rivers is there excessive heat and it is only during the hot and dry season. Also, see the Preface to this book.

[208] "Empty land"

[209] Alexander Grey Zulu, *Memoirs of Alexander Grey Zulu* (Ndola: Times Printpak Zambia Ltd., 2007), p. 4

[210] See Firstbrook, *The Obamas*, p. 104

[211] *Ibid.*, p. 99

[212] *Ibid.*, p. 100

If we take a look at the historical facts, we shall see, in the first place, what legality used to be taken to mean in Africa and what it was which used to be called "African law" as opposed to "the public law of Europe"; an African law illustrated – if one can apply the term – in the monstrous blunder committed by the authors of the Act of Berlin, the results of which have not yet disappeared from the African political scene. It was a monstrous blunder and a flagrant injustice to consider Africa south of the Sahara *terra nullius,* to be shared out among the Powers for occupation and colonization, when even in the 16th Century Vitoria had written that Europeans could not obtain sovereignty over the Indies by occupation, for they were not *terra nullius.*

By one of fate's ironies, the declaration of the Berlin Congress which held the Dark Continent to be *terra nullius* related to regions which had seen the rise and development of flourishing states and empires. One should be mindful of what Africa was before there fell upon it the two greatest plagues in the recorded history of mankind: the slave-trade, which ravaged Africa for centuries on an unprecedented scale; and colonialism, which exploited humanity and natural wealth to a relentless extreme. Before these terrible plagues overran their continent, the African people had founded states and even empires of a high level of civilization.[213]

Ammoun raises five very scintillating issues. In the first place, the consideration of Africa south of the Sahara *terra nullius* was robbery of gigantic proportion to Africa. Europe could not deny that it had neither the moral nor legal justification in branding Africa an empty land. In the second place, declaring Africa an empty land was a clear disregard for African law.[214] For even before borders and boundaries were demarcated in Africa, powerful states and great empires had existed which secured their spheres of influence through conquests.

---

[213] Fouad Ammoun, "Separate Opinion of Vice-President Ammoun," in M. Hamalengwa, C. Flinterman & E.V.O. Dankwa, (eds.), *The International Law of Human Rights in Africa* (Dordrecht: Martinus Nijhoff Publishers, 1988), pp. 137-138

[214] In Zambia, for example, "The first law that existed…was the indigenous law of the tribes." See John Hatchard and Muna Ndulo, *The Law of Evidence in Zambia: Cases and Materials* (Lusaka: Multimedia Publications, 1991), p. 1

Charles Mwewa

Even up to now Africa continues to face debilitating mutinies through tribal and civil wars because many of its clans were displaced through the scramble for land by the major European powers following the Berlin Congress. The imperial scramblers cared less what would result from the vicious dislocations.[215] In Zambia for example, to date, there exists dislodgments among people who presently occupy the eastern part of Zambia. The Chewa people of Malawi and of eastern Zambia are one and the same people who were dislodged by boundaries drawn by the colonists. The same could be said regarding the people who inhabit the Luapula Province. These people do not only share the border but both the cultures and traditions with the people in southern Congo DR.[216]

In the third place, the Act of Berlin designation of areas in which great states and empires had thriven *terra nullius* was meant to dominate Africa, and in doing so, take advantage of the plentiful human and natural resources to power the accoutrements of the Industrial Revolution in Europe. Ambition and a relentless quest to occupy other territories to exert imperial supremacy was the ultimate motivation for declaring Africa an empty land.

In the fourth place, Europe advanced the principle of *terra nullius* in Africa because of Africa's strategic advantage for mobilizing resources. Ancient kingdoms in Africa were

---

[215] Mbulo argues in the case of the Makololo and the Luyi or Lozi people whom he conceives were one people before colonization, thus, "[Dr.] Livingstone tried to deal with the Makololo and Lozi (the Borotsi, later Barotse, as David Livingstone called them) throughout as separate peoples, an aspect of the European colonial attempt to rationalize African peoples by tribalizing them. The fact still remains that Africans are one people. People of southern and central Africa all originated from the Luba-Lunda kingdoms speaking the Bantu languages" (Potpher Mbulo responding to "President Banda Should Set up Barotse Commission of Inquiry" by Henry Kyambalesa on *Zambia News Features*, October 31st, 2010)

[216] Also see Chapter One

established in regions with enormous environmental and climatic conditions suitable both as protective castles and mineral wells. Europe had learnt this from political and Christian missionaries who had expedited to Africa in the last half of the 19th Century.

Fifth and last, both slavery and colonialism were an affront to the future interest and well-being of Africa. Slavery has moral and economic consequences wherever it has been experienced. The longevity of slavery is tantamount to the potential human and economic losses a group of people suffers. In Africa, slavery lasted for over four hundred years. In human and economic terms, this meant depletion in human capital and future productivity.

The implicit consequence of slavery is the breaking, dehumanizing of the human spirit, which in the long run reduces a people to less than humans, unable to exercise independent rational thinking, and perpetually depending on others for intellectual and creative advancement. Per M'Bokolo, "Four million slaves [were] exported via the Red Sea, another four million through the Swahili ports of the Indian Ocean...nine million along the trans-Saharan caravan route, and eleven to twenty million across the Atlantic Ocean."[217] Slave trade is an international crime.[218]

Colonialism, on the other hand, is anathema to a people's political and economic gains. Colonialism did to Africa's political destiny what slavery did to its emotional and intellectual esteem. As argued previously, and more than slavery, it was colonialism that set the foundation for civil wars and ethnic tensions in Africa:

> For full three months, the European nations haggled over the partition of the continent, completely ignoring any of the cultural or linguistic boundaries already established by the indigenous

---

[217] Elikia M'Bokolo, "The Impact of Slave Trade on Africa," (April 1998) *Le Monde diplomatique* (English edition)

[218] See Firstbrook, *The Obamas*, p. 91; however, it would be improper not to mention that slave trade was rife in Zambia where the last slave cargo was stopped at Chipata in 1898.

populations. By the end of February 1885, Africa had been carved up into fifty irregular countries. In this "imperial" map of Africa, borders were often drawn arbitrarily, with little or no regard for ethnic unity, regional economic ties, migratory patterns of people, or even natural boundaries.[219]

Thus, to date this pattern of ethnic-based conflicts can be found in Chad, Liberia, Ethiopia, Congo DR., Sudan, Guinea, Kenya, Nigeria, and so on. The way Africa was shared was highly injurious to the future of African peace. Queen Victoria, the most acquisitive of all imperial forces, even suggested acquiring 'The big mountain [Kilimanjaro] in Africa' for her grandson, the Kaiser of German![220]

§5.5 Theories of Domination

It seems in the history of civilization that for a people to dominate another people, such a people first must advance a theory or thesis against the dominated. In the case of Africa, there was an overwhelming theoretical basis why the Black people of Africa deserved to be enslaved and colonized. Europe and America used a two-pronged hook of racism and H. Rider Haggard's *King Solomon's Mines*[221] to justify the enslavement and colonization of the Black Africans, respectively. Historian Basil Davidson writes:

> The racism that we know, was born in Europe and America from the cultural need to justify doing to Black people, doing to Africans, what could not morally or legally be done to White people, least of all to Europeans. To justify the enslavement of Africans, in short it was culturally necessary to believe...that Africans were inherently

[219] *Ibid.*, p. 104
[220] *Ibid.*, p. 106
[221] H. Rider Haggard, *King Solomon's Mines* (London: Cassalle and Company, 1885)

and naturally less than human.... That was the cultural basis...of the slave trade and of the modern imperialism of Africa which followed the slave trade.[222]

As modern as 2007, biologists such as James Watson[223] still promulgate the Kantian racial sobriquets that "Africans have received from nature no intelligence that rises above the foolish,"[224] joining the long line of the so-called Western *thinkers* like Votaires, David Hume, Georg Hegel and Hugh Trevor-Roper who have fed imperialistic avarice with impetus which has contributed to the subjugation and plunder of Africa.

Colonialism was founded on a very strong theoretical base. In *King Solomon's Mines Revisited: Western Interests and the Burdened History*, Minter asserts, "[Haggard's] *King Solomon's Mines* came off the press in London in September 1885, only six months after the European powers had met in Berlin to set the rules for dividing up Africa."[225] This book gave impetus to what would become of European imperialism in Africa. It, in part, informed the doctrine of *terra nullius,* and this resonated with the thinking of the time. Hegel's claim that Black Africans exist in the *Infancy of Humanity* became "the ideological justification for colonialism."[226] Zambia, just like Africa in general, lost more than a thousand years that not even hard labor could compensate

---

[222] Carina Ray, "We Have a History," (January 2008), *New African*, No. 469, p. 24

[223] James Watson was involved in the discovery of the structure of DNA. In 2007, he declared that the people of African descent were not as intelligent as the people of European descent. This is despite the fact that research has shown that race is indeterminate of intellectual dexterity. Consequently, Watson's pontificating has gone a long way in dealing a dearth blow to the people of African descent, especially in perpetuating inequalities in the workplace. His racist stance was so influential that he has adamantly stated that "people who have to deal with Black employees find this not true" that all people are equal!

[224] See Carina Ray, *supra.*

[225] William Minter, *King Solomon's Mines Revisited: Western Interests and the Burdened History* (New York: Basic Books, Inc., 1986), p. 3

[226] Ray, *supra.,* p. 24

Charles Mwewa

in Europe's scrambling for Africa's territories. Europe and the Americas on the other hand, gained much more than they could possibly need for a long time to come.

Consummate with historical ideation, in 2010, Pat Robertson suggested that the earthquake-ravaged Haiti was cursed by a pact to the devil, thus:

> "Something happened a long time ago in Haiti, and people might not want to talk about it," he said on Christian Broadcasting Network's "The 700 Club." "They were under the heel of the French. You know, Napoleon III, or whatever. And they got together and swore a pact to the devil. They said, we will serve you if you'll get us free from the French. True story. And so, the devil said, okay it's a deal.[227]

It is inimical of the lowest derogation to condemn a nation under the shackles of colonialism of Satan worship because the people wanted to be free from the colonial rule. Pat Robertson may be wrong in this. Somewhere in this book this argument is dealt with.[228] What is vital at this juncture is to overrule some justifications that those who put others in bondage advance. In this case, for example, Haiti is accused of Satan worship to justify its colonial-injected historical poverty.

It is against this background that the story of pre-independence Zambia will be detailed, bearing in mind that what is discussed is a quintessential analysis of Zambia's genuine desire to rubble off the shackles of unjust enrichment by colonial powers, the legacy of unequal treatment, and to celebrate the tremendous bravery of those who struggled with their might and life for Zambia's political independence.

---

[227] Danny Shea, "Pat Robertson: Haiti 'Cursed' By 'Pact to the Devil'" *The Huffington Post*, May 25th, 2011
[228] See §7.4

94

§5.6 Invasion of Zambia

Life as we know it in Zambia, concentrated mostly in urban areas, was an invention of European expedition to Zambia. About 2000 years ago, there about the time of Jesus Christ, the indigenous Zambians were hunter-gatherers. They lived by collecting wild fruits and hunting game for food and using the skins of the animals as marts. Between the 15th and 19th centuries, these indigenous Zambians were displaced by advancing Bantu[229] speaking tribes migrating from the Luba and Lunda kingdoms in what is present day Congo DR and Angola. They were flanked by the Ngoni people from the south towards the end of the 19th Century. To understand the composition, expedition and migratory adventures of these people, it is important to pay attention to their oral traditions and local myths and legends. One such rich tradition, which also forms part of the historical recollection of the people we call the Bemba in Zambia happened between the 15th and the 19th centuries.

Young[230] has argued against tribal histories, contending that, "Most of them describe in more or less picturesque detail, how a tribe was founded by a band of adventures."[231] He admits that these stories may contain, in general, a large kernel of truth, "But it is important to realize that they do not necessarily give us the literal truth."[232] Accordingly, he devalues them as mere myths. Their main purpose, he reminds, is not to record what really happened, but rather, to explain and justify the customs and institutions of the present day.[233]

However, it is vital to understand that these stories are based on historical facts. Indeed, their memory has been compressed and transformed into moral lessons for today, and that should not

---

[229] Human beings or simply people
[230] Andrew Young, *A History of Zambia* (New York: African Publishing Company, 1973)
[231] *Ibid.*, p. 63
[232] *Ibid.*
[233] *Ibid.*, p. 64

be a nefarious assumption why they should be believed. For the most part Western history is recorded, but it was not always so. Homer depended on local myths and legends to write the *Odyssey* and the *Iliad* in 800 B.C. Similarly, most of Zambian history in pre-European invasion period can only be deciphered from local myths and legends, and now through anthropology as well as archaeology.

The Bembas are those who consider themselves subjects of the Chiti Mukulu, the Bemba's only paramount chief. They live in villages of 100 to 200 people and numbered 250,000 strong at Zambia's independence.[234] There are over thirty Bemba clans, named after animals or natural organisms, such as the royal clan, "The people of the crocodile" (Bena Ng'andu) or the Bena Bowa (mushroom clan). They were the people who finally put a halt to the northward stride of the Nguni, Sotho-tswana and Ngoni people.

Reference shall be made to the Bembas as a way of illustrating the incomprehensive nature of the doctrine of *terra nullius*, dispelling the notion that the descendants of Zambians were landless before colonialism. Similar histories such as of the Lozi people[235] of Zambia provide irrefutable evidence of the

---

[234] Jay Samungole, "History of the Bemba People" (Lusaka: Unpublished, 2010)
[235] From "History of the Lozi People" by Jay Samungole, (Lusaka: Unpublished, 2010), used by permission:

> The Barotseland region of Zambia represents a large autonomous kingdom in the Western Province. The earliest known tribe of the Lozi people to settle in the area, the Luyi, migrated from Katanga in the Congo. They were ruled by a long line of female rulers until their settlement on the Bulozi flood plain. The earliest of these rulers was named Mwambwa, who was succeeded by her daughter, Mbuyuwamwambwa.
>
> Per legend, they both married Nyambe, the "maker of the world, the forests, the river, the plains, all the animals, birds and fish." Mwanasolundwi Muyunda Mumbo wa Mulonga, a.k.a, Mboo, the

flamboyant and booming kingdoms in the area which came to be called Zambia.

§5.7 Kola[236]

In a country called Cula or Kola, there was a chief called Mierda. He had several sons by different wives, but one day he heard of a woman with ears as large as an elephant's, who said she came from the sky and belonged to the crocodile clan. Her name was Mumbi Mukasa, and the chief married her. They had three sons, Katongo, Chiti and Nkole, and a daughter, Chilufya Mulenga. The impetuous young men built a tower that fell and killed many people. Mukulumpe was furious. He put out

---

son of Mbuyuwamwambwa, was chosen as paramount ruler of the Lozi, becoming the first male ruler in history. Thereafter, all his successors, as Litunga, have been males. A revolution in 1840 removed the ruling dynasty from power. The whole of Barotseland then fell under the rule of the Kilolo, led by Sibitwane, brother of the great Moshesh of Lasotho, for the next twenty-four years.

The Lozi dynasty continued to oppose them wherever possible, and maintained its leadership and traditions in exile. A rebellion again in 1860 enabled Lutangu Sipopa, a son of Litunga Mulumbwa, to seize his chance to establish his claim to the throne. He defeated and virtually exterminated the Kilolo four years later and restored the fortunes of the dynasty. Litunga Sipopa's assassination by his bodyguard in 1876 triggered a contest for the succession. Although his nephew, Mwanawina II, secured the throne, though powerful, he was deposed in favor of his popular cousin, Lubosi, two years later. Litunga Lubosi I or more popularly Lewanika, succeeded on the death of his cousin in 1878, was himself deposed and driven into exile in 1884. He escaped to Angola, gathered an army and regained the throne in late 1885. Highly intelligent and keen to modernize his kingdom, he embraced the missionaries as a means of educating his people. He also recognized the risk of White settlement and arranged to accept a British Protectorate in 1890 in order to protect his people and lands from encroachment.

---

[236] Samungole, *supra.*, used by permission.

Katongo's eyes, and banished Chiti and Nkole. Mukulumpe pretended to relent and called back the exiles. However, he had dug a game pit to kill the three of them. Katongo, though blind, warned his brothers by using his talking drum. When they arrived at the palace, the king humiliated them by subjecting them do menial work. Chiti and Nkole left the kingdom for good, and took with them their three maternal half-brothers Kapasa, Chimba and Kazembe and their entourage.

They fled east, until they came to the middle reaches of the Luapula River. Chief Matanda of the Bena Mukulo ferried them across. In their haste, they left behind their blind brother Katongo and their sister Chilufya Mulenga, who Mukulumpe had locked up in a house without doors. They dispatched their half-brother Kapasa to break out Chilufya Mulenga, which he did ingeniously. But on the way to Luapula, Kapasa fell in love with Chilufya. When it turned out she was pregnant, Kapasa was disowned by Chiti. The group meanwhile had fallen in with a 'White Magician,' Luchele Ng'anga. When they arrived at the Luapula, Kazembe decided to settle there, but Nkole and Chiti were uncertain. When Luchele Ng'anga conjured up a fish from a mortar, they took this to be an omen to head eastwards, and moved toward the plateau of the Chambeshi River, near Lake Bangweulu.

They crossed the Safwa Rapids, and the Luchindashi River, where there was a quarrel between two women, and part of the group stayed behind, forming the Bena Nona (mushroom clan), the royal clan of the Bisa people.

The others continued southwards where they encountered the Lala people, who asked them for a chief, and were given a man called Kankomba. The migrants then turned eastwards to the Luangwa Valley and among the Nyanja[237] and the Senga (or

---

[237] The people who are considered to be the Nyanja are actually the Chewa people. Nyanja is a dialect which developed in trading centers with its root being Chewa. In some instances, Nyanja and Chewa are taken as one

Nsenga) peoples, they encountered a chief called Mwase. Mwase's wife, Chilimbulu, was very beautiful, and her stomach was adorned with elegant cicatrizations. Chiti fell in love with Chilimbulu, and seduced her when Mwase was out hunting. When he returned, and caught them in the act, the two chiefs fought, and Chiti was grazed by a poisoned arrow, after which he died.

Nkole and his followers took Chiti's body with them, looking for a grove suitable for his burial. They encountered the magician Luchele Ng'anga again, and he directed them toward a majestic grove called Mwalule or Milemba. At Mwalule, they found a woman called Chimbala. They also found another visitor, the Bisa headman Kabotwe, who was there to trade and pay respect to Chimbala.

After Chimbala gave them permission to bury Chiti, they managed to get Chimbala to marry Kabotwe, ensuring Chimbala's ritual ability to purify those who buried Chiti. Kabotwe became the keeper of the grove, and received the title Shimwalule, which his matrilineal descendants inherited. However, Nkole had sent out a party to raid cattle from Fipa chief Pilula to provide an ox-hide shroud for Chiti. Then, he dispatched

---

because the difference between them if any, is minimal. There are presently over 1.5 million Chewa throughout Malawi and Zambia, however the Chewa are not considered people of Malawi, nor people of Zambia, but people from the Nyanja group of Bantu. The history of the Chewa people includes a number of stories of fact, tradition, ancestral beliefs, and spiritual influence creating the modern-day Chewa culture. Legend holds that over one thousand years ago, Bantu speaking people of Nigeria and Cameroon migrated to – among other places – the Luba area of Zaire, or what is now known as the Democratic Republic of Congo. The Nyanja group of Bantu settled within the Luba area known as Malambo and conquered more and more land from other Bantu peoples. Eventually their central locale shifted from Malambo to the region of Choma; a vast mountainous and plateau region known today as northeastern Zambia and northern Malawi (formerly Nyasaland). In Malawi, the Chewa are predominantly concentrated within the central region, surrounding the Capital City of Lilongwe, in areas such as Dedza, Kasungu, Dowa, Ntchisi, Mchinjui, Ntcheu, Salima, and Nkhota Kota.

a party to avenge Chiti's death, killing Mwase and Chilimbulu. Their bodies were burned at Mwalule, but the smoke overcame Nkole, who also died, and now also had to be buried at Mwalule.

The Kola migrants adopted matrilineal succession, and Chiti and Nkole were succeeded by their sister Chilufya Mulenga's son. He was also called Chilufya, and was too young to rule as chief, so Chiti's half-brother Chimba ruled in his place. The Kola migrants left Mulambalala, their site near Mwalule and crossed the Chambeshi River north. The disgraced Kapasa, however, settled on his own in Bulombwa, driving out Iwa chief Kafwimbi and his cattle.

The others traveled westward up the Kalongwa River, where two men, Kwaba and Chikunga found a dead crocodile. As the chiefs were of the crocodile clan, this was taken as a good sign. Here, the Kola migrants made their Capital, Ng'wena (Crocodile) on the Kalungu River and settled the surrounding country. The groups then living in the area were called Sukuma, Musukwa, Kalelelya and Ngalagansa. They were driven off or killed by the Kola migrants, who were by now called the Bemba.

When Chilufya the king grew up, Chimba handed him the royal bows belonging to his uncles Nkole and Chiti. Chilufya thereby gained the praise name 'Ca mata yabili' (of the two bows). Chilufya, however, insisted that Chimba keep Nkole's bow, allowing him to found his own village at Chatindubwi, a few miles north of the Kalungu River.

Thereafter, the Bemba became many. New villages and chiefs were founded, and many chiefs succeeded Chilufya. These paramount chiefs took the name of the original founder, Chiti Mukulu (Chiti the Great).

§5.8 Thriving Kingdoms

From this account, as too is from that of the Lozi or the Nyanja peoples, the descendants of Zambians were a well-organized people with thriving kingdoms, laws and order. They acquired lands and held claim to territories by conquests. In the places where they finally settled, whether by conquest or *jus soli*,[238] they set up political structures and hubs of power. Among the Bembas, for example, the Paramount Chief or Chiti Mukulu was the supreme ruler, who was assisted by chiefs and headmen. Similarly, among the Lozis, the Litunga is assisted by subordinates known as *indunas*.

By the 19th Century, the descendants of the modern-day Zambia had an established traditional legal system consisting of sound customs and conventions. Land was collectively owned by the people entrusted to the chief as the guarantor of land rights. The chief in turn delegated the demarcation and distribution of land to local headmen.

What was true of land policy in the present-day Zambia between the 15th and 19th centuries, was also true of Britain between the 11th and 13th centuries. In 1066, a Norman General from Normandy by the name of William the Conqueror, occupied what is known as England. He found no harmonized law and different groups resolving their disputes per the customs of that area. William introduced a Feudal System[239] and appointed a form of circuit court system to arbitrate land and criminal matters on his behalf. These circuit judges necessitated a common application of legal precedents throughout the land based on the principle of *stare decisis*.[240] These common customs became

---

[238] Right of soil

[239] Where land ownership was exclusively in the hands of the King

[240] The term *stare decisis* originate from the Latin maxim of *Stare decisis et non quieta movere,* which means "to stand by decisions and not disturb the undisturbed" or simply, "Let the decision stand." It is a theory of the common-law system which stipulates that the decision of a superior court is binding on an inferior court and on a court of co-ordinate jurisdiction so far

known as the common law.

By the mid of the 19th Century, Europeans comprising explorers,[241] traders and missionaries began to penetrate Zambia. Notable among them was David Livingstone, a medical doctor from England who, in the company of his African helper Chuma,[242] claimed to have discovered the Victoria Falls in 1855.[243] The Livingstone town in the Southern Province of Zambia is named after David Livingstone.

The brilliance and magnificence at the sight of the African continent could have stunned Livingstone. His explorations in the interior could have changed his view of what had been termed the Dark Continent forever.[244] Grant, attesting to this fact on

---

as it is a statement of the law which the court is bound to accept. This doctrine demands that rules or principles of law on which a court rested a previous decision are authoritative in all future cases in which the facts are substantially similar.

[241] Most of these explorers were ruthless against the Africans. For example, the journalist Henry Morton Stanley who met Livingstone at Ujiji on November 10th, 1871 and greeted Livingstone with those famous words, "DR. LIVINGSTONE, I presume," is believed to have used, "excessive violence, racial abuse, and condescending language towards Africans" (Firstbrook, *The Obamas*, p. 98).

[242] In 1997, this author wrote a poem called *Chitambo* (for this is the place in central Zambia where David Livingstone's heart is buried) in tribute to Chuma who helped Livingstone travel the almost impassable jungles of Africa. This poem is found on page 93 of *Song of an Alien*.

[243] David Livingstone did not discover the Victoria Falls; he renamed the falls which was called Mosi-oa-Tunya (or the smoke that thunders) by the indigenous people. This event informs us of the popularity of the doctrine of *terra nullius*, even before it was made official by the Act of Berlin in 1885.

[244] While to the White Europeans Africa was "dark", it was only in as far as Europe remained ignorant about both the thriving civilizations and booming trade taking place there way before a European stepped foot on Africa. Firstbook attests, "Trade with both the Arabs and the Chinese [as early as 1414, a huge fleet of 62 Chinese trading galleons and 190 support ships under the command of Zheng He had crossed the Indian Ocean and landed on the African coast] disproves the myth that Africa – the 'Dark Continent' – had little or no contact with the outside world until it was 'opened up' by

Livingstone's first view of Africa, nods: "A vivid sunrise of silver, gold and blood red tinged its beauty with something a little intimidating, even frightening. How must Livingstone and the early explorers have felt on seeing it for the first time?"[245]

The *first most significant event* that would shape Zambia's political and economic history happened in 1888. In that year, John Cecil Rhodes sent his emissaries Joseph Thomson, Frank Elliot Lochner and Alfred Sharp to make treaties with King Lewanika. In 1890, the emissaries arrived in Barotseland.[246] They obtained mineral right concessions from the local chiefs, including Chief Lewanika in what is the present day Western Province of Zambia.[247]

§5.9 British South Africa Company

In 1891, John Cecil Rhodes and his British South Africa Company (BSAC) or the Company brought the administration of the territory under the charter of BSAC and administered it as a colony in two units of North-eastern and North-western Rhodesias.[248] Attempts at unifying these two territories failed

---

Europeans" (Firstbrook, *ibid.*, p. 85; also see Korwa G. Adar and Isaac M. Munyae, "Human Rights Abuses in Kenya under Daniel Arap Moi, 1978-2001," (2001) *African Studies Quarterly*, Vol. 5, No. 1

[245] Grant, *Zambia – Then and Now,* p. 25

[246] However, prior, in 1872, the first English traders had arrived at the court of Sipopa in Barotseland.

[247] However, the emissaries penetrated far inland in search of mineral deposits. For example, in 1910, Moffat Thompson "discovered" Nkana (Kitwe) copper source.

[248] Section 14 of the Royal Charter of October 29th, 1889 entrusted the administration of Rhodesia to the BSAC and authorized thus: "In the administration of justice to the said peoples or inhabitants careful regard shall always be had to the customs and laws of the class or tribe or nation to which the parties respectively belong, especially with regard to the holding, possession, transfer and disposition of lands and goods, and testate or intestate succession thereto, and marriages, divorces, legitimacy, and other rights of property and personal rights, but subject to any British laws which

principally because of opposition from the White European settlers. The settlers abhorred the practice of employing Africans in administrative posts. This is very important and revealing to the future of Zambia.

The European settlers did not favor the idea of amalgamation because that would mean Africans taking up administrative posts. They feared this move because it would empower the Africans for leadership. The settlers preferred to relegate the Africans to low and general laborer jobs. This was the *second most significant event* in the history of Zambia. Zambia would, consequently, encounter massive shortages of educated leaders at independence. "In education, for example, Zambia had only 100 university graduates, about 1,500 had school certificates...and 7,000 had attained Form II certificates."[249]

In 1911,[250] the two territories of North-eastern and North-western Rhodesias were formally amalgamated and Northern Rhodesia was formed. Northern Rhodesia remained a charter colony of the BSAC as a British sphere of influence until 1924. On April 1st, 1924 Herbert Stanley was appointed Governor of Northern Rhodesia. Subsequently, the administration of Northern Rhodesia was transferred to the British Colonial Office and Northern Rhodesia became an official British Protectorate with

---

may be in force of the territories aforesaid and applicable to the peoples or inhabitants thereof." (Hamalengwa, "The Legal System of Zambia: Law, Politics and Development in Historic Perspective," in P. Ebow Bodzi-Simpson, (ed.), *The Law and Economic Development in the Third World* (New York: Praeger Publishers, 1992), p. 23). Thus, from the inception of colonialism, the British government had introduced a dual legal system in Northern Rhodesia (Zambia) of the African customary law and the English common law.

[249] *Times of Zambia,* "Zambia's Independence: 1964 Celebrations Relieved" (October 2004)

[250] See John J. Grotpeter; Brian V. Siegel; and James R. Pletcher, *Historical Dictionary of Zambia, Second Edition* (London: The Scarecrow Press, Inc., 1998); other records place this event in 1916!

its Capital City at Livingstone.[251] In 1935, the Capital City was moved to Lusaka.[252] Per Hamalengwa, "Zambia was incorporated into the world economy as a Company State beginning from the end of the 19th Century. The Company, British South Africa Company had been given mineral rights over the territory."[253]

The wealth and survival of Zambia is tied to copper. In 1895, Frederick Russell Burnham of the BSAC did not discover copper by accident. The BSAC had stated in its aim that it wanted to exploit the mineral wealth north of the Limpopo River, extend the railways and telegraph system, and encourage colonization, *et alia*: "To develop and work mineral and other concessions under the management of one powerful organization, thereby obviating conflicts and complications between the various interests that have been acquired within the region and securing to the native chiefs and their subjects the *rights reserved* to them under several concessions."[254] The BSAC had predetermined interest in Northern Rhodesia.

---

[251] "The colonial state and government were basically set up to cater for the interests of the Crown [British government] and colonial setters as well as international capital that was centered in the copper industry." (Hamalengwa, "The Legal System of Zambia: Law, Politics and Development in Historic Perspective," *supra.*, p. 22)

[252] The name Lusaka is derived from a village headman called Lusaaka who occupied the limestone area where the present Lusaka City is situated. His palace could have been located where the Manda Hill (National Assembly) is today.

[253] Munyonzwe Hamalengwa, *Class Struggles in Zambia 1889-1989 & The Fall of Kenneth Kaunda 1990-1991*(Lanham: University Press of America, 1992), pp. 21-22.

[254] F.L Coleman, *The Northern Rhodesia Copperbelt 1889-1962*, as quoted in Hamalengwa, *Class Struggles in Zambia 1889-1989 & The Fall of Kenneth Kaunda 1990-1991*, p. 25

§5.10 Treaties or Hoaxes

The supposedly "rights reserved" for the natives were only a hoax, as after 1889 the BSAC began, in effect, to plunder first the western portion of Zambia, and later the northern trail. It carried out manufacturing of commercial and trading businesses, searched and extracted diamonds, gold, copper, coal and precious stones. The Company further carried out business in banking, sold and manipulated metals, manufactured and imported arms and ammunitions, and administered the affairs of the Company and of the native Africans. As mentioned before, effectively from 1889, Zambia became a Company State under the Royal Charter of October 29th, 1889.

A treaty, like a contract, is a settlement or agreement arrived at through negotiation. A treaty gives rise to binding obligations between parties that make it. It may outline the rights and responsibilities of the parties as they are agreed upon. However, treaties are only binding on parties that have adhered to them, save for peremptory norms.

Modern treaties are sanctioned by international law and are consummated in the 1969 *Vienna Convention on the Law of Treaties* which defines a treaty as an agreement between two or more nation-states over matters that they have agreed upon. Enforcement and interpretation of these treaties is as well governed by international law. By extension, a treaty can also refer to any agreement or contract that describes an agreement made between parties other than nation-states.

Imperialists used two approaches to dominating other territories: Conquest or treaties. Through treaties, European nations, such as Britain, recognized the natives' occupancy, ownership and governance of the territories they wanted to colonize.

Northern Rhodesia was providentially positioned in the sense that treaties, rather than conquests,[255] were used to secure its territorial domination. But this providence came with inuendos. The representatives of the BSAC used concessions to grab mineral and other rights in Barotseland. The term *concession agreement* refers to a type of negotiated contract which gives a company the right to do specific business in an identified territory. In the case of King (Litunga) Lewanika and the BSAC, a mineral concession agreement meant an agreement which granted the concessionaire (the BSAC) exclusive right to do business in Barotseland in exchange for some carefully negotiated terms.

As shown earlier, by the last half of the 19th Century, most tribes in the territory that would become Northern Rhodesia had strong and well-established kingdoms. To secure their kingdoms, leaders of these kingdoms often solicited for alliances with other strong kingdoms, missionary organizations or, in the case of Litunga Lewanika, chartered companies.

Lewanika wanted British protection from the nearby Matabele Kingdom.[256] The Matebele had trekked upwards from the Zulu Kingdom of Shaka Zulu.[257] The Matebeles were under their leader Lobengula. Lewanika also wanted protection from the Portuguese and from some of his own dissident subjects. However, that was not enough reason to *sell* the entire territory

---

[255] Zulu attributes this approach to the subsequent peaceful and orderly independence transition as opposed to military operations in other colonized African countries: "In Northern Rhodesia [Zambia] and Nyasaland [Malawi] the nationalist struggle took a constitutional route mainly because these territories, although under the racial Federation, still enjoyed certain rights as protectorates under Her Majesty's government through the Colonial Office. The territories of Portuguese Africa were considered as 'overseas provinces, hence the intransigency of the minority to African agitation for self-rule." (Zulu in *Memoirs of Alexander Grey Zulu*, p. 5)

[256] Or the Ndebele Kingdom

[257] Shaka Zulu was an illegitimate son who became one of the most decorated warriors in Africa. He devised a short-specialized spear he called *Assegai* and coached his *Impis* (warriors) to fight barefooted and attack his enemies very early in the morning.

or most of the productive or mineral-laden land!

On June 26th, 1890 Lewanika signed a concession with Cecil Rhodes' representative, Frank Lochner.[258] "The concession covered *all* Lewanika's country, allowing the Company to engage in manufacturing, mining, banking, the provision of infrastructure works and the importation of arms and ammunition."[259] Basically, all the talk about signing treaties or concessions by the Africans with the Europeans at that time was a ruse. The Europeans, unlike the Africans, were on a mission on the African soil. They had left the comfort of their own lands for much more than just simple adventure or expeditions as they called them. They were wealth hunters, and wherever they found it, they used every arsenal at their disposal to acquire it.

It is travesty that Africa continues to fall for simple tricks even in the 21st Century. Africa tends to mistake openness to courtesy. The present must provide impetus to redeem the future.

The presence of the BSAC in Barotseland is the point in issue. The agreement Lewanika reached, if it can qualify to be an agreement at all, was for the most part a one-sided deal.

---

[258] The Lochner Treaty was signed by Lubosi Lewanika of the Second Regime of the Litunga Royal Establishment, himself the successor of King Lubosi of the First Regime. He was the 18th Litunga. The line of the Litungas or Lozi rulers from (1) Queen Mwambwa are: (2) Queen Mbuyawamwambwa (3) King Mboo Muyunda Mwana Silundu (4) King Inyambo (5) King Yeta I Ya Musa (6) King Ngalama wa Ingalamwa (7) King Yeta II Nalute Mucabatu (8) King Ngombala (9) King Yubya Ikandanda (10) King Mwanawina I (11) King Mwananyanda Liwale (12) King Mulambwa Santulu (13) King Silumelume Muimui (14) King Mubukwanu (15) King Sipopa Lutangu (16) King Mwanawina II (17) First Regime: King Lubosi; Second Regime: Lubosi Lewanika (18) King Tatila Akufuna (19) King Litia Yeta III, CBE (20) King Mwanang'ono Imwiko I (21) King Mwanawina III, KBE (22) King Mbikusita Lewanika II (23) King Ilute Yeta IV (24) King Lubosi Imwiko II

[259] Cedric Pulford, "Barotseland: A Unique African Kingdom" <http://www.pulfordmedia.co.uk/i_pages/i_features/african.htm> (Retrieved: May 31st, 2010)

Moreover, it cannot be said that Lewanika wanted the BSAC protection because he believed the Company would protect him entirely. Thirteen years after being swindled of mineral rights in Barotseland, the Company literally obliterated Lewanika's most feared neighbor, Lobengula of the Matebele people.

Pulford writes that within a few years Lobengula, Lewanika's arch-rival was dead. The 1893 Matabele war started over a small incident when the telegraph link was cut and wire stolen. The Chartered Company seized the opportunity and treated this as a *casus belli*.[260] Maxim guns made short work of Lobengula's *impis* (regiments). The king fled his Capital, Gubulawayo (close to today's Bulawayo), and soon died, probably of smallpox. However, the process of assimilation was by now unstoppable for Lewanika. Barotseland became absorbed into Northern Rhodesia at first under the Company and, from 1924, as a British Protectorate.[261]

The Company did not only sign more treaties, it went ahead and plundered Lewanika of resources.[262] One of the conditions for grabbing the wealth of the Lozi people of western Zambia was in exchange for some members of Lewanika to study in London. In 1898, Lewanika was again hoaxed into another concession called the Lawley Concession.

This concession "reduced Lewanika's annual subsidy from £2,000 to £850 and gave the Company judicial powers in disputes between Whites or Whites and Blacks. It was the blueprint for the Lewanika Concession of 1900. This affirmed the Company's

---

[260] "Justification for acts of war" from Latin *Casus* or case, and *Belli* or bellic, literally "of war."

[261] *Ibid.*

[262] Cecil Rhodes was not the only colonialist filled with avarice and disregard for the African continent. One called Karl Peters, described as the "Man with blood on his hands" by the people of East Africa, and the man whom both Kaiser Wilhelm II and Adolf Hitler later feted as the ideological hero of German, is said to have made a total of twelve bogus agreements with the Sultans, grabbing a total of 60 thousand square miles of the East African mainland. Peters is believed to have treated the Africans with cruelty and angst. See Peter Firstbrook, *The Obamas*, p. 105

administrative authority over the king's domains. It excluded prospecting in the Barotse heartland – and yet an astonishing postscript provided that if gold in worthwhile quantities was not found outside the reserved area, it could be sought inside the reserved area!"[263] The Company until 1909 soldiered on and grabbed all the arable land in Barotseland.

In 1917, Paramount Chief Yeta appealed to the British Government claiming that the Company's "rights were obtained in its capacity as the government – the inference being that without the responsibilities of administration it must also abandon its rights." In short, the African chief had come to realize too late that the Company had played the game of *cat and mouse*, plundering the area of its wealth and yet not taking full responsibility of developing or administering the area competently. From the beginning the relationship between the Company and the British Government was suspicious, described by some as "a peculiar one." In fact, the Company's revenue in terms of royalties from minerals had risen from £12,781 in 1925 to £300,000 in 1937.[264] This was nearly half of the total Northern Rhodesian government income from the mines.

The Company has been cited as an "accomplice in the intrigue of continued African servitude"[265] with the colonial establishment. The Company owned "large tracts of land throughout the territory from which it collect[ed] royalties or rent."[266] Thus, any agitations by the Africans for political independence were seen as treasonous to its business interests. Consequently, the Company did "everything to support Welensky and his gang."[267]

[263] *Ibid.*
[264] Richard Hall, *Zambia, 1890-1964: The Colonial Period* (London: Longman Group Ltd., 1976), p. 88
[265] Skeva Soko, "Independence for Zambia," (March 1962) *Africa Today*, p. 17
[266] *Ibid.*
[267] *Ibid.*

To return to the argument, the Company maintained that it signed legitimate concessions with the Africans. It had relied upon the bogusly created agreements to advance its thesis of the acquisition of land and mineral wealth in Barotseland. For all intents and purposes, the details of the Lawley Concession beg for elucidation. For "if gold in worthwhile quantities was not found outside the reserved area, it could be sought inside the reserved area" was a clear mark of the subtlety of the nature of these agreements.

For one, it is doubtful if Lewanika read it this way. For another, it is even cynical, because there is hitherto no record to show that a similar version of the agreement in the Lozi language in which the Litunga was eloquent was present. This line of thought is attested to by the article which appeared on the front page of the *Toronto Star*:[268]

> More than a century ago, a blind Ojibway chief from Northwestern Ontario named Missabay marked an 'X' on a treaty written in English, *a language he did not speak*. The chief *didn't have a lawyer acting for him* or his people from the Mishkeegogamang First Nation and played no part in negotiating the treaty (Emphasis added).[269]

The British MO in imperial conquest in colonial domination was the same everywhere. In Canada, it involved an Ojibway chief who was neither proficient in English nor did he seem to have understood what he had consented to. And yet the so-called James Bay Treaty No. 9 came into effect as a legitimate agreement.

And as mentioned above, for example, Yeta was himself confused of what he was doing; he thought he was signing the treaty with the British Government. Generally, "These treaties were hardly worth the paper they were written on, as it is unlikely

---

[268] Peter Edwards, "Lawsuit a Century in the Making," *Toronto Star*, (Tuesday, May 17th, 2011)
[269] *Ibid.*

111

that the Africans had any idea of what they were actually ceding."[270]

Subsequently, it is reasonable to believe that in the case of Litunga Lewanika, he could have construed the agreement as securing a smaller portion, as was customary for the African kings or chiefs in those days to do to their subjects and to the foreigners for temporary exploitation. In the absence of verifiable translation of the agreement to the contrary, the contract was at best a one-party formality and at worst a non-binding indenture.

The Barotseland Concession lacked credibility from the word go. The witness present, Col. Colin Harding, whose job was to attest to the signing of this resource-depleting exercise, was himself schemed into the process. He was, in fact, not told the details, and the activities surrounding the signing were highly suspicious. Harding is quoted as saying: "On more mature consideration [Lewanika] realized that it carried him further than he had meant to go."[271] Contrary to writers like Caplan[272] who contend that the concessions were desirable for the Litunga, a material witness vehemently disputes that fact.

Harding informs that Litunga Lewanika shortly after being lured into signing this agreement regretted. He realized that the Company representatives had hoodwinked him. Not only was the Litunga guilty of what he had been crooked into doing, Harding was also as culpable: "I would like to say here that although I was present when this Ratifying Treaty was signed and my name was appended as a witness to the other signatures, the full contents of the document were not divulged to me,"[273] Harding distances himself.

Pulford has examined this whole so-called treaty at length and has made scintillating discoveries. For example, he postulates

---

[270] Firstbrook, *The Obamas*, pp. 105-106
[271] Pulford, *supra*.
[272] See §5.14
[273] Pulford, *supra*.

that the 1890 and 1898 were not the only treaties the Company caused the Litunga to sign, *volenti non-fit injuria*; more were to come. By a simple exchange of letters in 1904, Pulford intimates that Lewanika gave the BSAC farming and settlement rights throughout his kingdom except the Barotse valley and the area near Sesheke.

To understand the nature of the treaties Lubosi Lewanika of the Second Regime signed with the Company, it is important to examine the person of the Litunga through whom the Company accomplished its dream. On November 4th, 1885, Lewanika recuperated his throne by a bloody battle which toppled Tatila Akufuna. From there he became the most sympathetic of all the Litungas to Western philanthropy. It is easy to understand why. He had just regained his throne after being deposed by Ngambela Mataa in September 1884. Mataa installed Tatila Akufuna. Fearing for another overthrow, he welcomed the Company with both hands. Immediately on June 27th, 1889, he signed the Ware Concession. Just a year after that, on June 26th, 1890, he signed the Lochner Concession.

Lewanika then attended the Coronation Ceremonies of King Edward VII and Queen Alexandra at Westminster Abbey in London in 1902 and was, subsequently, decorated with the medals of King Edward VII in the same year.[274] More to his tribute, he abolished slavery on July 16th, 1906 and was again decorated, this time, with the medals of King George V in 1911. He was succeeded by another ambitious Litunga, King Litia Yeta III, on March 16th, 1916. Yeta III continued the legacy of

---

[274] "Before 1900, Lewanika at one time protested to London and to Queen Victoria that the BSAC agents had misrepresented the terms of the concession, but his protests fell on deaf ears. Why? It is because he was in the first place chosen for convenience. The British were the masters of deception. They had just used the Litunga. The Litunga came back from London crowned as a British knight and he still wears that spectacular British uniform at the Kuomboka Ceremony while the British just laugh at our naïvety. We must be fools, indeed" (Mbulo)

Lewanika and won the title of the Commander of the British Empire (CBE) on January 1st, 1946.[275]

The above background is necessary to understanding why it was easy to dupe Lubosi Lewanika in signing treaties between 1889 and 1909. Consequently, the Wallace Concession was reached in 1909. Per Pulford, this treaty reiterated farming and settlement rights except in areas where prospecting was prohibited, such as the heartland. He adds that villages and gardens in Barotseland were uprooted, albeit with unconscionable consent and shoddy compensation. "The consent need not be that of the people affected, however. It could also be given by the High Commissioner of the territory – i.e. a Briton."[276] The colonialists had not only the ambition to invade another territory, but the courage, too, to usurp land rights and authority natively reserved for the African traditional rulers. Through a meager wage, they could buy most chiefs who in turn would render their services of soliciting for manpower for the colonialists. Per Dauti Yamba, a chief might be suspended from receiving his monthly wages, but to the people he stilled ruled.[277]

§5.11 Foundation for Democracy

If democracy was promulgated in Greece, and found its niche in the American Declaration of Independence, democracy was, however, a common feature of the African chiefs and kings in the territory we now call Zambia. What is more and this is in refutation of common assumptions to the contrary, the Africans,

---

[275] See Lubosi Muimui, "The Litunga of the Lozi People," Access Kuomboka and Cultural Affairs (September 5th, 2010)
[276] Ibid.
[277] M.C Musambachime, "Dauti Yamba's Contribution to the Rise and Growth of Nationalism in Zambia, 1941-1964," (1991) African Affairs, Vol. 90, p. 270

though militaristic in expanding their kingdoms, in governance, they pursued the Rule of Law to the letter. In the territory, we now call Zambia, the Rule of Law did not emanate from the British *Magna Carter*;[278] it was inherent in their customs, practices and government structures. In the case of Litunga Lewanika, Harding proffers evidence to this end:

> Colin Harding, who traveled up the Zambezi from Victoria Falls to Lealui, gave an account (in *Remotest Barotseland*, 1905) of Lewanika's daily routine. He sat in the courthouse between 9am and 10am, hearing complaints, promulgating laws and attending to other government business. The *indunas*, or senior officials, representing the people, sat on his right. They alone had the right to criticize the king. In *Far Bugles*, Harding praised Lewanika's "charming personality," his "loyalty and other inherent virtues." When the Litunga visited London for the coronation of King Edward VII, with Harding in attendance, the king and his retinue were found not to touch alcohol. "Lewanika's whole and consistent attitude was befitting a gentleman and a great native ruler," Harding wrote.[279]

Lewanika died an honorable man, a king of meritorious distinction. However, Zambian history will not forget the injustices the Barotseland, and by extension, Zambia has suffered through colonialism. There are those who still argue that the poverty and economic difficulties Zambia experiences in the 21st Century are far detached from historical corollaries. This author begs to differ, and the plunder of western Zambia by the BSAC over a period of 20 years justifies this assertion. Until Zambians revisit their history, Zambia will continue to be foreign-owned. Colonists hoodwinked local African chiefs into signing shoddy

---

[278] The *Magna Carter* or the Great Charter of England of 1215 required the English King John to proclaim certain liberties and to accept that his will was not arbitrary. The *Magna Carta* was the first document that limited the king's powers by law and protected the privileges of the barons or subjects of England. In essence, the *Magna Carta* introduced the Rule of Law to England where even the king himself was not to be above the law. Read more on the *Magna Carta* under §11.1

[279] Pulford, *supra*.

treaties and claim mineral and other rights, and this is a lesson our history books should never sideline.[280]

§5.12 Colonial Administration

It is a well-known fact that Zambia did not only inherit the British system of education, but the British edifice as well. The Zambian education system is itself full of British overtures. Sometimes one would think as though Zambians were being groomed to live in England rather than in Zambia. In England, presently, there could be as many as two million Zambians living there, approximately the entire population of Lusaka. From the Victoria Train Station in Central London to the African market at Shepherd Bush, what became of Zambia originated from Britain.

Since 1888 when the first BSAC officials entered Barotseland, the territory we call Zambia had come under British influence. Others would argue that, in fact, British influence extended earlier than the recorded history as the BSAC officials would have been to this area unofficially and surveyed the land, or how else could they have known of the existence of massive copper reserves in the territory!

John Cecil Rhodes[281] had a massive dream of connecting the dots of the British pockets into a great British Empire across Africa. He envisioned building a railway or road network running from Capetown in South Africa to Cairo in Egypt. The famous *Cairo Road* in Lusaka remains an essence of Rhodes dream.

---

[280] The 1890 Lochner-Concession sloppily gave BSAC the right to carry out mineral extraction in Barotseland. This treaty, in fact, represented the start of the colonization of what would become Zambia. This western part of Zambia became an English protectorate – the Barotseland Protectorate - under British protection.
[281] See §5.15

"Cairo Road – the name was a claim, a boast, then still a reality, if a tenuous one, that a person could drive right over the continent [of Africa] from Capetown in South Africa to Cairo in Eqypt without leaving the British-controlled territory."[282]

The British could be accused of anything, but lack of administrative prowess is none of it. In territorial vastness, the British Empire, at its peak, could have surpassed even its precursor, the Roman Empire. Good administration necessitated both its grandeur and influence. In Northern Rhodesia, the British administrative genius was everywhere.

At the helm, in London, was the Secretary of State for the Colonies. The Secretary of State appointed the Territorial Governor, who was the highest-ranking government officer in Northern Rhodesia. Under the Governor was the Secretary of Native Affairs who headed the Ministry of Native Affairs (MNA). The MNA "decided all appointments in... the Provincial Administration."[283]

In Northern Rhodesia, the Provincial Administration (PA) comprised districts under a Provincial Commissioner. Under him[284] were five districts each headed by a District Commissioner. The District Commissioner was assisted by District Officer Cadets – "It was therefore said that every [District Officer] Cadet carried a potential Governor's baton in his knapsack, but at the end that was a fallacy. After Sir Evelyn Hone, there would be no more Governors."[285]

District Officer Cadets were assisted by District Assistants, the only difference between them being, as Grant puts it, "That District Officers had degrees, usually honors degrees from 'good' universities, an achievement which was deemed to

[282] Grant, *supra.*, p. 26

[283] *Ibid*, p. 30

[284] Him but not her; the commonest feature of British colonial administration was the lack of gender equality - women were not appointed to administrative roles. So, in almost one hundred percent of the cases, the officers of the British colonial administration in Northern Rhodesia would be men.

[285] Grant, *supra.*, p. 30

convey superior ability."[286] Grant later writes that with the District Assistants he had a pleasure to work, there was no single sign of inferiority in terms of either efficiency or judgment!

Still under the District Assistants were Learner District Assistants, who later were assisted by African Administration Assistants and clerks.[287] After independence, the Learner District Assistants and clerks easily assumed the positions left behind by the district and provincial officers, and etcetera.

It is not a surprise that the colonization of Northern Rhodesia began in earnest in the western portion of modern Zambia. Shortly after the 1890 Lochner Concession, the BSAC took control of mineral and land rights in Barotseland. This western part of Northern Rhodesia became an English Protectorate, sometimes known as Barotseland Protectorate. Northern Rhodesia was officially a Company State until 1924 when the British Government took over full administrative control of the territory as a British Protectorate.

There is no denying that the western part of Zambia played a vital role in the journey to Zambia's colonization. Even though Lewanika might have been deluded into signing the treaties that gave the BSAC enormous freedom to exploit not only western Zambia, but the rest of the country as well, the treaties were, nevertheless, enforceable. If not intelligently handled, western Zambia would pose a big challenge to the vision of a united Zambia. However, Kaunda, Lewanika and the Queen of England had other plans through the Barotseland Agreement of 1964.

---

[286] *Ibid.*
[287] These were Africans who were being prepared to assume the administration of Northern Rhodesia after independence. One such was Freddy Achiume, who was one of the first Administrative Assistants in Northern Rhodesia, and who was enlisted in an Africanization program meant to prepare Africans for the hand-over of power!

§5.13 The Barotseland Agreement 1964

The Barotseland is Zambia's political Achilles' heel. As explained in this book, the area we now call the Western Province of Zambia was the first to enter treaties and concessions that would later define the nation of Zambia. By independence, these treaties were still in force. After independence, however, there was need to redefine the place of western Zambia, vis-à-vis, the new nation's geopolitical landscape. This was partially achieved through the Barotseland Agreement of 1964 (Agreement).

In the wake of the group calling itself the Barotseland Freedom Movement (BFM) and its attempt at lynching Alliance for Democracy and Development (ADD) president, Charles Milupi, on December 18th, 2010,[288] revisiting the Agreement is in order. Realizing that the Barotseland issue would come up at some point in Zambia's future, on April 16th, 1964, the government of Northern Rhodesia and the Litunga of Barotseland reached a provisional agreement to "conclude a permanent agreement."[289] This permanent agreement was concluded on May 18th, 1964 at the Commonwealth Relations Office in London. It was signed by Dr. Kenneth Kaunda, then Prime Minister of Northern Rhodesia; Sir Mwanawina Lewanika III, K.B.E, Litunga of Barotseland; and the Right Honorable Duncan Sandys, MP, Secretary for Commonwealth Relations and for the Colonies. Hon. Sandys' signature signified the approval of Her Majesty's government.

The Litunga acted "on behalf of himself, his heirs and successors."[290] This is very important in regards to the demands of the BFM. All the people of Barotseland, now Western

---

[288] *Zambian Watchdog*, "Soldiers Put on Alert as Barotse Secessionist Try to Release Prisoners," (Sunday, December 19th, 2010)

[289] Her Majesty Stationary Office, *The Barotseland Agreement 1964* (London: Eightpence Net, 1964); also available at Namakando Nalikando-Sinyama, "The Barotseland Agreement 1964," Namzybraveheart.Blogspot.Com (June 2009)

[290] *Ibid.*

Charles Mwewa

Province, were represented in the Agreement. Moreover, the people of Barotseland, through the Litunga, agreed to "proceed to independence as one country and that all its peoples should be one nation."[291] By signing the Agreement, the people of Western Province recognized that it was in the interest of Zambia's peace to be a unitary state. In addition, the Agreement did more than just uniting Zambia; it also terminated all "treaties and other agreements subsisting between Her Majesty the Queen of the United Kingdom of Great Britain and Northern Ireland and the Litunga of Barotseland."[292]

The Agreement came into force on Zambia's Independence Day. It guaranteed Western Province of the protection of human rights and freedoms. The people of Western Province acquired the same rights of appeal from the decisions of the Zambian courts and under customary law as all the peoples of Zambia. In addition, the Litunga of Western Province was recognized as the principal local authority for the government and administration of Barotseland. The Litunga would preside over issues related to customary law in the matter of land, forests, fishing, hunting, game preservation, control of bush fires, the supply of beer, and reservation of trees for canoes, among many others.

In stating that, "Government will provide peace and security to the Western Province"[293] in the wake of riots instigated by the BFM, former Home Affairs Minister Mkhondo Lungu was in order. The government of Zambia under the Agreement oversees keeping peace and order throughout the entire nation. Moreover, pursuant to the Agreement which has provision for unlimited "jurisdiction and powers of the High Court of Zambia in relation

---

[291] *Ibid.*

[292] *Ibid.*

[293] *Lusaka Times*, "Zambia: State Warns Western Province Rioters," (Monday, December 20th, 2010)

to writs or orders,"[294] demands for cessation can only be decided by the High Court of Zambia.

It is imperative to note that calls for cessation are reverting, and even unwarranted, in the case of Barotseland. The position adopted in this book is that calls for the cessation of Western Province from Zambia may be debatable at four fronts. First, it is highly unlikely that Western Province can stand on its own economically. The resources of Western Province cannot sustain the province for long. Indeed, the province is graced with land, rivers and minerals. However, and in relation to the overall survival of the area, the province stands to benefit from the collective allocation of the resources of Zambia.

Despite the Barotse Royal Establishment (BRE)'s vision, or indeed, of the Movement for the Restoration of Barotseland Agreement (MOREBA),[295] of a stand-on-its-own country, in the interest of Zambia as a unitary state, the cessation is a no-brainer. Mpombo agrees: "I am a solid supporter of Zambia as a unitary state but at the same time government must be cautious not to embark on reckless measures that can plunge this country into a serious political crisis." However, notwithstanding Mpombo's gallantry in settling political scores with former President Banda, the only reckless measure that can plunge Zambia into chaos is acquiescence to cessation.

Second, Zambia should cavil to any idea that misinforms of the long-established unity of the nation. Cessation of Western Province from Zambia may, in the main, portend travesty for the progress and development in terms of the economy and democracy. For over fifty years, the unity of Zambia has been perpetuated mainly through tribal compromises in the allocation of administrative boundaries, official language affiliation and, in the Second Republic, through the motto of *One Zambia - One*

---

[294] The Barotseland Agreement, *supra*.
[295] The coinage of MOREBA, namely, "Restoration of Barotseland Agreement," is itself an oxymoron; since by restoring the Agreement, they are consolidating Zambia as a unitary state.

Nation.[296] Thus, "We are all essentially one and the same people. And recognition of our oneness has, no doubt, been the lynchpin of the enhanced and unmatched national unity which our country has enjoyed since independence."[297]

Third, under the Agreement, the Litunga enjoys tremendous rights and privileges unequalled to any traditional chief in Zambia. The mineral rights and treaties Barotseland entered with the British Government terminated at independence. Consequently, and pursuant to first above, Barotseland could be deprived of its economic anchorage if the cessation became efficacious.

Fourth, politically, legally and morally, Western Province remains a significant part of Zambia. In more ways than one, Western Province has come to define the unity which has solidified Zambia's independence. In that sense alone, the Agreement is one of the most important instruments of Zambia's independence, and provides an anchor to the cause of unity, peace and development in Zambia. Notwithstanding, claims that the Litunga acquiesced to the colonization of Zambia as advanced by Caplan[298] needs confutation. Assertions like Caplan's have gone indubitably giving the impression that colonization could be justified.

§5.14 Caplan's Misleading

Equally as important to the mineral plundering debate of Zambia, is the fact that the copper deposits could be found

---

[296] The *One Zambia - One Nation* motto was effectuated by the then Western Province Minister, the late Sylvester Chisembele. See *Weekly Angel* of March 20th – 26th, 2006 at page 10.

[297] Henry Kyambalesa, "President Banda Should Set up Barotse Commission of Inquiry," *Zambia News Features*, (Sunday, October 31st, 2010)

[298] Gerald L. Caplan, "Barotseland's Scramble for Protection" (1969) in *Journal of African History*, x, 2, pp. 277-294

everywhere in the present day Copperbelt Province of Zambia in the 19th Century. Frederick found the natives wearing copper bungles, bracelets and local farmers using copper implements. The natives had been using copper even prior to the arrival of the European settlers. The Company can, thus, not claim it held mineral rights to the territory because it was responsible for "discovering" the deposits.

Most books detailing the history of Zambia deliberately omit these points. This is understandable. Most of the primary sources from which the history of Zambia is crafted were the works of European researchers and writers. The history of Zambia itself was written from this Euro-centric perspective. It is, therefore, expected that salient dynamics bordering on self-incrimination would be omitted.

Caplan contends that Africans actively sought for European domination.[299] In the case of Lewanika of Barotseland, Caplan concludes that Lewanika learned from the Shona and Ndebele revolutions of 1896-7 which were crashed. To avoid the Shona-Ndebele mistakes, Lewanika willingly entered the Lochner Treaty which Caplan describes as "The most important example of accommodation in that area of the continent."[300] This assertion is not only historically misleading, it is misplaced, too.

The Lochner Treaty which Caplan does assert was signed because Lewanika had learned a lesson from Lobengula of the Matebele or Shona-Ndebele revolution of 1896-7, happened before the fact. So Lewanika could possibly not have foreseen the clash. The Lochner Treaty was signed in 1890, way before the Shona-Ndebele clash! John Cecil Rhodes was driven by imperial motive, not altruism, when he exploited the territory which became Zambia. He was first and foremost a colonizer, then a businessman.

---

[299] *Ibid.*
[300] *Ibid.*

§5.15 John Cecil Rhodes

A quick glance at John Cecil Rhodes will reveal that he was an influential, shrewd and profit-motivated colonizer. John Cecil Rhodes was born in 1853. By the 1900, he was one of the most powerful personalities, businessmen and politicians in South Africa. His influence was felt both at home and abroad. Williams described the extent of Rhodes' influence in this manner: "He is the only colonial statesman who has to such extent struck the imagination and affected the thoughts of Englishmen at home and abroad."[301]

Caplan's assertion of Rhodes as an accommodator of the African interests is a falsity when one considers the *modus operandi* of his mission in Africa. First, he had wanted to conquer Africa at any cost, proposing a railway from the Cape to Cairo. In this quest, only imperial glory mattered, the interests of the natives did not. Second, Rhodes was not such a man who would accommodate the natives and Williams himself attests to this fact:

> Less than six years later the "cypher's" name was on every tongue as the *autocrat* of one of the greatest industrial undertakings in the world, as Prime Minister of his colony and as the founder of what promised to be a vast new dominion for the Empire. At home, indeed, the quality of his eminence was never so incontestable as at one time it was in South Africa. To many he was a bugbear - the type of the dishonest and unscrupulous politician, who uses politics to rig the market and the wealth thus acquired to corrupt politics, a man who filched away an empire and *slaughtered innocent savages* or plotted against a friendly state to put money into his own and his fellow-conspirators' pockets (Emphasis added).[302]

It is important to observe a few things here. Rhodes died in

---

[301] Basil Williams, *Cecil Rhodes* (New York: Henry Holt & Company, 1921), p. 4
[302] *Ibid.*

1902. The above words were written in 1921, barely two decades after his death. Rhodes is described as an autocrat. An autocrat is "A ruler who has absolute power, a person who expects obedience."[303] This is not a kind of a person who would accommodate the people who Williams calls "innocent savages."[304] The dictionary defines savages as people who are "primitive and uncivilized."[305] Evidently, Rhodes plundered the Africans both of their rights and natural resources to advance both his and the imperialistic *agenda* of the British Empire. Rhodes was a murderous, corrupt and dishonesty politician and imperialist.

§5.16 Second Scramble[306]

The *third most significant event* in history that would affect the Zambia of today was the scramble for Zambian copper deposits by two most powerful nations on earth, Britain and the US. In 1925, extensive copper deposits were discovered on the Copperbelt, 15 years after Thompson "discovered" copper deposits in Nkana (Kitwe). Two companies competed for domination of the copper fields. The first was the Rhodesian Anglo-American Corporation, a British company based in South Africa. The second was the Roan Selection Trust, a US company. Both companies began constructions on the Copperbelt.

---

[303] Angus Stevenson, (ed.), "Autocrat," *Oxford English Dictionary, Second Edition* (Oxford: Oxford University Press, 2002), p. 43

[304] Williams refers to "slaughtered innocent savages." Rhodes was, thus, a murderer of the Africans, whom they called savages. This explains why his successors cared less for the plight of Africans in Northern Rhodesia.

[305] *Ibid.*, p. 621.

[306] In May 2011, the Mandela Institute at the University of the Witwatersrand, Johannesburg, was offering a Ph. D scholarship at the University of Bern on the second scramble for Africa; also, see BBC of May 19th, 2011; David Blair, "Why China is Trying to Colonize Africa," *The Telegraph*, (August 31st, 2007); Julio Gody, "Second Scramble for Africa Starts," Blackpresence.co.uk (May 29th, 2009); and John Ghazvinian, *Untapped: The Scramble for Africa's Oil* (Orlando: Harcourt Inc., 2007)

In 1931, to increase investment profits, the American cartel started to restrict copper supply. This was bitter-sweet to Northern Rhodesia. Unable to meet demands, consumers sought alternative and cheaper materials instead of copper. The result was that the price of copper crashed. Many employees were sucked. White Europeans returned to South Africa while Africans went back to their villages to farm.[307]

A thorough investigation of the forgone is proper in the light of the future economic implications for Zambia. In a nutshell, and bearing in mind the 1931 restrictions on copper supply leading to the crash of the price of copper, commandist policies have always posed a challenge in the case of Zambia. Shortly after the attainment of independence, the economy of Zambia thrived despite very few educated Zambians. This economic boom would continue throughout the First Republic.[308] In 1972, through the Chona Commission, the UNIP government made one major error, a repeat of the scenario under investigation. Zambia's economy remained strong in the First Republic mainly due to the perpetuation of the free market practices and the absence of a command economy.[309]

The example of the 1930s in Northern Rhodesia is one future Zambia's political leaders and technocrats must not ignore. Even though only two companies dominated at the time, competition was still necessary to ensure maximum productivity. When this

---

[307] Fluctuation in copper prices is oft-cited as one of the causes of Zambia's economic malaise. However, the 1931 scarcities in the copper supply were artificially created by the cartel.

[308] Generally, the period between 1964 and 1972 is referred to as the First Republic. This period is synonymous with great economic boom, a thriving democracy and massive political pluralism in Zambia. However, it was just a matter of time before economic deficiencies inherited from the colonial administration would be felt.

[309] Chiluba, *Democracy: Challenge of Change*, p. 120

was denied and the *invisible hand*[310] completely obliterated, the economy of Northern Rhodesia broke down.

Something very dramatic needed to be done to offset the mini-recession of the 1930s. At the 1932 conference of copper producing nations held in New York, Rhodesian companies objected to interventions and sought for free competition in the copper marketplace. By 1933 normalcy had returned to the industry (thanks for a return to competition both at local and global levels), previous restrictions on competition had elapsed and Northern Rhodesia was once again in a very powerful position. Consequently, the BSAC sold all its mining rights to the Northern Rhodesia government.

This last move, together with the British style of Indirect Rule,[311] consolidated British colonization of Northern Rhodesia. A high-flying school of thought supposing why Britain decided to impose indirect, as opposed to direct, rule on Northern Rhodesia is that Britain did not have adequate resources to running direct governments. The official policy on Indirect Rule in Rhodesia was adopted by the British colonial administration in 1928. "This policy meant that the British settlers would utilize existing African institutions such as chiefs and local courts to govern Africans. To effectuate Indirect Rule, the Native

---

[310] First proposed by Adam Smith, the idea of *invisible hand* implies that human needs are best served by free competition in the economic marketplace. The only role of government is to enforce the rules of property and contracts to make competition possible but not to direct the process itself. However, as evidenced in the wake of the 2008 economic meltdown, regulation of key financial sectors is necessary if the market economy is to be saved from greed.

[311] The British concept of Indirect Rule was enumerated by Lord Lugard. Like the French policy of association, the system delegated power to local chiefs and others with pre-existing claims to local power. However, these powers were given to people sympathetic to British interests. The local chiefs collected taxes, decided outcomes of local disputes, and quelled any anti-British sentiments and riots among the people. The system worked so well that Britain did not have to expend any more capital than was necessary to control its African colonies. This had an added advantage of keeping Britain's financial and personnel costs to a minimum.

Charles Mwewa

Authorities Ordinance and the Native Courts Ordinance were passed in 1929."[312] It is alleged that for the most part, colonialism was hardly felt in areas ruled by chiefs such as the villages. However, colonialism meant occupying and controlling lands and resources which historically belonged to the Africans. Moreover, Indirect Rule gives credence to the veracity that the Africans had functional institutions even prior to colonialism. The notion that Africans could not rule themselves was, therefore, superfluous.

The distinction between direct and indirect rule was fundamental. Before 1924, the Company's Native Commissioner did not regard it as part of his functions to build up the role of the chiefs in local administration. But if that was the case, why then was Indirect Rule imposed? Lord Hailey explains: "The general effect of the policy was to preserve the outward form of the indigenous systems, but to *undermine the authority of the chiefs* both by making them depend on the administrative officer and by taxation which *obliged large numbers of men to leave their villages for considerable periods of time* (Emphasis added)."[313]

Indirect Rule was not designed to empower the African chiefs, it was a calculated policy aimed at destroying the power of the African chiefs. It was a cover-up designed to "undermine the authority of the chiefs." It was even more; it was meant to disrupt the African village so that able-bodied men could leave for service in the European haciendas for meager pay. In fact, Europeans knew exactly what they were doing. They, for instance, knew that one day the Africans would evict them from Africa, and the administration fashioned a stratagem: "For two or three generations we can show the Negro what we are: then we

---

[312] Hamalengwa, "The Legal System of Zambia: Law, Politics and Development in Historic Perspectives," in P. Ebow Bondzi-Simpson, (ed.), *The Law and Economic Development in the Third World* (New York: Praeger Publishers, 1992), p. 23
[313] Richard Hall, *Zambia* (London: Frederick A. Praeger, 1965), p. 103

shall be asked to go away. Then we shall leave the land to those it belongs to, with the feeling that they have better business friends in us."[314]

Colonialism was business as usual; it was a long-term investment in Western Capitalism. Indirect Rule constituted what in vernacular is called a *Mouse Bite*.[315] It was a ruse designed to tame the hatred and pain of domination in the Africans. But the colonialists knew too well that it was just a matter of time before the Africans would rise and claim their land back.

The mastermind of Indirect Rule, Sir Frederick Lugard,[316] thereafter, Lord Lugard, popularized what he called "dual mandate" in his book *The Dual Mandate in British Tropical Africa* published in 1922. The central thesis of the book, which became an essential reading for every ambitious cadet in the African territory, was that, "The imperial power would stay in [Africa] while it could, impact what it felt was good for the indigenous people and then retire gracefully but keeping her trade after the flag had been lowered."[317]

Implicit in this philosophy was the development of Indirect Rule. This did not happen as the Africans became more and more marginalized. After 36 years, the administration would again claim it was empowering the Africans for administration through an Africanization program. The truth is, the administration did not prepare the Africans for self-rule,[318] but for trade keeps "after the flag had been lowered." This trend of using Africa as a source

---

[314] *Ibid.*, p. 104

[315] A mouse is known to bite hard while cautiously tenderizing the wound so that the victim least feels the pain. In that way, the rodent can inflict a far-reaching damage.

[316] Lugard fought against the Arab slave owners in Nyasaland in 1888. He became the doyen of the British administrators in Africa. He retired in 1919 as Governor-General of Nigeria.

[317] Hall, *supra.*, p. 104

[318] Self-rule was not given to the Africans; it was fought for. Specifically, "Zambia's penultimate step in the progress towards independence, self-rule was attained as the result of the Order-in-Council of January 3rd, 1964." (See Grotpeter *et. al.*, *Historical Dictionary of Zambia*, p. 396)

of raw materials and capital has continued today imbued in such subterfuges as donor support or responsible philanthropies:

> Why do we with open eyes
> Let the thief in and rob
> Why do we with a piece of paper
> Surrender all we have
> Why have we allowed wealth-hunters,
> Who masquerade as democrats,
> To erase our memory of history
> Why all this while we say, nod and finally sign,
> Placing a dagger against hope?

§5.17 Africans Pay

The *fourth most significant event* in Zambian history that has had enormous impact on both the stability and conflict resolution dynamics of the Zambian society happened in 1935. This time it was not the moving of the Capital City from Livingstone to Lusaka. Rather, it was the first recorded shooting to death of six Black Africans by the White Northern Rhodesian police.

Just when relations between the White Northern Rhodesian government and the Black Africans were poised to be going in the right direction, mostly due to the announcement made by the British Government,[319] the unspeakable happened in Northern Rhodesia. The Africans were peeved with the shooting to death of their six countrymen. In 1935, the rates of the hut tax on the

---

[319] In 1930, the United Kingdom Secretary of State for Dominion Affairs, Lord Passfield, announced that the interests of the natives should be paramount in Northern Rhodesia. That proclamation meant that where conflicts arose over interests between the settlers and the natives, the interests of the natives should take precedence over those of the settlers.

Lord Passfield's announcement was a fundamental shift in British foreign policy given the imperialistic nature of the British Empire at the time. It is the position of this author that it was this softening in policy that would be responsible for Zambia's independence thirty-four years later.

Copperbelt were raised. This led to strikes in Mufulira, Nkana (Kitwe) and Roan Antelope (Luanshya). The shootings happened when the White police was sent in to restore *order* in Kitwe.

The struggle of the Zambian people has also been, for the most part, the struggles of a working class. And there is no contentious issue that brought more suffering upon the Africans than a hut tax. A hut tax was a tax on every dwelling, payable in hard currency. Firstbrook defines a hut tax as, "An iniquitous levy on a society that did not have a cash economy."[320] The hut tax was a precursor to the poll tax, which in the 1930s, was levied on all able-bodied males of 18 years and above. In *Historical Dictionary of Zambia*, Grotpeter et. al. inform that the hut tax was first proposed in North-eastern Rhodesia in 1901. It required every adult African man to pay three shillings per year for each hut he claimed, up to a maximum of six. The intent was to penalize polygamists and those supporting elderly relatives. It was payable in cash, as Firstbrook has alluded to, but this was only until 1905 when it could be paid in the form of rubber or forced labor services. By 1913, hut tax was adopted throughout the territory. Those who collected the hut tax came to be known as Collectors. However, the tax revenues paid only a fraction of administrative expenses. So, the real purpose of the hut tax was not to raise revenue; it was, rather, to encourage African men to seek work in the mines or on the White farms. The hut tax was dropped in the late 1940s, "making the poll tax the main tax upon Africans."[321] Removed from their lands in rural areas to work the mines and amass capital for the colonial capitalists, the Africans in Northern Rhodesia were underpaid, heavily taxed and harshly treated. In this way, therefore, colonialism manipulated capital and labor, two of the four means of production.[322] The other two are land and technology. In the communiqué, just before six of

---

[320] Peter Firstbrook, *The Obamas*, p. 121
[321] *Ibid*, p. 365
[322] Capital, labor and productivity constitute the three ingredients of economic growth.

their counterparts were brutally gunned down and several others wounded, they brought out their common concerns:

> Listen to this all who live in the country…we wish on the day of April 29th every person not to work, he who will go to work, and if we see him, it will be a serious case. *Know how they cause us to suffer, they cheat us for money, they arrest us for loafing, they persecute and put us in gaol for tax.* What reason have we done? Secondly, do you not wish to hear these words, well list this year of 1935, if they will not increase us more money stop paying tax, *do you think they can kill you, no.* Let us encourage surely you will see that God will be with us. *See how we suffer with the work and how we are continually reviled and beaten underground. Many brothers of us die for 22s. 6d., is this money that we should lose our lives for* (Emphasis added)?[323]

This incident is unprecedented in the history of Zambia. There are three observations here. First and foremost, it was "how they cause us to suffer, they cheat us for money, they arrest us for loafing, and they persecute and put us in gaol for tax." The statement is self-evidence of the brutality of the colonial administration against the plight of the African workers. The people of Northern Rhodesia endured cruel and inhumane treatment at the hands of the foreign entities in their own home country.[324]

Second, the Africans mine workers asked, "Do you think they can kill you, no"? Sadly, they were killed. Six of their comrades were short dead when they went on a strike and this was because they wanted equal pay and equal rights in the mines. To think that the colonial machine came to Northern Rhodesia to help develop

---

[323] Translated by an African Clerk who was present at the scene, quoted in Hamalengwa, *supra*, p. 30

[324] In many respects, Africans still suffer from systemic discrimination in employment, access to status bar, and in various other areas of life when they immigrate to other countries.

the colony would be an understatement and a grave injustice to those who perished for their rights.

Third and last, the mine workers take us down into the heart of the abyss; they allow us to see what happened underground: "See how we suffer with the work and how we are continually reviled and beaten underground. Many brothers of us die for 22s. 6d., is this money that we should lose our lives for?" The mine workers did not only suffer emotional, mental and physical abuse at the hands of the colonial masters, they also lost their lives, lives that could have been categorized as accidents in official reports.

Despite their infuriation, the Africans in Northern Rhodesia used the death of their six countrymen to get organized politically. They established the first Tribal Elders' Advisory Council and then the African Urban Advisory in the Copperbelt, Central and Southern provinces.

§5.18 World War II

In 1939, Britain entered World War II. This meant that Northern Rhodesia militias had to participate in the war on Britain's side. It was during this period that Northern Rhodesia experienced a great boom in the sale of copper which was in high demand for electric cables. As these events were unfolding in favor of the Africans in Northern Rhodesia, the White European workers were biting their nails. They threatened to strike but they feared that Africans would replace them. The Africans were willing to accept low pay.[325]

Moreover, the settlers' approach towards the Africans was that of marginalization. The Africans were expected to work in

---

[325] It is important again here to see. Whereas Britain's policy of Indirect Rule gave relative freedom to African chiefs to control their own people – although such freedom only existed on paper – economic opportunities did not come that easy for the Africans. This same pattern would follow shortly after Zambia became independent. The colonialists were willing to grant the Africans political independence but not economic independence.

the mines but not to earn a good pay, to carry out the theory of Indirect Rule, but not to aggrandize its substance. Sadly, in 21st Century Africa, this injustice has been allowed to mushroom and take root. To many in Europe and the West, Africa is a lost cause, just as it was a Dark Continent in the 19th Century.[326] But it should never be forgotten that it was, in part, the hydro-power of Southern Rhodesia that illuminated the Industrial Revolution, the gold of South Africa that brightened the world's economic portfolios and the copper of Northern Rhodesia that won the war!

In 1939, thirteen Africans were killed in Kitwe when they threatened a strike for pay raise. This was just four years after the six perished. In 1935, the six Africans were killed for protesting a hut tax increase. In 1939, the thirteen were killed for seeking a pay raise. In the light of these two unfortunate events, the settler government did not see Africans as equal partners in

---

[326] In fact, there has been a tremendous misrepresentation of Africa as a Dark Continent. As argued in this book, Europeans have written *our* history, mostly, from *their* perspective. By the time Europe was "discovering" Africa in the 15th and 16th centuries, Africa had been the cradle of life and civilization. Between B.C 285 and 247, Ptolemy II, King of Egypt had translated the first portion of the Hebrew Scriptures (the Torah or "Law") into Greek at Alexandria. Thus, "Africa [is] the cradle of Biblical translation" (see Bigelow, *White Man's Africa*, p. 2). If, therefore, the Bible is the symbol of *light*, why would a continent that received the first Biblical translation be *dark*? Moreover, Africa is also the first main home of Christian literature. In B.C 300, the earliest Latin version of the Scripture was made in Africa in the Coptic language of Egypt. And by 1200 A.D, Christian bishoprics were still in existence in Nubia, Africa.

Not only was Africa the cradle of life, civilization and *light*, Africa was also one of the first places to establish authentic trade. In 1150 A.D, Songhai merchants of Jennê founded Timbuktu, which became the center of trade in western Sudan. And politically, between 1308 A.D and 1331 A.D, the Mandingo Empire of Melle had reached its height of power under Mansa Musa. In fact, the empire was so extensive that it covered the whole of western Sudan. These historical facts, are, therefore, in direct contradiction with the popularized notion that Africans inhabited a "Dark Continent" and were devoid of economic, political or, indeed, religious organization.

development. However, in the context of historical fairness, these shootings were insignificant in comparison to the Lumpa Uprising[327] which resulted in the "death of 700 church members during police and army attack."[328] But it should not be forgotten that it was due to colonialism and the struggles for independence that the Lumpa Uprising took place.

A breakthrough partially came in 1946 when some few educated Africans in Northern Rhodesia formed the Federation of African Welfare Societies.[329] It is important to note here that

---

[327] The story of the Lumpa Uprising is one rarely talked about in Zambia. The Lumpa Church was founded by a woman called Alice Lenshina Mulenga Mubisha. The Lumpa (literally "better than all others") movement was formed in 1953 and by Zambian independence, had a following of over 100,000 members. Lumpa's attack on witchcraft, alcohol and polygamy seemed to have been well received by the people in villages. However, the movement was getting more powerful and becoming a threat first to the colonial, and in 1964, to the new Zambian government. In 1958, it built a grand cathedral at Zion and by 1964, it openly opposed earthly authority, rejected both government registration of the Lumpa Church and paying taxes. The church formed its own villages in defiance of established order and an affront to the traditional authority. The movement challenged the legitimacy of the Nationalist Party and of UNIP. Adherents of the Lumpa movement and UNIP cadres clashed violently. In 1964, the Prime Minister of the African majority government, Kaunda, sent in two battalions of the Northern Rhodesia regiment. Violence erupted leading to the death of between 700 and 1500 Lenshina followers. Many villagers fled in thousands to Katanga in the Congo. Kaunda banned the Lumpa Church in August 1964 and proclaimed a State of Emergency that was retained after independence and lasted until 1991. Lenshina was arrested, imprisoned, released in 1975 and arrested again in 1977 for disobeying a probation order by holding a church service. She died in 1978.

[328] Norbert C. Brockman, "Lenshina Mulenga Mubita, Alice c. 1924 to 1978: Lumpa Church, Zambia" in *An African Biographical Dictionary* (1994)

[329] This was the first association of Africans, unlike the earlier African Urban Advisory Council, that conducted its affairs in English. Generally, the period between 1941 and 1964 saw the rise not only of the spirit of nationalism, but also of men and women whom history has unfairly silenced. Indeed, works like those of Henry Meebelo, David Mulford or Robert Rotberg, have attempted to cover the mass evolution of nationalism in Zambia. However, even such impeccable works seem to omit on certain men and women who worked relentlessly to birth the new nation of Zambia. Thus, Musambachime

the Africans had already been organized in this way as early as 1912 at Mwenzo Mission.[330] However, the 1912 associations were village-based and conducted their business mostly in vernacular languages.

In 1948, the Federation of African Welfare Societies was changed to Northern Rhodesia Congress with Godwin Mbikusita Lewanika as its leader. This development could have reinforced the existing African Urban Advisory councils because they sent in delegates in 1948 and formed regional councils whose representatives met as the African Representative Council (ARC). In 1949, the African Mineworkers Union (AMWU) was formed.[331] In 1952, Godwin Lewanika was succeeded by Harry Mwaanga Nkumbula as head of the Northern Rhodesia Congress, which was shortly changed to Northern Rhodesia African National Congress (ANC).

---

has charged, "Mentioned in passing or simply forgotten are veteran politicians who pioneered the fight for independence" ("Dauti Yamba's Contribution to the Rise and Growth of Nationalism in Zambia, 1941-1964," (1991) *African Affairs*, 90, p. 259). He mentioned some of such men as Dauti Lawton Yamba, Dixon Konkola, Miles Kaweche Banda, Nelson Nalumango, Paskale Sikota, Safeli Chishala, Henry Kasokolo, among so many.

[330] Mwenzo Mission was opened by the Church of Scotland in 1895

[331] Other records have 1948 instead of 1949, see, for example, Grotpeter *et. al.*, *Historical Dictionary of Zambia.*

6| Struggles for Independence

They fought as a band of soldiers;
They died while fighting, as martyrs,
Some are presidents if they lived,
And others have scars to show for.

Chapter Focus

At the end of reading this chapter, you should be able to:

- Understand that Zambia's independence was achieved through bloody resistance
- Identify the last significant event before Zambia got its independence that would impact greatly on Zambia's political direction
- State the motivation for the formation of the Federation of Rhodesia and Nyasaland
- Trace the genesis of political organization in Zambia

BRIEF INTRODUCTION

This chapter discusses the last of the five significant events before independence that would impact the political and economic direction of Zambia. It also discusses the struggles for independence in greater details, including the genesis of political organization in Zambia.

§6.1 The Resistance

Zambian independence was achieved through struggle. From the outset, the Africans knew that gaining independence from the colonial government would not be without resistance. The struggles for independence, and indeed, struggles for equality and freedom in general, are viewed from different angles by different players affected differently. For colonial Britain and the European settlers, agitations by the Africans were viewed as lawless propaganda against the legitimately legislated laws.

For the Africans, however, fighting for freedom was unalienable right. There is no price to match the value of freedom. These assiduous men and women gave up all, including life itself, to liberate their people from slavery and colonialism. Their spirit is captured in two statements made by two of Zambia's greatest freedom fighters.

Brave Alexander Grey Zulu writes: "My love for Zambia and the African continent can only be surpassed by those who died during the struggle for independence."[332] This is the spirit that fought for Zambia's independence as will be explained in the following pages. The Zambian fathers and mothers who fought for independence did not do so only because of the likelihood that they would be leaders of an independent nation. But they also fought for the unlikelihood that they would live to see an independent nation. They were living martyrs and patriots at best.[333]

In *Looking Back, An Extraordinary Life*, the daring Mwaanga elucidates, "I held the view that the struggle for independence

---

[332] Zulu in *Memoirs of Alexander Grey Zulu*, p. 462
[333] We their brood their glory will save
Never to forget the blood they shed,
In their footsteps, we fondly wade,
Attesting to hearts strong and brave
("Heroes of Freedom," from: Mwewa, *Song of an Alien*, p. 83)

had of necessity to entail hardship and sacrifice on the part of those who were involved. No freedom fighter leads a comfortable life."[334] Zulu and Mwaanga reveal the philosophy and spirit that enabled the Zambian fathers and mothers to soldier on in their freedom quest.

A Catholic Landowner of Hungary orates, "Woe to the nation which raises no protest when its rights are outraged! It contributes to its own slavery by its silence. The nation which submits to injustice and oppression without protest is doomed."[335] There is no doubt that in Europe those who led expeditions to Africa and secured lands and territories are immortalized and celebrated. Indeed, they brought great wealth and prestige to the Empire and survived the harsh and dangerous terrain and predacious forests of Africa. To them, too, this Hungarian Oracle may apply.

However, there is no continent or a people in recorded history who suffered at the hands of other human beings like the Africans. Don Taylor in his book, *The British in Africa*[336] has not found any comparison in all of history with all its barbarities and cruelties a major race of people separated from the rest of humanity, civilization and denied basic human freedoms, even to exist as a free people, like the Africans have.

From the background given in the preceding paragraphs, the story of Zambia's struggle for independence is written. It is also vital to mention that the Zambian freedom fighters had to contend more with the *impistic*[337] resistance of the White settlers in Northern Rhodesia than with the Colonial Office in Britain.

To solidify its base and ensure that the Africans did not achieve their independence objective, the White settlers resorted

---

[334] Vernon J. Mwaanga, *Looking Back, An Extraordinary Life* (Lusaka: Fleetfoot Publishing Company, 2000), pp. 13-14
[335] Zulu, *supra.*, p. 1
[336] Don Taylor, *The British in Africa* (New York: Roy Publishers, 1964)
[337] Shaka, the greatest king of the Zulus was the first to invent a short-spear called *Assegai*. His soldiers who used the *Assegai* were known as *Impis*. "Impistic" is thus used in this fashion here, albeit in a negative connotation.

to the use of questionable political tactics and legal instruments.[338] In letter as well as in spirit, it was the same colonial regime that had instituted apartheid in South Africa which oppressed the Africans in Northern Rhodesia.

The regime, like in apartheid South Africa, passed laws like the *Preservation of Public Security Act,*[339] the *Public Order Act*[340] and the *Emergency Act.*[341] These instruments were "administered brutally and indiscriminately."[342] Like apartheid South Africa, the regime of some "70,000 Whites [ruled] three million Africans interpreting [the Africans'] political ideals as communistic."[343] And, too, like Apartheid South Africa, the regime allowed every White in Northern Rhodesia to own a gun

---

[338] Both Sir Evelyn Hone and Sir Roy Welensky had stakes in the continuity of the oppressive Federation and colonialism. Hone was born in Northern Rhodesia, and naturally felt he had the right to the land. Hone, in particular, did not take in well to the rising of UNIP; he adopted terror and intimidation techniques to cower the Africans from seeking for independence. He divided the African chiefs into superior and inferior categories so that those chiefs who refused to ban UNIP in their areas were removed from positions of power and privilege. Welensky, similarly, was adamant to the independence of Zambia. Using the concept of a "multiracial society" as a ruse, while reacting aversely to Macleod's constitution, he devised ways and means of delaying independence. More importantly, Welensky knew of the strategic importance of Northern Rhodesia; it was the life-blood of the Federation through its copper mines. More than Hone, Welensky went even as far as doctoring knighting privileges on some selected African chiefs in order for them to denounce any African political party that would seek for the independence of Northern Rhodesia. Indeed, it is strongly believed that the federal regime was responsible for the knighting of Sir Mwanawina so that he could ban UNIP from Barotseland (See Soko, "Independence for Zambia," pp. 16-17).

[339] *Preservation of Public Security Act*, Cap. 112 of the laws of Zambia

[340] *Public order Act*, Cap 113 of the laws of Zambia

[341] *Emergency Act*, Repealed by 5 of 1960

[342] Goodson Machona, "A Harvest of Treason Trials." <http://www.c-r.org/resources/occasional-papers/african-media-and-conflict-part-four-machona.php> (Retrieved: June 11th, 2010)

[343] Soko, "Independence for Zambia," p. 16

or "encouraged [them] to purchase one. The Africans, on the other hand, [were] legally not permitted to own firearms."[344]

Sadly, UNIP, the MMD and the PF have used these same repressive colonial laws to limit political participation in the Second Republic, to quail dissidents in the Third Republic, and to silence political opponents in the Fourth Republic, respectively.

In part by applying hated colonial-era public order laws, the PF Government moved methodically to silence critics in opposition parties and civil society. It also decided to implement a restrictive law on nongovernmental organizations (NGO), which it had vehemently opposed while in opposition. The legislation gave the government sweeping powers to deregister organizations and allowed substantial interference with freedom of association. The MMD government declared a State of Emergency under the *Emergency Powers Act* in March 1993. And the Sata government carried out similar oppressive tactics:

> Sata and the PF have repeated specious and hackneyed accusations that prodemocracy and human rights activists are doing the bidding of hostile, foreign interests, creating a permissive climate that emboldens the government's more radical supporters. In May 2013, peaceful demonstrators were prevented from protesting in a public space. Gathering in a church, they were besieged and beaten by thugs armed with hoe handles, machetes, and chains. The assailants were believed to be members of the ruling party's youth wing. The government's growing intolerance for criticism has extended to the media. Journalists have been unlawfully arrested, websites shut down, and nationwide broadcasting licenses revoked in a thinly disguised campaign by the authorities to circumscribe free speech and encourage self-censorship.[345]

Even in independent Zambia, there are those who cannot exercise their political and human rights because those who govern are detached from those who are governed.

---

[344] *Ibid.*
[345] Robert Herman and Cathal Gilbert, "Reversing Zambia's Authoritarian Drift," Freedom House, December 12th, 2013

Charles Mwewa

The *last significant event*[346] before independence that would impact not only the political direction of Zambia, but its economic survival as well happened in 1953. In that year, Northern Rhodesia (Zambia), Nyasaland (Malawi) and Southern Rhodesia (Zimbabwe) entered what is historically known as the Federation of Rhodesia and Nyasaland (the "Federation").[347] It was not only the naming of this Federation which was very important to the future of Zambia; it was also the role that each territory in the Federation played. For one, the Federation fused Zambia and Zimbabwe into one Rhodesia. For another, Zambia was used only as raw material supplier to operate the booming industry in both Zimbabwe and South Africa. Malawi supplied the much-needed manpower to the Federation.

Not only is the foresaid historical fact, it is a truth attested to by the British Colonial Officers themselves. Grant, for example, explains his first impressions when he first came to the territory then under the Federation, explaining, "As we crossed the

---

[346] See the first four in Chapter 5

[347] Prior to 1891 when the BSAC set up a Company State, it had "discovered" Zambia's copper and other mineral wealth. These motivated the formation of the Federation of Rhodesia and Nyasaland also known as the Central African Federation. Under the federal structure, which came into being in 1953, despite vehement African opposition, the Capital City was located in Salisbury (Harare), in Southern Rhodesia (Zimbabwe). The federal legislature and the government were in White-run Southern Rhodesia. Whites were a miniscule minority in the Central African Federation, but they were the political majority in the federal government and Parliament. White settlers wanted to use the Federation as the Boars had used the Union of South Africa to consolidate their power and load it over the Africans. Understanding these ramifications, the African nationalist leaders in Zambia and Malawi mobilized themselves to stop the federal idea from being implemented. Opposition from African nationalists in Southern Rhodesia was there, but it was not as vocal or strident as in the two northern territories. Whites in Malawi and Zambia favored the Federation, as did their Southern Rhodesian counterparts, because it would augment their regional numbers and make it less likely that Zambia and Malawi could be turned over to the Black majority.

borders...we were entering a new, recently-created, *ill-fated political entity*, the Central Africa Federation. This had been formed by the British Government, amalgamating Northern and Southern Rhodesia with Nyasaland under the leadership of an ex-pugilist and former railway unionist, Roy (later Sir Roy) Welensky, *against the clearly-expressed wishes of the Africans* in Northern Rhodesia and Nyasaland, which was to cause constant trouble."[348]

If the Federation was ill-fated, it would, however, be Northern Rhodesia that would pay for its ills. Northern Rhodesia would not only be a reservoir for cheap human labor, but would also be the most neglected territory of the three regions. From the beginning, the Africans in Northern Rhodesia did not wish to join the Federation. Britain was in a hurry to impose the Federation because as Grant exposes, "Everywhere lurked the shadow of the British Empire, even in its terminal decline."[349] Surely, in Central Africa the Federation was the last attempt at salvaging whatever was left of the glorious British Empire!

Indeed, to claim that the Federation created the poverty foundation for Zambia and Malawi is an understatement, because it did. Copper was mined from Zambia and exported to other territories and to Britain leaving Zambia empty-handed. Because most of the British administration of the Federation was carried out in Southern Rhodesia, infrastructure development also took place there to the negligence of Zambia and Malawi. Moreover, since Northern Rhodesians where required to work in the mines, which were mostly concentrated on Zambia's Copperbelt Province, most able-bodied Northern Rhodesian men had to leave their villages to work in the thriving copper mines of the Copperbelt. The Northern Rhodesian villages were left with feeble men, women and children. This was the beginning of rural poverty.[350]

---

[348] Grant, *Zambia – Then and Now*, p. 25
[349] *Ibid.*
[350] See §4.2

There is a popular claim asserting that Zambia's lack of competence in political and economic administration at independence is responsible for the economic conditions Zambia currently experiences. This thesis advances the view that Africans in general and Zambians prematurely acquired political independence and inadvertently chased away European administrators.

This reasoning is flawed in two significant ways. First, it fails to consider the resource-depletion character of the Federation as detailed above. Second, it fails to appreciate the administrative and civic activities of the Africans in the Federation. In fact, Zambians were much more prepared economically to govern themselves at independence than in 1991.[351] As early as 1912, Donald Siwale and others had raised the issue of self-rule, albeit indirectly, and by that time some of these great Africans were principals of mission schools. Above and beyond, the Africans had established political institutions even prior to the arrival of colonization.

§6.2 Livingstonia Mission Institute

The history of political organizations or associations in Zambia is as old as the history of Church or missionary influence in Northern Rhodesia. Mission stations and churches served as centers for ecclesiastical indoctrination and *quasi*-political propaganda. The former was explicitly engaged in while the latter was inherent in Africans' struggles.

The first crop of Africans who would bring structure and provide impetus to the African cause in Northern Rhodesia was former students of the Livingstonia Institute in Nyasaland (the "Institution"). Indeed, it has been observed that, "The Institution provided an intellectual ferment which awakened their

---

[351] See Chiluba, *Democracy: The Challenge of Change*, p. 122.

[Africans'] imagination to the concept of progress, and gave them [the Africans] a new role and sense of authority as Christians and educated people in bringing about the advancement of their people."[352]

Between 1902 and 1912 there were two isolated developments at the Institution that would permanently awaken the consciences of the future Zambian leaders. First, in 1902 a debating society was formed there. The society discussed issues ranging from native trade to industrial development to "the future of Africa."[353]

(Debates open a vista of ideas and views which create a reservoir for future innovation and invention. One of the reasons, albeit an innocuous one, why Africa continues to depend on mostly borrowed technology and ideas, is because young ones are not fully engaged in meaningful debates. A culture of debate from early maturational years has the propensity to creating a citizenry well vested in the intricacy of social, economic and political experimentation).

The second development at the Institution that would awaken the African consciousness and necessitate the formation of the first welfare association in Northern Rhodesia happened in June 1912. In that year, an institutional periodical, the *Livingstonia News*, "devoted seven of its sixteen pages to a full report of the Tuskegee Conference on Negro advancements held in the United States of America and concluded its report: 'If Dr. Booker Washington could become what he is and do what he has done, why should not some of the natives of this land, by the grace of God, follow his steps.'"[354]

Indeed, this charge was seriously taken by the Africans at the Institution, because in that same year, 1912, at Mwenzo

---

[352] Terrence O. Ranger, *Themes in Christian History of Central Africa* (Los Angeles: University of California Press, 1975), p. 107
[353] *Ibid.*
[354] *Ibid.*

Mission[355] in Northern Rhodesia, a group of teachers headed by Donald Siwale with Levi Mumba, formed the first welfare association called the Mwenzo Association. It is important to understand two dynamics here. The first one is that the 1912 Mwenzo Association was a local and village effort by the educated Africans in Northern Rhodesia to put a voice to their struggles for recognition as humans who deserved respect and equal treatment. Moreover, these would be the pre-World War I efforts by the Africans, because as will be discussed later, there were other efforts at Mwenzo by the Africans to advance their grievances after the war. These post-war efforts would concentrate mostly in the urban areas.

The second dynamic is that these first African intellectuals were more driven, as expected, by the Booker Washington's principle of accommodation of the Africans' and settlers' interests. It was only in the mid-1940s that more radical politically-minded Africans became vocal. These, to put it matter of factly, were more of a Dubois than of the Washington type.

§6.3 Quasi-Political Agitations

The history of the foundation of the Zambian political associations was a monopoly of political-minded Church Ministers like Edward Boti Manda, Donald Siwale, Levi Mumba, David Kaunda, Peter Sinkala and Hezekiya Nkonjera Kanoso, and others. It was with Levi Mumba and Edward Boti Manda that Donald Siwale discussed the need for an association to put the educated African viewpoint, and to discuss why it was that "Africans were being called boys by Europeans although they

---

[355] Mwenzo Mission was opened in Northern Rhodesia by the Livingstonia Mission in north-eastern Rhodesia in 1894.

were grown [up] men."[356] By the time they were contemplating forming the first welfare association, the Africans at Mwenzo had ascended to positions of school inspectors.

The express aim of the Mwenzo Association was captured in their 1914 constitution spearheaded by Donald Siwale. The African association wanted, "recognition of Africans as human beings, and advancements of their conditions, *not independence from colonial rule.*"[357] It is believed that despite their assertion to the contrary, the Africans at Mwenzo were more politically-minded than just for their recognition as human beings. The wisdom of our fathers, in stating "not [seeking] independence from colonial rule," is herein revealed. In concealing their real political motives, they were both playing to right timing and engaging in self-preservation. Both were essential to the progress of their cause.

The efforts of the pre-World War I Mwenzo Association would soon collapse at the onset of the war in 1914. This was not due to the fault of the Africans. As the war intensified, Mwenzo Mission was evacuated because of the fighting near the border with Tanganyika.

Shortly after the war, Donald Siwale, with the help of Jonathan Mukwasa Simfukwe and Andrew Sichula, revived the old Mwenzo Association. In 1923, they transformed the old Mwenzo Association into the Northern Rhodesia Native Association (NRNA). The naming of the NRNA is self-telling. Unlike the old Mwenzo Association, the new NRNA was broader in outlook and took the interest of the whole of Northern Rhodesia into account. The very first thing the NRNA did was to bring the "Native Commissioner to Mwenzo to explain to the teachers how the taxes were used."[358] Moreover, in the same year, the Secretary for Native Affairs received a copy of the NRNA constitution.[359]

---

[356] Terrence O. Ranger, *supra.*, p. 107

[357] *Ibid*, p. 108

[358] *Ibid*, p. 109

[359] The Secretary for Native Affairs was responsible for African interests in Northern Rhodesia.

This act would both legitimize the efforts of the Africans and bring to the attention of the authorities in Northern Rhodesia the desires of the Africans.

The Africans in Northern Rhodesia were suspicious of foreign influence in their territory even before they were brought into the British orbit at the end of the 19th Century by the BSAC which administered Northern Rhodesia on behalf of the British Government until 1924. Arguments have been made that Caplan's assertion of Rhodes as an accommodator of the African interests was a falsity.[360] It is suspected that the British Government decided to take direct control of Northern Rhodesia in 1924 because it perceived that the Africans were disgruntled with the Company.

For one, the Company's approach to native administration was profit-motivated. For another, it employed force, and not law, to administer the territory. For example, the Company "burned villages and put chiefs and headmen in chains to intimidate them into sending their people to do carrier service."[361] Headman Kasichila ardently opposed to not only the Company's presence in Northern Rhodesia, but also to the erection of a mission "because it stood on his land."[362]

Just before the British Government took over the administration of Northern Rhodesia from the chartered Company, Judge McDonnell was tasked with the responsibility of inquiring into the disturbances in the territory. In a letter to the administration of May 5th, 1919, he said: "As one listened to pleas and evidence which showed that the old words, obedience to the elders, headmen and chiefs, obedience to the *Boma*, had lost their meaning, we realized the delicate and fragile nature of

---

[360] See §5.14
[361] Terrence, *supra.*, p. 108
[362] *Ibid*, p. 110

our hold over these people and at times we saw the abyss opening."[363]

Analyzing from this angle, it is plain knowledge that the Africans in Northern Rhodesia did not desire the imposition of colonial rule over them. Contrary to the general assertion, the Africans did not acquiescent to colonialism. As records, have shown, the Africans resisted colonialism with all their might. Thus, "The British found that the imposition of colonial rule was opposed practically everywhere. Between 1895 and 1914, the British organized several military raids – 'punitive expeditions' – against what they called 'recalcitrant tribes.'"[364] The British, further, used well-armed soldiers to force the ill-equipped African tribes into submission to colonialism.

It is strongly believed that whatever can be sourced on this topic is only a piece of the ice-berg. It is common knowledge that the British administration would not want to give an impression that the Africans abhorred the colonial regime. The way the administration did this was in either by spreading propaganda supposing that African acquiescence to colonialism was efficacious or by completely obliterating any information detailing the resistance efforts of the Africans from public record.

Arguments have been made that, "Throughout much of the Third World, basic dates and data on decision making, let alone reliable empirical evidence on the intimate functioning, formal as well as informal, of political systems, are typically not readily accessible."[365] In fact, it is assumed that such evidence rarely exist at all.[366] If this assertion merits its premise, that is great news for Zambia. However, in practice, it is Zambia that needs to probe into records that might provide a little window of how much in terms of resource depletion colonialism inflicted on the

---

[363] Terrence Ranger, "Making Northern Rhodesia Imperial: Variations on Royal Theme, 1924 – 1938, *African Affairs*, p. 349

[364] Peter Firstbrook, *The Obamas*, p. 115

[365] Douglas G. Anglin, *Zambian Crisis Behavior* (Montreal: McGill-Queen's University Press, 1994), p. xii

[366] *Ibid.*

nation. The plain truth is that such records are hard to come by either because they were shredded at independence for fear of self-incrimination or they are classified.[367] Fortunately, bits and pieces from here and there are sufficient to provide an informed opinion, and even conclusion of what transpired.

The Africans' agitation continued even during the World War II period. This period, from 1939 to 1945, would not only see the spread of welfare associations in urban areas, but the massive exposure to information the Africans had hitherto been denied. Smyth[368] conceives that Africans in Northern Rhodesia experienced World War II vicariously, rather than directly. In other words, through war news and propaganda, the Africans could see the intentions and ruthlessness of the British administration beyond the *Bwana*-servant façade.[369]

The war produced something of an information explosion in Northern Rhodesia. The war news and propaganda to which the African population was suddenly exposed hastened the emergence of an African political voice. The need to mobilize public opinion in support of the war effort led the Northern Rhodesian government to pay more attention to African public opinion than it had done before the war. Indirectly, the war stimulated some educated Africans to use the press, government as well as commercial, to engage in political dialogue with the administration and with White settler politicians.[370]

The vitality of information cannot be overemphasized. Then as now, information gives a people a soft pad for revolutionary

---

[367] See Governor John Alexander Maybin's secret memorandum to Malcolm MacDonald in the following pages who feared that the activities of the new Information Office might unsettle the natives.
[368] Josaleen Smyth, "War Propaganda During the Second World War in Northern Rhodesia," (July, 1984) JSTOR: *African Affairs*, Vol. 83, No. 332
[369] A *Bwana* was a term given to white European masters in Northern Rhodesia. In the Bemba language, it means a superior or a boss!
[370] Smyth, *supra*.

emancipation.[371] To the Africans, it did. Is it any wonder why in Zambia vital information is so hard to come by? Information is power, and the one who has it can wield tremendous leverage over the information have-nots.

It is little wonder, too, that when the Information Office was created in Northern Rhodesia, one of the Governors[372] was infuriated. Governor John Alexander Maybin, in a secret

---

[371] For example, the pro-democracy agitation by the youth of the Arab nations and North Africa in February 2011 was necessitated by the social network media. The simple fact is that the revolution was only possible because of information explosion.

[372] From April 1st, 1924 to October 24th, 1964, Northern Rhodesia had nine Governors. This list gives the names, dates when the term began and ended, and any additional details, if necessary: Sir Herbert James Stanley (April 1st, 1924 - June 1927); Sir James Crawford Maxwell (June 1927 - October 27th, 1932); Sir Ronald Storrs (October 27th, 1932 - February 19th, 1934; resigned due to ill health); Major Sir Hubert Winthrop Young (February 19th, 1934 - May 5th, 1938); Sir John Alexander Maybin (May 5th, 1938 - April 9th, 1941; died in office); Sir Eubule John Waddington (May 30th, 1941 - December 16th, 1947); Sir Gilbert Rennie (December 16th, 1947 - April 1st, 1954); Sir Arthur Edward Trevor Benson (May 1st, 1954 - April 23rd, 1959); Sir Evelyn Dennison Hone (April 23rd, 1959 - October 24th, 1964). Three of these Governors: Sir Herbert James Stanley, Sir Arthur Edward Trevor Benson and Sir Evelyn Dennison Hone held the KCMG, *the Most Distinguished Order of Saint Michael and Saint George,* which is an Order of Chivalry founded on April 28th, 1818 by George, Prince Regent, later George IV of the United Kingdom, whilst he was acting as Prince Regent for his father, George III; Sir Ronald Storrs held the KCMG, and the CBE, the *Most Excellent Order of the British Empire,* which is an Order of Chivalry established on June 4th, 1917 by George V of the United Kingdom. The Order comprises five classes in civil and military divisions. In decreasing order of seniority, these are: *Knight Grand Cross* (GBE) or *Dame Grand Cross* (GBE), *Knight Commander* (KBE) or *Dame Commander* (DBE), *Commander* (CBE), *Officer* (OBE) and *Member* (MBE); Major Sir Hubert Winthrop Young held the KCMG, and the DSO, the *Distinguished Service Order,* which is a Military Decoration of the United Kingdom, and formerly of other Commonwealth countries, awarded for meritorious or distinguished service by officers of the armed forces during wartime, typically in actual combat; the other four never held any orders, namely Sir James Crawford Maxwell, Sir John Alexander Maybin, Sir Eubule John Waddington, and Sir Gilbert Rennie.

memorandum to Malcolm MacDonald in 1939, feared that the activities of the new Information Office might "unsettle the natives."[373] It is not technological prowess that sets Europe above Africa; it is because the former is better informed on certain critical issues than the latter.[374]

§6.4 ANC, ZANC AND UNIP

There are several Zambian leaders who were key to Zambia's political independence. These included Dauti Yamba, Godwin Mbikusita Lewanika, Harry Mwaanga Nkumbula, Mainza Mathew Chona, Simon Mwansa Kapwepwe, Sylvester Chisembele, Kenneth David Kaunda, to mention but a few. All of them, diverse in educational, tribal and professional affinities, were brought together under one cause – Zambia. They all provided critical leadership towards Zambia's independence, and some even beyond.[375]

Indeed, the term "Zambian fathers,"[376] apply to them. Their story, sacrifice and exceptional leadership prowess cannot, in all

---

[373] Public Record Office Kew: CO 323/1663/6281/1B, "Comments on Secret Memorandum" as quoted in Josaleen Smyth, *supra.*

[374] It is the position of this author that neither science nor technology differentiates Zambia from the West; it is, rather, access to scientific and technological information that is a factor. The late President Mwanawasa was, like so many Zambians, of the view that, "The difference between White and Black people was not due to the color of their skins but due to science and technology," ("Zambia's Economic Future Lies in Technology - Levy," *Times of Zambia,* retrieved: March 10th, 2011).

[375] All, that is, except Godwin Lewanika.

[376]
      Thou art Yamba, never just a number
      Thou art Chona, reader, thinker and winner
      Thou art Lewanika, formidable and broker
      Thou art Nkumbula, the prized lion's molar
      Thou art Kapwepwe, pathfinder of a new way

fairness, be adequately exhausted within the ambit of this section. Suffice, nevertheless, to mention that shortly after joining the ANC in 1956, in August, Kapwepwe became Treasurer of the Lusaka-based ANC. In 1958, there was a rift in the Nkumbula-led ANC over the perceived autocratic leadership of Nkumbula and his willingness to participate in the national elections. Other leaders in ANC, including Kapwepwe protested this participation because it only allowed 25,000 Africans to vote.

In October 1958, Kapwepwe, Kaunda, Sikota Wina and a few others, broke away from ANC and formed the Zambia African National Congress (ZANC).[377] In March 1959, ZANC was declared illegal and its leaders were gaoled.[378] Those ZANC nationalists, who were not jailed, led by Mainza Chona, formed the United National Party (UNP). The name was later changed to the United National Independence Party (UNIP). Other records stem UNIP from an amalgamation of the United Freedom Party (UFP) and the African National Independence Party (ANIP) leading to UNP. Mainza Chona was not the first president of UNIP, Dixon Konkola was. However, Konkola was suspended within weeks of his presidency and was replaced by Paul Kalichini who also was replaced by Mainza Chona. Chona himself had only recently left ANC.[379] When Kaunda was released from prison in 1960; Chona stepped down and handed the presidency of UNIP over to him.[380] Chona might have

---

Thou art Kaunda, leader, nation's defender

[377] ANC was mostly organized on tribal lines, the largest chunk coming from Southern Province among the Tongas. ANC propaganda stipulated that UNIP would wipe out the cattle owned by the Tongas and give the Tonga wives to Bemba men if UNIP won the elections and became the governing party!

[378] Placed under banning orders

[379] See K. Makasa, *Zambia's March to Political Freedom* (Nairobi: Heinemann Educational Books, 1985), pp. 115-116)

[380] Chona remained loyal to UNIP, serving as UNIP's Vice-president (1960-61); UNIP National Secretary (1961-69), and as Republican Vice-president (1970-72). He never wavered from the party he helped found even when he suffered repeated humiliations at the hands of UNIP and Kaunda.

Charles Mwewa

stepped down "because [he] did not feel he possessed the necessary qualities to lead an independence movement."[381]

The Northern Rhodesian nationalists were not deterred by the doors of jail or the bars of prison.[382] After the October 1962 elections,[383] in which Africans won convincingly, UNIP and ANC formed a coalition government.[384] Kaunda became leader of the coalition with Kapwepwe as his Minister of African Agriculture.

§6.5 Kenneth Kaunda

With respect to Northern Rhodesia, an oft-made observation is that the Africans ill-timing of independence, and the subsequent removal from office of the White European masters was a mistake. This author begs to differ. The Africans in

---

[381] Mwaanga, *Looking Back: An Extraordinary Life*, p. 13

[382] In November 1953, Harry Nkumbula and Kaunda were arrested for publishing the second issue of the *Congress News*. On January 6th, 1955, Nkumbula, Kaunda and Sikalumbi were arrested and their homes thoroughly searched for allegedly possession of prohibited publications. Nkumbula and Kaunda were sentenced to two months in prison with hard labor and sent to Lusaka Central Prison. On March 12th, 1959, Kaunda was arrested at his Chilenje home and on June 20th, 1959 sentenced to nine months in prison with hard labor at Lusaka Central Prison before being transferred to Salisbury Central Prison. Kaunda was released from prison on January 9th, 1960.

[383] In 1962, the British government accepted Nyasaland's desire to opt out of the Federation. At the local level, in 1948, two Africans were named to the Northern Rhodesian Legislative Council, which was the beginning of the recognition that Blacks needed representation in the legislature. After negotiations among the Africans, the Whites, and the British government, a new constitution was agreed upon. It came into effect in 1962 and, for the first time, it seemed obvious that Africans would form the majority in the new Legislative Council.

[384] A coalition happens when two or more political parties join forces with other parties during periods of conflict of interest.

Northern Rhodesia neither ill-timed their independence nor did they prematurely remove the White colonialists from power. Perhaps more than any freedom fighter,[385] Kenneth Kaunda both epitomizes and personifies the struggles of Zambia's independence. In that sense alone, Kaunda is the hero of Zambia's struggles for independence.

Described as "Very shy, polite and friendly"[386] in his childhood, and "as he grew up, he openly resented the discrimination against Africans practiced and perpetuated by the White people in Northern Rhodesia because of color,"[387] Kaunda was born Kenneth Buchizya[388] Kaunda on April 24th, 1924 at Lubwa Mission in Chinsali in Northern Zambia.

Kaunda's father, David Julizya Kaunda,[389] a Tonga by tribe, was born in 1878 at Lisali in Bandawe in Nyasaland. David Julizya Kaunda introduced "education and the Gospel to the inhabitants of Chinsali and the Bemba-speaking people of

---

[385] Kaunda is discussed here in more details not because he was the worthiest of the Zambian fathers, but because he was the first of the founders of Zambia to lead both as Head of State and head of government.

[386] Chisala, *The Downfall of President Kaunda* (Lusaka: Co-op Printing, 1994), p. i

[387] *Ibid.*

[388] Buchizya literally means one who is not expected. Kaunda could have been named Buchizya because as the last of the eight children by David Julizya and Helen Tengwera Nyamunyirenda Kaunda, he was born twenty years after his parents were married.

[389] Kaunda's father was born Julizya Kaunda. About 1885 Julizya was baptized by the United Free Church of Scotland (UFCS) at Nyuya in Malawi and christened David. David Julizya Kaunda married Nyamunyirenda at Livingstonia in 1900 before relocating to Lubwa in Chinsali under the auspices of UFCS in 1905. There flanked by Rev. Robert McMinn, Maxwell Robertson, Dr. Brown and R.A Young, David Julizya Kaunda introduced Christianity among the Bembas of Chief Nkula (Bwalya Changala). David Julizya Kaunda died in 1932, his widow, and Kaunda's brothers and sisters were permanently settled at Shambalakale in honor of David Julizya Kaunda's missionary work there. The Bemba people of Lubwa Mission would later inscribe on the church building the following: *Kaunda Brought the Gospel Here in 1905.* Helen Kaunda died at Shambalakale at the age of 87 years in 1972.

Northern Province."[390] Kaunda did his primary education at Lubwa up to 1938 when he began to teach at the tender age of sixteen at Lubwa straight from completing his two-year elementary teacher's course. In 1941, Kaunda joined Munali Secondary School, and in 1943, he completed his Form Two. "Although he fared well in his examinations, he was unable to proceed to Form Three. Instead he was recalled by the missionaries to become Boarding Master at Lubwa for Boys. By any standards, the education he had attained at that time was very high considering the level of illiteracy in the country then."[391]

On August 24th, 1946 Kaunda married[392] Betty Mutinkhe Banda Kaunda,[393] the daughter of a Mpika local and successful businessman called John Kaweche Banda. Soon Kaunda relocated to the Copperbelt where he got a job as a clerk at Mindolo. He later moved to Chingola where he worked as a Welfare Assistant in the Nchanga Mines before resigning and

---

[390] Chisala, *supra.*, p. 2

[391] *Ibid.*, p. 3

[392] Initially Kaunda had intended to marry Gloriah Chellah, a pretty daughter of Amon Chellah, a Head Clerk, first in Mazabuka and later in Chinsali. Gloria was born on August 24th, 1930; the same date Kaunda and Betty had wedded. While still married to Betty, Kaunda had a child out-of-wedlock in 1948 with Gloria, and they named her Catherine Kaunda. Six months earlier Kaunda and Betty had a son whom they called Panji Kaunda. Gloria later got married to Golland Sichivula in 1950. Gloria died on January 30th, 1994.

[393] Betty Kaunda was born on November 17th, 1928 at Chitungulu village in Lundazi. She completed her Standard Four in Mpika before attending boarding school at Mbereshi Girls Boarding School in Kawambwa, Luapula Province, where she pursued teaching. Mbereshi was established by one Adam D. Purves of the LMS in 1900 before his death in 1901. By independence, Mbereshi was one of the leading centers for nursing training. One of the early missionaries who worked at Mbereshi was Mabel Shaw, and upon the transformation of the school into a girl's secondary school, it was renamed Mabel Shaw Girls Secondary School in 1915. Betty died on September 18th, 2012

relocating to Mufulira where he acquired a job as a Boarding Master at Mufulira Upper School between 1948 and 1949.[394]

It was in Mufulira where Kaunda started to become politically conscious, which had been launched by the formation of Welfare Associations.[395] The first of these was, in fact, pioneered by Kaunda's father: "During the inception of the Welfare Associations, most Africans including Kaunda became politically conscious. It is also on public record that David Kaunda, the father of Kenneth Kaunda, was one of the founders of the first African Welfare Associations together with Donald Siwale at Mwenzo in Northern Province."[396] While in Mufulira, Kaunda became the Vice-secretary of the local Urban Advisory Council, and subsequently of the Provincial Advisory Council. In 1949, Kaunda, together with his friend Simon Kapwepwe, returned to Chinsali where he formed the Chinsali Young Men's Farming Association. Kaunda would later become leader of UNIP and eventually first president of the Republic of Zambia.

---

[394] The Headmaster of Mufulira Upper School then was the Rev. Fergus Macperson.

[395] The first known African Welfare Association was formed by the duo of David Kaunda and Donald Siwale. In 1933, the first general meeting of the United African Welfare Association was held in Kafue, and later Welfare Associations were transformed into political organs. One of the leading champions of the Welfare Associations in Northern Rhodesia was Dauti Yamba, who helped found the Northern Rhodesian version of the African National Congress (ANC) party after visiting South Africa in 1942. Yamba was a teacher and a nationalist politician in the 1940s and 1950s. He visited South Africa and came back with the idea of forming an ANC. Northern Rhodesia African National Congress (NRANC) was formed in 1946. Yamba voted against the Central African Federation (CAF) in 1953, "One of the only four to vote against" (Grotpeter *et. al., Historical Dictionary of Zambia,* p. 464).

[396] Chisala, *supra.,* p. 7

§6.6 Seventy Years of Foreign Rule

Zambia's 75 years of colonialism can be divided into three phases. Phase one is the Company State (1889 – 1923), Phase two is the Protectorate State (1924 – 1952), and Phase three is the Federal State (1953 – 1963). Of the three, the most ruthless was also the shortest period, the Federation of Rhodesia and Nyasaland, also known as the Central African Federation (CAF) or simply called the Federation.

Under the protection of the British Government, Northern Rhodesia enjoyed a relative period of good human rights record and security of the Africans' interest. It was during this same period in 1935 when the Secretary of State for Dominion Affairs, Lord Passfield, announced the pre-eminence of the interests of the natives in Northern Rhodesia. That proclamation meant that where conflicts arose over interests between the settlers and the natives, the interests of the natives should take precedence over those of the settlers.

§6.7 The Federal State

The architects of the Federation had more ulterior motives than the British Colonial Office.[397] Godfrey Martin Huggins,

---

[397] The Colonial Office was met by another rival organization in deep ideological and political interest, the Dominion Office. The Dominion Office was abolished and replaced by the Commonwealth Relations Office in 1947. In principle, the objectives of the Commonwealth Relations Office remained the same as those of the Dominion Office. The Colonial Office was in charge of the northern territories of Nyasaland and Northern Rhodesia; the Commonwealth Relations Office was indirectly in charge of Southern Rhodesia. The Northern Rhodesia and Nyasaland opposed a Southern Rhodesian hegemony which the Commonwealth Relations Office supported. The Commonwealth Relations Office was for the settler populations and against the interests of the Africans in Northern Rhodesia and Nyasaland.

who was the first Prime Minister of the Federation from 1953 to 1956, favored an amalgamation of the three territories to create a single state.[398] He was succeeded by Sir Roy Welensky from 1956 to the end of the Federation in 1963 who remarked that he "would not accept Northern Rhodesia [to] become an African state."[399]

The Federation was designed to be a semi-independent state. It comprised Southern Rhodesia, Northern Rhodesia and Nyasaland. At the time of the Federation, Southern Rhodesia was a self-governed state while Northern Rhodesia and Nyasaland were British protectorates. The Federation, in more ways than one, adopted an image of its own. Unlike most British dominions, the Federation was neither a colony nor a dominion. It was a federal realm of the British Crown although the British Sovereign was represented by a Governor General as is usual for dominions. In due course, the Federation was being wired to become a dominion in the Commonwealth of Nations just like Canada.

When the Federation was created on August 1st, 1953, it was meant to last forever. Nevertheless, the Federation crumbled on December 31st, 1963 for two major reasons. First, the Black African nationalists wanted a greater share of power in the Federation. The dominant minority White population was unwilling to concede. Southern Rhodesia dominated the property and income franchise because of its much larger European population. The Africans who comprised the majority in the Federation were prevented from owning property and franchise in the Federation.

---

[398] Godfrey Martin Huggins was the Prime Minister of Southern Rhodesia for 23 years and the first Viscount Malvern, Prime Minister of the Federation for its first three years. Perhaps more than any other piece of evidence, the longevity of Godfrey Martin Huggins in office shows that Western leaders are as culpable as their African counterparts to dictatorial tendencies if not restrained by powerful democratic forces.

[399] Zulu, *Memoirs of Alexander Grey Zulu*, p. 1

Charles Mwewa

§6.8 Plundering Zambia

The second major reason why the Federation crumbled was because it depleted Northern Rhodesia and Nyasaland of their economic potential. Zambia was the culprit with its enormous copper deposits: "The central economic motive behind the [Federation] had always been the abundant copper deposits of Northern Rhodesia."[400]

The Federation was patterned upon the racist South African regime under the apartheid government. The Black Africans were seen as mere labor force. Their economic well-being was not a priority. For example, in 1946 the population of Black Africans in the territory that would constitute the Federation was over five million as opposed to the Whites who constituted a mere 104 thousand people. In the Federation, there were over two million Black Africans in Northern Rhodesia as opposed to only about 72 thousand Europeans.[401] Towards the end of the decade-old Federation, the Africans protested the White minority rule of the Federation.

Per Robert Blake, the Federation perpetuated apartheid and "in that sense, apartheid can be regarded as the father of Federation."[402] Although Nyasaland (Malawi) was "economically the poorest, politically the most advanced and numerically the least Europeanized of the three territories,"[403] it, nevertheless, led the upheaval to end the Federation.

---

[400] Retrieved from:
www.wikipedia.org/wiki/Federation_of_Rhodesia_and_Nyasaland (July 25th, 2010)
[401] Zulu, *supra.*, p. 171
[402] Robert Norman William Blake, Baron Blake (December 23rd, 1916 - September 20th, 2003) was an English historian. He is best known for his 1966 biography of *Benjamin Disraeli, 1st Earl of Beaconsfield!*
[403] *Ibid.*

160

The way Welensky handled the disturbances[404] arising out of the protests against the Federation, led to British Tory Prime Minister Harold Macmillan to commission an inquiry into the fracas. (This is the same Macmillan who made the famous *Wind of Change* speech in the South African Parliament in 1960). A Monckton Commission was constituted to advise Macmillan on the future of the Federation.[405] The commission came up with twelve recommendations. Eleven of the 12 recommendations of the Moncton Report are: (1) Allotment of a higher proportion of seats to the Africans who occupied 12 out of 59 seats in the Federal Assembly; (2) Extension of the franchise to ensure broader representation of both European and African opinion in the Federal Legislature; (3) Establishment of a common roll of European and African voters. Further, a committee to be established to recommend voting qualifications, which would ensure that African members were fully represented and had real support of communities; (4) Transfer of a number of functions from the Federation to the Territorial governments, leaving external affairs, defence and control of the economy with the Central Government; (5) Strengthening of the machinery of co-operation between government establishments of the economic council to co-ordinate all development planning at ministerial

---

[404] The Africans in the Federation protested against the Federation. Hastings Banda of the African National Congress (ANC) of Nyasaland (later Malawi Congress Party) returned to Nyasaland in July 1958. In 1959, unrest broke out in Nyasaland. In Northern Rhodesia, Kaunda of the Zambian African National Congress (ZANC), a faction from the Northern Rhodesian ANC had his ZANC banned in March 1959, and was subsequently imprisoned in June 1959 for nine months. While Kaunda was in jail, Mainza Chona with other African nationalists created UNIP.

[405] This royal commission was led by Walter Monckton and included, among other members, Habanyama (Northern Rhodesia) and Wellington Chirwa (Nyasaland). The African representatives dissented arguing, "The continuation of the Federation not based on consent was unacceptable, and that the inhabitants of each territory should be asked in a referendum, whether they wished to remain in the Federation, and that the British government should provide for immediate succession of any territory whose people desire it" (Zulu, *supra.*, p. 170).

levels; (6) Introduction of legislation by all legislative councils making discriminatory practices illegal; (7) Introduction of a Bill of Rights in the Territorial and Federal constitutions, which was to be re-enforced by the establishment of a Council of State to protect persons against the enactments of legislation that might be unfairly discriminatory on grounds of race, color or creed; (8) Federal Capital to remain in Salisbury for the time being and subject to review upon relaxation of racial regulations in Salisbury which had made it inaccessible to Africans; (9) Rotation of meetings of Federal legislatures in each of the three Territories; (10) The question of secession to be discussed at the Federal Review Conference and that the British government should declare its intention of permitting secession, subject to certain conditions; (11) A new constitution for Northern Rhodesia and such constitutional changes that may be desirable in Southern Rhodesia, and should not wait on a full revision of the Federal structure.[406] However, the recommendations from one to nine "failed to meet the demands and aspirations of the African population."[407] Rather than dismantle the Federation, the recommendations were merely intended to reform the Federation. This did not go well with the Africans in Northern Rhodesia and Nyasaland.[408]

In December 1960, a Federal Constitutional Review Conference was held in London, England pursuant to Article 99

---

[406] Adopted from Zulu, *ibid*, pp. 169-170

[407] *Ibid.*, p. 171

[408] For example, a Mr. Habanyama who represented Northern Rhodesia, and a Mr. Wellington Chirwa, who represented Nyasaland, dissented on the report declaring that the continuation of the Federation was unwarranted and called for a referendum to inquire whether Northern Rhodesia and Nyasaland wanted to remain in the Federation any longer. And if anyone of the two Territories desired to opt out of the Federation, the British government should allow it.

of the *Constitution of Rhodesia and Nyasaland.*[409] The commission was attended by Kaunda, Kapwepwe, Chona, and Nkumbula. Most historians attribute the commencement of the end of the Federation to this conference. As Welensky feared, hosting the conference in London, Macmillan favored Legislative Council consisting of thirty candidates, sixteen being Africans while 14 were to be Europeans.[410] Under a frustrating electoral environment on October 30th, 1962, the African parties in Northern Rhodesia achieved political milestones that were indicative of the election success in subsequent years.[411] In 1962,

---

[409] The article stated: "Not less than seven or more than nine years from the date of the coming into force of this constitution there shall be convened a Conference consisting of delegates from the Federation, from each of the three Territories and from the United Kingdom, chosen by their respective governments, for the purpose of reviewing this constitution."

[410] Sir Roy Welensky, *4000 Days* (London: Collin, 1964), p. 307

[411] Because of a deadlock at the Federal Constitutional Review Conference, on February 20th, 1961, British Colonial Secretary Iain Macleod presented his own plan. The plan provided for a 45-member Legislature based on a two-tier system comprising an Upper Roll and a Lower Roll. The Upper Roll consisted of 15 seats and the Lower Roll also consisted of 15 seats. There were 15 national constituencies in total. The plan also insisted that at least two Africans and two non-Africans be included among the six "Unofficials" (Unofficials in the Legislative Council did not hold their seats because of membership in the official colonial administration. It was a particularly important step for the territory when, in 1945, the number of Unofficials in the territory's Executive Council outnumbered the officials. Many of the Unofficials in the 1930s were Europeans who urged amalgamation with Southern Rhodesia. For many years, the leader of the Unofficials was Sir Stewart Gore-Brown (who also became a staunch supporter of UNIP), but he was replaced in 1946 by Sir Roy Welensky) on the Executive Council.) The constitution demanded high qualifications for candidates to the Upper Roll in terms of income, property ownership and educational attainments. The Africans lacked all the three. Kenneth Kaunda and UNIP protested that Africans would be unable to get Upper Roll support for the national seats but reluctantly accepted the plan. Sir Roy Welensky and his United Federal Party were critical of the plan and immediately sought for its revision. For example, "Welensky feared that it would allow an African majority to be elected" (Grotpeter et. al., *supra.*, p. 237). The Macleod constitution was, however, only in force until January 1964, but it conveniently allowed the

163

the Africans won control of the Northern Rhodesian government.

Consequently, Northern Rhodesians demanded greater participation in the Federal government. The British feared losing political control to the Northern Rhodesians and the people of Nyasaland as the election results of 1962 revealed.[412] In that year, the Africans won the majority in the Legislative Council. The council subsequently, passed a resolution calling for Zambia's secession from the Federation. In addition, the Africans made three demands: Self-government, a new constitution and a new National Assembly based on a broader democratic franchise.

On December 31st, 1963, the Federation was formally dissolved. The assets belonging to the Federation were distributed among the territorial governments. As expected, the bulk of assets went to Southern Rhodesia, including the Federal army. It took less than a year and Northern Rhodesia became an independent nation on October 24th, 1964.

While to the Zambians independence was inevitable, to some, especially those of the colonial establishments, independence was said to have come too soon or even unwarranted. For one, all peoples have the right to self-determination. It is an ultimate truth that all the peoples of the world ardently desired the end of colonialism in all its manifestations. Colonialism militated against the ideals of universal peace, democracy and justice.[413]

For another, since April 6th, 1320 when the Scottish people demanded independence through Scotland's Declaration of

---

Africans to win control of the Northern Rhodesia government. This was the signal that the end of CAF and the independence of Northern Rhodesia were imminent. The ensuing elections in 1962 saw great spurts in terms of turn-out and enthusiasm among the African populations.

[412] Welensky, *supra.*

[413] On February 7th, 2011, Matthew Pennington of the *Associated Press* quoted President Obama as having said that, "After decades of conflict, the image of millions of southern Sudanese voters deciding their own future was an inspiration to the world. He also said it is another step forward in Africa's long journey toward *justice and democracy.*"

Arbroath; to 1776's US Declaration of Independence; to August 28th, 2008 when the Parliament of Georgia passed a resolution declaring Abkhazia a "Russian-Occupied Territory;" and to July 9th, 2011 when South Sudan became independent; the sounds of independence have never ceased to ring. Chapter Seven will establish that Zambian independence was inevitable.

§6.9 Requiem for a Freedom Fighter

This section briefly discusses Sylvester Mwamba Chisembele whom Valentine Kayope described as, "The gallant and indomitably courageous freedom fighter and humble and selfless servant of the Zambian people."[414] For a comprehensive review of his life, agitations, political contributions and death, read his wife, Sophena Chisembele's latest book, *Zambia, The Freedom Struggle and the Aftermath.*[415]

Sylvester Chisembele was born on March 1st, 1930 in Fort Rosebery (Mansa).[416] His father Michael Filalo and his brother Romans Filalo Lupando established the Catholic Church in Mansa, "a fact that was recognized by His Holiness the Pope in Rome."[417] In 1948, Chisembele was booted out of a seminary because "his questions on racial equality were considered too radical for that period in time."[418] He rose to be a very successful businessman in Mansa, a feat that did not go too well with the White District Commissioner and his police department. It is recorded that by 1952, at the time when the highest paid White miners received £200 per month, his "trade alone brought him a

---

[414] In a eulogy on Thursday, February 9th, 2006
[415] (London: Sylsop Books, 2015)
[416] See also the brief history of Sylvester Mwamba Chisembele in *The Guardian* of Friday, December 8th, 2006
[417] *Weekly Angel*, "S.M. Chisembele: Death of a Hero," (March 13th – 19th, 2006), p. 6
[418] *Ibid.*

net profit per month of £400."[419] At this same time, the highest paid African mine workers received not more than £10 per month.

Because of the harassment and frustrations Chisembele continued to suffer at the hands of the District Commissioner, he was forced to "detest and hate the existence in the country of colonialism and anything about it."[420] He braced for the independence of Zambia as the way of equalizing benefits for the indigenous people of Zambia. He joined the banned ANC and "became one of Zambia's greatest fearless freedom fighters, who put his call to freedom fighting before his own personal life and family."[421] Consequently, in 1955, Chisembele organized a firm ANC base in Mansa using his own resources of money and buildings to further the causes of freedom. His efforts spread over to Samfya. In 1956, Chisembele was arrested for political agitation and spent the whole year in prison. Upon his release in 1957, he was appointed Provincial General Secretary of ANC in Luapula. An assassination attempt on his life in 1958 left him with a permanent disability in his right ear and with only a partial hearing in his left.[422] In the same year, due to wrangles in ANC of Harry Nkumbula, Chisembele joined the newly formed ZANC, a precursor of UNIP.

In 1959, Chisembele was arrested for the second time and detained at Kalabo Prison for nine months under the orders of Governor Sir Arthur Benson. His real estate property in Luapula was confiscated, denying him any means of livelihood. In 1961, Chisembele was arrested for the third time, this time on the allegation of harboring explosives. Shortly after a meeting with the Governor of Northern Rhodesia, Sir Evelyn Hone, mainly for

---

[419] *Ibid.*
[420] *Ibid.*
[421] *Ibid.*
[422] This was when two security officers armed with two long batons beat him up leaving him permanently disabled.

his role in drafting UNIP's Five-Point Master Plan, he was arrested and detained for the fourth time. Cha-Cha-Cha the civil disobedience movement launched by UNIP,[423] was said to have been fiercest in Luapula Province under the leadership of Chisembele.[424] Chisembele was one of freedom fighters who managed to burn the *Fitupas*[425] throughout Luapula Province. For this, Chisembele received a three months' detention at Milima Prison in Kasama. This was his fifth arrest and detention.[426]

In *Zambia: The Politics of Independence 1959-1964*,[427] Mulford writes, "Sylvester Chisembele, perhaps the most widely known and respected of Luapula's ZANC restricted persons, returned to Fort Rosebery on January 8th, 1960, bearing a duplicating machine and 1,000 new UNIP membership cards, an important advance had been achieved by UNIP in Luapula province."[428] By 1960, Luapula had the fastest growing branches of UNIP and membership in the country.[429]

As a strategic move in 1962, UNIP decided to allow Kaunda, then UNIP's president, to stand in Luapula. The move was motivated by Chisembele's superior organization skills and proven leadership success.

This highest degree of political organization prompted the UNIP National Council to select the party president, then

---

[423] The name itself was derived from a song, "Independence Cha-Cha," composed by a Congolese rumba singer, Joseph Kabasale, at Congo's Independence. (Source: *Unegual to the Task?* by Elias C. Chipimo, Jr.)
[424] This is attested to by Nephas Tembo who in 1984 wrote about the movement of Cha-Cha-Cha and its impact on Zambian political struggles.
[425] *Fitupas* were colonial identity cards and were considered by the Africans as symbols of enslavement.
[426] Consequently, between 1956 and 1962, Chisembele was arrested and detained severally for addressing meetings without permits.
[427] David C. Mulford, *Zambia: The Politics of Independence 1959-1964* (Oxford: Oxford University Press, 1967)
[428] *Ibid.*, p. 138
[429] For example, between April and December 1960, UNIP branches rose from 28 to 482, with Luapula accounting for 305 of these with an estimated membership of 69,000. See Mulford, *ibid.*, pp. 161-162.

Kenneth Kaunda, to stand in the Luapula constituency in the ensuing controversial Ian McLeod 15 Constitution and Chisembele was asked to be his election agent. Chisembele asked Kaunda to campaign for UNIP candidates in other provinces, since he, Chisembele, could deliver all the Luapula seats to UNIP.[430]

However, things for Chisembele began to turn sour when he registered his disapproval for the leaders of the party to be chosen, *inter alia*, by one person.[431] This challenge to UNIP's stance cost Chisembele senior government positions after independence.[432] Despite this repudiation, Chisembele distinguished himself as a conciliator.[433] Upon his retirement from active politics in 1983, Chisembele proved himself as an assiduous farmer and businessman, yet again.[434]

Chisembele's real fallout with the MMD government began when he challenged the incumbents on corruption. His "stance against corruption was not always acceptable and made him

---

[430] *Weekly Angel, supra.,* p. 11

[431] At the UNIP Magoye Conference, it was decided that UNIP leaders would be appointed by Kaunda alone. This did not augur well with Chisembele who had been imprisoned five times already for his fight for equality and democracy.

[432] Despite his spurts in agitating and organizing the struggles for independence, at independence, Chisembele was only appointed as Deputy Minister of Agriculture to Elijah Mudenda. Many believed that he deserved better.

[433] For example, in 1966, he was involved in negotiating peaceful resolution to the heated debate over the name of Baluvale between the Luvales and the Lundas. Through his efforts, the name was changed from Baluvale to Zambezi. This move settled the issue permanently. Moreover, Chisembele served as Minister of Copperbelt, Eastern and Western provinces. It was in Western Province in 1970 where Chisembele won the hearts of the Lozis, including the Litunga, to return UNIP once more as a popular party following embarrassing defeats before he was transferred there.

[434] He owned such restaurants as the Garden Restaurant in Cairo Road, Ethel's Restaurant in Cha-Cha-Cha Road and the Filalo Farm in Chisamba.

enemies."[435] Besides, before his death on February 5th, 2006, he had presented his version of how the constitution should be adopted to be a "proper people-driven constitution [which] would solve most of Zambia's problems including corruption."[436]

Chisembele's battle with the MMD incumbents, was in their neglect and brutal treatment of the Zambian freedom fighters. Before his death, he had launched a protracted fight for the honor and respect of the men and women who had fought and won Zambia's independence. Chisembele was approached on October 16th and 20th, 2004 by representatives of the Office of the Vice-president with the suggestion that he should accept an Award for the Order of the Eagle of Zambia, 4th Division during the Independence Day celebrations of that year. Chisembele declined emphatically since, "H.E. President Patrick Levy Mwanawasa has refused to see me concerning a case which I have against the government involving victimization and appalling corruption which the government has refused to address. To accept an Award under such circumstances would be impossible."[437]

---

[435] *Weekly Angel, supra.*, p. 11
[436] *Ibid.*
[437] Chisembele had indicated his unwilling to accept an Award he considered a joke in the various correspondences he made to the following people: to the Secretary to the Cabinet on October 25th, 2004; a general letter circulated by Mr. Chisembele in October 2004 to individuals he considered should be informed of the correct circumstances; notes of the meeting with the Secretary to the Cabinet, Dr. Joshua Kanganja on November 1st, 2004; Secretary to the Cabinet on November 5th, 2004; the Hon. Dr. Sipula Kabanje, MP, Deputy Minister of Lands on November 10th, 2004; the Hon. Andrew Mulenga, MP, Minister of Education on November 10th, 2004; the Hon. George W. Mpombo, MP, Minister of Energy & Water Development on November 10th, 2004; the Hon. Lt. Col. Patrick Kafumukache, MP, Minister of Labor & Social Security on November 10th, 2004; Hon. Amusaa K. Mwanamwambwa, MP, Speaker of the National Assembly on November 10th, 2004; a reply from Secretary to the Cabinet on November 17th, 2004; Mrs. D.K.K. Mwinga, Clerk to the National Assembly on December 2nd, 2004; from the Deputy Minister in the Office of the Vice-president on December 29th, 2004; the Hon. Kennedy Mpolobe Shepande, MP for Nangoma Constituency, Deputy Minister of Works & Supply on December

Chisembele's central argument was that government had neglected the freedom fighters. Hence, Chisembele charged, "In my opinion, giving an honor implies that the recipient is being shown genuine respect and treatment, which I feel has not been the case in my situation."[438] Moreover, Chisembele had his business and farms confiscated by the same government he fought for and brought to power. Sophena Chisembele, the widow of Chisembele, writes, "The farm and property confiscation issues, which might appear personal…are, in fact, political in nature, and will…be of historical value to later generations, wishing to know more of their founding fathers and the on-going human struggles for democracy and justice."[439]

Neither presidents Chiluba nor Mwanawasa was oblivious to Chisembele's fight for the plight of the Zambian freedom fighters, Chisembele alleged. Chiluba acknowledged: "I am glad that despite the obvious anxiety and psychological torture you were subjected to, the matter has been laid to rest and you have retained ownership rightfully of a property on which you have spent all your time and resources to develop."[440]

As mentioned earlier, in 2004, government decided to decorate Chisembele with an Award for the Order of the Eagle of Zambia, 4th Division. He declined. In correspondence after correspondence to and from Cabinet Office, Chisembele demanded to be removed from being gazetted as a recipient of the Order of the Eagle of Zambia, 4th Division. Ironically, Chisembele's name was included even before he was informed: "You may be aware since you were in government leadership that by the time recipients of Honors and Awards are informed,

---

31st, 2004; and the Hon. Mrs. R.C. Banda, MP, Deputy Minister in the Office of the Vice-president on January 17th, 2005.

[438] Chisembele, in a letter to the Hon. Mrs. R.C. Banda, MP, Deputy Minister, Office of the Vice-president on January 17th, 2005

[439] Sophena Chisembele, "The Hon. Sylvester Mwamba Chisembele: March 1st, 1930 – February 5th, 2006," (October 10th, 2008)

[440] President Frederick Chiluba, in a letter to Chisembele of March 31st, 2000

government has had already printed their names."[441] Eventually, after a long and protracted battle, Chisembele had his name de-gazetted.[442]

The *Chisembele Case* is one of the saddest episodes in the history of our young nation, Zambia. Barely fifty years ago, had the Zambian fathers and mothers fought with their life and blood for Zambia's independence. When history should have stood in awe of their sacrifice, instances like the one concerning Chisembele stand as testament to the politics of exclusion. Chisembele was one of the first Zambians to demand for reparations: "Chisembele was the first and only…Zambian to attempt in 2004 to claim compensation from the British Government for atrocities and imprisonment [Zambian freedom fighters] suffered during the non-violent struggle for independence."[443] Despite the Zambian Government unwillingness to push this matter further with the British Government, Chisembele brought the matter before the European Court of Human Rights which threw out the case on October 12th, 2004.[444]

In view of the *Chisembele Case*, three issues emerge. First, it is whether the freedom fighters in Zambia are ignored and neglected. "Freedom fighters are totally ignored by government except for a few words of praise and gratitude once every year. Words of praise which are hallow and hypocritical."[445] If this allegation holds, it portends a serious national omission, especially for a nation like Zambia which made many sacrifices to obtain independence from Britain. As shown in Chapter 5,

---

[441] Hon. Mrs. R.C. Banda, MP, Deputy Minister, Office of the Vice-president's reply of December 29th, 2004 to Chisembele who wanted to know why his name was included despite the fact that he had expressed unwillingness to accept the Award.

[442] See Gazette Notice Numbers 629 of 2004 and 640 of 2004.

[443] Sophena Chisembele, *supra.*

[444] The case failed only because the Human Rights Convention came into force after 1966, the year it was ratified.

[445] Sophena Chisembele, "General Comments on the Treatment of Zambian Freedom Fighters Today," (2004)

colonialism was brutal and devastating to the future economic well-being of Zambia. The men and women who fought for Zambia's independence, therefore, deserve the highest sustained honor the former colonial state could not afford them.

Second, is whether freedom fighters should be honored both in words and deeds: "Many once fearless, patriotic freedom fighters have grown old and been allowed to die in miserable poverty."[446] It is not a question of casting offhand aspersions to insisting that some so-called freedom fighters are undeserving of the honor they receive. Some were not quintessential freedom fighters; they can best be described as collaborators. The true and authentic freedom fighters are condemned to the solitaries of indecency and poverty.

Third and last, is whether Zambia, like many former colonies, has not pursued the issue of reparations by the former colonial masters frantically. Evidence proffered in Chapter 5 shows that Africa and Zambia did not only lose in terms of economic propensity, but also in human terms. The Federation plundered Zambia economically. The colonial forces inflicted chagrin and pain on peaceful freedom agitators. Thus, and sadly, "State-backed crime against an African during the colonial era is not considered at all."[447] Britain retired from Northern Rhodesia with enormous wealth at the expense of the future of Zambia. To demand that reparations be made is only just and fair:

> Independent Zambia was created poor even before it began to crawl. In Part I, I showed how Zambia was declared independent but still required to undertake to pay for all the retirement packages of its former colonial masters. In fact, as we saw, right at independence, Zambia would be indebted to Great Britain to a "total of £5¾ million in financial aid, composed of a £2¾ million grant in respect of the ex-federal short-term debt and a £3 million loan towards the cost of compensation to members of her majesty's

---

[446] *Ibid.*
[447] *Ibid.*

overseas civil service." Mr. John Tilney, Member of the House of Commons representing Liverpool Wavertree and who moved the Bill to create Zambia for a Second Reading, confessed that, "My own regret is that I have never visited Northern Rhodesia, though I have long wished to do so." Isn't it ironic that, like the way Africa was parted from Germany (without even most of the partitioners having set foot on the land of Africa), Zambia's future would, similarly, be determined by those who had not even visited it?[448]

Others, like Gabi Hesselbein,[449] have done extensive research on the deleterious effects of colonialism in Africa. Lord Aikins Adusei[450] argues vehemently for the colonial and slave reparations of Africa by the US and European nations involved. He maintains that, "The lack of development in Africa and the poverty of millions of African-Americans have been blamed on...slavery and colonialism."[451] He contends that centuries of slavery and colonialism deprived Africa of its able human and economic resources. These human beings[452] "traveled in very deplorable conditions, often without adequate food, water and air."[453] His basis for reparations is that, "While in the New World, [the Africans] were made to work for centuries without pay. The slave trade deprived the continent of her energetic men and women a vital resource in any development process and sunk the continent into intellectual wilderness."[454]

European powers scrambled for Africa, "an act that can only be described as robbery."[455] He cites the example of Congo DR where, "King Leopold II of Belgium enslaved the Africans, forced them to work without pay, killed about 10 million and

---

[448] Charles Mwewa, "In their Own Words: Debates that created Zambia, Part II," *Zambian Eye*, October 30th, 2015

[449] See G. Hesselbein, *Reparations for Colonialism?* (2002)

[450] Lord Aikins Adusei, "US and Europe Must Pay Reparations to Victims of Slavery and Colonialism," *Modern Ghana*, (Thursday, February 12th, 2009)

[451] *Ibid.*

[452] In all about 30 - 40 million people

[453] Adusei, *supra.*

[454] *Ibid.*

[455] *Ibid.*

Charles Mwewa

looted the country of her resources and virtually nothing was used to invest in the country except guns [with] which the Belgium army used to terrorize and kill the Africans."[456] Adusei cites other atrocious examples like the case of the Africans who resisted the illegal activities in South West Africa (now Namibia) who were killed by the Germans between 1904 and 1907, committing what he refers to as "The first genocide of the 20th Century with the killing of the Herero and the Namaqua people."[457]

Clearly, the story of colonialism, the suppression and oppression of the Africans' interests during colonialism, and indeed, the plundering of Zambia, deserve much debate. The issue of colonial reparation is not dead, and must be revisited in this or the generation to come. Until then, the story of colonialism will remain an elephant in the room.

§6.10 The Freedom Statue

Freedom in Zambia was achieved through sweat, lashes and blood. This is loudly depicted by the Freedom Statue "standing defiantly along Independence Avenue in Lusaka."[458] The statue portrays "Zanco" Mpundu Mutembo, "The flesh behind the stone."[459] Mpundu Mutembo was a *mposa-mabwe* (literally, "Stone-thrower" or rubble-rouser) during the struggle for freedom. The stone is based on a true picture depiction of Mpundu Mutembo; "[It] is a true-life event that got captured on

---

[456] *Ibid.*
[457] *Ibid.*; see also Hesselbein, *supra.*, p. 11
[458] Chibamba Kayula, "Zanco Mpundu Mutembo, Symbol of our Nation," June 26th, 2013
[459] *Ibid.*

174

camera and frozen solid by casting experts."[460] Chibamba Kayula narrates how this was done:

> [Zanco Mpundu Mutembo was] born in 1936 in Mbala. Mpundu Mutembo and his twin brother, Arnold, got involved in the freedom struggle for independence when they were just teenagers. This was after dropping out of school following their father's demise. In 1957 having already earned his place in the political struggle in Northern Province which was led by Kapasa Makasa and Simon Mwansa Kapwepwe, Mutembo along with seven others were sent to Kenya where Dedan Kimathi was leading a rebellion against the British. Their mission was to learn how to carry out their own rebellion back home. When he returned, Mutembo worked closely with Kapwepwe and [Kenneth] Kaunda, following them on their campaign trails.
>
> On October 24th, 1958 at a location in Chilenje, Mutembo got his pet name "Zanco." It was also here that the unborn nation was christened.... The nation's name was proposed by Kaunda and Kapwepwe. "We had wanted to call it Zambezia, but we settled for Zambia. When we chanted the name 'Zambia, Zambia!' it sounded very nice and we all started dancing like little children,' Mutembo recalled."
>
> Per Mutembo the motto, "One Zambia-One Nation," was also coined at the same meeting which also marked the birth of the Zambia Africa National Congress (ZANC). Later, on December 31st, 1963, after Mpundu was chosen by Kaunda and the UNIP leadership as the symbol of the soon to be born nation, he drove with Sir Evelyn in his official vehicle with a mounted police escort down King George Avenue (now Independence Avenue) to police force headquarters. At force headquarters after being interviewed, he was taken to a room where eighteen military officers stood with guns at the ready. He was then handcuffed to a chain [and] ordered to break free.
>
> "Zanco, break the chain. If you fail, we will shoot you!" the soldiers [shouted]. "[It] was hard and I was sweating. After pulling so hard the chain snapped and the Governor raised his hands," Mpundu said. "You are now the symbol of the nation," the Governor announced.

---

[460] *Ibid.*

> Unveiled on October 23rd, 1974, the Freedom Statue has
> come to symbolize Zambia's freedom from the British. The
> statue has also earned its place on some of the country's
> most important articles, including its currency.

Before Mpundu Mutembo was chosen to be depicted onto the Freedom Statue as the symbol of Zambia's freedom, various symbols were contemplated, including the Victoria Falls and the Muchinga Escarpment. "Kaunda, however, had other plans on his mind. He called Mpundu Mutembo a strongly-built-teenaged freedom fighter from Mbala...to die for the nation."[461]

It is ironic that the freedom statue cenotaph had been in existence from October 1974 and Mutembo, after whom the statue is modeled, an old man by 2014, was still alive, and he was largely forgotten. For "It is traditional on the national calendar every year during Africa Freedom and Independence Day celebrations that the Republican President and other invited dignitaries have to lay wreaths on the Freedom Statue....This is symbolic as a way of paying respect to the fallen heroes and an honor accorded to them for their contribution to the freedom struggle which led to the independence of the country."[462] This story, like the previous one on Sylvester Chisembele, shows that Zambia has a long way to go in honoring its living heroes. Zambia is a sum-total of all those who fought for independence, whether they died or survived.

---

[461] *Ibid.*

[462] Darlington Mwendabai, "Zambia: 'Zanco' Mutembo - Forgotten Freedom Fighter," *Times of Zambia*, February 24th, 2007

7| Independence Theories

Thou built reason's mind, O Plato,
Shaped brain's wit, thou Aristotle,
And deified politics divine
Whence St. Augustine's city doth shine!

Chapter Focus

At the end of reading this chapter, you should be able to:

- Establish that traditional Zambian customs lean heavily towards democracy
- Establish that Africans can run their own governments
- Refute assumptions that the early failures in independent Zambia were due to lack of leadership acumen
- Review a critical racial theoretical scheme that propelled Europe to acquire colonies in Africa

BRIEF INTRODUCTION

In this chapter, the author offers a theoretical basis for Zambia's independence and ascertains that independence was inevitable for the Africans in Zambia.

§7.1 Democratic by Nature

Zambians are by nature democratic. The three demands proposed by the Africans in Northern Rhodesia in 1962 when they called for Zambia to secede from the Federation, namely: Self-government; a new constitution and a new National Assembly based on a broader democratic franchise, illustrate their quest for self-determination. It was also evidence that democracy in Zambia was not to be a creation of Britain, rather of the Zambians themselves. It was not in Britain's interest to willingly grant self-government to the Zambians. Even though towards the end of the Federation Britain had devised a course in Africanization, "in preparation for the hand-over of power to the African government,"[463] research shows that, in the mind of the British colonial administrators, independence was far removed from their immediate *agenda*.

As mentioned before, the imposition of the Federation itself was a contradiction in terms. Lessons could be learned from the 1930's when Lord Passfield's announcement that the interests of the natives were paramount was immediately met by the gunning to death of the natives who complained against slave wages and poor working conditions. This took place in 1935. It would take bloodshed, imprisonment and extraordinary bravery for the natives to gain independence. Grant admits that although Africanization was introduced, independence itself was perceived "to be many years away."[464]

Fundamental to the belief of the time was the perception that Zambians could never be democratic. As far as colonial Britain was concerned, Africans were devoid of democratic competence.[465] A former Colonial Officer has generously revealed that they suspected that democracy in Zambia was unworkable, or worse still, it could plunge the entire nation into chaos. He cites events after independence as testament to that belief:

> Maintaining law and order was our [District Officer Cadets'] most important single function. Progress in African standards of living

---

[463] Grant, *Zambia – Then and Now*, p. 30

[464] *Ibid.*

[465] In the movie, *Invictus*, released in 2010 and starring Morgan Freeman as Mandela, the former White rulers of apartheid-era South Africa farce again and again and ask, "He [Mandela] can win elections, but can he run a country?"

depended above all upon stability. Most Colonial Officers were essentially classical British conservatives, knowingly or not, disciples of Edmund Blake and his successors, who believed that freedom could only be considered in a context of order firmly rooted in traditional institutions: The Chiefs, the Crown, the Governor, and, of course, the District Commissioner. *Most were fundamentally suspicious of democracy and feared that Africa would dissolve into chaos if that were taken too far or too soon.* Sadly, events in the decades immediately after independence very quickly seemed to justify these fears only too well (Emphasis added).[466]

To be fair, the belief expressed in this statement may not be generalized to all Britons at the time, or to those in our time. However, a notation is warranted here to sufficiently understand why and how the colonial administration did what it did. Britain, like many liberal democratic societies, espouses freedom in dives of viewpoints. The line is usually drawn between liberals and conservatives. Among the liberals are those who tilt towards the right-center, and may be referred to as Classical Liberals. Those liberals who lean towards the left-center are referred to as Reform Liberals. Both sets of liberals believe in personal freedom,[467] limited government,[468] equality of rights,[469] and in the consent of the governed.[470]

Conservatives on the other hand, are situated to the right of the liberals on an ideological continuum. A leading American

---

[466] Grant, *supra.*, p. 45

[467] Liberals believe that for people to be truly free, coercion of any form should be eliminated. This means that people should be free to express themselves in speech, in the ownership of private property, and in the choice of political affiliation and religion.

[468] Liberals do not believe that government should do everything for the citizenry; rather, that government should serve a specific function in society, and should not be in general charge.

[469] Liberals believe in the Rule of Law, that laws which do not favor one sector of society at the expense of another, and which are impartially enforced, should be enacted.

[470] Liberals believe in popular sovereignty that the people are masters of the democratic arena – setting the *agenda* for running government affairs including hiring and firing politicians through a ballot.

writer has listed six common characteristics of all conservatives.[471] These are: A strong belief in order; affection for the proliferating variety and mystery of human existence; conviction that civilized society requires orders and classes; persuasion that freedom and property are closely linked; faith in prescription and distrust in economic abstraction; and recognition that change may not be salutary reform. Conservatives are suspicious of radical change, and may be eluded by progressive innovations.

Thus, it was under this conservative montage that the Africans in Northern Rhodesia endured under the wrath of *love for order*. But to accuse the Africans of being undemocratic, and to justify this assertion by the events following independence, was typical of the imperial attitude.[472] African democracy is usually judged from the Western perspective, or by the events of the first two decades of the 1960s and 1970s when most African nations acquired political independence.

The following are some of the reasons why in this book a contrary view has been taken. To begin with, it is the issue of time. While most Europeans and Western nations measure the plausibility of African democracy from the first few years after independence, a critical omission has been made. Democracy, even in Athens, did not take root in one day, as the expression goes – Rome was not built in one day! This is not to justify spurts of coups and irresponsible governance in very few African governments. Elsewhere, arguments for democracy and decry for the legacy of coups d'état in Africa have been made.[473]

---

[471] Russell Kirk, *The Conservative Mind*, 7th ed. (Chicago: Henry Regnery, 1986) as quoted in Mark O. Dickerson & Thomas Flanagan, *An Introduction to Government and Politics: A Conceptual Approach* (Toronto: Thomson Nelson, 2006), p. 150

[472] Sometimes, the claim is justified owing to some African nations' tendency of undemocratic removal from power of legitimately elected leaders through coups d'état.

[473] See Chapter 9

For the most part, Western democracy has gone through fire and trials to get to where it is. At the time, former colonial powers where itching to see what new African leaders would do with democracy, theirs had been in existence for hundreds of years. Surely, even God hates unfair scales.[474] The strength of African democracy cannot be equitably measured by the last four or five decades after independence.[475] In the case of Zambia, within the last five decades, there have been reliable signs of a firm democratic foundation. Judged objectively, Zambia has met three critical factors that define democratic progress: A political culture; a strong civil society, and a liberalized economy. Defined by these three indicators, Zambia is on the right path to democratic maturity.

The colonial establishment did very little, if anything, too late, to empower the Africans for leadership.[476] As mentioned above, the Africanization program came too late, and usually the colonial powers themselves did not even have faith in the ability of the Africans to rule themselves. Africans had to learn Western-style government at gun-point.[477] It is posited that, given the circumstances at the time of independence, the African leaders in

---

[474] Proverbs 11:1

[475] In the case of Zambia, which got independence in 1964

[476] Here leadership is defined in terms of the ability and sophistication of running Western-style institutions. It should be mentioned that the Africans had been adept at running local politics very well even before colonialism.

[477] During the colonial era, Africans who could rise to a clerk position were privileged. The majority served as messengers to the *Bwana* (bosses or masters) who were the White colonialists. At the *Boma* ("Home" in Swahili), the Africans were ironically never at home; they perpetually served as servants in the colonial officers' homes and farms. The closest Africans came to be self-motivated leaders were in the church circles, especially after the emergence of African Independent Churches. This soon paved the way for leadership, albeit on a limited scale, in administration as lowest ranking officers, and occasionally as teachers. This scenario, undoubtedly, meant that the newly installed African leaders would have to depend on expatriate help and on the same masters they had supposedly replaced for government and expertise.

Zambia did a commendable job to reach Zambia where the nation was in the 2000s, although more could and *must* be done!

§7.2 Ready to Self-Govern

The 1962 elections had shown that Zambians were ready to rule themselves and any attempt at another election would only favor the Africans. And this was what exactly happened, for on December 31st, 1963 the Federation was dissolved[478] and after ten months Zambia became an independent Republic on October 24th, 1964.

Although Zambians had demanded recognition and dignity, they, however, did not see independence as an option before World War I for strategic reasons.[479] The Mwenzo Association clearly stated in its 1923 constitution that independence was not one of its objectives. Nevertheless, the association existed to champion causes of human recognition and the assumption is that it was such movements which gave impetus to nationalism in the early parts of the 1960s.

During World War I, Mwenzo Mission was closed because of disturbances near Lake Tanganyika. Although this closure disbanded the first Mwenzo Association, it, however, paved the way for the Africans to experience the war on the side of Great Britain. More African troops joined World War II on the Allied

---

[478] On December 31st, 1963, just ten years after its founding, the Federation of Rhodesia and Nyasaland was declared dead. African nationalists had triumphed. After that, it was just a question of time before Northern Rhodesia and Nyasaland would join most of the rest of Africa in the 1960s in winning majority rule and independence from European colonial rule. Less than a year after the federation's dissolution, Northern Rhodesia became the independent Republic of Zambia on October 24th, 1964. UNIP which had succeeded the banned ZANC won most the seats under the new constitution.
[479] See §6.3

side. This last deployment would prove very decisive to African nationalism in Northern Rhodesia.

The Allied forces and nations emerged victors in World War II, and so did the Africans in Northern Rhodesia. What the war did directly for the Allied nations in the Northern Hemisphere did indirectly for the Africans in Northern Rhodesia in the Southern Hemisphere. The war exposed the Africans to information to which they would otherwise not have had access. As the Africans fought alongside their colonial masters, they began to realize that the Whites were after all humans and mortals. The façade[480] of infallibility that the colonialists had put on, the Africans found to be a sham.

The gun, which, in fact, had given the colonial forces maximum advantage over the Africans, could kill the Whites as well as the Blacks alike. The Africans began to realize that the colonialists were just as vulnerable, and far from being infallible. In World War II, Britain lost over 700 thousand men. The empire was crumbling, the smokescreen was lifting, and Britain's Achilles' heel was beginning to be exposed.

---

[480] When I was growing up in Chingola, Zambia, a myth surrounded the White race. For us, the White people were more than just human beings; they were almost like gods. Among our peers, we even embraced a notion that White people did not use a toilet. We believed strongly that they possessed superior powers which they could invoke at any time to acquire wealth or win wars or engineer technological advancements. This conjecture was strengthened by the fact that all the White folk in Chingola lived in wealthy neighborhoods, had African maids and servants, occupied very high positions in places of work, were very successful businesspersons and drove expensive cars.

As I grew up, I started to dispute the myth. I realized that White folks were just normal human beings who were subjected to the same human conditions as the Africans. This knowledge was what the early Africans who encountered the Whites lacked. Simple information like this one has the propensity to liberating a people and to cause them to demand for equal treatment and recognition. As I went abroad to the West for studies, I began to realize further that even an intellectual supposition of White Superiority or White Supremacy is just that, a myth. White folks are not predisposed to a much higher IQ than Africans. All races are capable of intellectual competence. These myths eluded my people for a very long, long time!

§7.3 The Waning Empire

On paper, the intentions of the colonialists seemed to have been, per Lord Passfield, that of protecting and advancing the native race of Northern Rhodesia. This was alleged to be the guiding principle for Britain's quest for colonies. However, the actual motive for the colonization of Africa was spelled out by the Berlin Act, *viz*, the acquisition of territories for raw material and cheap labor. Northern Rhodesia was, therefore, not regarded as a trust on behalf of the Africans. It was, rather, to be owned, with everything in it, as a possession.

After World War II, the British Empire was internally weakened in power, though in size it remained largely expansive. This internal weakness of the empire meant that Britain's interest in overseas territorial management was shifting towards that of reduction in investment. This move did not match the increasing interest of the colonial settlers who wanted more ascendancy and territorial dominance in Northern Rhodesia.

The 1953 imposition of the Central African Federation on the Africans was seen by the settlers to be an attempt at consolidating territorial supremacy in Africa. But the colonial administration in Britain saw this as the last attempt at salvaging the weakening empire's influence in Central Africa and possibly as step one in the preparation of the Africans for self-rule in an unforeseeable future. By 1955, London was no longer averse to granting the Africans political independence, a decision categorically resisted by the settlers from the beginning.

The colonial settlers understood that in granting or preparing the Africans for self-rule, the settlers were expending themselves. The preparation of the Africans for independence, though a topic of heated discussion towards the end of the Federation, was only remotely countenanced as a possible undertaking in a foreseeable future. The Africans sensing this naïvety, and encouraged by the exposure to information regarding Britain's vulnerability after World War II, pressed and demanded for self-rule.

When the Africans began in earnest to demand for self-rule in Northern Rhodesia, Britain's response was that the Africans were not prepared for it. The question remains: Who was to determine whether the Africans were well- or ill-prepared for independence? By what criteria and in whose interest, was the preparation supposed to be undertaken? In the following pages this argument is further explored.

§7.4 Theoretical Basis

Then as now, human beings have dominated one another by popular beliefs.[481] The conception of the notion of power and its origin, has given rise to theorization which in turn has occupied the human quest for domination. Europe, flanked by populist theories, banked on the postulations of the time to engineer empires and deduce guiding principles of domination.

In *The Republic*, Plato (427 – 347 B.C.) argues that human beings are by nature free and that a true democratic society hinges on liberty: "Liberty, I said. This is what you would hear in a democracy is its finest possession and that this is the reason it is the only *city* worth living in for a man who is *by nature free*."[482] Plato, father of classical political thought, makes argument that a city[483] in which liberty thrives is a democratic polity. By extension, Plato posits that a people under foreign domination are not free even if they may have their basic needs met by a foreign regime.

---

[481] See §5.4
[482] Jene M. Porter, ed., *Classics in Political Philosophy* (Scarborough: Prentice Hall Canada Inc., 2000), p. 84
[483] The idea of a city or *polis* was first canvassed by Plato and later Aristotle to be the basic building block of public political administration. The term politics is itself derived from *polis* or city.

For Aristotle (384 – 322 B.C), all human beings are capable of politics. In *The Politics,* he argues that humans are political animals: "From these things it is evident, then, that the city belongs among the things that exist by nature, and that *man is by nature a political animal.*"[484] Aristotle argues, in essence, that all societies are capable of political association. It is not what others impose on them. It has been established by divine providence and it is natural to them. Thus, the domination of one people by another, in Aristotelian thesis, is construed as oppressive and unnatural.

In *The City of God*, St. Augustine (A.D 354 – 430) argues that for a Republic to be properly defined, both the well-being of the people and their rights are to be taken into consideration: "A Republic, i.e. the affair of a people, exists when a people is governed well and justly."[485] First, St. Augustine defines a Republic as the "affair of a people." By a *people* he means a free, rational and dignified people. Second, in defining a Republic as comprising a free and rational people, St. Augustine advances a view that justice in ruler-ship is an integral part of political administration. Thus, where a people's well-being is neglected, and where injustices prevail, such a people are not, in St. Augustine's conception of a Republic, free.

St. Thomas Aquinas (1224 – 1274) in *Summa Theologica* advocates for the active resistance of a tyrannical government wherever it may exist: "A tyrannical government is not just, because it is directed, not to the *common good,* but to the *private good* of the ruler. Consequently, there is no sedition in disturbing a government of this kind, unless indeed the tyrant's rule is disturbed so inordinately, that his subjects suffer greater harm from the consequent disturbance than from the tyrant's government."[486] Aquinas justifies resisting a tyrannical

---

[484] Porter, *supra.,* p. 122
[485] *Ibid.,* p. 180
[486] *Ibid.,* pp. 220-221

government on two bases. First, when the rulers disregard the common good for their own private good. Second, when such resistance would not disturb public peace and subject the citizens to harsher consequences than the absence of such actions would portend. Per Aquinas, a government which does not look to the interest of the people must be resisted.

In *The Prince*, Niccolo Machiavelli (1469 – 1527) postulates that freedom is easily maintained through the means of its own people: "A city used to living in freedom is more easily maintained through the means of its own citizens than in any other way, if you decide to preserve it."[487] According to Machiavelli, to preserve freedom in a city, or a *polis*, or a political organization, the citizens of that polity must rule, and not "any other way." Thus, foreign domination, even in the Machiavellian conception, was incongruent to freedom.

Thomas Hobbes (1588 – 1679) distinguishes between what he calls a commonwealth by institution and a commonwealth by acquisition.[488] In *The Leviathan*, he speaks of the sovereign, subjects and sovereign power in this fashion:

> The attainment of this sovereign power is by two ways. One, by natural forces; as when a man maketh his children, to submit themselves, and their children to his government, as being able to destroy them if they refuse; or by war subdueth his enemies to his will, giving them their lives on that condition. The other is when men agree among themselves, to submit to some man, or assembly of men, voluntarily, on confidence to be protected by him against all others. This latter, may be called a political commonwealth, or commonwealth by institution and the former, a commonwealth by acquisition.[489]

---

[487] *Ibid.,* p. 226
[488] Hobbes' articulation on sovereignty is akin to two competing schools of thought on the origins of the state, the *Integrative* and the *Conflict*, illustrated by Hobbes' commonwealth by *institution* and *acquisition*, respectively. See also §28.4
[489] *Ibid.,* p. 302

The Hobbesian political thesis does not fit in the case of Northern Rhodesia as has been demonstrated in this book. The colonization of Northern Rhodesia was neither by commonwealth by institution nor commonwealth by acquisition. It was, as I prefer to call it, commonwealth by trickery. Therefore, the Hobbesian twelve-point[490] thesis does not apply to the situation under investigation. Hobbe's twelve points, though, apply in the context of a political commonwealth secured by the consent of the governed, and sanctioned by a constitution enacted by the will of the majority.

The greatest contribution of Hobbes to the concept of domination is in his definition of freedom. To Hobbes, to be free means that people are able to exercise their will, whenever their strength and intelligence can determine to do or not to do of what they are able to: "A freeman, is he that in those things, which by his strength and wit he is able to do, is not hindered to do what

---

[490] Hobbes postulates that where consent of the governed is, in fact, acquired the following twelve points applies: (1) the subjects cannot change the form of government; (2) sovereign power cannot be forfeited; (3) no man can without injustice protest against the institution of the sovereign declared by the major part [majority]; (4) the sovereign's actions cannot be justly accused by the subject; (5) whatsoever the sovereign doeth is unpunishable by the subject [the doctrine which supports the immunity provision of Heads of State for what they do while serving in official capacity]; (6) the sovereign is judge of what is necessary for the peace and defence of his subjects; (7) the right of making rules; whereby the subjects may every man know what is so his own, as no other subject can without injustice make it for him; (8) the right to hear and decide all controversies belongeth to the judicature; (9) the right of making peace and war with other commonwealths belongeth to the sovereignty; (10) the right of choosing all counsellors and ministers belongeth to the sovereignty; (11) the right of rewarding with riches, honor, etc., and punishing with corporal or pecuniary punishment or with ignominy, arbitrarily, belongeth to the sovereignty; and (12) to the sovereign belongeth the right to give titles of honor, and to appoint what order of place, and dignity, each man shall hold, and what signs of respects, in public or private meetings, they shall give to one another (Porter, *ibid.*, pp. 303-308)

he has the will to."[491] Thus, the domination of a people against their own free will, constitutes bondage, and is objectionable to the idea of freedom.

John Locke (1632 – 1704) writing in *The Second Treatise of Government* makes a conjecture that human beings are by nature free, equal and independent: "Men being, as has been said, by Nature, all free, equal and independent, no one can be put out of his estate, and subjected to the political power of another, without his own consent."[492] Locke was a privileged son of Puritan lawyer and he wrote his second treatise to justify the right of the English people to change governments. His thesis is in direct contention against the principle of colonialism. Locke argues that, "No one can be put out of his estate," by another power and "subjected to the political power of another, without his own consent." Not even the philosophies of one of Britain's most darling thinkers could dissuade the English from putting out the Africans from their estates and be subjected to slavery and unequal treatment.

A philosopher better suited to explore the topic under discourse is, in the judgment of this author, Jean-Jacques Rousseau (1712 – 1778). Rousseau was no admirer of Hobbes and he differs exponentially on all fundamental basis of human nature, except on freedom. In *Second Treatise* on human nature Rousseau writes, "Let us not conclude with Hobbes that because man has no idea of goodness he is naturally evil.... He [Hobbes] says precisely the opposite, because of having improperly included in the savage man's care of self-preservation the need to satisfy a multitude of passions which are the produce of society and which have made laws necessary."[493] Then Rousseau charges that, "Man is weak when he is dependent, and he is emancipated before he is robust."[494]

---

[491] *Ibid.,* p. 309
[492] *Ibid.,* p. 352
[493] *Ibid.,* p. 386
[494] *Ibid.*

To Rousseau, any form of oppression, whether through colonialism or slavery, weakens a people for it keeps them dependent on the goodwill of the master. Thus, foreign domination of one nation against the other, wounds the national spirit of the dominated. Freedom, for Rousseau, is the fertilizer that enriches the national spirit and causes a people to blossom.

Georg Wilhelm Friedrich Hegel (1770 – 1831)[495] speculates in *The Philosophy of Right* that individuals have a subjective right to be free or independent. He further theorizes that to be convinced that a people are free, an objective ethical order or a state of independence must be achieved. Thus, "The right of individuals to be subjectively destined to freedom is fulfilled when they belong to an actual ethical order [a state of independence], because their conviction of their freedom finds its truth in such an objective order, and it is an ethical order that they are actually in possession of their own essence or their own inner universality."[496] Therefore, a people may be well-provided for, cared for and given to acceptable economic conditions, but without being fully independent, they would be subjectively unfulfilled.

John Stuart Mills (1806 – 1873) makes a proposition that, "A people can only learn the art of governing by exercising it, and that it is preferable to make one's own mistakes than to be governed by others, even if the mistakes are thereby greater."[497] Mills postulates what was upheld by the Westphalia Conference in 1848 when major European powers jointly agreed to respect the sovereignty of nation-states. Arguments can be made that nation-states are a political entity and, therefore, by such virtue are deserving of national sovereignty.

---

[495] See also Georg Hagel in §5.4. Despite his postulation of "the right of individuals to be subjectively destined to freedom," he, however, did not consider Blacks as deserving of independence.

[496] *Ibid.*, p. 483

[497] Grant, *Zambia: Then and Now*, p. 134

However, a similar proposition should be extended to nations or peoples under foreign domination for, in the words of Hegel, they comprise a "subjective ethical order" until such a time when they attain to national independence and obtain an objective ethical order. In the state of subjective ethical order, a people are unfulfilled as a national entity. Independence completes the transition into what Hobbes calls a political commonwealth.

In *On Liberty*, Mills breaks down, in historical perspectives, the genesis of liberty and how it has evolved into a *landlord-tenant* relationship between the governors and the governed. Note especially his caveat on the dangers of domination by "oppressive" powers which the dominating power may use as a "weapon" against the subjects:

> The struggle between liberty and authority is the most conspicuous feature in the portions of history with which we are earliest familiar, particularly in that of Greece, Rome, and England. By liberty, was meant protection against the tyranny of the political rulers. The rulers were conceived as an unnecessary antagonistic position to the people whom they ruled. They consisted of the governing *One, or a governing tribe or caste*, who derived their authority from *inheritance or conquest*, who, at all events, did not hold it at the pleasure of the governed, and whose supremacy men did not venture, perhaps did not desire, to *contest*, whatever precautions might be taken against its oppressive exercise.
>
> Their power was regarded as necessary, but also as highly dangerous; as a *weapon,* which they would attempt to use against their subjects, no less than against external enemies. The aim, therefore, of patriots was to set limits to the power which the ruler should be suffered to exercise over the community; and this limitation was what they meant by liberty.
>
> It was attempted in two ways. First, by obtaining recognition of certain immunities, called political liberties or rights, which it was to be regarded as a breach of duty in the ruler to infringe, and which if he did infringe, specific resistance, or general rebellion was held to be justified. A second, and generally a later expedient, was the establishment of constitutional checks, by which the consent of the community, or of a body of some sort, supposed to represent its interests, was made a necessary condition to some of the more important acts of the governing power.

Charles Mwewa

> It appeared to [the people] much better that the various magistrates of the state should be their *tenants* or delegates, revocable at their pleasure. In that way alone, it seemed, could they have complete security that the powers of government would never be abused to their disadvantage. By degrees this new demand for elective and temporary rulers became the prominent object of the exertions of the popular party.[498]

The passage above is chosen for two reasons. First, it is to brainstorm on the political culture prevalent during Britain's colonial rule in Africa. As Mills as duly placed it, there were two approaches to domination and government going on at the time or previously before, one on another, and yet side by side. On one hand, was "One, or a governing tribe" in the form of a monarchy which derived its authority from "inheritance" superimposed by a toothless Parliament.

On the other hand, the governing tribe exercised so strong the power that it became a dangerous "weapon which [it] would attempt to use against [its] subjects, no less than against external enemies." Theoretically, per Mills, the British sovereign exercised such authority and power on its own subjects as was tyrannical and vexatious. Everyone served one tribe, the queen's tribe, and all Britons were subjects of one tribe, the monarchy.

By extension, the tribe which exercised such authority on its own subjects, "no less than against its external enemies," was the same tribe now dominating a faraway territory so-called Northern Rhodesia. The Africans in Northern Rhodesia, especially under the Company and Federal states, respectively, were less than British subjects; they were cheap laborers, maids and servants.

Second, it is to delineate the assumption often made by former colonial masters that independence may be undesirable by a people who wish to be brought under the dominion of another. Per Mills, mankind has graduated from being "content to combat

---

[498] Porter, *supra.*, pp. 505-6

one enemy by another, and to be ruled by a master," to regarding the rulers as "tenants or delegates, revocable at [the people's] pleasure." This liberal principle does not only apply to free and democratic social order, it also concurs with the spirit that moralizes the acquirement of independence.

Mankind has moved from being controlled to deciding its destiny, and it does not matter whether in doing so mankind makes greater mistakes. Friedrich Nietzsche (1804 – 1900) has advanced a moral and ethical thesis why a people should not only seek for political independence, but must "attack" to acquire it.

In the *Will to Power*, Nietzsche advances a hypothesis that power, whose impulse he calls freedom, is humankind's fundamental wish. However, Nietzsche sees power not as an end but as means to an end. The end is charity. But a people must first acquire freedom which power brings before they can be a just order, which itself is in transit to the highest order of charity.

Nietzsche puts forward a proposition that people seek power for three reasons: For the sake of the happiness it brings; for ambition; and for independence.[499] The third reason applies to the subject matter under investigation. But Nietzsche makes a clear distinction between the *will to power* and the *lust of power*, the latter, he posits, is decadent and akin to colonization.[500] To Nietzsche, the will to power is positive power and "the highest form of individual freedom, of sovereignty."[501]

Thus, for the oppressed and those in slavery conditions including nations under foreign domination, the will to freedom is the first step to attaining a state of just and charitable society. A people, therefore, must be free from domination to free their spirit towards innovation, creativity and actualization. Political independence is not a gamble or a prerogative of the governors or a debatable issue, it must be acquired at all cost – and there is no right or wrong timing to it – because it is the first step in the progression from *freedom* to *justice* and to *charity*, in that order.

---

[499] *Ibid.,* p. 649
[500] *Ibid.*
[501] *Ibid.,* p. 651

§7.5 Independence Inevitability

As shown above, independence like freedom is a people's right. A people under bondage do not need to wait another minute to obtain independence. A master-slave relationship is based on power-imbalance. The stronger loads over the weaker and is reluctant to part away with power. In this regard alone, people in bondage need not wait another day to acquire political independence.

In his book, *Zambia, Then and Now,* a former colonial *Bwana* to Northern Rhodesia muses: "Many have argued, particularly in the light of subsequent *events,* that the Africans were not ready for *self-rule* and should not have been granted it in 1964 for that reason."[502] There are fundamental difficulties with this assertion. Reasons will be proffered to the contrary in the following pages.

As theorized above, independence is necessary if a people should begin to actualize themselves and make progress from bondage to freedom to a just society to the love for the brotherhood. And as argued by Mills, a people can only learn the art of governing, in part, by exercising it, and that it is preferable to make one's own mistakes than to be governed by others, even if the mistakes are thereby greater. The Africans, however, did not need to learn the "art of governing," for they had been governing themselves way before the arrival of the Europeans on the African continent.[503]

---

[502] Grant, *supra.,* p. 134

[503] To many, except as shown in this book, Zambia did not have a history before colonialism. In line with the principle of *terra nullius,* Europeans considered Africa not only an empty territory but a land without a history as well. It must, however, be stressed that Africa in general and Zambia had a history stretching as far back as the 4ᵗʰ Century.

The argument repeatedly made by European scholars and historians that Africans were devoid of political leadership, let alone self-government, is a misconstruction. This assertion is said to be justified based on "subsequent events" that followed independence. By subsequent events is mainly meant political and, to a lesser extent, business corruption. The struggle for independence was an ultimate price paid by those Africans who had "chosen to stand up and fight for the rights of all humanity in love, respect and peace."[504]

Certain records, in fact, indicate that the Africans were extremely competent and dependable. The irony is that it was the ingenuity of the Africans that not only established but also sustained colonialism. The Europeans, who were strangers to the natural environs of Africa, both depended on the Africans and used the resourcefulness of the Africans to manage the African countryside. A poem that appeared in the *Northern Rhodesia Journal*[505] better illustrates this weathered ingenuity of the Africans:

> On Luapula's banks by rock and pool
> *Bwana* Kijana exercises rule
> Around his *boma* turmoil ceases not,
> Belgians intrigue and missionaries plot,
> Witchdoctors brew decorations to destroy him
> But all these things are powerless to annoy him.
> Unmoved, undaunted, undismayed he still
> Will not bend or break to their iron will.
>
> On Luapula is much zeal administrative
> I should like to be a native
> On Luapula where Harrington is ruler,
> Where the revenue is full and always
>   Growing fuller,
> Where the rubber and the pine tree grow.
> Oh, I wish I was a Negro

---

[504] Kornerstone Kreation, "Marley Tribute: A Tribute to Jah Rastafarai Chosen Child [Bob] Robert Nesta Marley," 1981
[505] H. T. Harrington, "The Taming of North-Eastern Rhodesia," (1954) *Northern Rhodesia Journal*, Vol. 2, No. 3

> For the revenue is bigger
> And always growing bigger
> Oh, what luck to be a Nigger
> On the Luapula where Harrington is ruler[506]

Thus, the Africans did not only provide the wisdom and know-how with which to manipulate the great African continent, their ingenuity was also evident to their colonial masters. The poem is very informing of the abundance of both human and natural capacity that the colonizers found in Zambia. Harrington refers to the *Bwana* exercising rule in Luapula area "Where the revenue is full and always growing fuller." He regrets that someday he would leave Zambia and the Africans would enjoy the bounty that Luapula offered: "Oh, I wish I was a Negro/For the revenue is bigger and always growing bigger/Oh, what luck to be a Nigger." By independence, the likes of Harrington had, unfortunately, plundered so much of the resources of Zambia that just after ten years of independence Zambians would begin to feel the pangs.

In Chapter Eight, the Second Republic is discussed.[507] Most of the foundational problems of pre-independent Zambia grew wings and began to fly in the Second Republic. The irony is, the very architects of the Zambian independence became also the heroes and villains of the newly-found freedom.

---

[506] *Ibid.*, p. 20

[507] No single chapter has been devoted to the discussion on the First Republic (1964 – 1972); rather, events and issues of the First Republic have been fused into the rest of the book. In Chapter Eight, it will be shown that soon after Zambia's independence, Kaunda moved systematically to eliminate the opposition and turn the country into a One-Party State, something that had become fashionable in Africa between the 1960s and 1980s.

8| The Second Republic

He rose up like a bright and morning star
A man shaped by many tribulations
He whimpered thither and tither but got far
Father to a people he barely won
Son of heroes, leader of two nations
Call him a Zambian, tactics lacked he none

Chapter Focus

At the end of reading this chapter, you should be able to:

- Understand that Zambia began on a multiparty trajectory
- Identify the Second Republic as the gravest detour in Zambia's democratic quest
- Ascertain that Kenneth Kaunda's silencing of vital opposition in banning Simon Kapwepwe's UPP was step one in declaring a One-Party State
- Explain what and why the Africans desired political independence

BRIEF INTRODUCTION

This chapter discusses the Second Republic and the reign and downfall of President Kaunda. Of interest is the institution of the One-Party State in Zambia which many have considered the greatest detour in Zambia's democratic quest.

Charles Mwewa

§8.1 Critical Themes

There are two themes emphasized in this chapter: Breaking the heart of oppression in Zambia and redirecting the soul of the nation on a full democratic trajectory. This is what is conceived to be the steepest detour in Zambia's democratic quest. This author will borrow significantly from the analysis of the Second Republic from Hamalengwa's 1992 work.[508] In this author's view, Hamalengwa's work proffers the most comprehensive review of the Second Republic.

The Second Republic is generally the period between 1972 and 1991. Zambia became a multiparty democratic Republic in 1964. With several parties[509] involved in the political process, Zambia was on its path to full democratic development. During the period from Zambia's independence to 1972, also referred to as the First Republic, Zambia's young democracy thrived with notable economic prosperity in many respects. It was only a matter of time before the magma of economic troubles would begin to erupt, mainly owing to depleted resources sanctioned by the Federation, and because of the policies espoused by the UNIP government after 1969.

§8.2 Undemocratic Tendencies

The Second Republic was necessitated by two major developments, both in the ruling party, UNIP, and in the country. First, it was the results of the 1967 elections for the members of

---

[508] Hamalengwa, *Class Struggles in Zambia 1889-1989 & The Fall of Kenneth Kaunda 1990-1991* (New York: University Press of America, 1992), especially Chapter 10 from page 135 to page 151.
[509] Including the NPP, a defunct of Sir Roy Welensky's UFP; ANC; and Hugh Mitcheley, an MP from Gwembe North who stood as an independent after ditching ANC!

UNIP's Central Committee. This was the first post-independence election in Zambia. It would go to test whether Kaunda was to remain the true hero of Zambia's independence and if he would kvetch under the puncture of "Absolute power corrupts absolutely."[510] Per Hamalengwa, "Posts in the [Central] Committee were crucial and those who held them wielded tremendous power and influence over the decision-making process which allocated scarce resources to regions, communities and individuals in Zambia."[511]

However, elections in the Central Committee were held on tribal lines, creating very stiff competition among the party faithful. Kaunda and UNIP had learned a lesson a year earlier when the United Party (UP) was formed by break away dissidents in UNIP. Per Hamalengwa, "The UP was a product of the growing disenchantment and relative deprivation felt by many political leaders of Lozi origin within UNIP over what they regarded as the neglect of Barotseland (now Western Province) in terms of system distributive outputs and in view of what they regarded as Bemba dominance of the party."[512] In other words, things in UNIP were not as palatable as Kaunda had envisioned. His own cling to power was endangered. Multiparty politics was proving to be a threat to Kaunda's continuation as president.

The above recitation warrants a brief review. Most leaders begin on a path of democracy until power gets to their heads. This was the case with Kaunda. What these leaders forget is that democracy is predicated upon competition. Democratic leadership is earned and not coerced upon the people. A leader who delivers in terms of economic growth may win majority support, while the one who fails to deliver stands to be booted out of office in an election. Kaunda understood perfectly well that the continued wrangles in UNIP over territorial supremacy

---

[510] John Emerich Edward Dalberg Acton, first Baron Acton (1834–1902)

[511] Hamalengwa1992, *supra.*, p. 137

[512] *Ibid.*, also see §5.13 and note specifically the rise of a group calling itself the Barotseland Freedom Movement (BFM).

portended a loss of grip on power. Moreover, Kaunda knew this when he movingly stated at a General Conference in 1967:[513]

We have canvassed so strongly and indeed, viciously, along tribal, racial and provincial lines, that one wonders whether we really have national or tribal and provincial leadership. I must admit publicly that I have never experienced in the life of this young nation, such a spate of hate, based entirely on tribe, province, race, color and religion, which is a negation of all that we stand for in this Party and Government. I do not think that we can blame the common man for this. The fault is ours fellow leaders – we, the people here assembled.[514]

Second, UNIP was in danger of defeat in the 1970 election especially following the resignation of UNIP's second highest ranking officer, Vice-president Kapwepwe. Kapwepwe's formation of the United Progressive Party (UPP) in 1972 gave Kaunda the most terrifying opposition, and by extension, a stiff competitor in the 1970 general elections. Kaunda understood this as well. However, Kaunda was ill-wired to withstand competition then.

To offset this weakness, he would resort to demagoguism, including the use of the very laws of the land to enslave people and curb rivalry. Kapwepwe's UPP, whose "constituency was based on the Copperbelt and in Northern Province quickly gathered support from some key members from UNIP, the Copperbelt, Northern and elsewhere. [Disgruntled] members of [the party were] also defecting from UNIP. There was a likely coalition with the ANC. And elections were just around the

[513] The General Conference was UNIP's highest governing body which also elected the UNIP president and 20 members of the Central Committee. Just below the General Assembly was the National Council which was the policy-making body of UNIP and met twice every year.
[514] Zambia Information Services, *Mulungushi Conference – Proceedings of the Annual General Conference of the United National Independence Party* held at Mulungushi 14th - 20th August, 1967, as quoted in Hamalengwa 1992, *supra.*, p.137

corner in 1972. It was clear UNIP was in trouble and something had to be done or it would go down in defeat."[515] Consequently, Kaunda and UNIP accused Kapwepwe and UPP of threatening public security, detained[516] Kapwepwe and banned UPP.

The detaining of Kapwepwe and the banning of his UPP was a deep blow to multiparty democracy in Zambia. By eliminating tangible opponents, Kaunda was slowly moving towards a One-Party State, a state in which there would be no competition, and a state in which Kaunda would be the sole candidate in an election. To do so, he had to look for a plausible justification.

§8.3 Which People?

Not surprisingly, Kaunda found ample justification among the very people he deemed to represent; the people of Zambia. It is

---

[515] Hamalengwa 1992, *ibid.*, p.138

[516] Hamalengwa gives a succinct review of the law of detention in Zambia from page 146 of his book *Class Struggles in Zambia 1889-1989 & The Fall of Kenneth Kaunda 1990-1991*: By Ordinance No. 5 of 1960, the Legislative Council of Northern Rhodesia enacted the Preservation of Public Security Ordinance, which empowered the Governor to detain people, or require people to do work or render services. On July 28th, 1964, Government Notice No. 376 proclaimed Ordinance No. 5 into force. On the same date, the Governor by Government Notice No. 377 amended the Preservation of Security Regulations by introducing Regulation 31A which gave the Governor more powers. For example, under Regulation 31A, the Governor could exercise control over any person and directing that such a person be arrested and detained. It was these powers which were immediately used to quash the Lumpa Uprisings in the northern parts of Zambia. Ironically, upon independence on October 24th, 1964, the new law, the *Zambia Independence Act*, 1964, in ss. 2(1) and 4(1) provided for the continuation of all former laws and ordinances. This meant that the emergency declaration of July 28th, 1964 continued even after independence, subject to extension *actioned* by a resolution passed by the National Assembly in blocks of six months' renewals. *The Constitution (Amendment) (No. 5) Act* of 1969 in s. 8 made the emergency declaration permanent. Thus, Kaunda and UNIP perpetuated the same repressive laws they fought hard to get rid of in their struggles for independence against the colonial regime.

argued that democracy is the rule of the people, by the people, for the people.[517] There are three "people" involved in this definition and each of those "people" mean differently to different constituencies. Traditionally, the rule "of the people" has always been interpreted to mean that the people of Zambia have the right to rule their own country. However, the people who rule are politicians, thus, the rule "of the people." "By the people" means those who have found entrance into political power, the political elites, like those in the ruling party. And "for the people," which "people" here mean the same as punching bags.

Kapalaula asks, "Which people?"[518] The way in which people are perceived to participate in the governance of their country is redundant. Democracy is not the best form of government; it is only the least evil of all forms of government. Democracy tends to pay only lip-service to the participation of the people in governance. The opinion of one single person, usually the Head of State, may be enshrined in political jargons and interpreted as the will of the majority. Kaunda's One-Party State is a good example.

Moreover, the people who legislate and suppose to make decisions for the people may be completely out of touch with the general populous. Yet, whenever they make decisions, they consider them the will of the people. This is attributed to the representative nature of constitutional democracy. Arguably, rule by referenda comes much closer to representing the will of the people. But the task is daunting, the exercise time-consuming and the undertaking very expensive.

Weak as democracy may be, One-Party rule is the weakest of them all. Whereas in representative or plural politics the people

---

[517] The term "democracy" comes from the Greek: δημοκρατία – (dēmokratía) "rule of the people" coined from δῆμος (dêmos) "people" and κράτος (Kratos) "power." Democracy literally means people power!
[518] Mwamba Kapalaula, "Constitutional Impasse," *The Post*, (May 10th, 2008)

may have a chance to elect people who hold different views from the ruling elites, in a One-Party regime, only the will of the president prevails. Thus, by its nature, a One-Party State is a form of dictatorship, albeit a *Tyranny of the Majority*. This happens because instead of one all-powerful leader making all the decisions in a typical dictatorship, in a One-Party regime, the elected majority, who only represents one political view, and by extension that of the leader, makes all the decisions for a diverse nation.

The greatest threat to dictatorial establishments is the people.[519] However, the people must be organized politically and constitutionally to exert their power against a dictatorial regime.[520] People can wield tremendous power over an elitist political regime only if they are unified as a "general countrywide voice, since it is more resistant to political upheavals and reversals and difficult to manipulate."[521]

The political elites use people in more less like the boxer would use a punching bag. While the punching bag makes a boxer, it is disregarded until the next boxing match. When facing a next bout, a boxer would again think of the punching bag. In other words, the punching bag, as too is its sister the boxing gloves, is only a means to the boxer's end, the end to which the boxer only will benefit.[522]

---

[519] This was demonstrated by the people of Egypt in what came to be known as *Match of a Million* in February 2011. Mubarak, who had held power for 30 years, was forced to negotiate with the Muslim Brotherhood, a thing he would never have contemplated before the people rose up against his dictatorial regime. See *The National Post* (Canada), "I am a Survivor," Tuesday, 8th, 2011, p. A16

[520] The pro-democracy revolutions in Tunisia, Egypt, Libya, Morocco, Yemen, Bahrain, and generally in North Africa and the Mid-East in the first quarter of 2011 illustrate what the people can do if they are organised as one voice against dictatorial regimes.

[521] Kapalaula, *supra*.

[522] Caroline Katotobwe defines the people as "anyone and everyone, regardless of their position in society" in a *Post* article of November 18th, 2005 titled, "Democratic Rule."

Charles Mwewa

In Zambia, historically, the people, sadly, have both made and unmade its autocrats. The example of Kaunda regime informs of this tendency. It has been argued that the penchant of the Zambian society to hero-worship its presidents, created, in the case of Kaunda, "an autocrat out of a democrat."[523] Initially, Kaunda was elected on the platform of unity under UNIP,[524] which itself, like the MMD, emerged as a crisis party from an amalgamation of the UFP and African National Independence Party (ANIP). UNIP's first president, Dixon Konkola, was suspended within weeks and replaced by Paul Kalichini. Shortly after, Kalichini was also replaced by Mainza Chona who had just left ANC. Elsewhere it is mentioned that Chona, in principle, handed the presidency of UNIP over to Kaunda because as Mwaanga observes, Chona, did not feel he possessed the necessary qualities to lead an independence movement.[525] On January 31st, 1960, Kaunda was elected UNIP's national president.

---

[523] Bizeck J. Phiri, "Colonial Legacy and the Role of Society in the Creation and Demise of Autocracy in Zambia, 1964-1991," (2001) *Nordic Journal of African Studies* 10(2), p. 241

[524] Kaunda was naturally seen to be a unifier owing to his Malawian parentage. He was used to be an agent for quailing anti-tribal sentiments (see Makasa, Zambia's march to Political Freedom, p. 94). Accelerated by the ideology of togetherness, which was propounded by Harry Nkumbula, and backed by Sikota Wina in his letter to Nkumbula of October 20th, 1963 (see Keesing's *Contemporary Achieves 1963-64*, p. 19889), Kaunda harnessed the spirit of nationalism by appealing to unity. However, as discussed in this book, Kaunda would later in the name of unity engineer what he termed a One-Party Participatory Democracy. Historical evidence suggests that Kaunda did not prefer a One-Party State to multiparty because he deemed it a unifying mechanism, but because of "UNIP's failure to capture four seats in the Southern Province by-elections in 1968 (see T. Rasmussen, "Political Competition and One-Party Dominance in Zambia," (1983) *Journal of Modern African Studies,* Vol. 7, No. 3, pp. 410-411).

[525] See Mwaanga, *Looking back: An Extraordinary Life*, p. 13

204

§8.4 One-Party Dictatorship

Per Phiri, "The One-Party State system of government in post-independence Zambia, and indeed elsewhere, was perceived as a form of dictatorship."[526] In his book, *Memoirs of Alexander Grey Zulu*, Zulu explains why he chooses to discuss the subject of the One-Party State. He states, "I am doing this for posterity...so that they are able to know and understand the circumstances under which the One-Party Participatory Democracy was established as well as the reason why such a system existed for 17 years."[527] Zulu is convinced that the creation of the One-Party State was necessary to quail disturbances in the nation and to augment the spoils of independence into a united nation. Unity and peace are, thus, advanced as the basis for the decision.

To Kaunda, similarly, the One-Party State was the people's idea. He considered the popularity of UNIP and its electoral success as a sign of the people's desire to return UNIP as the sole political party in Zambia. He categorically stated this in a speech at Mulungushi Rock of Authority in Kabwe on August 15th, 1967:

> If what has been happening at both the parliamentary and local government levels is anything to go by, we are obviously very *close to the attainment of the One-Party State*...being honest to the cause of the *common man* we would, through effective Party and government organizations, *paralyze and wipe out any opposition* thereby bringing about the birth of a One-Party State.... We go further and declare that even when this comes about we would *not legislate against the formation of opposition parties* because we might be bottling the feelings of certain people no matter how few...I repeat, One-Party State is coming to Zambia because the *masses of our people recognize that we are sincere and true to each one of them*.... The masses of our people trust us because we have said that the One-Party State was going to come about as a result of

---

[526] Bizeck J. Phiri, *supra.*, p. 225
[527] Zulu, *Memoirs of Alexander Grey Zulu*, p. 428

the people voting for the party freely for a people's democracy and this has continued to be our guideline (emphasis added).[528]

This statement by the Zambian Head of State in 1967, in principle, ushered in a One-Party State in Zambia. For all those who still doubt the pre-meditative nature of the creation of the One-Party State, this statement offers irrefutable evidence. All the justifications for the creation of the One-Party State ought to be investigated. In fact, Grotpeter has considered the emergence of the One-Party State in Zambia, "admittedly gentler, under Kenneth Kaunda, than in other African states,"[529] as a false start.[530]

First, Kaunda and, indeed, other senior UNIP officials, claimed that what was happening at both the parliamentary and local government levels were an indication that Zambia was ripe to ditch multiparty democracy in preference for a One-Party State. Certainly, UNIP had a good share of electoral success from 1964 to 1967. However, as pointed out above, and Kaunda knew this, the posts were shifting very fast. UNIP was no longer enjoying overwhelming support at provincial levels. Besides, the continued factions and sectarianism in UNIP portended defeat for that party in the coming elections. All Kaunda wanted was to move fast to avoid electoral defeat which he foresaw was imminent. In a way, tribalism played a part but it was only a scapegoat: "The inauguration of a One-Party (UNIP) State by Kaunda in 1972 was made to arrest the trends perceived towards ethnic and provincial parochialism."[531]

Second, Kaunda attributed the urgency of a One-Party State to the common man. This is the best case illustrating how politicians may use the common person as a punching bag to

---

[528] Zambia Information Services, *supra.*

[529] Grotpeter *et. al., Historical Dictionary of Zambia, Second Edition*, p. xi

[530] *Ibid.*

[531] World Socialist Movement, "Zambia's Tribalist Politics," (August 13th, 2006)

achieve their hidden *agendas*. The composition of the Chona Commission (the Commission) itself leaves much to be desired. Initially, the Commission comprised 19 people[532] under the chairmanship of Mainza Chona and deputized by Humphrey Mulemba.[533] In considering the composition of the Commission one thing that strikes out is that from the first glance it might have looked like a true reflection of the diversity of the Zambian society. But it was not. Apart from Harry Nkumbula and Nalumino Mundia, who also "declined to sit on the Commission,"[534] the Commission was only left with UNIP loyalists and stooges.

Moreover, apart from the composition of the Commission which inherently favored UNIP, when the so-called common man was consulted to submit their views of the One-Party State through the Chona Commission, most of their recommendations were rejected through a White Paper. For example, the Commission discussed the need for a "Preamble to the proposed constitution of a One-Party Participatory Democracy which would among other things, reflect the sentiments of the people of Zambia."[535] The White Paper naively accepted this, but then diluted it by incorporating Kaunda's ideology of Humanism.

Per Hamalengwa, "Incorporating [Humanism] in the preamble – the aim here was to legalize President Kaunda's thoughts and prescriptions for Zambia and to institutionalize

---

[532] This number was reduced to 17 when Harry Nkumbula and Nalumino Mundia refused to sit on the Commission.

[533] At the time Mainza Chona was Zambian Vice-president and Humphrey Mulemba was Minister of Mines. Other members were: Clement Mwananshiku (Minister of State); Daniel Lisulo (MCC); Frank Chitambala (MCC); Timothy Kandeke (District Governor - ANC); Lavu Mulimba (Business & Industry); David Phiri (Anglo-American); Daniel Katungu (Defence Force); Benjamin Mibenge (UNZA); Kasuka Mutukwa (UNZA); Elijah Mutale (Luapula); Rev. J. Mwape (UCZ); Valerian Lavu (PS – Education); Lily Monze (House of Chiefs); Chief Undi (President – House of Chiefs); Chief Chikumbi (VP – House of Chiefs); Harry Nkumbula (President – ANC); and Nalumino Mundia (VP – ANC).

[534] Zulu, *supra.*, p. 428

[535] Hamalengwa, 1992, *supra.*, p. 139

Humanism as the official ideology of the new system and a guiding campus of all the people as a whole."[536] This, in earnest, was not what the common person wanted; it was what Kaunda and UNIP wanted. The government was playing a perception game; to make it look like the people were involved from start to finish when the entire process was doctored to produce a pre-meditated result.

Third, Kaunda clearly intended to paralyze and wipe out any opposition thereby bringing about the birth of a One-Party State. It is important to note that this statement was made in August 1967, by 1972, Kapwepwe was detained and his party banned. Obviously, this was not a coincidence. Kaunda was the architect of the One-Party State, and not the common person as he alleged. In fact, Kaunda and UNIP had declared Zambia a presidential One-Party system, neither in 1973 when the 1964 constitution was replaced, nor on December 13th, 1972 using the government's White Paper. Zambia's One-Party State was sanctioned on January 22nd, 1968 when the National Assembly Speaker Robinson Nabulyato refused to recognize ANC as an official opposition in the National Assembly because, "It was too small a minority to constitute an official opposition."[537]

Phiri has observed that the decision not to accord ANC recognition as the official opposition had serious implications for the role of the opposition in both Parliament and the nation. He further observes that the decision ultimately destroyed the democratic process, since without an officially recognized opposition party Zambia had become a *de facto* One-Party State.[538]

---

[536] *Ibid.*
[537] Bizeck J. Phiri, "Colonial Legacy and the Role of Society in the Creation and Demise of Autocracy in Zambia, 1964-1991," (2001) *Nordic Journal of African Studies* 10 (2), p. 232
[538] *Ibid.*

Thus, the events of 1972 and 1973 were only a camouflage for concealing the real motive of the creation of a One-Party State. Article 4 of the 1973 *Zambian Constitution* put the nail in the coffin of plural democracy by stating that:

(1) There shall be one and only one political party organization in Zambia, namely, the United National Independence Party
(2) Nothing contained in this constitution shall be so construed as to entitle any person lawfully to form or attempt to form any political party or organizations other than the Party, or to belong, assemble or associate with or express opinion or do any other thing in sympathy with, such political party or organization.

In his keynote address to the General Conference in August 1967, Kaunda said, "We would not legislate against the formation of opposition parties because we might be bottling the feelings of certain people no matter how few." Of course, that was untrue, because within less than five years the constitution was amended and the sections above are a complete opposite of what Kaunda promised. Hamalengwa has observed that, "The beneficiary of the new system was obviously the president who was given wide powers."[539]

On the question of wide powers, Kaunda hijacked just everything that was required to maintain himself untouchable, powers that made him Zambia itself personified. First, Mwaanga admits that Kaunda had sweeping powers:[540]

---

[539] Hamalengwa, 1992, *supra.*, p. 144
[540] That historian and moralist, that first Baron Acton (1834–1902), otherwise known simply as Lord Acton or simply as John Emerich Edward Dalberg Acton, in an opinion letter to Bishop Mandell Creighton in 1887 aptly said: "Power tends to corrupt, and absolute power corrupts absolutely. Great men are almost always bad men." As if in concert with this historical salutation, that honorable English politician, namely, William Pitt, the Elder, that once Earl of Chatham and British Prime Minister from 1766 to 1778, also truthfully said in that august UK House of Lords in 1770, thus: "Unlimited power is apt to corrupt the minds of those who possess it."

> It is an indisputable fact that the Legislature has given the President of the Republic many powers. Indeed, having had a great deal of time during the past year to read various Acts of Parliament, I am frightened to discover just how much power the president enjoys. Even as a former Cabinet Minister and Member of the Central Committee, I am ashamed to admit that I had no idea quite how sweeping were these powers, with virtually no checks and balances. It is part of human nature to succumb to temptation, even the most just and greatest of men use and abuse this excessive power at some time or the other.[541]

On August 29th, 1985 Mwaanga was issued a Detention Order signed by President Kaunda on suspicion of using the illegal substance of Mandrax, and was subsequently detained under very despicable conditions until April 4th, 1986. Mwaanga made the statement above after going through a brutal detention at the mercy of the same president who had raised him for power and influence since the age of 21 years.

Mwaanga regrets, "At no time in my life prior to my detention did I ever think that I would sleep, eat and drink next to a filthy toilet located in the cell."[542] It is also important to note that what Mwaanga experienced in a period of close to ten months in detention is what a common person experiences daily for as long as earth can sustain them!

Mwaanga's story is a mind opener. His, is a critical look into the inside of a beast which swallows even those it purports to protect. If there is anything we learn from Mwaanga's two books, *An Extraordinary Life* and *The Other Society*, it is not about the "meteoric rise to positions of power, prestige and influence,"[543] or what the *Times* magazine cogitated as, "One of the eight African potential world leaders under the age of 40 years." [544] It

---

[541] Vernon J. Mwaanga, *The Other Society* (Lusaka: Fleetfoot Publishing Company, 1986), pp. 311-312.
[542] *Ibid*, p. 315
[543] *Ibid*, back cover story
[544] *Ibid.*

is rather, the ruthlessness, the unpredictability and even the disenchanted nature of African politics in general, and of Zambian politics. Mwaanga lets us see into the mind of Second Republic leaders in Zambia, but he also fundamentally unravels the best disclosure of the, sometimes, hypocrisy of Zambian political leaders, which if not corrected, may plunge the next generations of Zambian leaders into the same doldrums the predecessors fell.

The Other Society is a disclosure of the soul of many a Zambian politician, and heightens the need to reform the Zambian prisons and criminal justice systems. In discussing this aspect in Chapter 14, the testimony of three Zambians who suffered under the emergency regime of President Kaunda, *viz,* Munyonzwe Hamalengwa, VJ Mwaanga himself and Fostino Lombe, will be used.

Mwaanga had an attractive political upstart many of us can only dream possible. Ambassador to the Soviet Union at just 21 years of age and Permanent Secretary in the Office of the President at 22 years of age. The Permanent Secretary is a non-political civil service position. In other words, a Permanent Secretary is one of the highest non-political positions in the civil service. In principle, Mwaanga had a rare chance to see what goes on both in the inside of and outside of the political system.

Mwaanga's detention without trial reveals the dictatorial tendencies of President Kaunda, *viz*, that everyone was politically expendable. Mwaanga recounts how he "had risked his life to campaign for the United National Independence Party in a very hostile area which was under the control of the late Harry Nkumbula's African National Congress."[545] Despite all this risk, however, Kaunda went ahead and detained him. Again, Kaunda would recuse himself by claiming, "I want to assure the nation that there is no way I Kenneth David Kaunda, President of the Party, the nation and Commander-in-Chief of the Armed Forces, can protect anybody who commits an offence. I operate on the

---

[545] Mwaanga, 1987

basis of truth, love, social justice and fair play."[546] Of course, that was only a publicity stunt; in reality former president Kaunda was doing just the opposite.

The question to pose is: Were the people really all that important, and did the people really architect the Chona Constitution? The recommendations of the Chona Commission were the wishes of the people for the most part. The recommendations of the White Paper constituted UNIP government's, and by extension, Kaunda's wishes, aspirations and whims.

Contrary to popular belief, the Chona Commission made some very progressive recommendations under the circumstances. For example, the Commission recommended that the Prime Minister should be appointed by the president amongst Members of Parliament subject to the approval of Parliament and that he should be responsible for the execution of the following functions: (1) to serve as the Head of Cabinet and to preside over Cabinet meetings; (2) to serve as the chief spokesman on government matters; (3) to appoint Ministers and Deputy Ministers in consultation with the president; and (4) to appoint the Attorney-General of the Republic amongst the Members of Parliament in consultation with the president.

The above four recommendations were in line with sound democratic principles. Accepting these recommendations would have meant instituting strong checks and balances on the powers of the president. They would have also delineated the function of the president as Head of State and those of the Prime Minister as head of government.

However, as would have been expected, Kaunda and UNIP rejected these recommendations, opting instead for the full Executive powers to be vested into the Office of the President. The Prime Minister was to be appointed by the president, and

---

[546] *Times of Zambia*, "Ignore Lies – Kaunda" (Monday, November 18th, 1985) as quoted in Mwaanga, 1987

"should continue to retain his office at the pleasure of the president."[547] Hamalengwa notes that the UNIP government decided to restrict the functions of the Prime Minister to that of the head of government administration and as leader of government business in Parliament. In the absence of the Prime Minister, the president should appoint a Minister to act. It was also decided that the Secretary-General of UNIP should be *ex-officio* member of Cabinet.[548]

The Chona Commission made recommendations on the size of Parliament in the One-Party State including the number of nominated members and institutional requirements in Parliament. Per Hamalengwa, "Government made only a slight modification with regard to the required qualifications for elections to the National Assembly."[549] While the Commission recommended 18 years with respect to the age of an MP, the White Paper extended that age to 21. However, "it later turned out that people who wanted to stand for parliamentary elections had to be approved by the Central Committee. The aim may have been to create a 'dummy Parliament.'"[550]

Plural politics is overtly determined by the presidential term of office. The Chona Commission had recommended a five-year presidential term of office. The incumbent would be eligible for a second term of five years. To accommodate the whims of the incumbent, the Commission further recommended that upon the completion of his second term of five years the president should not be eligible for a period of at least five years. The incumbent would be ineligible to stand for a third term until after five years had elapsed since he or she last served as president.

Kaunda knew that once he had served two terms, he might not be re-elected as president after a five-year absence. As could be expected, government rejected this recommendation. Government through the White Paper decided that, "There

---

[547] *Ibid*, p. 142
[548] *Ibid*, pp. 142-143
[549] *Ibid*, p. 143
[550] *Ibid*.

should be no limitation on how often a man or woman can serve his or her country in the Office of President."[551] Of course, the *man* referred to in this quote was Kaunda himself. As Hamalengwa has observed, this move sanctioned a life presidency under the One-Party State system.[552]

For those who had not heard or read Kaunda's August speech at Mulungushi in 1967, all they knew was the justification government made regarding the creation of a One-Party State, *viz*, that, "Zambia had many enemies surrounding her and therefore the implementation of the One-Party Participatory Democracy as well as Humanism, together with the attendant problems, require a unified command under an Executive president."[553] Moreover, UNIP believed a One-Party State would unite and bring peace to the nation.

Yet, as observed earlier, the UNIP government had pre-meditated a One-Party State to avoid an election defeat in subsequent general elections and Kaunda knew that the tribal wrangles in UNIP did not portend well for the safety of his presidency. But the One-Party State would not be established without problems. For some, the One-Party State was synonymous with repression. People considered it as Kaunda's solidification of a totalitarian state where opposition to his leadership was wiped out. The first event that would threaten the very existence of the One-Party State was a coup plot led by Edward Shamwana.[554] The omnipotence nature of Kaunda's

---

[551] Republic of Zambia, *Reports of the National Commission on the Establishment of a One-Party Participatory Democracy in Zambia: Summary of Recommendations Accepted by Government,* as quoted in Hamalengwa, 1992, p. 141

[552] Hamalengwa 1992, *ibid.,* p. 142

[553] Republic of Zambia, *Reports of the National Commission on the Establishment of a One-Party Participatory Democracy in Zambia: Summary of Recommendations Accepted by Government,* as quoted in Hamalengwa, *supra.,* p. 142

[554] This issue has been canvassed at length in Chapter Nine

single-man rule created him many enemies who believed that removing him through a democratic mean was difficult, if not, impossible. However, the events of 1991 would prove that circumstances external to the system were stronger than an entrenched dictatorial wrench.

§8.5 Kaunda Loses Power

In 1968, Kaunda embarked on the process of nationalization, thereby creating what is called African Socialism. However, the events of the early 1970s and late 1980s poured scorn on all the efforts at Kaunda's programs. There were massive increases in the price of oil and a slump in copper prices in 1973 and 1975, respectively. These events reduced Zambia's export earnings. Due to total dependence on copper and its price diminution, Zambia began to experience balance-of-payment problems. To curb this deficit, the Kaunda government had to borrow from the International Monetary Funds (IMF). By the 1980s, Zambia had become a highly-indebted country. There were calls from the IMF to restructure the economy and offset copper dependence. To the socialistic regime, that was a bitter pill to swallow. It meant three things for the UNIP government: (1) devaluation of the copper, (2) ending of price controls, and (3) cancellation of subsidies, mainly on farm inputs. These measures spelled serious economic and political consequences. Economically, Zambia had introduced Soviet-style socialistic policies of National Development plans. Shortly after the adoption of the Chona report which declared Zambia a One-Party Participatory State, Zambia's move towards Socialism was completed.

Between 1970 and 1973 there was the First National Development Plan; between 1974 and 1977, Second National Development Plan; and lastly between 1978 and 1983, the Third National Development Plan.

The Third National Development Plan, however, backfired due to the collapse of the Soviet Union and Eastern Europe, whose socialistic ideology Kaunda had followed. Politically, and coupled mainly with the IMF's insistence that Zambia endorse new economic recovery programs, the urban populations of Zambia began to feel the pinch of the global Socialism collapse.

First, there were riots as the people protested Kaunda's removal of food subsidies. Second, the IMF charged Kaunda to de-nationalize the major national parastatals. In 1990, Kaunda was forced to make a policy shift, to partially privatize the economy. The economic, more than the political commotion in Zambia, cost Kaunda power in the 1991 presidential election in which the Frederick Chiluba and the MMD emerged the winner.

Specifically, between 1987 and 1990, food shortages and very harsh economic conditions had continued to ravage the nation. Lockhart captures the year 1990 concisely in this fashion:

> Unrest permeated the nation that year as Zambians from every province demanded multiparty elections. Dr. Kenneth David Kaunda (respectfully referred to as "KK" by Zambians) and his Freedom Fighters had broken the chains of British colonialism off of the Zambian people, emancipating the nation on 24 October 1964. They promptly changed the name of the country from Northern Rhodesia to Zambia. Former president Kaunda and his socialist leaning United National Independence Party or UNIP...had been in charge ever since. The Zambian people were indebted to Kenneth Kaunda as their father and founding Head of State, but after 26 years, they clearly desired a democratic voice in selecting Zambia's leader.[555]

There were rioting in various parts of the nation. The police who ran Zambia in the UNIP era were brutal at worse and notorious at best. They were feared like an inferno. In Kapisha Compound where this author lived at the time, the people never mentioned the name of Kaunda in public for fear that the police or intelligent agents would find them out. The police had placed

---

[555] Kirbey Lockhart, *Zambia Shall Be Saved* (Lethbridge: Paramount Printers Ltd, 2001), p. 40

such fear in the people that they almost deified the president. The only time they talked about him was when they praised him, sometimes for nothing.

The people of Kapisha revered Kaunda. The mention of his name brought shivers. He was like a god. People saw his image on the national currency on both notes (the Kwacha) and coins (the Ngwee). He was the first topic and last in the social studies textbooks. He was the first on the radio news and people heard about him from the local UNIP branch officials on almost every corner of their streets. He was the first and last news on local Television.

It seemed as if the indomitable Kaunda was unchallengeable. That is why when people began to hear rumors of political shifts taking place at Garden House Motel in Lusaka, shock and excitement began to run incessantly into their veins. (Garden House Motel was the venue for the plans and meetings that hatched the MMD. The initial plan was to hold the meeting in Livingstone. However, due to possibly lack of funding, the organizers instead moved the meeting to Garden House Motel in Lusaka on July 20th, 1990 where 130 delegates attended). Hitherto, Kaunda was *Wamuyayaya*, untouchable and invincible. There was no public thought in Zambia that anybody could challenge Kaunda's power.

Prior to the meeting at Garden House Motel, the organizers of the meetings there which would eventually usher in multiparty politics in Zambia were steered by the tensions in the country. For example, in 1988 nine persons were detained for alleged subversive activities.[556] However, many people, including Western diplomats, said that the detentions revealed UNIP government's growing sensitivity to potential political opposition ahead of the parliamentary and presidential elections on October 26th that year. Since independence from Britain in 1964, UNIP had endorsed only Kaunda as the sole presidential candidate, including for the 1988 elections.

---

[556] *New York Times*, "Zambia Detains 9 as Rumors of Coup Plot Fill the Capital," (October 9th, 1988).

It can be argued that, while the 1988 detentions worried Kaunda, they did not shake the UNIP government. This is because when UNIP met for its Extraordinary Fifth National Convention from the 14th to the 16th of March, 1990, at Mulungushi International Conference Center, UNIP "rejected the re-introduction of multiparty system saying the One-Party had worked remarkably well."[557]

It was the Luchembe-led attempted coup of 1990 which sent a vivid message to UNIP government that if plural politics were not in sight any time sooner, something worse would happen.[558] After the Luchembe attempted coup, even the late Betty Kaunda reminisced over moving out of State House and was alleged to have poured hot porridge on a worker who confronted her on this issue.[559] This shows that the Kaunda's did not take it well to the notion or attempts to remove them from State House. It had become like their personal-to-holder item. However, this is understood in consideration of the longevity the first couple had spent in State House.

§8.6 Humanism

The Second Republic is the period of grave undemocratic tendencies, and at worst, Kaunda's near-dictatorial reign. For 19 years, Kaunda would consolidate his power by proclaiming himself *Wamuyayaya*.[560] That phrase had become synonymous with UNIP itself. Kaunda and UNIP portrayed themselves

---

[557] Chisala, p. 341

[558] Luchembe's attempted coup is canvassed at length in §9.2

[559] Chisala writes in his book, *The Downfall of President Kaunda* that, "Former president Kaunda refuted a strong rumor that his wife had poured hot porridge on a State Lodge worker following a dispute. The worker was alleged to have asked the former First Lady where her family would go if MMD won the elections." (p. 348)

[560] Or life president

humanly, exemplified by Humanism. Humanism is a philosophy that has a central emphasis on the human realm. Historically, Humanism was commonly applied to the cultural movement in Renaissance Europe characterized by a revival of classical letters, an individualistic and critical spirit, and a shift of emphasis from religious to secular concerns. "The movement dates to the 14th Century and the poet Petrarch, though earlier figures are sometimes described as humanists. Its diffusion was facilitated by the universal use of Latin and the invention of movable type."[561] However, Kaunda's Humanism had a face of its own.

Kaunda's Humanism was not supposed to be interpreted from its generic etymology, it was a modified version tailored towards the resistance of Capitalism. It was a "political philosophy which endeavored to devise a social, political and economic order which was based on Man's truth rather than on Man's untruth."[562] In that sense, it was a means of achieving what Kaunda called an African Democratic Socialism. However, that order was to be later defined as the last stage in pursuit of Communism.

Kaunda's version of state order was from a Pre-Historical Age to Primitive Age to Slavery. Slavery stage progressed towards Capitalism and to Socialism. Socialism gave birth to Humanism, which was "the end of all this."[563] However, Kaunda's Humanism, unlike universal Communism, acknowledged the Supremacy of God as Kaunda reiterated, "A true communist believes not in the Super-being and after-life. His religion is his ideology. On the other hand, a humanist believes in the presence of a Super-being – the source of all life."[564]

Since the inception of Humanism in 1967, Kaunda contended that it centered on Man. But that Man was not the universal Man, it was the African person. To Kaunda, the inherent cooperative

---

[561] *Britannica Concise Encyclopedia*, "Humanism"
< http://www.answers.com/topic/humanism> (Retrieved: January 17th, 2010)
[562] Kenneth D. Kaunda, *Humanism in Zambia and A Guide to Its Implementation* (Lusaka: Kenneth Kaunda Foundation, 1967), p. 65
[563] *Ibid.*, p. 67
[564] *Ibid.*

nature of the African society necessitated his philosophy of Humanism: "African society was progressive and humane,"[565] he exhorts. It was depopulated by slavery only to be repopulated by science and technology. The infusion of the money economy disturbed this "mutual aid society which was an accepting and inclusive community."[566]

While Humanism as was postulated by Kaunda paid due regard to the social patterns of Zambia's past, that past was overtly archaic in outlook and taken by events. Thus, Kaunda's Humanism was an attempt at repeating old Zambian village life. It evolved not as much into a Man-centered society, as later, especially after nationalization, into a State-Controlled Capitalism.

Kaunda was determined to preserve the inherent communal nature of the African society without sacrificing the benefits of science and technology. He opted for a society where Man was supreme, only below God: "It is people above ideology; Man, above institutions."[567] To effectuate it, he decided to establish a Chair of Human Relations at UNZA.[568]

While Humanism as postulated by Kaunda paid due regard to the social pattern of the Zambian past, it was not, however, practical as a social order in the modern era in which Zambia was expected to be a key player in the community of nations. Critical examination of Kaunda's Humanism reveals that it did not promote Man as the center of attention. Rather, it used Man as a means of production, just like Capitalism uses Man as a means of mass production. What Kaunda ended up creating was a society in which only one man was supreme, and that man was Kaunda himself.

---

[565] *Ibid.,* p. 7

[566] *Ibid.*

[567] Kaunda, *Humanism in Zambia: A Guide to Its Implementation, supra.,* p. 8

[568] This move was later rejected by the students at UNZA. See §3.5

However, Kaunda's initial conception of Humanism was closely tied to *Ubuntu*, a central-southern African term meaning humanness. In Zambia, a *Muntu* (singular, whereas *Bantu* is plural) is a human being with rights and duties as opposed to a slave or a person without rights. Thus, Kaunda's promulgation of the humanistic dogma stood within the ambit of the African concept of *Ubuntu*. In a sense, Kaunda's Humanism was conceived with due credence, because it connoted the very values of the Black people of Africa. Consequently, on October 21st, 2007, the National Heritage Council (NHC) of South Africa honored Kaunda for what it termed, "His work in demonstrating the values of *Ubuntu*."[569]

Moreover, in the inception, Kaunda opted to use Humanism as a weapon against what he called the four problems, *viz*, hunger, poverty, ignorance and disease.[570] At the writing of this book, these four problems have not only grown bigger, they have become complicated as well. Thus, any political approach that would solve these problems, including Humanism, then as now, is welcome.

Despite his belief in Humanism, Kaunda was a political tactician. In later years, he grew too powerful and disregarded the very Man he promised would be important. Upon the recommendation of Mainza Chona and the Chona Commission to create a constitution of One-Party Participatory Democracy, Kaunda proclaimed the Second Republic in 1972. Kaunda's leadership took on more autocratic characteristics. He personally appointed the Central Committee of UNIP, which he asserted "is now more supreme than the Cabinet."[571] To legitimize the process he provided for the pre-approval of the National Congress of UNIP, which was just a front.

---

[569] Namibia Online Community, "South Africa: Kenneth Kaunda Honored for His Humanism" from < http://www.hellonam.com/governance-democracy/2606-zambia-kenneth-kaunda-honored-his-humanism.html> (Retrieved: January 18th, 2010)
[570] Kaunda, *supra.*, p. 38
[571] Kaunda, *supra.*, p. 76

Kaunda controlled the parliamentary elections. He did this by requiring the names of candidates to be submitted to UNIP's Central Committee. The Central Committee then selected three people to stand for any constituency. The Central Committee was so powerful that it could veto anyone without giving reasons. This solidified the concept of the *Party and its Government* because UNIP was supreme and its decisions could not be challenged. "Using these methods, Kaunda kept any enemies at bay by ensuring that they never got into political power."[572]

Authoritarianism is detrimental to the overall political and democratic development of a nation. In Zambian politics, especially in the Second Republic, people knew about Kaunda's dictatorial tactics, but they were hopeless. Kaunda could easily have his way claiming the legitimacy of the Chona Commission and even as a façade for advancing Humanism. Even if some quarters had wanted to raise a counter voice, Kaunda would still silence them in an election.

For example, what Kaunda called elections in the Second Republic were not elections at all, at least in the modern democratic sense. Kaunda was, in fact, the only human candidate on the ballot.[573] The other *candidate* was a frog. The frog represented nothing at all. Voting for a frog meant voting for no candidate, which still left Kaunda the winner, even if only one person (who, of course, was Kaunda) voted in the election. Lockhart explains it this way:

---

[572] Wikipedia: The Free Encyclopedia, "Kenneth Kaunda." (Retrieved: February 7th, 2010)

[573] If Humanism meant Man-centered, then that Humanism was given a massive test in the conduct of elections. Did Kaunda decide to make a frog more important that Man; choosing, rather a frog to contest elections against him and not Man? Did Kaunda judge Man of no human worth than an amphibian? If so, did the choice of his political competitor reveal that only Kaunda was Man in Zambian politics?

Previous Zambian "elections" used a simple ballot. Zambian citizens…were instructed to check the picture of a garden hoe if they wanted Kenneth Kaunda and his UNIP to stay in power. If not, they were to check the picture of the frog. That the frog represented nothing was never explained to the voter.[574]

Kaunda would advance his tactics of political exclusion by using UNIP's Central Committee for over 19 years. It would make him a sole candidate in elections and further frustrate any attempts at bringing Zambia back to democracy:

> This was the tactic he used when he saw off Nkumbula and Kapwepwe's challenges to his sole candidacy for the 1978 UNIP elections. On that occasion, the UNIP's constitution was "amended" overnight [so that] Kapwepwe…could not stand because only people who had been members for five years could be nominated to the presidency (he had only re-joined UNIP three years before); Nkumbula was outmaneuvered by introducing a new rule that said each candidate needed the signatures of 200 delegates from *each* province to back his candidacy. Less creative tactics were used on a third candidate called [Robert] Chiluwe; he was just beaten up by the UNIP Youth Wing to within an inch of his life. This meant that he was in no state to submit his nomination.[575]

The tactic of exclusion portended the worst scenario for the future of democracy in Zambia. This tendency has passed on to the Fourth Republic. It has created a culture political entitlement, a sort of a political career.[576]

§8.7 Voices against Oppression

The national political temperature was getting hotter and hotter by day. Kaunda's tactics soon gave way to the wrath of

---

[574] Lockhart, *Zambia Shall Be Saved, supra.*, p. 40

[575] *Ibid.*

[576] In April 2011 on Zambia Blogtalk Radio, Winter Kabimba, the then PF Secretary-General, frantically admitted that politics in Zambia was a career, and not a service, for most of the politicians.

student activism at UNZA. In the past, Kaunda had managed to squash student *rumpenism* and rampage by either closing the institution or detaining the agitators or both. Between 1971 and 1990, UNZA had been closed six times[577] owing to student activism. Some closures were politically motivated while others were purely academic.[578]

However, the 1990 UNZA closure was material to the downfall of Kaunda. In the late 1980s, the IMF and the World Bank had introduced SAPs in Zambia. The students felt that the conditions attached to these stabilization programs ignored the structural problems of the developing nations. Coupled with the gradual withdrawal of the subsidy[579] on maize announced on June 19th, 1990 by the then Prime Minister, Malimba Masheke, "Dissension over the increase reached such a feverish peak that the writing was evidently seen on the wall for the government."[580] On June 26th, 1990, the students marched on Cairo Road in demonstration against the food shortages and price increases.[581] Through the student incitement, the mob grew and widened its tentacles to include cigarette sellers,[582] marketeers and unruly youth. The mob transformed itself into a demolisher of supermarkets, shops and government buildings. Looting and rioting married and gave birth to a *Dark Tuesday*.[583]

---

[577] Wele cites five closures, see §3.5

[578] See Chapter 3

[579] Subsidy on mealie meal was gradually withdrawn from K114.50 to K269.00 for "Breakfast meal" and from K82.30 to K198.00 for "Roller meal."

[580] Wele, *Zambia's Most Famous Dissidents,* p. 74

[581] Frederick J. T. Chiluba, *Democracy: The Challenge of Change* (Lusaka: Multimedia Publications, 1995), on page 64, places this date on June 25th, 1990

[582] Also known as *Mishanga-Sellers* in vernacular

[583] Tuesday, June 27th, 1990, prompted by an erroneous revelation that Kaunda had a stack of US$5 billion in foreign banks insinuated by Gen. Christon Tembo, from UNZA to Chilenje, the mob ransacked and looted

Per Wele, while events in the country, and specifically the closure of UNZA, were simmering, a pressure cooker was seething at ZNBC. It began with the surprise announcement: "Due to the escalating cost of living followed by the food riots, the Zambia Army has decided to take over the government. This is Lt. Mwamba Luchembe."[584] The event was too much for Alexander Grey Zulu who announced the coup foil by the commandos under the command of Brigadier General Weston Chanda.[585] President Kaunda, who was opening a Trade Fair in Ndola, was awakened to the "Lord is My Shepherd."[586]

The events surrounding UNZA demonstrations and closures, and the riots that rocked the City of Lusaka leading to the Luchembe coup attempt and the shaking up of the UNIP regime under Kaunda have been well captured in Frederick Chiluba's book, *Democracy: The Challenge of Change*: "The University of Zambia has always been a center of political agitation. By the end of 1980s students and academic staff alike were predisposed to be dissatisfied with the government, which on several occasions had closed the university and disrupted the academic program, sometimes in retaliation against their political outspokenness."[587]

The immediate pressure put up at the UNIP's Fifth National Convention held in March 1990, the riots and attempted coup, forced Kaunda to call for a referendum for plural politics. From July 20th to July 21st, 1990, gathering at Garden House Motel in Lusaka, a group of determined Zambians including Frederick Chiluba[588] and flanked by VJ Mwaanga, Arthur Wina and Sikota

Kabulonga Supermarket, mistaken to have been owned by the Kaunda family. In fact, the supermarket was owned by Lendor Burton.
[584] Wele, *supra.,* p. 171
[585] As Secretary-General of UNIP, Grey Zulu was the second most important politician in Zambia, and at ZNBC he announced that the coup was the work of one undisciplined-soldier.
[586] Psalms 23
[587] Chiluba, *Democracy: The Challenge of Change*, pp. 64-65
[588] On November 2nd, 1991, Frederick Jacob Titus Chiluba became Zambia's second republican president. Born on April 30th, 1943, Chiluba became the President-General of the Zambia Congress of Trade Unions (ZCTU) in 1974

Wina, formed the National Interim Committee for Multiparty Democracy. Arthur Wina became the committee's chairman. Frederick Chiluba became head of the committee's operations, Levy Mwanawasa[589] for legal affairs, VJ Mwaanga for public relations, Ephraim Chibwe for finance, and Andrew Kashita for transport. Chiluba suggested the change of name from National Interim Committee to Movement for Multiparty Democracy (MMD) and the name was adopted. In 1991, Chiluba and the MMD led Zambia back to multiparty politics in what is now known as the Third Republic.

Life under the MMD was not completely free from police brutality as was envisaged of the Third Republic. Political *caderism*[590] continued to agitate the innocent citizens in Zambia. The case of Father Frank Bwalya showed that Zambia's democracy was still bleeding. On Monday, March 15th, 2010, Father Bwalya, a catholic priest, was arrested by the Kitwe police for showing what he referred to as a Red Card against President Rupiah Banda.

---

before agitating his fellow trade unionists in 1990 to defeat Kaunda in the nation's first multiparty elections since 1968. He is credited with the introduction of liberal economic policies in Zambia. He died on June 18th, 2011.

[589] Levy Patrick Mwanawasa, Zambia's third Republican president, was born on September 3rd, 1948. He experienced a minor stroke in 2006. While in Sharm-Sheikh in Egypt for an African Union Summit, Mwanawasa was hospitalized due to a brain hemorrhage on June 29th, 2008. On July 2nd, 2008, a rumor escalated that Mwanawasa had died. The Office of the Vice-president and the Ministry of Foreign Affairs in Lusaka issued a joint statement on July 3rd, 2008 that the Zambian President was alive. He was however, in the Intensive Care Unit at Percy Clamant Military Hospital in Paris, France until he finally died on August 19th, 2008. He is credited with the solidification of the Rule of Law and the curbing of corrupt practices in government.

[590] *Caderism* is a practice whereby political parties intend to frustrate the citizens' expressions of their political freedoms or/and human rights. It may manifest itself in the use of organized police by the ruling political party to silence those who may be against government's policies.

9| Coup Attempts

A World Food Program worker describes evil as being told to rape your mother in front of your father, then being told to kill your father in front of a mob, and then being stupidly turned into a child soldier.

Chapter Focus

At the end of reading this chapter, you should be able to:

- Understand the meaning of repression in the Second Republic
- Identify the critical masterminds of the attempted coups in Zambia and the goals that motivated them
- Ascertain that the preservation of democracy far outweighs any justification for staging a coup
- Explain the reasons why coups failed in Zambia but succeeded elsewhere in Africa

BRIEF INTRODUCTION

This chapter explores coup attempts in Zambia and the factors that have led to their failure. In view of the future of Zambia, this chapter investigates the political implications of attempted coups to the nation's young democracy.

§9.1 Shamwana-Musakanya Trial

Despite their uncouthly implications, coup attempts and coups in general provide a chance to consider the minds of the plotters. But for Zambia, they provided a rare opportunity for the ruling

politicians in the Second and Third republics to re-examine the
One-Party regime and autocratic tendencies, respectively. For the
future generations, they should provide a lesson to avoid pitfalls
that might lead to successful coups d'état.

In Zambia, change for multiparty politics was accelerated by
several coup attempts. One of the most organized of these was
the so-called Shamwana Treason Trial.[591] A few Zambian
statesmen were infuriated with the prospects of a One-Party
State. Among them were Elias Chipimo and Valentine
Musakanya.[592] Per Mundia Sikatana, Pierce Annifield's law firm
partner, who appeared to have been the leak of the plot to the
state, either Musakanya or Edward Shamwana was to be the
leader of government if the plot succeeded.[593]

---

[591] This coup attempt did not only have all the features of a well-plotted
coup, its protagonist had a very special place in the Zambian legal industry.
Shamwana was just about to be appointed Chief Justice of Zambia before the
coup was foiled. The allegation was that the plot involved bringing a band of
foreign forces from Congo to be organized by a Congolese, Deogratias
Symba. Symba had led a failed invasion of Shaba Province with his
Katangese forces from Angola. Brigadier General Godfrey Miyanda was to
bring in army support and also divert weapons imported for the Zimbabwean
liberation movements to the farm. Air Force Chief, Christopher Kabwe, was
to divert Kaunda's plane to a military base and force him to surrender and
resign.

[592] In April 1980, Elias Chipimo, as chairman of Standard Bank, and a close
friend of Musakanya issued a public statement condemning the One-Party
State, urging African leaders to abandon this political system if they were to
prevent coups d'état against them. Kaunda quickly accused Chipimo and
other members of the flying club of being involved in the plot to remove
him. Kaunda also forced Standard Bank to fire Chipimo.

[593] Emmanuel Mwamba, "The Musakanya Papers; Rare Insight into 1980
Coup," *Zambian Watchdog*, (July 6th, 2010). For a comprehensive review of
the Shamwana-Musakanya coup plot, read Chapter 5: Shamwana Treason
Trial of Patrick Wele's *Zambia's Most Famous Dissidents* from pages 90 to
145.

The books, *The Musakanya Papers* edited by Miles Larmer[594] as well as *Zambia's Most Famous Dissidents* written by Patrick Wele, give us the loop-hole into the political gymnastics of the Second Republic. Politics thrives on perception. It is common practice in politics for the seasoned politicians to use the errors of judgment of opponents to their advantage. Argued on its face, the Shamwana-Musakanya coup plot had merits in the mind of the plotters, although the means of delivery contradicted the principle.

The coup was prompted by the plotters' refusal to bow to UNIP's imposition of a One-Party regime on Zambia. Among legal counsel Edward Shamwana's masterminds were Valentine Musakanya.[595] "Musakanya was always fearless and refused to be cowed by the existing political environment. Whilst still holding the position of Bank of Zambia Governor, he submitted to the Chona Constitution Review Commission in 1972, far reaching proposals."[596] Basically, Musakanya condemned the proposed One-Party State and the tribal balancing proposed by UNIP. He argued that it promoted tribal and ethnic based politics at the expense of good governance.

Musakanya "advocated for the retention of multiparty system,"[597] referring to the One-Party State concept as the "Rape of the State." Among other things, Musakanya advocated for a constitution that limited presidential powers, called for the publication of government records to stem the rise of corruption and bribery in government, and nodded constitutional guarantees for individual civil liberties and human rights. While these

---

[594] Miles Larmer is a British historian and Sheffield University lecturer who also has written *Mineworkers in Zambia: Labor and Political Change in Post-Colonial Africa.*
[595] Valentine Musakanya was born in 1932 and was one of the first few Zambians to acquire a university degree. He served as Secretary to the Cabinet at independence and as Minister of State (a deputy ministerial position). He later served as Bank of Zambia Governor before being removed by former president Kaunda for opposing the One-Party State.
[596] Mwamba, *supra.*
[597] *Ibid.*

proposals portend well in contemporary Zambian political times, in the Second Republic, these sentiments did not go well with the establishment.

However, Musakanya's affront to Kaunda's leadership came when he proposed "for the presidency to be limited to two terms and that such a presidential candidate should be born from indigenous parents! Clearly the proposals were directed at excluding the now all powerful Kaunda."[598] This last charge threatened the incumbent's own survival and Kaunda conveniently fired Musakanya from his position as Bank of Zambia Governor.

§9.2 "Second" President

The reign of Zambia's *second* president lasted only three hours, and was, "achieved single-handedly without the alleged organized support from fellow soldiers."[599] Lieutenant Mwamba Luchembe[600] claimed the coup was prompted by escalating cost of living followed by the food riots. However, in the wee hours of June 30th, 1990, General Weston Chanda announced that, "The coup has failed and anybody who will be on the streets will be shot."[601]

When Luchembe attempted a coup on former president Kaunda in 1990, this author was with Goodson Sanga. He remembers this day very well. The condition of the day was mild to cold. Goodson and this author were going just past the Kapisha Catholic Church. There are certain days one cannot forget because what happened then was significant.

---

[598] *Ibid.*
[599] Wele, *supra.*, p. 171
[600] Mwamba Luchembe was born on February 14th (Valentine's Day), 1960 in Mpika to Mubanga Luchembe and Kapinda Chilangwa. In 1978, he joined ZNS and in 1980, he joined the Zambian Army. Luchembe was discharged from the Zambia Army on June 30th, 1990, the day of the attempted coup.
[601] Wele, *supra.*, p. 173

On June 30th, 1990, this author looked at the sun, and it was almost dropping tears.[602] He looked to the west of Kapisha Compound[603] and could hear the silence. Everyone was glued to the radio, being the only main source of information and news in Kapisha. You could feel the fear in people's eyes. That near thirty-minute gap as the people were tuned to the radio is perhaps the greatest sign to this author that Zambian people are naturally democratic, an argument made earlier in Chapter Seven.

The Luchembe coup was significant by every Zambian standard at the time. For one, it "brought happiness to some,"[604] and for another, it "provided unwarranted detentions for the innocent few."[605] If Luchembe had intended to remove former president Kaunda from power through unconstitutional means, his feats surely set in motion a revolutionary escapade that culminated into the presidential elections of 1991.

§9.3 Coups d'état

A coup or its attempt should not be justified. Coups insult the very foundation upon which democracy is based. They thwart people's will to decide their own political destiny. They send a nation into an irretrievable political spin that in many cases would not stabilize the nation again. Nations that have

---

[602] Shortly it was announced the coup had been foiled. The fracas lasted only few hours. A great calm and relief came back to Kapisha. It seemed like the entire nation had gone into a trance or a numbed state of existence. People started talking, but not like before. Luchembe was a near-hero, but even that no-one would talk openly for fear they could be arrested by the police. If there is anything the Luchembe coup attempt accomplished, it was not only the fuelling of the dissatisfaction of the people of Zambia with Kaunda's reign. It was also the attestation to the fundamental truth that Zambian's preferred democratic means of removing a government from power to democratic disparage.

[603] See §2.2

[604] *Ibid.*, p. 174

[605] *Ibid.*

experienced the bitter taste of coups cannot boast of stable governance thereafter. Between 1952 and 2011, there were 85 successful coups d'état in 35 countries in Africa. The very first coup in Africa took place in 1952 in Egypt by General Col. Abdel Nasser and Anwar Sadat. Among other nations to experience coups in Africa are Ghana in 1966 in which Kwame Nkrumah was deposed. In 1969, Muammar Gaddaffi overthrew King Idris in Libya. Other countries include Mauritania where about 16 coups d'état have taken place and Nigeria with about 12 and a civil war of 1967-70. There have been coups d'état in Togo, Mali and Uganda with the overthrowing of presidents Silvio Olympio, Modibo Keita, and Milton Obote, respectively. Other coups d'état have taken place in Fiji by the Acting Prime Minister Frank Bainimarama on December 5th, 2006; in Mauritania by President Mohamed Ould Abdel Aziz on August 6th, 2008; Guinea Bissau where on March 2nd, 2009, President Bernado "Nino" Vieira was overthrown and on March 17th, 2009 when Andry Rajoelina became the President of the High Transitional Authority in Madagascar.

The civil war of 1960 in Congo DR saw the assassination of Patrice Lumumba by Mobutu Sese Seko. Botswana, Malawi, Tanzania and Zambia have been fortunate to escape coups d'état. In addition, there have been over 180 attempted coups d'état in Africa which prompted the first President of Tanzania, Mwalimu Nyerere to declare, "There is a devil in Africa."

Salou Djibo staged a coup in Niger on February 18th, 2010.

Where coups have been attempted or succeeded, a bad precedent is set and coming generations find it tempting not to resist staging one, wherever progress in the land is stalled, or because of the selfish political ambitions of one person or a few people.

Best interest is usually cited as motivation for staging a coup. The plotters would claim that they were doing so in the democratic or economic interest of the nation.[606] The

---

[606] To some extent, especially from the 1980s, some coups in Africa have been fuelled by drastic economic conditions imposed by the rich

consequences of coups outweigh their benefits. In Zambia, in the late 1990s, one would argue a coup attempt was justified because of the dictatorial tendencies of the Kaunda regime. However, by parity of argument, such conception falls short. Sabella Ogbobode Abidde has candidly reasoned that military coups d'état can never be justified not only because the broadcasted reasons for staging such coups are usually bogus and anomalous, but also because military governments usually end up exacerbating the socio-political and economic conditions of the country.[607]

Despite the poverty and corruption situations in Zambia, Zambia still stands a better chance, politically, in terms of democracy. Future Zambian leaders will be able to build on this tradition to create for themselves and for posterity paths that will eventually lead to sustained economic prosperity. This is the cardinal reason why democracy ought to be preserved at all costs.

§9.4 Coup Attempt Implication

Amenable with the popular attitude that independent Zambia has been relatively peaceful, is the unsuccessful attempts at dislodging the government, thrice under the UNIP watch and thrice under the MMD's.

The first alleged coup plot against the Kaunda government, as discussed above, was in October 1980 by Edward Shamwana, Valentine Musakanya, Godwin Mumba, Anderson Mporokosa,

---

governments and IFIs on the developing nations. When faced with runaway inflation some of the more common measures prescribed by the IFIs have been price control, strict currency control, increased taxes and devaluation. Unfortunately, these have not always been popular measures and have instead tended to generate countrywide dissatisfaction and national outrage. Military intervention has often occurred in these circumstances.

[607] Sabella Ogbobode Abidde, "Of Rumored, Attempted and Successful Coups," (2004) <http://www.nigerdeltacongress.com/oarticles/of_rumored_attempted_and_s uccess.htm > (Retrieved: March 18th, 2010)

Charles Mwewa

Thomas Mulewa, General Godfrey Miyanda, Deogratis Symba, Albert Chimbalile and Laurent Kanyembu. At trial Gen. Miyanda was acquitted but the rest were found guilty. The second alleged coup attempt on Kaunda took place on October 5th, 1988. Sixteen men were arrested including: General Christon Tembo, Ben Mwila, Colonel Bizwayo Nkunika, Bob Litana, Wilfred Wonani, Emmanuel Hachipoka, Peter Vundamina, Harrington Chishimba, Major Patrick Shula, Major Knight Mulenga, Major Nixon Zulu, Captain Wamulume Maimbolwa, John Kalenga, Donald Sadoki, Warrant Officer Christopher Chawinga and Matiya Ngalande. The third and final coup attempt under the Kaunda regime was one led by Lieutenant Mwamba Luchembe on June 30th, 1990.

The three coup-attempts under the MMD watch were as follows: First, it was the Zero Option of 1993 when a group of high rankings UNIP cadres were accused of a ploy to overthrow the MMD government. Second, it was the case of eight top UNIP officials who, together with a clandestine organization called the Black Mamba, were charged of treason and murder in 1996, shortly before Chiluba signed the May 28th, 1996 constitution which contained a controversial presidential clause, Article 34(3)(b), which required any presidential candidate to prove that their parent or parents were Zambians by birth or descent. The third one was a four-hour coup attempt by Captain Steven Lungu, a.k.a., Captain Solo, who had claimed a government takeover by his Supreme National Council citing intolerance by the MMD government. This coup took place on October 28th, 1997.

For future Zambian leaders, these events are worth of notice. The implications for the young Zambian democracy are huge, but their preventive advantage cannot be disputed. Generally, Zambia has been saved from the unfortunate predicaments in which successful coups leave the victim nations. However, sometimes there is a thin line between the response from international donors and human rights organizations to the state of emergency and the duty of government to enforce national security measures to protect themselves and their citizens.[608]

It has not always been true that the Zambian nationalists conducted themselves peacefully or non-violently. Just before independence, Kaunda's UNIP had mobilized civil disobedience campaigns through the Cha-Cha-Cha uprising,[609] and the sponsorship of Adamson Mushala to China to train in guerrilla tactics was meant to overthrow the colonial government if all democratic means failed.

Between 1975 and 1982, Mushala dissented from UNIP. Having been trained in China in guerrilla tactics, Mushala was well-equipped to give Kaunda and UNIP enough trouble to earn the name as the most notorious dissenter in the history of Zambia. Even by the time this author was growing up in Mibenge as a small village boy, Mushala's name ringed trouble and danger. Mushala was disgruntled with UNIP that it had failed to honor its pre-independence promise of giving Mushala a prominent position either in UNIP or in government. After being refused a position as Chief Warden, Mushala first joined the opposition UP, and thereafter went into exile to South Africa. There together with his comrades, he prepared to return to Zambia to wage a guerrilla war, against the same party that had trained him in the first place. Mushala's war of terror continued until 1982 when on November 26th, he was gunned down by the Zambian army. Alexander Saimbwende succeeded him. On September 25th, 1990 Saimbwende surrendered through Alexander Kamalondo who in turn handed Saimbwende to Kaunda. Kaunda later pardoned Saimbwende.[610]

---

[608] See Julius O. Ihonvbere, "The 'Zero Option' Controversy in Zambia: Western Double Standards vis-à-vis Safeguarding Security?" (1995) *Afrika Spectrum,* Vol. 30, No. 1: 93-104

[609] Cha-Cha-Cha was both a civil disobedience campaign and an armed struggle resistance against the colonial government. Believed to have been first organized by Kaunda in 1960 shortly after his release from prison, the resistance organized protests and was even prepared to take on arms against the British colonial government in Northern Rhodesia.

[610] Wele, *supra,* covers this subject in greater details

To the larger extent, from the struggle for independence Kaunda marshaled enough tactical resources to help him consolidate power for such a long time.[611]

Before the coup failure of Luchembe of June 30th, 1990, UNIP had held its Fifth National Convention to deliberate political issues. It was during that meeting that independent voices called for a referendum for multiparty politics in Zambia.[612] However, the referendum would not be held because of the coup attempt.

The coup challenge in Africa has been mostly addressed from a contemporary viewpoint, ignoring the historical corollaries that have made Africa an open oven for military takeovers. It is unarguable that in some countries[613] tribalism and ethnic tensions have played parts: "Governments have tended to be more tribal than national in structure, with inter-tribal oppression becoming common practice."[614] This observation is, however, only partially true, or a symptom of a much deeply entrenched cause.

---

[611] Thus, despite condemning the enactment of the *Preservation of Public Security Act*, under which Kaunda and other nationalists were detained, Kaunda conveniently continued to use the same law on the pretext that it was needed to ensure stability in the newly independent Zambia.

[612] This would not be the first-time Zambia was embracing notions of plural politics. During what is commonly termed as the First Republic, from 1964 to 1972, Zambia was a multiparty state. On page one of his book, *Democracy: The Challenge of Change,* Chiluba informs that even before independence, the country was characterized by political pluralism and contestations, features that all theorists of liberal democracy agree are vital to democratization. There were two major parties comprising mainly Africans, the African National Congress (ANC) of Harry Mwaanga Nkumbula, and Kenneth Kaunda's United National Independence Party (UNIP). In addition, there were two other parties, the Liberal Party led by Sir John Moffatt, which had some sympathy among Africans, and the United Federal Party led by John Roberts and Sir Roy Welensky, and which was mainly for Whites. Following the attainment of independence in 1964, plural politics was retained and the procedures of democracy were established, so that in 1968 general elections, for instance, UNIP won eighty-one seats and the ANC increased its representation to twenty-three seats in the Legislature.

[613] This is true in Congo DR, Sudan, Burundi and Rwanda, to mention but a few.

[614] Jimmi Wangome, *supra.*

The cause is, as argued constantly in this book, historical in nature.

The first problem must do with the treatment of the Africans by the colonial soldiers.[615] During the sensitive days of struggle for freedom and independence the general populace and the local politicians had developed an almost allergic fear and mistrust for soldiers. The ensuing tribal imbalance necessarily made more difficult than it would otherwise have been the army's achievement of national status as an institution.[616]

The other cause is the plunder of the African economic reserves by the colonialists. It did not take the ordinary citizens long to realize that new African governments were not delivering the goods fast enough. Although corruption played a part, it was mainly because these governments had inherited structures without resources. Indeed, "A protracted economic crisis has in most cases led to the failure of the political leadership."[617]

The other cause is foreign in scope, such as regime changes mostly instigated by the CIA or other Western intelligence and investigation wings. For instance, Salvador Allende of Chile is believed to have been overthrown in 1973 with the help of the CIA.[618] The "1976 Church Senate Select Committee Report with Respect to Governmental Intelligence" and the "Pike House Select Committee Report with Respect to Governmental Intelligence" were two reports that were most comprehensive US congressional reports on CIA interventions in "form of electoral

---

[615] Gutteridge has observed that nationalist politicians saw them as agents of imperial rule suppressing political demonstrations and protecting European property. Though they had won glory by serving overseas in the two world wars, their imperial activities caused them to be regarded in some quarters as armies of occupation or at best as mercenaries in the service of a foreign power. This impression was assisted by a recruitment policy that defined them as 'martial races' or 'worthwhile soldiers.' See Gutteridge, *infra*.

[616] Thus, the colonial soldiers were not only mistrusted, but they were also responsible for fuelling ethnic and tribal tensions. See, W.F. Gutteridge, *Military Regimes in Africa* (London: Methven & Co Ltd, 1975), p. 6

[617] Wangoma, *supra*.

[618] See Ariel Dorfman, "Now, America, You Know How Chileans Felt," *New York Times*, December 16th, 2016

Charles Mwewa

interventions, *coups*, assassination of foreign leaders, military interference, bribery, dirty tricks, and etc., perpetrated by the CIA against foreign governments in aid of American foreign policy from the postwar to 1976. The value of these reports is that they are not foreign propaganda, they are official US congressional reports that resulted from exhaustive congressional hearings and studies after public outcry that the CIA had shamed American democracy by excessive and brutal foreign intervention."[619]

It does not, however, pay or benefit Zambians or indeed, Africans, to play a blame game. And although Wangoma has charged that, "As long as there are economic and political instability military coups will continue to occur; the future of Africa is that bleak,"[620] The future of Africa, however, can be bright. For Zambia, that bright future is in the inculcation of sound democratic tendencies even in the military.[621]

For one, political squabbles, inefficiency of the civilian governments, corruption, maladministration, internal political problems within the ruling elite, and foreign interference, are all problems which have a political solution. For another, "Coups have been linked directly or indirectly with personal ambitions and the craving for power by some specific key players."[622] Zambia is a quintessential epitome of a nation where those in the military with political ambitions have democratically joined the political ranks without resorting to the barrel of the gun.[623] The Zambian democratic model stands the best chance and portends hope for Africa. Zambia has repeatedly proven that democracy can thrive despite ethnic diversity or economic underdevelopment.

Zambia has been cited as one of the African nations that have

[619] Munyonzwe Hamalengwa, "Rumors of an election coup in the United States," *The Zambian Observer*, December 13th, 2016
[620] Wangoma, *supra*.
[621] See §10.7,
[622] Samuel Decalo, *Coups and Army Rule in Africa* (Clinton: The Colonial Press Inc., 1976) p. 231
[623] Good examples are Gen. Godfrey Miyanda, Gen. Christon Tembo, Gen. Ronnie Sikapwasha, to mention but a few.

established the "means of civilian control that have stood the test of time."[624] This commendation is backed by a basic realization that it is easier to accomplish a coup than to maintain peace. It is clear from the evidence that any African army which resolves to launch a coup against a civilian regime has very good prospects of success. Given its dominant role in controlling the technology of violence, there are seldom any insuperable physical obstacles in its path. The sword usually proves mightier than the pen.[625]

Indeed, in Zambia, the continued dominance of the pen over the sword is a testament to the determination of the people of Zambia to live in peace and forge the ideals of democracy in their progeny. Zambia has not only averted coup attempts on its soil, but has been instrumental in hosting numerous foreign nationals who have run away from political oppression.[626]

From the foregone, it is apparent that a political culture that promotes order and social solidarity is rife in Zambia and has been, together with the other factors mentioned earlier, responsible for the failed coups. However, this is an ongoing commitment as it conveniently shelters the people from the cumbersome Catch-22[627] of having to choose between a bad democracy and a good dictatorship.

---

[624] Claude E. Welch, Jr., "Civilian Control of the Military: Myth and Reality," in Claude E. Welch, Jr. (ed.), *Civilian Control of the Military: Theory and Cases from Developing Countries* (Albany: State University of New York Press, 1976), p. xi

[625] David Goldsworthy, "Civilian Control of the Military in Black Africa," (January 1981) *African Affairs*, Vol. 80, No. 318, p. 52

[626] See Balamn Yeko, "Exile Politics and Resistance to Dictatorship: The Ugandan Anti-Amin Organizations in Zambia, 1972-79," (1996) *African Affairs*, 96, p. 97

[627] *Catch-22* was a post-modernist satirical novel written by Joseph Heller in 1961. It poses a logical and psychological conundrum. A *Catch-22* situation has a disambiguation, idiomatic usage meaning a "No-win situation" or "A double bind" situation.

10| Presidential Politics

A president I will, rather than a king
For a precedent is only one thing
To follow the rule they create for him
To borrow peace and kill joy they seem.

Chapter Focus

At the end of reading this chapter, you should be able to:

- Differentiate between the presidency as the person who occupies the office and the Office of the President (O.P)
- Identify the relationship between civil control and military command
- Identify qualities that define the presidency in the 21st Century
- Recognize that women are key to presidential politics
- Understand the dual function of the O.P in Zambia
- Explain the "Leader Principle" and demonstrate how it offends democracy

BRIEF INTRODUCTION

This chapter focuses on the presidency of Zambia. As an institution called the presidency, and as a person who occupies that office, the presidency in Zambia has been pivotal to the very ethos of national politics. The presidency is discussed in relation to the military. The historical interaction between the presidency and the military in Zambia explains why even under extreme national distress, a coup has never materialized (See Chapter Nine). Qualities that will define the president of Zambia, including women presidents, in the 21st Century are discussed.

§10.1 The Presidency

The Zambian Republican president is the most powerful person in the nation. He or she is constitutionally the Head of State and head of government. The presidency, also known as the Office of the President (or "O.P"), is an institution. The Zambian president is vested with extensive powers that include presiding over the Cabinet (comprising the president, vice-president, the Secretary to the Cabinet and twenty-four MPs appointed by the president), initiating or vetoing legislation, establishing or dissolving ministries (with legislative approval), and immunity from criminal prosecution for acts committed while in office. Rounding out the Executive branch are the vice-president and Cabinet. The later formulates policy, answers to the National Assembly and oversees government operations. The president is commander-in-chief of the armed forces.

The *Zambian Constitution* assigns presidential powers. After gaining political independence from Britain on October 24th, 1964, Zambia went through three systems of governance. These are plural politics from 1964 to 1972; One-Party system from 1973 to 1991; and a reversion to plural politics from 1991 onwards. Although Zambia is made up of ten[628] administrative provinces, most political activities happen in the national Capital of Lusaka and on the Copperbelt Province. Historically, these two provinces have been hubs of political agitation and operation.

Politically, the governance of Zambia rests in the central and, to some extent, local governments: "Government power is, however, concentrated in central government, which administers government functions at national, provincial and district levels. Local authorities (councils) enjoy only limited administrative authority."[629] Political representation is distributed among 150

---

[628] Up until October 2011 with the addition of Muchinga Province by President Michael Sata, Zambia had nine provinces

[629] Government of the Republic of Zambia, *Interim Report of the Constitution Review Commission*, Lusaka, June 29th, 2005, p. 12

constituencies. These 150 constitute elective seats in the National Assembly. The Republican president is also the president of the National Assembly. He is represented in the National Assembly by the Republican vice-president. The Republican president nominates eight more members to the National Assembly. Thus, the Republican president, the Republican vice-president, the 150 MPs, and the eight nominated members comprise the Zambian Parliament. The Zambian Parliament consists of 160 members in principle. Parliament legislates on behalf of the Zambian people.

§10.2 Power Hubs – State House

The most important person who lives at State House in Zambia is the Republican president. Every time the president awakes at State House, he[630] has the larger national *agenda* in mind. Today, he could dictate over the national defence establishment, he could appoint new ministers or even reshuffle them, and he could receive investment representatives from any country on the globe.

State House politics is predicated upon an administrative *octopus'* system. Like an octopus with tentacles, the president achieves his daily diary activities through an army of officials and operatives. Sometimes the president may not even know, individually, what is obtaining among his Ministers except through special officials assisting him on that front. It is important, therefore, that the president selects these officials very carefully, because they could, if incompetent, endanger effectiveness and efficient running of government business.

As stated earlier, the President of Zambia holds sweeping powers which make him the most powerful man in the nation. The *Zambian Constitution* can be described, in economic terms, as consisting of too much centralization of economic and political powers in O.P. Review of the Zambian constitutional legacy will

---

[630] In this chapter, "he" is gender neutral, it also means "she".

reveal that such powers as vested squarely in one office (practically, in one person) is too strenuous even for the most assiduous of men that only two outcomes are possible.

One, the president must be a-jack-of-all-trade and *must* be a master of all. Or two, the president may falter under the weight of constitutional force and may ultimately either collapse mentally or, in a worst-case scenario, lose their lives. From independence to 2016, Zambia elected six presidents, namely, Kenneth Kaunda, Frederick Chiluba, Levy Mwanawasa, Rupiah Banda, Michael Sata, and Edgar Lungu.[631] Chiluba died out of office; Mwanawasa and Sata died while in office.

The Office of the President of the Republic of Zambia begins with a presidential election held every five years. The functions of that powerful office, however, begin with a simple oath:

> "I, ____ having been elected to the high office of President of the Republic of Zambia do (in the name of the Almighty God swear) (solemnly affirm) that I will be faithful and true to the people of the Republic of Zambia; that I will at all times preserve, protect and defend the Constitution of the Republic of Zambia; and that I dedicate myself to the service and well-being of the people of the Republic of Zambia and to do right to all manner of persons. I further (solemnly swear) (solemnly affirm) that should I at any time break this oath of office, I shall submit myself to the laws of the Republic of Zambia and suffer the penalty for it."

This oath ushers one into one of the most strenuous offices of any nation within the community of nations. The first power of the president is in regards to, and in tandem with, the Rule of Law mandate. The president must assent to the Bill to gain legal effect and become law. This quasi-legislative power places the president right in the middle of the Third Branch of Government

---

[631] President Edgar Lungu was inaugurated on September 13th, 2016 after the Constitutional Court dismissed an opposition petition to nullify elections held on August 11th, 2016. Lungu succeeded Michael Sata as president after winning the January 25th, 2015 elections. Sata died on October 28th, 2014 without completing his tenure.

as "Chief" of the Judiciary, with implications on the eternal doctrine of the Separation of Powers. By constitution law, the president is mandated with the proclamations of laws.

Second, the constitution grants the president enormous powers of attrition (of wear and tear). The president is bestowed with the prerogative of mercy powers, which he may exercise in respect of any criminal offence committed.[632] The president appoints an advisory committee on the prerogative of mercy and presides at any of the meetings of the said advisory committee. In addition, the president must report to the National Assembly on the progress made in the fulfillment of the fundamental human rights and freedoms.

Moreover, the State, through the president, must provide a *peaceful, secure and stable political environment which is necessary for economic development.* This is commonly christened as providing an "Enabling Environment."

The president may, at any time, refer to the Constitutional Court[633] the case of a person who has been or is being restricted or detained pursuant to a restriction or detention order. And in addition, he may declare a State of Emergency if the State is threatened with war or natural disaster.

The president appoints the Ethics Commission subject to *ratification* by the National Assembly. It is important to clarify that the principle of ratification, as it applies to Zambia, is a redundant procedure. This is because the National Assembly cannot unreasonably refuse or delay the ratification. This, and the fact that the ruling party may enjoy majority in Parliament, makes the ratification exercise just a mere formality. Therefore, ratification, for the most part, is presumed or even guaranteed.

---

[632] In this, and subsequent sections dealing with the *Zambian Constitution*, the author has attempted to deliberately omit reference to constitutional provisions. The reason is that since independence Zambia has repeatedly changed its constitution.

[633] The Zambian Constitutional Court is a higher court that deals with constitutional law or any other constitutional matter related to human rights. Its mandate is contained in clause 127 of the Zambian Constitution (2016).

The president has enormous powers to confer honors and awards on deserved persons. He may, thus, confer honorary citizenship on deserved individuals.

Third, the above powers as may be exercised by the president emanate from the overarching constitutional *fiat* that, as president, the person occupying the office is the Head of State and government, and commander-in-chief of the defence forces. He is, quintessentially, the Chief Executive Officer (CEO) of the State.

Residue powers contained in that prerogative, "Head of State," cloaks the president with invincibility captured constitutionally in such terms as "dignity," "leadership," and "execution." The president presides over Cabinet, accredits and appoints diplomats, dignitaries and plenipotentiaries. He also receives and recognizes foreign ambassadors and heads of international organizations. And as discussed under the power of attrition, may pardon or reprieve offenders unconditionally.

The president is constitutionally expected to negotiate and sign international agreements. This, he must do bearing the economic implications of such actions in mind.

The appointing (delegated) prerogative of the president is, perhaps, the single most frequent preoccupation of his august office. The constitution makes the president the quintessential appointing authority of the State. He may, thus, appoint commissions of inquiry on any matter of public interest or concern; ministers; deputy ministers; provincial ministers; and the Secretary to the Cabinet (the chief civil servant).

Fourth, if the president in Zambia is the quasi-head of the Judiciary, he is, in state as in function, the "head" of the Legislature, the Second Branch of Government. In Zambia, Parliament does not exist apart from the president. Both the National Assembly (elected and nominated MPs) and the president must be present to constitute Parliament. Therefore, if the legislative power of the Republic is vested in a Parliament, it is the president who is "President of the Legislature."

The *Zambian Constitution* requires the president to execute dates in relation to first sittings of Parliament. By notice in the *Gazette*, he must appoint a date of not more than thirty days after a general election for the first sitting of the National Assembly. Moreover, he may, in writing, request the Speaker to summon a special meeting of the National Assembly to consider *extraordinary* or urgent business! The Zambian president may dissolve Parliament, and thereafter if there should exist a state of war or emergency, he may re-call the National Assembly that he dissolved to meet. And like the powers rarely exercised under the political concept of "Responsible Government," in parliamentary democracies, the Speaker, in consultation with the president, may *prorogue* the National Assembly by proclamation. Parliament is his to attend at will or from time to time. Even more, he may cause anything he so desires to be read there on his behalf, or as the case might be.

The only thing the president may never do, and rightly so, with the National Assembly, is that he has no *final* judicial power. This principle is a fundamental premise upon which democratic societies thrive. The idea of the Independence of the Judiciary, is thus in this way guaranteed under the constitution. But as any student of the *Zambian Constitution* knows or ought to know, this brisk guarantee is obviated by the extra-judicial powers granted to the president by the same constitution.

The president may appoint, subject to ratification of National Assembly and in consultation with the Judicial Service Commission (members of the Judicial Service Commission and its Chief Administrator are themselves appointed by the president), the Chief Justice and the Deputy Chief Justice. He may also designate a Judge of the Supreme Court to perform judicial functions at the Highest Court in the land. In addition, he appoints Judges of the Court of Appeal and of the High Court.

The Judicial Complaints Commission reports the results of their investigations, dubbed "petitions," to the president. The president supervises the Medical Board, so that anyone investigated or examined and found wanting may be removed, vicariously, by the same president.

Fifth and revisiting the appointing powers of the president, nearly all the heads of important bodies are appointed by this one person. The House of Chiefs – its Clerk and officers; the Attorney-General (with National Assembly ratification and at the recommendation of the Judicial Service Commission); the Solicitor-General; the Director of Public Prosecutions; and the Permanent Secretary are all appointed by the president. The Public Services Commission only exercises "delegated" authority on behalf of the Zambian President. The members of the Public Services Commission are all appointed by the president.

The president also appoints the Auditor-General on the recommendation of the State Audit Commission, and, of course, ratified by the National Assembly. As with most state departments, the members of the State Audit Commission themselves are appointed by the president. And, indeed, the president appoints the *Chief Money Man* of the land, the Governor of the Central Bank. If currency control, or even decontrol, on interest rates has any bearing on national economics, the president holds that in balance.

There is one public official who derives no direct appointment from the president, the Parliamentary Ombudsman. He is appointed by the Parliamentary Service Commission subject to ratification by the National Assembly. However, here is a caveat, the Ombudsman must first surrender a copy of his or her report to the president, and most of his or her missions or services are recommended by the president.

Sixth, the position of commander-in-chief, in the *Zambian Constitution*, bequeaths an enormous weight on the president's shoulders. To begin, the president chairs the Defence Council.[634] The Defence Council consists of the Minister of Defence; the Minister for Home Affairs; the Minister for Foreign Affairs; the

---

[634] See §10.5

Army Commander; the Air Force Commander; the Director-General of the Intelligence Security Service; and one other person appointed by the president. The president also chairs the National Intelligence Council with supervisory powers over the Director-General of the Security Intelligence Service; the Army Commander; and the Air Commander. The chairperson of the Police and Prisons Services Commission is appointed by the president; together with all its members.

This supervisory power over the security chiefs is unequivocal to the president as commander-in-chief. For instance, the president determines their emoluments and other terms and conditions of service in close consultation with the Emoluments Commission.

Not only does the president chair or appoint the chairpersons of some security services, he also appoints other persons to hold or act in office in the Defence Forces or any of the national security agencies. The president may receive advisory help from either the Service Commission or Security Council.

Seventh, the president is instrumental in securing accountability in the financial wing of government. One can immediately vouchsafe that the president will control and administer the *Appropriation Act*[635] in respect of a financial year. In that capacity, the president may authorize the withdrawal of money from the Consolidated Fund (the same fund that determines presidential pension in part) to meet expenditure, if need be. The president must know and should be informed of any loans obtaining under such themes as the source and the extent of total indebtedness by way of principal and accumulated interest. This alone, may call for the exercise of enormous economic intelligence on the part of the president. In addition, the president must both oversee the provision made for servicing or repayment of the loan and tenor as well as for the utilization and performance of the loan. The level of intelligence and good judgment required here, especially for highly indebted poor

---

[635] No. 32 of 2011

nations, is material to both the sustainability and the management of economic debt.

Land is the largest natural and national resource of any nation. The president is the guardian of land, both of state land and customary land. He holds land "in trust for and on behalf of the people of Zambia." And through the National Lands Commission (which the president appoints), and to some extent by the chiefs or local authorities, the president may alienate land to citizens or to non-citizens as he sees fit.

The Office of the President of Zambia is surrounded by a team of individuals who ensure that day to day affairs at State House are well-looked after, including administrative, political, economic, national security, media, legal or other personal matters: The Office is attended to by the Chief of State House Staff, Principal Private Secretary, Three Senior Private Secretaries and Five Special Assistants (Press, Economics, Politics, Legal, Projects Monitoring and Implementation). Two Chief Personal Secretaries serve directly in the Office where the president works, supported by his Aide De Camp.[636]

§10.3 Commander-in-Chief

The Zambian Defence Force, over which the President of Zambia is Commander-in-Chief, is defined as consisting of an Army (comprising the Regular Force of the Army, the Territorial Force of the Army, the Army Reserve and the Territorial Army Reserve) and an Air Force (comprising the Regular Force of the Air Force, the Auxiliary Air Force, the Air Force Reserve and the Auxiliary Air Force Reserve). The Army and the Air Force are mandated to charge the Defence Force with the defence of Zambia and with such other duties as may from time to time be determined by the president; and to provide for the creation of a

---

[636] "The President's Office," http://www.statehouse.gov.zm/index.php/about-state-house/the-presidents-office (Retrieved: June 2nd, 2010)

Defence Council to advise the president in matters of policy and matters affecting the command, discipline and administration of the Defence Force.[637]

Phiri[638] has brilliantly discussed the military history of Zambia. However, it suffices to point out that the Zambian Army emanated from the Northern Rhodesia Regiment which also grew out of the Northern Rhodesia Police to "protect the colonial power."[639]

The civil control of the military in Zambia was established in 1933 at the time of the creation of the Armed Forces during the colonial era. Since then civilians have controlled the military. This may explain why there has never been a successful coup in Zambia.[640]

The army is part of the civilian majority. It has the monopoly of arms and is an expert in the management of violence. In Zambia, the civilian authorities interact with the military institutions. The military provides national security by defending Zambia both internally and externally.

§10.4 Civil Control

Civil control of the defence forces is an essential aspect of democracy. Zambia has one of the best military-civilian relationships in Africa. This relationship has been instrumental in securing a relatively peaceful climate for the Rule of Law and order. Zambia has continued to foil coups and maintain cordial relationships between the military and the civilian authorities because of four principles.

---

[637] *Defence Act*, Cap. 106 of the Laws of Zambia (preamble)
[638] Bizeck J. Phiri, "Civil Control of the Zambian Military since Independence and its Implication for Democracy," (2007)
[639] *Ibid.*
[640] There have been four attempted coups in Zambia in the Second Republic (1976, 1980, 1986 and 1990). All these were nipped in the bud because the intelligent system was well organized.

Charles Mwewa

First, in Zambia, a civilian Chief Executive Officer (CEO), the president, is supported by civilian subordinates and is also the head of the military chain of command. The High Court has the jurisdiction to hear cases involving military infringements on the rights of the citizens. The Commander-in-Chief is, similarly, empowered by the courts to determine the operational use of the armed forces and he has the power to appoint members of the armed forces.

A clear delineation is made in terms of controlling the powers of the military by a civilian body. Thus, "Civil control of the defence force is meant to guard against military subversion while ensuring that military strategy remains a tool of national political goals under the civilian government."[641] But where a civilian government is empowered to control the military without checks and balances, the Executive branch of government is bound to abuse its powers leading to catastrophic ends, the resumption to arms by the military to restore order. In that way, in Zambia, civil control of the military is also regulated by Parliament to oversee "the exercise of powers conferred upon the president."[642]

The above scenario, therefore, explains how the three branches of government interact in ensuring that the military is subjected to strict discipline in averting possible coups. This is achieved through the Separation of Powers. The Separation of Powers itself is an essential element in the strengthening of the Zambian democratic process.

Second, the design of the Zambian defence forces has made it possible for the military to be an instrument for the enhancement of national security and democracy. The nature of the presidential duo roles both as the CEO of the civilian government and Commander-in-Chief of the armed forces necessitates this. As CEO of the civilian government, the president guards against possible military subversions. However, this is put in check by the National Assembly (Legislature) which checks on the Executive branch of government. The Judiciary completes the

---

[641] Phiri, *supra.*
[642] *Ibid.*

252

picture under the principle of the Separation of Powers by an extended jurisdiction to hear infringements related to the military's abuse of civilians' human rights.

Third and consequent to second above, the military's subordination to political civilian authorities ensures two things. It ensures the defence not only of the nation but also of the *Zambian Constitution*. The military, in peaceful times, embodies special machinery for the safeguard of democracy in Zambia.[643] Mphaisha quotes Kenneth Kaunda who on March 22nd, 1966 reminded the Third Battalion of the Zambia Regiment in Kabwe to "protect and defend the constitution of the land as well as other institutions emanating from the provisions of the constitution."[644] This charge came handy in the light of events in Africa where the defence forces had taken over constitutionally elected governments mainly through coups d'état.

§10.5 Defence Council

The military's subordination to political civilian authorities predicated upon the creation of the Defence Council, which the president chairs, ensures that the benefits of democracy are not undermined by possible military subversion. The Defence Council of Zambia was created in 1955 by an Act of Parliament to advise "the president in such matters of policy and matters affecting the command, discipline and administration of the Defence Force and shall perform such other functions and duties as may be referred to it from time to time by the president."[645]

---

[643] Phiri defines democracy in Zambia as "a political system that accommodates multi-party or plural politics. Democratization in the context of Zambian politics means the process of change from a One-Party system to plural politics in 1990" (Bizeck J. Phiri, "Democratization and Security Sector Reform in Zambia.")
[644] Chisepo J. J. Mphaisha, (ed.), *The State of the Nation Volume I: Politics and Governance* (Lusaka: Kenneth Kaunda Foundation, 1988), p. 172
[645] *Defence Act* of Zambia, section 8(1)

Since 1991, the composition of the Defence Council has differed sharply from the composition it had in the Second Republic.[646]

The Defence Council is chaired by the president or the Minister for Defence in the absence of the president. Members of the council are the Minister for Home Affairs, the Minister for Legal Affairs, and the Minister for Finance. Other members are ruling party representatives, commanders of the Zambian Army, Zambia Air Force (ZAF) and ZNS, and the rest are the Investigator-General (IG) and the Director of Intelligence. The Director of Intelligence acts as the secretary of the Defence Council of Zambia.

Fourth, and last but not the least, cordial relationships between the military and the civilian authorities have been necessitated by the *apolitical* nature of the military. A multiparty democracy calls for the non-politicization of the military. To be legitimate, the military should reflect "the spirit of nationalism in general."[647] However, this should be coupled with a clear redefinition of democracy as it applied then to the Second Republic and now to the Third Republic. In the Second Republic, with only one party in the system, the Kaunda regime idealized the military with the "myth that One-Party Participatory Democracy was an alternative form of democracy."[648]

With the attainment of multiparty politics in Zambia after 1991, military allegiance is no longer based on party lines or ideology. Allegiance does not depend on the wishes of those the military receives authority from, either. The military personnel are required not to "participate in politics while actively serving in the defence force."[649] This does serve to maintain the professionalism of the military personnel and all the members of

---

[646] In the First and Second Republics, the Zambian Defence Council comprised the president, the Minister for Finance, and the commanders of the Army and the Air Force.

[647] Van Donge, "The Military and the Crisis of Legitimacy," in J. van Donge & G. Harries-Jenkens (eds.), *The Military and the Problem of Legitimacy* (London and California: SAGE Publications, 1976), p. 22

[648] Phiri, *supra.*, p. 9

[649] *Ibid.*

the defence forces. Phiri informs that, "The MMD believed that only a professional defence force would defend the constitution and protect the ethos of democracy [in Zambia]."[650]

For example, in 1993, the MMD government, for the first time in the history of the Zambian Defence Forces subjected the Ministry of Defence Estimates of Expenditure to parliamentary debate and scrutiny. This move, together with other measures,[651] helped to facilitate continued improvements in civil-military relations in Zambia, and to enable civilians, both in and outside Parliament, to debate military expenditure without the fear of being accused of undermining national security.[652]

§10.6 Military and Politics

An aura of reality exists in Africa that there is imminent possibility of military takeovers. No country in Africa is immune. The sad reality is that, "The record of the African military has been one of disaster."[653] There is generally consensus that military governments are undemocratic, and are incapable of initiating, nurturing and consolidating democracy.[654] Today, the coup d'état phenomenon still looms over Africa, which in the least, has not improved the African economic conditions. The coup has not been a source for political stability, either. Rather than solve African contemporary political and socio-economic

---

[650] *Ibid.*, p. 12

[651] Such as the introduction of the Parliamentary Committee on Foreign Affairs, National Security and Defence

[652] G. Haantobolo, *The Role of the Zambian Legislature in the Transformation of the Zambian Defence Forces 1964 – 2000*; A Paper submitted to the Civil-Military Relations SADC Project, June 2000, p. 22

[653] Julius O. Ihonvbere, *Economic Crisis, Civil Society and Democratization: The Case of Zambia* (Trenton & Asmara: Africa World Press, Inc., 1996), p. 36

[654] *Ibid.*

problems, military coups d'état in Africa have tended to drive the continent into even further suffering and turmoil.[655]

Military governments may resort to brutal force to martial policies and may easily silence opponents of the junta whenever cause for criticizing government arises. Thus, independent voices may be put to rest and the only tactical way of ruling is through intimidation and control. There is abundant evidence that military rule relies on "wanton human rights abuses to stifle civil society and assert its own control over society."[656]

The general attitude is, therefore, that the military is devoid of democratic conception akin to democratic mindedness. Kaunda observes:

> With certain brilliant exceptions, the military mind is not adept at the art of politics. It knows little of the compromises, accommodations and persuasion which underlie political decisions. Because the military leader must have an unquestioning conviction that he knows what is best for those under him, he is prone to translate this possibly unwarranted self-confidence into the political sphere with disastrous results, for there are no representative mechanisms through which he can be curbed.[657]

Military rule is a quintessential dictatorship. It is not, however, a dictatorship by choice, but rather by design. Military leaders are wired to dictate authority and command loyalty. Military men and women are in turn trained to obey without question and to carry out orders and ask no questions. These are tendencies which do not rhyme with democratic principles.

---

[655] Jimmi Wangome, "Military Coups in Africa - The African 'Neo-Colonialism' That Is Self-Inflicted," (1985) http://www.globalsecurity.org/military/library/report/1985/WJ.htm (Retrieved: January 10th, 2011)

[656] See Julius O. Ihonvbere, *Nigeria: The Politics of Adjustment and Democracy* (New Brunswick, NJ: Transaction Publishers, 1994) as quoted in Julius O. Ihonvbere, *supra., ibid.*

[657] Kenneth Kaunda, as quoted in Henry Kyambalesa, "MMD'S Quest for Statutory Media Regulation," *Zambia News Features* (August 29th, 2010)

To preserve democracy, there must be a clear delineation between the civilian rulers and the military officers. The former must be entrusted with political leadership while the later should defend the interests of democracy. In this way, therefore, civilian leadership and the military are related.

President Kaunda understood the place of the military in democracy. While Zambia has been fortune to elect democratically-minded leaders, many countries in Africa have not. "Without doubt, in Liberia, Nigeria, the Sudan, Somalia, Rwanda, Burundi, Togo, [Congo DR and Sierra Leone] (to mention only the hotspots of crisis in Africa), the democratic *agenda* has taken a back seat to efforts to resolve the national question, reconstitute the state, and mediate contradictions and conflicts within and between political constituencies."[658]

This sad state of affairs continues to undermine efforts meant to solidify democracy in Africa. The Zambian case offers a concrete testimony to the rest of Africa that democracy can thrive without military interference. However, many still fear that democracy in Zambia could be a false start, especially in the wake of plural politics in 1991. This fear, though, is not sustained given the many coup attempts that have failed and the resilience of the Zambian people to see democracy take root.[659]

If the success of democracy in Zambia is measured in terms of lack of military takeovers,[660] then Zambia is a beacon of

---

[658] Ihonvbere, *Economic Crisis, Civil Society and Democratization: The Case of Zambia, supra.,* p. 38

[659] See Chapter 9 for a sustained discussion on Attempted Coups in Zambia.

[660] With regards to military takeovers in Africa, Western influence has been cited. For the most part, tribalism and other factors have played a role. However, for the other, the West and other powerful nations have used Africa as a battle ground for their own interests. In *Barrel of a Gun: A Correspondent's Misspent Moments in Combat* (Havertown, PA: Casemate Publishers, 2010), see especially pages from 17, Al J. Venter, recounts how Western forces have been at the forefront of civil wars and coups in Africa. Does it, therefore, matter if the Africans lose their lives and devastate their already precarious economies as a result, as long as foreign interests acquire their much-coveted oil, precious stones, minerals or strategic enclaves for continued military domination?

Charles Mwewa

democracy in Africa. However, a crisis-ridden political economy continues to downgrade the gains of democracy. This has prompted a Nigerian researcher and scholar to describe the democratic change in Zambia since 1991 as "change without change."[661]

§10.7 President of the Entire Nation

Many credit the relative stability and peace of Zambia to Kaunda's philosophy of Humanism and the slogan of *One Zambia – One Nation*. Historically, a contrast has been made between Zambia's *de jure* president, Kenneth Kaunda, and Simon Kapwepwe, "The president who never reigned." Both Kaunda and Kapwepwe were born in Chinsali and attended the same mission school. They were casually referred to as the two twins. Kaunda and Kapwepwe had been political colleagues since childhood.

Kapwepwe could easily have become Zambia's second Republican president. He was "second only to former president Kaunda in influence among Zambian decision makers."[662] The two twins, however, differed in one fundamental respect. Kapwepwe was more identified with the traditional Zambian society than Kaunda. This difference is owed to Kaunda's Malawian parentage.

Although Kapwepwe was naturally the "acknowledged leader of the Bemba-speaking peoples who dominated the northern provinces and the Copperbelt,"[663] he was politically considered a liability abroad. The diplomatic circles viewed him as an extremist and a hardliner socialist. "Admittedly [Kapwepwe's] proclivity for indulging in rhetoric overkill, his calculated

---

[661] Ihonvbere., *Economic Crisis, Civil Society and Democratization: The Case of Zambia, supra.*, p. 40

[662] Douglas G. Anglin, *Zambian Crisis Behavior* (Montreal & Kingston: McGill-Queen's University Press, 1994), p. 40.

[663] *Ibid.*

258

disregard of diplomatic niceties, and his characteristic impatience contributed to his reputation as a radical."[664]

Kapwepwe's blunder was not his making.[665] He was perceived to be pro-Bemba, despite being primarily concerned with "the material well-being of the Zambians in general."[666] On the contrary, Kaunda was perceived as a unifier, a fact that made him more presidential than Kapwepwe.[667]

In Zambia, it is imperative that presidential candidates and reigning presidents articulate in plain language the inherent united nature of the Zambian social mosaic. It is this miscellany which has been responsible for the relative peaceful and united character of the Zambian society. The perception that only people from northern and eastern provinces can become presidents in Zambia is phony and should not be entertained.

§10.8 Great Presidential Qualities

Zambia needs not only good presidents but great presidents as well. The problem of poverty and the challenge to safeguard the young democracy, Zambian presidents ought to be exceptional men and women. They must strive to achieve with high aspirations for their own self and for Zambia. They must be

---

[664] *Ibid.*, p. 41

[665] Presidential politics, like politics itself, is perception. Potential presidents have gaffed their way through to defeat, or they were simply tactically uncalculated. In presidential politics, popularity at home does not necessarily translate into electoral victory, either. The Kaunda - Kapwepwe saga is a good illustration of the point in question.

[666] Anglin, *supra.*

[667] Many Zambian politicians, especially from the Western and Southern provinces, continue to make this mistake today. Anderson Mazoka was perhaps the most intelligent politician to hurl from the southern sands of Zambia. However, Mazoka's political fortunes were gravely reversed by the tribal card. Most Zambians believed, erroneously or not, that the United Party for National Development (UPND) was the party for the Tongas and the Lozis. Michael Sata's Patriotic Front (PF) could be repeating the same mistakes Kapwepwe made.

ambitious and endeavor to perform their duties with personal competence. Such competence should include superior intellectual abilities as well.

There is no substitute for hard work for presidential success. They must set ambitious goals for themselves and move heaven and earth to meet them. Great presidents have exceptional ability to tolerate stress and adversity. This quality is translated into assertiveness, one of the most celebrated marks of presidential greatness.

Successful Zambian presidents must keep an open mind. Because ideas are not a monopoly of a few, open-minded presidents tend to respond to challenges in time. They must be attentive to their emotions and be risk-takers; willing to question traditional values and try new ways of doing things. It is important for Zambian presidents to value matters of faith and morality. A traditional approach to morals is ideal for presidents. However, as much as possible, they should rely on leadership from Church and religious establishments to help guide the nation into righteousness.

No matter their personality,[668] great presidents of the past were more imaginative and more interested in art or poetry and beauty than the less successful presidents. In other words, they were tender-minded, and had a great concern for the less fortunate.

The not-so-popular or non-traditional[669] qualities of most

---

[668] Psychologists have recognized eight personality traits of great world presidents. These are those who are dominators, the introverts, the good guys, the innocents, the actors, the maintainers, the philosophers, and the extraverts (extroverts).

[669] The more traditional qualities of presidents articulated by Kyambalesa include: "Emotional stability, humility, patriotism, selflessness, impartiality, patience, compassion, tolerance, respect for the Rule of Law, ability to conceive of leadership as a temporary mandate to serve the people, ability to conceive of oneself as just another mortal with limited knowledge and aptitudes, ability to make compromises with people who have dissenting views, and the ability to accept criticism and dissent as necessary evils in public life" (Henry Kyambalesa, email of March 12th, 2011).

great presidents are stubbornness and disagreeableness.[670] Unlike other qualities, these two show that presidents have a mind of their own, and can make independent decisions. It has been recognized that great presidents are disorganized as well.[671]

Inspiration is a great asset for successful leadership. Most presidents were great leaders because they knew how to guide and to inspire the people, especially at critical moments.[672] They were persistent, resilient, and they demanded excellence. Moreover, most of them had sympathy and compassion and were good communicators.[673]

By their office, great presidents tend to develop esteem and have the nerve or courage to face challenges. They practice team leadership and share a common vision with the governed. Great presidents, however, can be all these and still be overwhelmed until they lead from the heart by following core values.

§10.9 "For the President's Eyes Only"

The above presidential qualities, notwithstanding, it, however, seems that there is only one prized quality. It is called intelligence. Nations all over the globe have secret departments known as the Secret Service. In Zambia, it is an extension of the

---

[670] Traditionally, all great leaders including presidents are expected to be visionaries, honesty people, credible and trustworthy. They must also have the ability to motivate others, be willing to accept mistakes and correction, and be dedicated and disciplined. The last two traditional qualities are charisma and consensus building.

[671] Most of the research done on presidents before they were elected to office, show that most of them did not keep their offices tide, were frequently unkempt and were visibly enraged with lack of progress.

[672] Critical moments may include when the nation faced a natural catastrophe, when there was an attack on the safety and security of the nation, or in times of national anguish and emergency.

[673] In addition to being good communicators, great presidents were frequently in touch with their people. Some moved *incognito* to assess and listen to the problems of their people. They informed the nation about what was happening and were decisive.

O.P and it is called the Zambia Intelligence Security Service (ZISS). In the wake of the *Chiluba Matrix*,[674] a great deal has been revealed about this most secluded department. But even twenty years before Chiluba became the second Republican President, in 1965, an event that revealed the heart-beat of this department took place. It was captured in Roy Christie's *For the President's Eyes Only*.[675]

Almost four decades ago, Christie saw what is as plausible in the 21st Century. He observed that, "It is a characteristic of African political organizations that they tend to be very much a one-man band."[676] While this practice favors the president in terms of leverage with the electorate, it, however, disadvantages true democratic progression. For one, it creates only a company of "yes, yes, men" who are devoid of their own independent rational judgment. For another, it pours scorn on one of the most fundamental principles of presidential character, persuasiveness. Presidential power constitutes the politics of leadership.[677]

The people the president would persuade must be convinced in their own minds that the president has skill and will enough to use his or her advantages.[678] Thus, intelligence is a double-edged sword. It must be in the president so that the right men and women can be positioned to deliberate national issues and policy.

---

[674] Read Volume Two

[675] Roy Christy, *For the President's Eyes Only* (Johannesburg: Hugh Keartland Publishers, 1971). The book details a true story about John Henry Poremba-Brumer, an agent who shrugged President Kaunda.

[676] *Ibid.*, p. 10

[677] By definition, presidential politics is anchored on persuasion. Both the person of, and the office itself, needs a scintillating persuasive force in order to get consensus of the peers on matters of public concern. Presidential persuasiveness with other stakeholders in government depends partly on bargaining. First, the president must choose men and women who should form the core of public decision-makers. Second, the president must persuade these leaders to move the country in a particular direction. To do so, the president needs something more than the advantages for bargaining.

[678] See Speech (under "Communication Classics"), which is a basic persuasive technique, as adequately discussed in Charles Mwewa, *The Seven Laws of Influence* (Baltimore: PublishAmerica, 2010), pp. 32-37

It also must be in the people the president chooses to oversee the management of public interest. The *modus operandi* or method of operation (MO) of intelligence is contained in the information gathered itself.

Indeed, it is documented that the Rhodesian Special Branch charged Brumer in 1964, to feed President Kaunda with genuine high-level intelligence (information) because "they wished to strengthen him through knowledge."[679] That is the key principle of intelligence; it is believed that the better informed the president is, the better decisions he or she will be able to make and the more secure and safe his or her state will eventually remain. Thus, the president protects his or her power stakes in his or her own acts of choice. The people who are privileged to share in governance must be inveterate observers of the president.[680]

In presidential politics, there is no distinction whether one belongs to the presidential Cabinet, is a member of the provincial or local administration, is a part of the military command in the fields, or belongs to the cohort of the leading politicians, or simply represents private organizations, the diplomatic core or the common citizen on the ground: all are at the service of the president for the accomplishment of *national* goals. However, events in North Africa and the Arab world in the wake of revolutionary chants for democratic change in 2011 and the demonstrations in the first week of the Trump administration in early January 2017, have proven that governments must now be more answerable to the people than ever before.

---

[679] Christie, *supra.*, p. 42

[680] In other words, the presidential operatives are the objects of the president's personal persuasion. They are even more; they are the most attentive members of the president's audience. They are the doers, who comprise in spirit the notion of the *Zambian Nation*. This follows that in presidential politics, the notion of a *nation* itself cuts across the president's own constituencies.

§10.10 Leader Principle Offends Democracy

The tendency by the Zambians to hero-worship their presidents has led to autocratic predispositions in the Zambian leadership formation. Phiri argues that, "Former President Kaunda was not born an autocrat."[681] He was made one by the people of Zambia. When the people see their president as one above reproach, a form of a political savior and as a father-figure, they quickly create a platform for him or her to autocratism.

Kaunda, for example, "was made an autocrat by the masses and fellow UNIP leaders who placed him above reproach."[682] It is officially recorded that Sikota Wina considered the name of President Kaunda as above reproach, noting, "The name of His Excellency the President of this Republic must never be taken in vain."[683] Indeed, Kaunda was unarguably, one of the "best minds on the continent of Africa."[684] However, that did not make him infallible.

Similarly, Kaunda was considered as one who was beyond ridicule. Kapwepwe is quoted as saying: "When you make a mistake with your father [Kaunda], he whips you,"[685] and that Kaunda was a man who, "listens to all complaints small and big from rich and poor, the real humanitarian, a man that we may not find again in our generation."[686] Indeed, it was sentiments like these which made Kaunda into what Phiri calls a "Frankenstein's Monster."[687] In fact, "Little did Kapwepwe and other UNIP leaders realize that they were creating a personality cult around

---

[681] Bizeck Phiri, "Colonial Legacy and Role of Society in the Creation and Demise of Autocracy in Zambia, 1964-1991," (2001) *Nordic Journal of African Studies* 10(2), p. 229
[682] *Ibid.*
[683] Hansard No. 4, 1965, p. 189
[684] Skeva Soko, "Independence for Zambia," (March 1962) *Africa Today*, p. 16
[685] See Hansard, No. 4, 1965, pp. 199-200
[686] *Ibid.*, p. 201
[687] Phiri, *supra.*, p. 231

President Kaunda whereby his name became synonymous with 'His Excellency the President.'"[688]

Five years after the fact, Kapwepwe and others would feel the weight of the 'monster' they had created, resulting into Kapwepwe's unceremonious burial, for all that he had done for the country.[689] Hero-worship creates autocrats. Good people can become dictators overnight where they are given undeserved adulations. Only God is infallible and a "Father."[690]

Hero-worship in Zambia did not end with Kaunda; it persisted in the Third Republic.[691] Although President Chiluba has been credited with "The end of an era,"[692] the twenty years of autocratic rule in Zambia, "did not seem to have taught Zambians the dangers of surrendering their political rights to one individual."[693] Hero-worship tendencies were still rife during the Chiluba rule.[694] However, in rejecting Chiluba's third term bid, the people of Zambia had shown tremendous resilience in ditching the tendencies of the regime that serenated one man as a demigod.[695]

---

[688] *Ibid.*, p. 230

[689] See §13.5

[690] In Zambia, this tendency to regard leaders as fathers has transcended politics into religion itself. Many congregants see their Bishops and Reverends as father-figures, offending Jesus' charge that no human factor should be regarded as father, noting, "You have only one Father in Heaven" (Matthew 23:9).

[691] Under President Banda, for example, it is Rumored that one called William Banda, the Lusaka Province Chairman, is said to control the Neo-Patrimonial *agenda*. Someone once told me that it is easier to see President Banda through William Banda than through government bureaucratic channels.

[692] See John M. Mwanakatwe, *End of an Era* (Lusaka: Multimedia Publications, 1994); *The Economist* (July 7th, 1990)

[693] Phiri, *supra.*, p. 240

[694] See *The Monitor*, No. 134 of November 2000

[695] For example, as far as the Zambians were concerned, Kaunda was a god. The UNIP motto went something like: *"One Zambia, One Nation; One Nation, One Leader; that Leader, Dr. Kaunda Wamuyayaya (Forever), Umutende (Peace) Na Ubuyantanshi (and Development)."* Other slogans were even more explicit, like: *"In Heaven, God; On Earth, Kaunda!"*

Hero-worship is pegged on *Leader Principle*, as Bishop Imakando used to preach, "Everything rises and falls on a leader!" This is a very dangerous prognosis, because at the least, it entails that a leader determines the success or failure of an enterprise. It goes even further than that; it sees the leader as a sort of a *savior*. In other words, a leader is idolized and the followers are meant to think that without the leader, the organization, and indeed, a nation, may not make progress.

When it gets deeply entrenched into the followers, they begin to believe that they are condemned to follow and obey the leader. The result is a culture of hero-worship. This leads to the creation of sycophantic relationships between the leader (patron) and the people (clients).[696] Dictators are made by people who support them.

As argued elsewhere in this book, history has played an important role in the culture of hero-worship in Zambia. Indeed, "The nature of colonial rule made it easier for the new African leaders to become autocrats."[697] Colonial rule in Africa did not reflect the ideals of liberal democracy, either.[698] For one, the *Northern Rhodesia Constitution* did not permit for the formation of opposition parties.[699] For another, British rule in Northern Rhodesia did not encourage the development of leadership redolent to liberal democracy. In 1958, for example, the colonial government developed an impromptu *Africanization* program, "in preparation for the hand-over of power to an African government."[700] Thus, "At independence neither UNIP nor most

---

[696] This kind of sycophantic relationship is known as Neo-Patrimonialism, and is said to be the catalyst for predatory behaviors like public corruption. See Chapter 32.

[697] Phiri, *supra.*, p. 228

[698] See J. S. Coleman, "Economic Growth and Political Reorientation," in M. J. Herskovits and M. Harwitz (eds.), *Economic Transition in Africa* (Evanston: Northwestern University Press, 1964), p. 396

[699] H.C Donald Mackenzie-Kennedy, Northern Rhodesia Chief Secretary to Stewart Gore-Brown, in R. I. Rotberg, *Black Heart: Gore-Brown and Politics of Multiracial Zambia* (Los Angeles: Berkeley, 1977), p. 168

[700] Grant, *Zambia, Then and Now*, p. 30

politicians were sufficiently prepared to nurture liberal democracy, which Britain had hurriedly put in place in 1958."[701]

More seriously, however, was the dictatorial nature of colonial rule. Abroad, the colonial regime gave the impression that democracy was thriving at home. In 1962, Soko wrote that, "Contrary to fact, the Whites and their supporters [were] fond of saying that the Africans [were] represented in the federal and territorial legislatures."[702] Soko then informs that, that was, in fact, "A deliberate distortion of the truth: the Africans who [sat] in…legislatures [were] hand-picked by the White political parties. They [could] not be said to represent their fellow Africans but [were] in fact the tools of their masters."[703]

"Tools of their masters" indeed, they were, and even worse. They were enslaved to an oppressive regime "operating as a police state."[704] In this police state, "Democracy as the Whites [saw] it [could] be achieved only under their continued dictatorship."[705] It is little wonder that when they attained political independence, the first Zambian leaders did not have a democratic model to emulate.

At independence, leadership was fashioned at gun-point. Those who had served as clerks, a position akin to middle district management, emerged as the governors of an independent nation. Those who still distinguished themselves became the new idols. Through them, the people perpetuated a *Kapitao Syndrome*. Emerging Zambian Leaders should work relentless and hard to annihilate such dictatorial tendencies of hero-worship in the Zambian polity. A president is not a god; he is a fallible human being subject to making mistakes.

Moreover, pursuant to the doctrine of the Separation of Powers, the presidency is not the supreme institution in the country. The president is, therefore, not above reproach, not

---

[701] Phiri, *supra.*, p. 229
[702] Soko, *supra.*, p. 16
[703] *Ibid.*
[704] *Ibid.*
[705] *Ibid.*

beyond ridicule, and his or her name can be taken in vain, just like any person in the nation. Hero-worship produces politics based on instincts rather than issues; and parochialism is said to taunt posterity.

In a democratic arrangement, a president is two things: He or she is the epitome of democracy personified; and he or she must be seen to champion the widely acceptable tenets of democracy. Thus, the president must be seen to obey and operate within the law, even when such law or laws work against the president's best interest. For this reason, "The president should stay out of particular cases. He should not participate in certain cases because that is politicizing them."[706]

Hero-worship defeats democracy. It sets the president both above the people and the law. By its nature, hero-worship is inherently anti-Rule of Law. In Zambia, there is a presumption that the nation is democratic: "The premise under which we live is that Zambia is a democratic society."[707] This is not only because the *Zambian Constitution* states so, but also because democracy was the premise on which independence was fought and achieved.

The Zambian freedom fighters did not sacrifice all, including life itself, to gain independence and surrender their rights to a president. They, rather, sacrificed all to establish a society pegged on the Rule of Law – and where the president was to be a symbol of the new nation's quest for democratic manumission. Until the Zambian political psychology is transformed to viewing the presidency as a national right not privilege, the culture of hero-worship will not only be deeply entrenched, it will defile all the efforts at being truly a free society.

Hero-worship damns political pluralism and tolerance. It is no wonder the UNIP regime naturally skewed towards a One-Party dictatorship because of this unpalatable social behavior. Where there is hero-worship, you least expect, "Political pluralism and

---

[706] *Africa News*, "Zambia; Levy's Order to Arrest Sata Was Improper - Prof Chanda," (Thursday, July 28th, 2005)
[707] *Ibid.*

political tolerance and freedom of the media."[708] Emerging Zambian Leaders must abash hero-worship, preach unadulterated equality of all persons, and insist that Zambia does not fall back into the doldrums of political serfdom.

§10.11 Women and the Presidency

It is prudent and in order that the discussion of the presidency should be concluded on the women's note. Recent global, political developments have tended to favor women in decision-making process. In this section, ten reasons are offered why women may make great presidents. As implied in §11.1 under the discussion of the Magna Carta, women issues in politics are (and will continue to be) important.

The first of the Magna Carta's principles requires that those who govern rule by the same laws as those they govern obey. Clause XXIX of the Magna Carta states, in part, "...we will not deny or defer to any man [woman] either justice or right." It had to take more than 500 years before this principle would be realized for women, and even then, it has mostly been in the Northern Hemisphere. Most women even today remain second class citizens, mostly relegated to child-bearing and sexual palavers. Among the liberties denied to women for centuries, the right to vote (and to be elected to positions of power) and the right to contract for highest ranks available, feature prominently. As a result, in many countries, those who hold highest political and economic offices are still males.

Although, historically, there have been variations in how women were regarded from culture to culture and civilization to civilization (for example, ancient Nigeria and Egypt had women who could hunt and rule, respectively) most of what has come to be Western civilization discriminated against women. In another instance, Greeks ostracized women (they were not persons, in

---

[708] *Ibid.*

fact); the Chinese bound their women's feet; and the Romans denied their women a vote. In Bible days, women roles were strictly restricted. It is ironic that modernism frowns upon the Islamic woman who, historically, had been relatively better-protected than her pre-Islamic Arabic and medieval European counterpart!

In Zambia, women who have held influential positions are far and few. Here is an incomplete list, and by no means a comprehensive line-up, of women who have trail-blazed the leadership and political echelons. Time and space will not allow showcasing all the deserved women. This list is restricted to the period between 1964 and 2010:[709]

Margaret Mwanakatwe, head of Barclays Bank in Ghana; Ireen Muyenga, managing director of the Zambia State Insurance Company; Anne Chifungula, Auditor-General; Doris Mwiinga, clerk of the National Assembly; Nkandu Luo, first Zambian woman professor; Lombe Chibesakunda, first Zambian woman high commissioner and former Chief Justice, and currently serving as Chief Justice of SADC court; Mama Kankasa, head of UNIP Women's League for 16 years; Mama "UNIP" Julia Chikamoneka, woman freedom fighter; Mukwae Nakatindi Nganga Yeta, MP for Nalikwanda constituency; Esther Banda, MP for Roan constituency; Margaret Mbeba, MP for Kazimuli constituency; Edith Madeline Robertson, nominated Member of Parliament (MP); Nakatindi Nganga, later Chieftainess Nakatindi of Sesheke, served as Parliamentary Secretary to the Minister of Labor and Social Development.

Others are: Monica Chintu Nanyangwe, MP for Mbala North constituency; Walumweya Monze, nominated MP and served as Minister of State for Planning and Finance Minister of State in the Office of the Prime Minister for a year and as Minister of State for Economic and Technical Cooperation; Dr. Mainga

---

[709] Between 2011 and 2016, there have been credible women in Zambia who easily fit this list; but space and time will not allow to list them here.
However, special inclusion is given to the first female Vice-President of Zambia.

Mutumba Bull, MP for Nalolo, first woman full Cabinet Minister and who also served as Minister of Health, Minister of State (Minister of State in the First and Second Republics was equivalent to Deputy Minister) for Information, Broadcasting and Tourism. Dr. Bull was also the first Zambian woman to obtain a PhD. and the first Zambian woman to lecture at UNZA. She also served as Minister of State for Foreign Affairs and as Minister of State for Civil Service; Phyllis Lombe Chibesakunda, MP for Matero constituency, Minister of State for Legal Affairs and Solicitor-General; Senior Chieftainess Nkomeshya, Minister of State for Home Affairs, Minister at National Commission for Development and Planning and also served in the Ministry of Decentralization; Elizabeth Peggy Mulenje, MP for Chilanga; Grace Chilufya Mulule, MP for Shiwan'gandu; Mary Kaluluma Mwango, MP for Kabwata; Zenia Ndhlovu, MP for Kazimuli and served as Minister of State for Youth and Sport and as Minister at the National Commission for Development and Planning; Alice Pearce Lloyd, MP for Kabwe constituency and also served as Minister of State; Mavis Muyunda, MP for Kabwata constituency, Minister of State for Decentralization, Minister at the National Commission for Development and Planning and Minister of Foreign Affairs.

The other women who deserve mention here are: Bathsheba Ng'andu, Minister for Lands and Natural Resources; Esther Mwanakatenya Chande, MP for Ndola; Matildah Kolala, MP for Mkushi South; Alina Nyikosa, nominated MP; Kabunda Kayongo served as Deputy Education Minister and Youth Sport and Child Development Minister; Edith Nawakwi, Nakonde MP, Cabinet Minister for Labor and Social Security, Energy and Water Development Minister, Agriculture, Food and Fisheries Minister, first woman appointed Finance Minister in Zambia and President of Forum for Democracy and Development (FDD); Princess Nakatindi Wina, MP for Kanyama and for Sesheke; Katongo Mulenga, MP for Chinsali; Wendy Wakapembe Sinkala, MP for Maine and Bwacha and also served as Deputy Minister; Inonge Mbikusita-Lewanika, MP for

Senanga and Zambia's Ambassador to the United States; Letizia Mwanza, MP for Lumezi; Chilufya Kapwepwe, MP for Lunte; Matildah Chakulya, MP for Nkana; Dr. Mbikusita Lewanika, first woman to head a political party called Agenda for Zambia; Gwendoline Konie, ambassador and one of the first women to head a political party called Social Democratic Party; Gladys Nyirongo, Cabinet Minister for Lands; Chileshe Kapwepwe, Deputy Minister of Finance and National Planning; Marina Nsingo, Cabinet Minister for Works and Supply; Sylvia Masebo, Cabinet Minister for Health and etc.; Judith Kapijimpanga, Cabinet Minister for Science and Technology; Mutale Nalumango, Cabinet Minister for Labor; Patricia Nawa, Deputy Minister for Defence; Rosemary Banda, Deputy Minister in the Office of the Vice-president; Julianne Chisupa Chipwende, Deputy Minister for Works and Supply; Angela Cifire, Minister of Health; Vera Tembo (formerly Vera Chiluba), Deputy Minister of Tourism; Gladys Lundwe, Deputy Minister of Energy and Water Development as well as Deputy Minister in the Ministry of Sports, Youth and Child Development; Alice Simango, Deputy Minister for Southern Province; Sarah Sayifwanda, Minister of Gender and Women's Development; Dora Siliya, Minister of Transport and Communications as well as Minister of Education.

It will not be prudent to end this list without mentioning two illustrious women who have trail-blazed the Zambian frontiers in recent years: Irene Mambilima, former chief at the Election Commission and Chief Justice of Zambia (2016); and of course, former Minister of Gender, Inonge Mutukwa Wina, first female Vice-president of the Republic of Zambia (2016).

What is so heartbreaking about these women is not that some of these make it in the list of some influential women in Zambia; two observations are warranted. First, it is that the numbers have been disproportionate to the role and place of women in Zambian decision-making positions. For a long time, Zambian women's participation in politics has ended at voting. Calls by the Southern African Development Community (SADC) to a goal of 50 percent women in decision-making positions as well as previously by the Beijing Platform for Action, have necessitated awareness for women participation, including a proposal for equal ministerial appointments in the constitution.

Second, it is the fact that the positions so rightly enumerated are mostly political offices. This is liability, and in the main, is based on a faulty assumption that only politicians are true leaders. It is vital in future to improve this list to include women trailblazing in all other disciplines such as religion, academia, entertainment, and so on.

Women are necessary to law and development in the following ten (10) ways: First, women bring greater social returns to a country *per capita*. It is more than just a motherly instinct that women possess; women and the idea of targeted investment initiatives have proven that it leads, in the short term, to strengthened individual resilience and self-reliance. This, in the long term, provides a cost-effective alternative that reduces pressure on public expenditures. Women, more than men, tend to consider the broader social implications of their actions, and are more likely to challenge authority and tradition. It is this quality that makes women less corrupt than men. Most of those implicated in corruption in Zambia have been men.

Second, women are more socially responsible than men. Both companies and nations are realizing that advancing more women to senior leadership roles has many benefits. One of these benefits is increased financial performance and sustainability. Women may donate more to altruistic causes, may be committed more to agenda, and may be more likely to keep their promises than men. These are the same qualities that are in short supply nowadays for political leaders. In the same vein, women are more likely than men to care more for the environment as well as transacting in policies that have as their long-term goal the preservation of social relationships necessary for social solidarity.

Third, women decision-makers grow and then sustain the economy. This may be very germane to the quandary most developing countries, like Zambia, face. For the most part, men leaders are good sustainers and rarely grow the economy. Since independence, most African nations have performed worse than when the colonial powers managed the same economies. Most of these post-independence Africa leaders have been men.

And since the 1960s, and popularized in the 1990s, the mantra has been economic sustainability. This has been a faulty prioritization. In the first place, this has been a masculine approach to economics. Men, by nature, sustain, women, improve. The best model suitable to Africa and Zambia should center on progressiveness, not sustainability only. And in the second place, Zambia needs progressive leadership and mindsets. Leaders of this kind will move the nation from the quagmire of economic and political quandary into the limelight of progressive ideas, creative experimentation and new thinking. Women, better than men, are naturally equipped to do that.

Per a study focused on women,[710] women's effect on business and the economy are measurable. For example, "…more women are linked to a 53 percent higher return on equity, per one study, and their companies go bankrupt less frequently. (The presence of even one female director can reduce the risk of going belly up by 20 percent.) Others were more qualitative: Women ask more questions, rather than nodding through decisions." Moreover, women fare better at making consistently fair decisions when competing interests are at stake and they tend to be natural problem-solvers than men.

Fourth, women make better leaders than men. The reasons are not far from reality. Women can forge better and stronger relationships and can be trusted. Women make better teams and are more respected in leadership positions than men. "They think more accurately about the resources needed to accomplish a given outcome."[711]

---

[710] Carol Toller, "New research shows women execs really do think differently—that's why we need more," *Canadian Business*, May 7th, 2013
[711] Erika Andersen, quoting Jack Zenger and Joseph Folkman in *Forbes* in 2012 based on a research study they did of 7,280 leaders in 2011

Fifth, women are better performers than men. Statistics show that children who grow up with single fathers end up worse than those reared by single mothers. Science has come to the same conclusion that those who have been raised by mothers know that nurturing a child early in life may help them develop a larger hippocampus. This is the region in the brain which is very important for learning, memory and stress responses.[712] Put a seed inside of woman's womb, she turns it into a baby; put instruments of power in the hands of women, and they turn them into productivity, prosperity and innovation!

Sixth, there is industry in diversity. A research by Illuminate Ventures found that where there is diversity, performance and innovation increase.[713] The same research found that, "Organizations that are the most inclusive of women in top management achieve 35 percent higher return on equity (ROE) and 34 percent better total return to shareholders versus their peers – and research shows gender diversity to be particularly valuable where innovation is key."[714]

The cardinal factor that has contributed to the under-performance of women in the economy stems from the fact that men have set things upside down. Boys and girls begin at par in Primary School. However, boys end up out-numbering girls later. This disparity is easily observable in employment and leadership as well.

If this trend is reversed, we will begin to see the magic of contribution which only women can bring. Nations like Zambia need to harness this untapped human resource and put it to work at the highest echelon. Women should not be used only as labor force and end there; they should be encouraged to reach high levels of learning and to attain to higher positions of power to transform both peoples and processes for the benefit of all.

---

[712] Joseph Castro, "How a Mother's Love Changes a Child's Brain," *Live Science*, January 30th, 2012
[713] See Geri Stengel, "11 Reasons 2014 Will Be a Breakout Year for Women Entrepreneurs," *Forbes*, January 8th, 2014
[714] *Ibid.*

Seventh, women never stop learning. It is a truism that *readers are leaders*, and this is where the rubber hits the road for women. Women do better than men in self-development, and more than men, they listen more, read more and attend professional development trainings more. If a woman is a president and she attends high-powered meetings, be assured that what she learns from there will be for everyone in the country. This privilege may not exist for men.

Eighth, Zambian women have been there when they were needed most. When called upon to do a national task, Zambian women have stood to the challenge. The list of Zambian influencer women enumerated above is a good example. Government must continue to give women more roles to help them continue to break the glass ceiling. Their success is the success of everyone.

Ninth, Zambian women suffer more from the negatives of economic mismanagement than men. When a man has money, he takes it to the tavern; when a woman has money, she fends for her family. Extrapolated economic-wise, the same is true when women occupy highest positions in the nation.

Tenth, women in general have been marginalized, abused and deprived of human rights more than men have. It is time that historical injustices were reversed in favor of women. With all the power that men have executed historically, it has been the woman who has been the loser because of men's errors. When a woman loses, the entire nation loses. And this is one of the reasons that in countries where women are marginalized or violated, those countries also struggle to achieve social integration, and sometimes, even economic freedom. Women have proven that they can do anything a man can do. They should be considered as partners together with men in development.

11| The Rule of Law

The vile wars of Banguanaland:
Let me lament for the beloved
And compose a dirge to her plot
Refugee camps stripe my beloved
Just like the skin of a leopard
And the world believes it is free!
Poverty, like locusts, invades,
Ballots are nothing but a ruse
While laws only favor the rich!

Chapter Focus

At the end of reading this chapter, you should be able to:

- Understand the historical connection between the Rule of Law and the Magna Carta
- Understand the relationship between law and politics
- Define "Crimes of Poverty"
- Understand how law links the Three Branches of Government
- Identify ways in which law has ruled Zambia
- Link law to development
- Define Judicial Independence and Constitutionalism
- Review the history of constitutional review commissions in Zambia
- Define who a democrat is

BRIEF INTRODUCTION

This chapter introduces the Rule of Law and answers the question of whether law rules in Zambia. The discussion of the Rule of Law in Zambia is related to the historical

Magna Carta, a document believed to have introduced the Rule of Law to the British Empire in 1215.

§11.1 Magna Carta

For over 70 years, Imperial Britain presided over what would become known as the Republic of Zambia. Since its protégé and great colonialist, John Cecil Rhodes, determined to connect the Cape to Cairo, Zambia was cited as a mineral-rich territory deserving of mining prospection and settlement. This British vision was realized by the 1890s when through the British South Africa Company (BSAC), the Lochner Concession of June 1890 was signed and assigned mineral and trading rights of Barotseland to the BSAC. This agreement was reached, practically, without a full understanding of what the agreement said or of its implications. The Barotseland chief was of a belief that he was signing an agreement with the British Government. When he learned the truth, he was powerless to reverse it.

This British ingenuity of taking land by treaties permeated through all and everything the British did and omitted to do, in Africa. Every territory which had come under the British colonial impulse would in later years feel economic revulsions. And Zambia is one of those nations. However, Britain had bequeathed to the world (and by extension to Zambia) something just short of immortality – something which even Britain itself had come to regard as the greatest instrument for the protection of the liberties of the people –The Magna Carta.

Despite the praise for this vetted document, however, initially, it protected only the liberties of the powerful barons. While it would one day become a basic document of the *British Constitution*,[715] democracy and universal protection of

---

[715] Unlike most modern states, Britain does not have a codified constitution but an unwritten one formed of Acts of Parliament, court judgments and conventions. The Magna Carta is part of the *British Constitution*. See Robert

fundamental liberties, protecting the commoners' interests was not among the barons' objectives. It was a feudal document. It was meant to protect the rights and property of the few powerful families in England: "In fact, the majority of the population, the thousands of unfree laborers, is only mentioned once, in a clause concerning the use of court-set fines to punish minor offenses."[716]

The Magna Carta celebrated its 800th anniversary on June 15th, 2015. June 15th in 1215 was the date when the English barons and King John of England agreed to the pith and substance of the "Great charter."[717] John and his predecessors had ruled *vis et voluntas*. Previously, John had taken executive and arbitrary decisions, always justifying his indiscriminate commands on the basis that *a king was above the law*. The barons disagreed. With the help of the Church of England, they drafted the Magna Carta. The principles underpinning the Magna Carta now permeate all civilized and emerging democracies. The Charter has outlived its earlier creators' intentions. It has become an instrument of political freedom and constitutionalism in many parts of the world. The governed must now be ruled according to law, not to the governors' caprice and whim.

The Magna Carta, in principle – immediately – and thereafter, in practice, ended the *Rule of Men* and gave way to that eternal principle of the Rule of Law. The king as well as his subjects were all under the law and must abide by its precepts. The Magna Carta diminished the political capital expended by those in power that they could act at will and with force against the liberties and freedoms of the people. It equalized prospects for the governor as well as the governed.

Blackburn, "Britain's unwritten constitution," http://www.bl.uk/magna-carta/articles/britains-unwritten-constitution (Retrieved: October 10th, 2016)
[716] "Legacy of the Magna Carta,"
http://www.magnacharta.com/bomc/legacy-of-the-bomc/ (Retrieved: September 30th, 2016)
[717] Magna Carta

The American Declaration of Independence (first of the American Charters of Freedoms – in 1776) was penned pegged on the Magna Carta. In the late 18th Century, the *United States Constitution* (US Constitution) became the supreme law of the land, recalling the way the Magna Carta had come to be regarded as fundamental law. In fact, the US Constitution's Fifth Amendment guarantees that "No person shall be deprived of life, liberty, or property, without due process of law," a phrase directly derived from the Magna Carta.

The relevance of the Magna Carta to Zambia is in two ways. First, the Magna Carta is a vicarious part of the Zambian legal and political tradition. In section two of Zambia's 2016 constitution, the corpus of Zambian law or its "existing law" is defined as "…all laws, whether a rule of law or a provision of an Act of Parliament or of any other enactment or instrument whatsoever (including any Act of Parliament of the United Kingdom or Order of Her Majesty-in-Council), having effect as part of the law of Zambia, immediately before the effective date, and includes any Act of Parliament or statutory instrument made before the effective date and coming into force on the effective date or thereafter." Thus, Zambia inherited from Great Britain the rules and principles of law (including British jurisprudence) and all the trappings that come with it.

And second, it is in what the Magna Carta promised where Zambia stands to benefit. The Magna Carta promised the protection of church rights, protection from illegal imprisonment, access to swift justice, as well as placing limitations on taxation. The Magna Carta played a vital role in curbing the excesses of tyrannical monarchs. "Both King Richard and his brother-successor, King John, were levying crushing levels of taxation on their subjects and seizing property virtually at whim."[718]

There is a lot to be done in Zambia to instill an awareness of the citizens' liberties. Clause XXIX of the Magna Carta states

---

[718] Edwin J. Feulner, "Saluting a 'Great Charter' of Liberty," Heritage.org, June 17th, 2015

that, "No freeman shall be taken or imprisoned, or be disseized of his freehold, or liberties, or free customs, or be outlawed, or exiled, or any other wise destroyed; nor will we not pass upon him, nor condemn him, but by lawful judgment of his peers, or by the law of the land. We will sell to no man, we will not deny or defer to any man either justice or right." It is wildly believed that implied in this clause are five key principles:

That no-one is above the law of the land;
That women's rights are important and are to be protected;
That there is equal justice at all levels of society;
That universal human rights apply to all; and
That the protection of the liberties of the governed is fundamental to democracy.

§11.2 Law is Politics

Law is part of politics. Politics is about who gets what and how in a certain political order. To do so, there must be the Rule of Law. In fact, "Government cannot live long unless its foundations are laid on principles of justice."[719] The first principle of the Rule of Law is that everyone is equal before the law. "It does not matter whether one is a wealthy professional, unemployed, or a member of the political bureaucracy; one is subject to the same laws."[720] Maiko Zulu has aptly put it, "The law knows no personality,"[721] because it should not.

The second principle of the Rule of Law establishes what law should do. This principle means that there is an objective set of

---

[719] Poultney Bigelow, *White Man's Africa* (New York & London: Harper & Brothers Publishers, 1898), p. i
[720] Shirley V. Scott, *International Law in World Politics* (New Delhi: Viva Books Private Limited, 2005), p. 13
[721] Zulu remarked when Danny Mwikisa, a renowned Zambian singer who rose to fame with the hit song *Ichiloto Ukuwama,* was sentenced to four years' imprisonment for theft of K26 million in 2007.

rules by which people ought to be governed. In the application of the Rule of Law the governor and the governed, must in principle, operate at the same level and must be governed by the same rules.

§11.3 Crimes of Poverty[722]

In developing countries, there exists an economic chasm between the governors and the governed. The governors are said to belong to an elitist club while most of the ruled grope into the very jaws of poverty. The ruling class, or the politicians, usually in power, enjoys all the economic benefits of the land while the ruled are eluded by wealth. The governed struggle to earn and keep a living and are subjected to oppressive and demeaning working conditions. Most are unemployed and are used as capitalistic pawns. Capitalism needs them as operators and propellers of the free-market system that keeps the elites comfortably in power.

In such a system, law is said to perpetuate disparities that keep the poor where they are and elevates the rich and powerful to an even loftier glory. To survive, the poor tends to commit what are known as crimes of poverty. Poverty, and the subsequent crimes arising from it, undermines the Rule of Law. As a Zambian statesman, has succinctly put it, "An empty stomach knows no law."[723] Muhammad Yunus, founder of Grameen Bank and winner of the 2006 Nobel Peace Prize, argues:

> Poverty is perhaps the most serious threat to world peace, even more dangerous than terrorism, religious fundamentalism, ethnic hatred, political rivalries, or any of the other forces that are often cited as promoting violence and war. Poverty leads to hopelessness, which provokes people to desperate acts. Those with practically nothing have no good reason to refrain from violence.[724]

---

[722] See §4.7

[723] Zulu, *Memoirs of Alexander Grey Zulu*, p. 290

[724] Muhammad Yunus, *Creating a World Without Poverty* (New York: PublicAffairs, 2007), p. 105

He adds that nations whose people are brutalized by poverty find it easier to resort to vices like crime or war.[725]

In Zambia, the Rule of Law must move in tandem with the fight against poverty. People are reluctant to obey good laws when such laws bring them no benefit. The Good Lord would argue: "What does it profit a person to gain the whole world and lose their own soul?"[726] The poor would answer, what does it profit a poor soul to obey all the laws and still lose this world?

In December 2002, the Quebec National Assembly adopted the *Act to Combat Poverty and Social Exclusion (Poverty Act),* becoming the first jurisdiction to do so in the world. The *Poverty Act* deals with the "future of the poor"[727] and provides a "model of participatory democracy."[728] Law has, thus, a prominent role to play in the fight against poverty. Fighting poverty itself contributes to the "promotion and protection of human rights, and more specifically of economic and social rights."[729]

Moreover, the Rule of Law means that government is bound in all its actions by fixed rules. These rules should be "announced beforehand so that it is possible to foresee with fair certainty how authorities will use its coercive powers in given circumstances and to plan one's individual affairs on the basis of this knowledge."[730] The principle of the Rule of Law may not always match the realities of the legal system, but it is necessary to set parameters along which certain behaviors may be contained.

---

[725] *Ibid.*

[726] Mark 8:36, "For what does it profit a man to gain the whole world, and forfeit his soul?" (The New American Standard Bible)

[727] Lucie Lamarche, "The 'Made in Quebec' Act to Combat Poverty and Social Exclusion: The Complex Relationship between Poverty and Human Rights," in Margot Young; Susan B. Boyd; Gwen Brodsky & Shelagh Day, (eds.) *Poverty: Rights, Social Citizenship, and Legal Activism* (Vancouver, BC: UBC Press, 2007), p. 139

[728] *Ibid.*

[729] *Ibid.*

[730] F. A. Hayek, *The Road to Serfdom* (London: G. Routledge, 1944), p. 39

Charles Mwewa

§11.4 Balance of Powers

In a perfect world, there would be no power imbalances as all the people would be equal based on birth or nationality. However, in the real world, society is highly imbalanced. The rich are more powerful than the poor, and those who govern are more influential than the governed.

The Rule of Law brings balance to society. The Rule of Law limits the extent to which power can be used as leverage against the weak and the poor. In principle, it gives the weak of society the same access, privileges and rights the strong of society enjoy. By ensuring that everything that is done officially be according not only to law, but to well-defined and popularly enacted law, the Rule of Law puts premium on equality and, in principle, strengthens the ideal of equal benefit before the law.

The Rule of Law preserves democracy. "History has also shown that countries which, come out of violent conflicts, often face the same problems."[731] Thus, war-like behavior produces war-like effects. Nations that began on a path of violence have followed the same course to their own peril. The Rule of Law safeguards democracy and ensures that the benefits of hard work and diligence are not negated by the pulsations of war.

To guarantee the balance of power, the Rule of Law must entail three things: The presence of the Bill or Charter of Rights; an understanding and accessibility to the law; and independence of the Judiciary. Part Three of the 1996 *Constitution of Zambia* constituted the Zambian Bill of Rights[732] - which contained twenty-one articles ranging from Article 11 on Fundamental Rights and Freedoms to Article 32 on Interpretation and Savings.[733]

However, the Rule of Law is futile if citizens cannot understand or access the law. "Unless people understand and

---

[731] Mwaanga, *The Long Sunset* (Lusaka: Fleetfoot Publishing Company, 2008), p. 24
[732] Or the Protection of Fundamental Rights and Freedom of the Individual
[733] This constitution was replaced by one of 2016

know [the law's] provisions,"[734] the Rule of Law will have no benefit on the common person. This is the reason why citizens should insist that a constitution to last the test of time is enacted with the people's absolute consent. This constitution must be accessible.

Philosophically, law must by itself be just to guarantee the protection and safety of the members of society. A good law is defined not by what the law is, but by why it was enacted. A bad law, that is a law that discriminates or gives unnecessary powers and privileges to one sector of society, say to political leaders, cannot be good even if a sane and well-meaning Judiciary interprets it. However, with an independent Judiciary, laws, good or bad, may serve as an umpire for the cause of justice.

In a democratic society, law must be above men. In Zambia, this must be the case: "The absolute supremacy or predominance of regular law as opposed to the influence of arbitrary power, and excludes the existence of arbitrariness, of prerogative, or even of wide discretionary authority on the part of the government."[735] Putting it simply, the Rule of Law is founded on the premise that whatever is done officially must be done in accordance with law.

In the charge to his most noble knights, King Arthur of the Kingdom of Camelot played by Sean Connery in the *First Knight* says, "Let all the citizens see that the law rules in Camelot." This was to be the case even if it had to do with Lancelot himself,[736] that great deliverer of Queen Gunevere, the wife of King Arthur and Lancelot's future lover!

To actualize this rule, the Judiciary must operate independently of the Executive. Independence of the Judiciary is necessary if law must prevail over arbitrary force. For this to happen, the courts ought to not be seen to be instruments of government or the state. The courts should not exhibit marked deference to the political organs and should, where and if

---

[734] Mwaanga, *supra.*
[735] Dice
[736] Lancelot was played by Richard Gere.

necessary, be seen to challenge the "validity of legislation and Executive acts (those that seriously [limit] liberties)."[737]

To guarantee the independence of the Judiciary in a democratic society, the appointment and removal of judges must be regulated by a system based on merit and not political association or lack of it. In 2002, a retired Zambian High Court judge, Kabazo Chanda, and Dr. Frederick Nga'ndu of UNZA, remarked that, "The Zambian Judiciary has never been independent."[738] The duo accused Zambian judges of cowardice and that the said judges would rather dance to the tune of government than maintain judicial independence.

The thread of self-censorship and general cowardice runs through the history of the High and Supreme courts of Zambia. The traditional conduct of the Zambian Judiciary in political cases has generally been one of leaning towards the Executive. In political matters between an ordinary citizen and the state, or between an opposition party and the state, the courts have almost invariably, decided in favor of the state, even in cases where evidence clearly showed that the private citizen or the private organization deserved justice.[739]

This conjecture is saddening, and should induce in every democrat a sense of repugnancy towards the so-called arbiters of justice in society. Zambia should seek to elect to office action-oriented individuals who would stand by the Rule of Law, whether it chops off their heads or portrays them as derring-doers. Courts have a duty to society, to ensure that they interpret the law fairly whether it concerns the state or the individual.

---

[737] Munyonzwe Hamalengwa, "The Legal System of Zambia: Law, Politics and Development in Historic Perspectives," in P. Ebow Bondzi-Simpson, (ed.), *The Law and Economic Development in the Third World* (New York: Praeger Publishers, 1992), p. 27

[738] Reuben Phiri, "'Judiciary in Zambia has Never been Independent,' says Judge Chanda," *The Post,* (Wednesday, June 5th, 2002)

[739] Phiri, *ibid.*

On April 3rd, 2009, in an article famously dubbed *The Captive Chief Justice*, the Law Association of Zambia (LAZ)[740] refused to endorse Mwamba Chanda. Critics observed that Chanda, though a rising star of the Judiciary, possessed no special discernible qualifications and her Curriculum Vitae (CV) was replete with workshop qualifications. However, Chanda had topped the list[741] and Justice Sakala insisted she should be appointed or ratified as High Court Judge.

§11.5 Rule of Lows

Mwaanga has argued that, in fact, most African countries have not been ruled by laws, but by *lows*: "At a time when there was…increasing usage of the line 'Governments of Laws and not of Men.' An attempt has been made to show that what we were, in fact, experiencing was 'Government of lows and not Men' as could be seen in [Zambia]."[742] Mwaanga's emphasis, though, is on the US, which has risen in a unipolar[743] world victimizing the developing countries for "regime change"[744] where it has other self-interests. He gives the example of Iraq where the US waged

---

[740] LAZ is established by the *Law Association Act* as Zambia's bar association whose membership consists of all lawyers and judges in Zambia. It furthers the development of law as an instrument of social order and social justice, as well as providing all lawyers in Zambia with a forum to contributing to the development of the Zambian society. It deals with legal ethics as well as ensuring that legislation related to legal aid is effectuated.

[741] The list also included Edward Luputa Musona, Jones Chinyama (who acquitted Chiluba in the *Matrix* Case), Egispo Mwansa and Chilombo Maka Phiri.

[742] Mwaanga, *supra.,* p. 119

[743] The rising of China is, however, creating a duopolistic world of China and America, what the historian Niall Ferguson calls Chiamerica.

[744] Mwaanga has warned that, "We must guard against accepting or legitimizing the principle of 'regime change' which does not form part of the United Nations *Charter* or any of the U.N Security Council resolutions. If we accepted the principle of 'regime change,' where is it going to end? Which regime will be next? Will it be [Zambia]?" (Emphasis mine)

an unpopular war even when Hans Blix did not find any Weapons of Mass Destruction (or WMDs) there.[745]

Although some people argue vehemently that the legal system in Zambia is weak, the argument holds no provable basis. As illustrated above and taking Judge Kabazo and Dr. Nga'ndu's charge that Zambia, "has never been ruled by a democrat"[746] into consideration, referring to former presidents Kaunda and Chiluba, it becomes apparent that the people entrusted with leadership, whether at the Executive or judicial levels, make the law of no effect.

The Laws of Zambia have been amended, and where necessary, repealed many times more than new ones have been enacted. For the most part, the Laws of Zambia conform to the changing times and are adequate, when applied fairly, to satisfy the fundamental requirements of justice.

Despite heaps of praise accredited to Mwanawasa for upholding the Rule of Law in Zambia, critical review will indicate that, of Zambia's first three presidents, Mwanawasa was the most unsophisticated on the abuse of his presidential powers. For example, in a letter dated July 5th, 2002 and addressed to Newstead Zimba,[747] Mwanawasa commands, "What the Vice-president should have mentioned categorically is that your Ministry is issuing licenses to people like Richard Sakala *who do not mean well to this administration.*"[748]

---

[745] In fact, on Wednesday, February 16th, 2011, Ed Pilkington, Helen Pidd and Martin Chulov of the *Guardian* in an article titled, "Colin Powell Demands Answers over Curveball's WMD Lies," reported that Curveball or Rafid Ahmed Alwan al-Janabi gave dubious information on Iraq's secret biological weapons program. In other words, the CIA acted on lies that Saddam Hussein had WMDs. A regime change occurred, and with it the death of thousands of the Iraqis and Americans all for nothing. This admission by a former refugee whose only motivation was to get employed and acquire a Mercedes Benz, questions the credibility of some intelligence the US and other governments rely upon to change regimes.

[746] Phiri, *supra.*

[747] Then Minister of Information and Broadcasting Services

[748] Richard Sakala, *A Mockery of Justice* (Lusaka: Sentor Publishers, 2009), p. 22

This statement borders on the abuse of presidential powers. A president vows on the constitution to uphold the Rule of Law and to govern fairly despite political polarity. In this case, not only does Mwanawasa display tyrannical attitudes, but he advises that Sakala be denied a TV license because he does not "mean well to this administration." This act bordered on denying a citizen the right to earn a living which is against fundamental human rights anywhere on the planet.

On December 16th, 2003, Mwanawasa to Mark Chona, wrote: "I spoke to Mr. Mutembo Nchito this morning when I learnt that the Director of Public Prosecution had directed him to withdraw from the Sakala's case. I am glad that Mutembo accepted my request and I believe that as I dictate this letter he is cross-examining."[749]

This is an instance of disservice to the law and a grave disrespect to the office of the DPP. The DPP has been mandated by the Zambian law to prosecute cases on behalf of government. Such mandate is even beyond the dictates of the Republican presidency. In the statement above, Mwanawasa overruled the constitution and substituted it with the "rule of a man." Clearly, when the Rule of Law is mentioned in political speeches, it makes all sound like passionate democrats. However, when a president can allow the courts and the prosecution and defence establishments to go about doing the business of justice without political interference, even when he or she knows that the outcome may disadvantage him or her, only then will it be said that the Rule of Law is taking shape in Zambia.

§11.6 Does Law Rule in Zambia?

The answer to the question, "Does law rule in Zambia?" is both yes and no. Pursuant to the charge raised by Chanda and Ng'andu above, *viz*, that, "The traditional conduct of the

---

[749] *Ibid.,* p. 23

Zambian Judiciary in political cases has generally been one of leaning towards the Executive," it would be in order to assess this issue in relation to political, rather than criminal,[750] perspectives.

In delivering judgment of the 2002 Presidential Election Petition, his Lordship the former Chief Justice of the Republic of Zambia, Earnest Sakala, referring to the first two petitioners,[751] noted, "They argued that the role of the court...is to resolve disputes between different parties of the society so that society does not degenerate into anarchy, otherwise parties to presidential elections would have, as their only recourse, to take their grievances to the street."[752]

Thus, it seems, when it comes to expediency, as also His Lordship further noted, that, "It cannot be said that it was the court's intention that [the petition trial] goes on *ad infinitum*,"[753] and in regards to high profile political cases, that the Zambian Judiciary tries to do everything to adjudicate cases in reasonable time. In that juncture alone, therefore, the law seems to rule.

However, citizens are wary, not only of the procedural excellence of the justice system, but also of the outcome. It is an irony, therefore, that in the petition under investigation, the court ruled in favor of the incumbency, despite the allegation that, "Levy Patrick Mwanawasa by himself and or through his agents *corruptly* and *illegally* paid several voters including chiefs, to induce them to vote for him and his party, MMD."[754] The court found Mwanawasa not guilty of electoral corruption on or after November 30th, 2004. At this point in time, the former accused was now ruling as president. Miti-Banda called the judgment,

---

[750] See chapters 13 and 14 for discussions on criminal justice and the law in Zambia
[751] There were three petitioners: Anderson Kambela Mazoka, Gen. Christon S. Tembo and Brig. Gen. Godfrey K. Miyanda. There were also three respondents, namely: Levy P. Mwanawasa, the Electoral Commission of Zambia and the Attorney-General of the Republic of Zambia.
[752] Supreme Court of Zambia Judgment, "Presidential Election Petition - 2002," p. 11
[753] *Ibid.*, p. 8
[754] Petition, *ibid.*, p. 270

"judicial nonsense."[755] And Pule "charged that President Mwanawasa was himself muddled in corruption and should resign as president."[756]

On July 11th, 2002, less than six months in his presidency, Mwanawasa urged Parliament to lift Chiluba's immunity to be prosecuted on *corruption*, and other charges. It was Chiluba who allegedly engineered Mwanawasa's electoral victory, the victory Mwanawasa denied was marred by electoral fraud.[757] If the court ruled in 2004 that the Chiluba engineered Mwanawasa victory was not fraudulent, when Mwanawasa himself in 2002 in Parliament admitted that Chiluba's presidency, including his presiding over the campaign that made Mwanawasa president, was corrupt and fraudulent, it raises serious issues.[758]

§11.7 Rule of Law and Development

Law must be an instrument for transforming society. It must prescribe the role government and legal organs should play to establish the necessary infrastructures for realizing political, economic and social change leading to development. The practice of law for its own sake, derogates the fundamentals of justice in a nation in which the majority is poor.

To achieve the above, legal power[759] should be strengthened to supersede state power. Legal power is defined as "the performance of legislative functions by an organ that is

[755] Laura Miti-Banda, "Woodlands Police Station," *The Post,* (June 29th, 2005)
[756] Speedwell Mupuchi, "Pule Joins ZADECO as President," *The Post,* (Friday, June 24th, 2005)
[757] See Malupenga, p. 140
[758] For a full discussion on the *Chiluba Matrix*, see Volume 2
[759] As opposed to state power. State power "underscores the supremacy of the Executive and/or the party organs. State power, however, is usually a whimsical, one person show that inherently is potentially unstable," (Hamalengwa in *The Law and Economic Development in the Third World*).

independent of the Executive and/or party organs,"[760] is more likely to be stable and durable and is because of "deliberate and tempered decision-making."[761] Legal power gives credence to democracy and is vital to the concept of freedom.

The Rule of Law must be distinguished from rule by law. Under rule by law, the law can serve as a mere tool for government to suppress divergent views in a legalistic fashion. The Rule of Law, on the other hands, checks on the way the Executive uses power prescribed by the constitution. In fact, Mazuba Mwiinga has branded Chiluba as, "The man who served this country with a rule by law formula in which he unleashed the snaring dogmatic repressive laws on his opponents."[762] By "dogmatic repressive laws," Mwiinga is indirectly asserting the fact that Zambian laws[763] are in dire need of surgery to

---

[760] Hamalengwa, *supra.*, p. 21

[761] *Ibid.*

[762] Mazuba Mwiinga, "Chiluba the Scared Man," *The Post,* (Wednesday, June 2nd, 2010)

[763] Since 1996 the Laws of Zambia have been compiled into 26 volumes containing all the laws and the entire respective various Republican constitutions since independence. Volume 1 contains the Index of the of the Laws of Zambia and Chapter (Cap.) 1 of the Laws of Zambia which is the *Constitution of Zambia Act*; Volume 2 contains Cap. 2: *The Interpretation and General Provisions Act* to Cap. 22: *Zambia Institute of Diplomacy and International Studies Act*; Volume 3 contains Cap. 24: *Judicature Administration Act* to Cap. 28: *Subordinate Courts Act*; Volume 4 contains Cap. 29: *Local Courts Act* to Cap. 49: *Zambia Institute of Advanced Legal Education Act*; Volume 5 contains Cap. 50: *Marriage Act* to Cap. 56: *Persons with Disabilities Act*; Volume 6 contains Cap. 68: *Defamation Act* to Cap. 84: *Deeds of Arrangement Act*; Volume 7 contains Cap. 87: *Penal Code Act* to Cap. 98: *Mutual Legal Assistance in Criminal Matters Act*; Volume 8 contains Cap. 106: *Defence Act* to Cap. 110: *Firearms Act*; Volume 9 contains Cap. 111: *State Security Act* to Cap. 127: *Census and Statistics Act*; Volume 10 contains Cap. 134: *Education Act* to Cap. 147: *Zambia Institute of Human Resources Management Act*; Volume 11 contains Cap. 153: *Hotels Act* to Cap. 170: *National Arts Council of Zambia Act*; Volume 12 contains Cap. 173: *National Heritage Conservation Commission Act* to Cap. 208: *Common Leasehold Schemes Act*; Volume 13 contains Cap. 213: *Mines and Minerals Act* to Cap. 220: *Zambian Mines Local Pension Fund (Dissolution) Act*; Volume 14 contains Cap. 224: *Agricultural Credits Act* to

acclimatize them to the changing needs of a modern society. A critical look will reveal that Zambia has fared well on law vis-à-vis amending and repealing those laws which have outlived their effectiveness. For example, Zambia had by 2011 over 400 enacted laws and as early as 1911 when the first Order-in-Council was proclaimed or when the North-western Rhodesia and North-eastern Rhodesia Deeds Registry was amended and then repealed by 15 of 1914,[764] to as early as January 5th, 2016 when the president assented to the newest amended *Zambian Constitution Act (2016)*, Zambia has repealed and or amended more laws than it has enacted.

§11.8 Independent Judiciary

In this section, "Independent Judiciary," or "Independence of the Judiciary," or indeed, "Judicial Independence," mean one and

---

Cap. 238: *Tobacco Levy Act*; Volume 15 contains Cap. 243: *Veterinary Surgeons Act* to Cap. 280: *Non-Designated Expatriate Officers (Retiring Benefits) Act*; Volume 16 contains Cap. 281: *Local Government Act* to Cap. 291: *Gwembe District Special (Dissolution) Act*; Volume 17 contains Cap. 295: *Public Health Act* to Cap. 317: *Medical Aid Societies and Nursing Homes (Dissolution and Prohibition) Act*; Volume 18 contains Cap. 321: *Zambia Revenue Authority Act* and Cap. 322: *Customs and Excise Act*; Volume 19 contains Cap. 323: *Income Tax Act* to Cap. 341: *Insurance Levy Act*; Volume 20 contains Cap. 347: *Finance (Control and Management) Act* to Cap. 379: *Development Bond Act*; Volume 21 contains Cap. 385: *Investment Act* to Cap. 392: *Insurance Act*; Volume 22 contains Cap. 393: *Trades Licensing Act* to Cap. 401: *Trade Marks Act*; Volume 23 contains Cap. 402: *Registered Designs Act* to Cap. 426: *National Savings and Credit Bank of Zambia (Dissolution) Act*; Volume 24 contains Cap. 432: *Engineering Institution of Zambia Act* to Cap. 442: *Zambia Institute of Architects Act*; Volume 25 contains Cap. 444: *Aviation Act* to Cap. 463: *Rhodesia Railways Act*, 1949; and Volume 26 contains Cap. 464: *Roads and Road Traffic Act* to Cap. 475: Appendix 1-12. Readers should consult the Zambian Parliament website for updated listings.
[764] Volume 1 of the Laws of Zambia

the same thing. The history of constitutionalism[765] can be traced to two historical landmarks. The first is the American Revolution and the second is the implosion of the Eastern Bloc of the Berlin Wall in 1989. After armed struggles with the British Empire, thirteen American states formed a new constitution "after engaging in extensive debate as to the proper form of popular government."[766] This tradition of "extensive debate" is a permutation of the dynamism of the force of the Rule of Law. The Rule of Law should, therefore, encapsulate the idea of how law itself is made and interpreted. The fall of the Berlin Wall marked the end of the Cold War. Many Republics of the former USSR began to pattern their governments on the principles of constitutionalism.

The idea of an Independent Judiciary should be a vital presence in Zambian politics and should be part of its constitutional order. There is no such a thing as an independent Judiciary because independence means, "not subject to control of any person...free to act as one pleases."[767] The Judiciary,[768] especially the judges and justices, is so constrained by

---

[765] The idea of, or spirit of, constitutionalism stipulates that governments are not the controlling force of societies. They are simply instruments within societies. Governments must exercise the powers of authority and coercion for the general welfare of the people. Constitutionalism, thus, connotes the idea of limited state. The constitution, which sets out the fundamental rules and principles by which a state should be organized, expresses governments' limitations. It does so by stipulating the powers to the people or bodies to exercise privileges for the sake of the people. For more discussion on constitutionalism, see §11.9

[766] Mark Kozlowski, *The Myth of the Imperial Judiciary* (New York: New York University Press, 2003), p. 51

[767] Ernest L. Sakala, *Autonomy and Independence of the Judiciary in Zambia: Realities and Challenges* (LL.M Thesis, 2000), University of Zambia, p. 119

[768] The roles or core functions of the Judiciary include the following: Dispute resolution; interpretation of the Laws of Zambia; promotion of Order and the Rule of Law; protection of human rights; and safeguarding of the *Zambia Constitution* (source: http://www.judiciary.gov.zm/tiki-index.php, retrieved: May 12th, 2011)

administrative and procedural requirements that it is not feasible to be said to be independent. As Sakala notes, judges do not act as they may please, "otherwise one good, namely justice, would be sacrificed on the altar of another, namely, independence."[769] Rodger Chongwe argues that judicial independence is necessary but should be augmented by judicial accountability: "Thus, judicial independence must not be pursued to a point where judges become totally unaccountable for their actions. In short, judicial independence must be balanced with an appropriate measure of judicial accountability."[770]

The independence of the Judiciary is predicated upon the premise that judges are at least able to decide matters free of political or any other form of interference. Judicial independence encapsulates at least three facets: (1) That judges would assess facts and understand the law applicable without any improper influence;[771] (2) that judges would be impartial in deciding matters;[772] and (3) that judges would be free to do justice in their communities, protected from the power and influence of the state and made as immune as humanly possible from all other influences that may affect their impartiality.[773]

Precedent to the above three facets, and bearing in mind that judicial interference is not only limited to the state and the Executive, but to the corporate masterminds as well, there are two principles of an independent Judiciary. These two principles

---

[769] Sakala, *supra.*

[770] Rodger Chongwe, "Judicial Accountability," *The Post*, (Wednesday, July 30th, 2008)

[771] International Court of Jurists, 25-26 *CIJL Bulletin*, April – October, 1990 as quoted in Sakala, *ibid.*, p. 120

[772] See Macgarvie R. E., "The Ways Available to the Judicial Arm of Government to Preserve Judicial Independence," (1992) Journal *of Judicial Administration*, Vol. 1, No. 235, as cited by Nicholson R. D., "Judicial Independence and Accountability: Can They Co-exist" reproduced in Sakala, *supra.*, p. 120

[773] Stephen N., "Judicial Independence," The Inaugural Oration in Judicial Administration, The Australian Institute of Judicial Administration Incorporated, July 31st, 1989 in Sakala, *supra.*, p. 121

relate to how judges should be selected and remunerated and the relationship between the Judiciary and the other two branches of government.

First, there should be the employment of the standard of good behavior for the continuation of the office of judicial magistracy. Judges should not be appointed and removed at will by the governors. Similarly, courts should not be created without legislative approval. Both practices help to curtail the overarching power of the appointed authorities. The standard of good behavior for the judges ensures that there is a "steady, upright and impartial administration of laws."[774]

Courts are very important in the overall administration of justice. Like judges, courts should be approved by Parliament, lest they become weapons against all those "who don't mean well to this administration." The judicature should be fair and unbiased. From the magistrate, to the justice of the peace, to the judge and the Chief Justice, the judicature should not be dismissed at the governors' *fiat*. For example, in 1969, Kaunda summonsed Chief Justice James Skinner[775] to explain a judgment passed by Justice Evans. Apparently, the president did not agree with it. Such actions go against the very pathos of judicial autonomy and they are bathos to the ideals of a free and democratic society.

In matters of court structures and procedures the state Legislatures should not exercise unchecked powers. Judicial decisions should not be overturned simply because of legislative

---

[774] Kozlowski, *supra.*, p. 52

[775] Sinner supported the African nationalists in the campaigns for self-rule. He had joined UNIP in 1960 and he was the legal advisor to UNIP as well as one of its principal campaign advisors in 1962. He wrote the *Election Workers Handbook* in 1962, a 22-paged manual that was sent to UNIP officials at all levels to guide them through the election procedure. He was appointed Attorney-General in September 1964 and also as Minister of Justice. He was Attorney-General until 1969 and as Minister of Justice until 1965. In 1967, he was appointed Minister of Legal Affairs and as Chief Justice of Zambia in March 1969. (See Grotpeter *et. al*, *Historical Dictionary of Zambia*, p. 408)

fiat. Judicial discretion should be minimized to the greatest extent possible. "The aim is to end eccentric impulses of whimsical, capricious designing man."[776]

A viable Judiciary is one which does not absorb all the powers into its own hands and does not carry out all the tasks of government through its committees. To perform this neutral role, the Judiciary must be distinct but mutual to the Executive and the Legislature.

Second, to ensure the independence of the Judiciary, the Judiciary should constitute a distinct branch of government. Montesquieu argues, "There is no liberty, if the Judiciary power be not separated from the Legislature and Executive."[777] Not only will liberty be jeopardized, where there is no independence of the Judiciary, "the Legislature and Executive branches might use judges to further their own oppressive designs."[778] However, the Judiciary needs the other two branches of government because on its own it may not administer justice to the fullest.

William Blackstone fears that the alliance among the Judiciary, the Legislature and the Executive, where they are not kept independent, may harm life, liberty and property: "Were [the Judiciary] joined with the Legislature, the life, liberty, and property, of the subject would be in the hands of arbitrary men."[779] In other words, lack of independence of the Judiciary is detrimental to the very foundation of freedom and democracy.

In Zambia, especially in the first decade of the 21st Century, emphasis was on the Executive branch of government. The presidential office attracted enormous attention in wake of the *Chiluba Matrix* and the *Captive Chief Justice*. However, this should not be advanced at the expense of the Legislature which has been used, for example, in the Mwanawasa administration to

---

[776] Goldon Wood, "Comments," in Amy Gutmann, (ed.), (1997) *A Matter of Interpretation*, 50, 51

[777] Montesquieu, *The Spirit of the Laws*, 152 (Hafner, 1949), p. 1

[778] Kozlowski, *supra*.

[779] William Blackstone, (1765) *Commentaries on the Laws of England*, Vol. 1: 259-60

lift the immunity of a former Head of State.

Zambia, a presidential democracy, is considered by the United Nations to devolve an extreme concentration of powers upon the president. This concentration of powers is considered illicit and excessive. Concentration of powers in the presidency is said to aggravate the corruption situation in the country. Thus, excessive presidential powers, "Significantly increase the level of corruption in the country; influence the president's refusal to drive a constitutional review process forward and to address seriously electoral reforms; and does not respect the principle of independency among the Legislative, the Executive and the Judiciary."[780]

Like in the Second Republic where "meetings of the National Assembly were not supposed to offer criticism of policy,"[781] the Third Republic was flanked by similar attitudes. For example, criticisms of the Judiciary when the decisions go against government, "have continued even in the Third Republic if not even more vicious."[782] James Madison warns, by extension, that the compilers of the *Zambian Constitution* should not allow the National Assembly to be "everywhere extending the sphere of its activity and drawing all power into its impetuous vortex."[783] This caveat should apply to the government of the day as well.

To avoid falling back into the doldrums of illiberal tendencies such as was espoused in the Second Republic, and from time to time perpetrated in the Third Republic, government must be restrained through the doctrine of the Separation of Powers.

People should voice out when the law is relegated to obliviousness. The case of *Silva and Freitus v. The People*[784] illustrate how the public may demonstrate against the decisions

---

[780] United Nations Offices on Drugs and Crime (UNODC), "Anti-corruption Strategies: Comparative Cases from Indonesia, Pakistan and Zambia," (Vienna, 2010)

[781] Frederick Chiluba, *Democracy: The Challenge of Change*, p. 44

[782] Sakala, *supra.*, p. 198

[783] James Madison, 48, (Mentor 1961), *The Federalist*, Clinton Rossiter, (ed.), pp. 308-309

[784] (1969) ZR 121 and to *Kaunda v. The People* (1990/1991) ZR 215

of the courts regarding the acquittals of those with power and means. Similar incidents in the Third Republic happened when in 1996 the Supreme Court of Zambia declared section 5(4) and section 7 of the *Public Order Act* unconstitutional. This government protestation saw the venerated parliamentary procedure of legislation thwarted as the Bill went through all the procedure for passage in one day! In 2009, the public expressed dissatisfaction when President Chiluba was acquitted of corruption charges. There have been criticisms of the Judiciary from both government and the public in Zambia from time to time. Former Chief Justice Earnest L. Sakala thinks that such criticisms of the Judiciary ought to be accepted as healthy in a democratic society.[785] Apart from retaining the powers of the Executive, the Judiciary, headed by the Chief Justice,[786] must be reformed to operate autonomously against the vagaries of the Executive branch.

The president in Zambia possesses enormous powers in the appointment of the Chief Justice. Although the constitution stipulates the procedure whereby the appointment is subject to parliamentary ratification, the practice has favored naïvety at the expense of serious vetting. A system like the US whereby Senate grills and drills the appointee prior to approval should be favored in Zambia.

---

[785] See Sakala, *supra*.

[786] The question of "A Captive Chief Justice" is at issue here. It is said that a Chief Justice of a country should be allowed to be as independent as possible, for citizens to access fairness and justice. But if he or she were unfortunate to be held captive, he should be a captive of the state and its institutions only. But Zambia portended a different scenario where a few private individuals had held the Chief Justice captive by promising to hide his questionable *agenda* while they made him help settle their personal political and legal scores. Mutembo Nchito faced Chief Justice Mathew Ngulube demanding cooperation. Ngulube thought that Mutembo was attempting to blackmail a sitting Chief Justice who enjoyed constitutional protection and security of tenure. Ngulube was dismissed after being implicated in a ZAMTROP controversy. Mutembo himself was implicated in some corruption by the PF Government.

A vetting process like this one will ensure that the person chosen as Chief Justice is not a political puppet of the incumbent. It will also make certain that he or she does not exist merely to convey the wishes of the ruling party. A system like this will induce credibility into the process and make the Judiciary autonomous.

Zambia's electoral record needs commendation. Zambia's elections are relatively free and fair. The presidential term of office is firmly fixed and the transfer of power has been very impressive. Emerging Zambian Leaders have a moral and legal obligation to perpetuate this tradition.

As Zambia espouses the ideals of free and fair elections, resolution of political conflicts via a ballot, smooth transfer of power, two-term presidential tenure of office and the Rule of Law, Zambia should not pay a blind eye to the experiences of neighboring countries. It is common observation that nations which take short-cuts to power reap bitter political legacies. Once a nation losses its grip on democracy it also bids farewell to peace and order.[787]

Examples of Congo DR and Nigeria, to mention but two, illustrate the fact that once a nation resorts to coups d'état, it is very difficult to reinstitute it to democracy. Although, in the long run, democracy may be attained, undemocratic tendencies will shoot up from time to time, sinking down progressive strides which have been achieved already at great cost and sacrifice.

In Zambia, people's rights and freedoms must continue to be explicitly guaranteed in the constitution. For the most part, Zambian laws have been adequate. However, modern laws should take into consideration women,[788] children, the disabled, minority and the environment, and as it has been argued in this book, gay-lesbian rights. A society that recognizes that minorities, gays and lesbian people, women and children have the same inalienable rights and freedoms as everyone else is progressing towards a sound democratic culture. The rights of

---

[787] See Chapter Nine
[788] See §10.11

every person in Zambia, regardless of age, gender, or sexual orientation, must continue to be protected under the Zambian Bill of Rights.

§11.9 Constitutionalism

Constitutionalism is related to the idea of limited government and the Rule of Law. There is an ancient expression that rule should be of laws and not of men. By that is meant that the governed should not be subjected to the unhindered discretion of the governors. The governors, as well as the governed, should all obey "known, predictable, and impartial rules of conduct."[789] Thus the laws, which the governors should rule by, must not only be legitimately legislated, but must also be well-known to the common person. What is germane to Zambia is the idea that democratic pluralism, which Zambia has embraced, is itself a "foundational principle of constitutionalism."[790]

§11.10 Constitution Reviews

The history of constitutionalism in Zambia is as old as Zambia itself. Pre-independence constitution reforms were tailored towards solidifying colonial power in Northern Rhodesia. Reforms in the First and Second Republics were, like the Intelligence System itself, "centered on the president."[791] Under the Second Republic everything from politics, to party politics,

---

[789] Mark O. Dickerson and Thomas Flanagan, *An Introduction to Government and Politics* (Toronto: Nelson, 2006), p. 82

[790] Errol P. Mendes, "Democratic Pluralism: The Foundational Principle of Constitutionalism in Canada," in Linda Cardinal & David Headon (eds.) *Shaping Nations: Constitutionalism and Society in Australia and Canada* (Ottawa: University of Ottawa Press, 2002), p.39

[791] Roy Christie, *For the President's Eyes Only* (Johannesburg: Hugh Keartland Publishers, 1971), p. 148

to secret service and to security, were based on the principle of royalty to the president.[792]

President Chiluba's political and rhetorical charm and finesse raised an aura of change from politically motivated constitutional reforms, away from the political rat-race of the Second Republic. Consequently, shortly after the beginning of his second term in office, President Chiluba and the MMD began to put in place a new constitution. In speeches as well as in campaigns, Chiluba pledged to create a constitution that "would reflect higher goals of national interest."[793] The gist of the new constitution would center on non-partisanship and would represent different Zambian interests.

On November 22nd, 1993, Chiluba appointed John Mwanakatwe to head the Mwanakatwe Commission. In 1995, John Mwanakatwe, Zambian's first Minister of Education, academician and lawyer, was the same person who appended the forward to Chiluba's book, *Democracy: The Challenge of Change*.[794] The Mwanakatwe Constitution Review Commission, as it is known in full, has been one of the many attempts[795] at creating a constitution that is truly representative of the wishes and aspirations of the Zambian people.

Zambia's constitution review process, like the constitution itself, grants both the president and the government tremendous power. Its history has only favored government whims at the expense of the wishes of the people.

---

[792] *Ibid.*

[793] Goodson Machona, "A Harvest of Treason Trials" Conciliation Resources http://www.c-r.org/resources/occasional-papers/african-media-and-conflict-part-four-machona.php (April 10th, 2010)

[794] Frederick Chiluba, *Democracy: The Challenge of Change,* p. xi.

[795] Zambia's constitutional making process is powered by *The Inquiries Act.* This Act requires that a Commission of Inquiry be first established. Government is empowered to accept or reject recommendations of the people from the public inquiry. Moreover, government can make any modifications that it deems desirable through a document commonly referred to as the government White Paper. See §11.11.

§11.11 Historical Context

To have a concise grasp of the constitutional review process and the rumpus this has caused in the case of Zambia, it is prudent to begin the analysis from far before independence. In 1953, at the dawn of the Federation of Rhodesia and Nyasaland, an Order-in-Council was drafted to allocate powers to the federal government and to the territorial governments. This was followed in 1962 by a constitution to accommodate the participation of the European settlers and the Africans in the Legislative Council. This constitutional review granted more electoral privileges to the settlers than to the Africans. In 1964, just before independence, another constitution was drafted to provide a more representative framework leading to the independence of Northern Rhodesia. It also dissolved the Federation after the secession of Nyasaland. These so-called Westminster model constitutions were not the phathomation of the Africans. They were designed for the emerging nations of former British Colonies and Protectorates.

The real first Zambian constitutional review was the creation of the 1973 constitution which eliminated all political opposition. It emerged from the recommendations of the Chona Commission for a One-Party Participatory Democracy. Kaunda and UNIP realized that the only way of sorting out internal conflicts in Zambia was the proscription of all political parties with the sole exception of UNIP, mandated by article 4 of the 1973 constitution.

In 1991, arising out of the public's demand for a return to multiparty politics, Kaunda passed a resolution for constitutional amendment. This resulted in the *Constitution Act* of August 30th, 1991. It was this constitution, whose commission was chaired by the Solicitor-General, Mphanza Patrick Mvunga, which re-introduced multiparty politics to Zambia.

Due to the emergent nature under which the *Constitution Act*, 1991, was enacted, the immediate concern of the newly installed MMD government was to re-enact a constitution it believed was comprehensive and broad-based enough to represent the general wishes of the people. The 1991 constitution was no longer seen as a legitimate document. It had already outlived its mandate, which was the facilitation of the transition to multiparty politics.

In 1993, both as part of an election promise and as a search for a comprehensive constitution, Chiluba appointed a Constitution Review Commission, chaired by John Mwanakatwe. Upon the completion of making substantive recommendations the draft constitution was presented to Chiluba in June 1995.

Final amendments were made to the constitution in 1996. These amendments, however, met two cardinal drawbacks: First, the MMD government rejected the following recommendations of the Mwanakatwe Constitution Review Commission, namely (1) a Bill of Rights to include women, children, economic, social and cultural rights; (2) the introduction of a Constitutional Court; and (3) the adoption of the constitution through a Constituent Assembly. Second, people were infuriated for government's refusal to consider most of the submissions they made.

Consequent to this constitutional unrest, the 2001 eleven presidential contenders all pledged to review the constitution if elected into office. In 2003, the Wila Mung'omba Constitution Review, also known as the Dragged Constitutional Review Commission was constituted. It was the initiative of late President Mwanawasa and it came about by Statutory Instrument Number 40 of April 17th, 2003. The Mung'omba Commission comprised 31 terms of reference which included the protection of human rights, the examination of the death penalty, the elimination of discriminatory provisions in the Zambian constitution, and the promotion of good democratic governance, among other recommendations.

One of the recommendations of the Mung'omba Commission under Chapter 27 of its report dubbed, "Methods of Amending the Constitution" was the adoption of the constitution either through a Constituent Assembly or a Constitutional Conference. The latter method was chosen. Consequent to this recommendation, under the *National Constitutional Conference (NCC) Act*, Number 19 of 2007, the National Constitutional Conference (NCC) was established. In this way, and for the first time since constitutional history, the will of the people of amending the constitution through a constitutional conference seems to have been respected. The NCC sat under the chairmanship of Chifumu Banda flanked by three vice-chairpersons – Faustina Sinyangwe, Regina Musokotwane and Leonard Hikaumba – with Mwangala Zaloumis as its spokesperson.

The NCC adoption process was designed as follows: After 14 months of debate, recommendations and comments, the final text of the new constitution would be decided either by submitting to the Minister the entire adopted constitution for submission to a National Referendum or by any one of the two options (1) presenting to the National Assembly for enactment if the Draft Bill did not contain any provisions to alter Part III or Article 79 of the *Zambian Constitution* or (2) submitting to a referendum, if the Draft Bill contains provisions to alter Part III or Article 79 of the Zambian Constitution or any provisions in the Mung'omba Draft Constitution on which there was no agreement either through consensus or secret ballot. In 2011, the NCC failed to pass a vote in the National Assembly.

Since 1970, the first three presidents of Zambia, except for President Rupiah Banda[796] have constituted five[797] constitution review commissions to amend the *Zambian Constitution*. The late Michael Sata failed to create a lasting constitution. President

---

[796] President Rupiah Banda served as vice-president to President Mwanawasa. Upon the death of the later in July 2008, Rupiah Banda acted as president until the presidential by-elections of October 2008 in which he emerged as the winner over Michael Sata, becoming the fourth president of Zambia since independence.

[797] Since independence, Zambia has had five constitutional review commissions. These are the Chona Commission of 1970; the Mvunga Commission of 1990; the Mwanakatwe Commission of 1993, the Mung'omba Commission of 2003; and the National Constitution Conference (NCC) of 2007.

Lungu succeeded President Sata, and immediately changed the constitution. Each attempt, without exception, has either fallen short or has enacted a one-sided politically-motivated constitution aiming at consolidating the power of the ruling party.

The Inquiries Act requires that a Commission of Inquiry be constituted to ascertain the feasibility of amending the constitution.[798] The law gives the government power to accept or reject or modify through a White Paper the recommendations of the people. This power has made it very difficult for Zambia to create a constitution which is truly representative as government has from time to time used the White Paper power to veto the people's will. Mwale[799] bemoans the lackadaisical attempts at reforming the *Zambian Constitution* for over fifty years, vis-à-vis *The Inquiries Act*. In the last fifty years Zambia has been in existence, successive administrations have unfortunately initiated constitutional reforms under *The Inquiries Act* much to their advantage and have defied the collective wisdom of the people and popular sovereignty. And, "Using *The Inquiries Act,* the government hindered people's demands of a constitution-making process that is broad-based, inclusive and representative, in order to give the constitution the necessary legitimacy."[800]

In 1996, the people of Zambia reached a place where they were fed up with the constitution innuendos of government. The people rejected the White Paper released by the Chiluba government. Among other things, the White Paper had added some recommendations to those in the Mwanakatwe Commission. The most controversial one was Article 34(3) (b).[801] People saw this as targeting Kaunda whose parents hurled

---

[798] *The Inquiries Act*, Cap. 41 of the Laws of Zambia
[799] Simson Mwale, "Constitutional Hiccup," *The Post,* (August 30th, 2005)
[800] *Ibid.*
[801] This clause required that the presidential candidate prove that their parents were Zambians by birth or descent. At its face, this clause is reasonable; after all, most countries demand the same. But in the context of the 1996 general and presidential elections, this clause was seen as an attempt by the Chiluba government at barring Kaunda from contesting the

from Malawi. This assertion is supported by other commentators as well. What made matters worse was that the ruling MMD had successfully pushed through a clause in the 1996 *Constitution (Amendment) Act* - Article 34(3) - which centered on the requirement for presidential aspirants to have "both parents" being "Zambians by birth or descent." This effectively discriminated against the then UNIP's Kaunda, who had Malawian parentage. It also effectively barred from the election race UNIP Vice-president, Senior Chief Inyambo Iluta Yeta, because there was another contentious clause - Article 129 - which provided that no person, while remaining a chief, would join or participate in partisan politics.[802]

Besides, from the prior attempts at reforming the constitution, government's all-powerful mandate to change or modify the report, had always left the people out of the process, the process which is supposed to be the people's making. This time, people had had enough. It was time to eliminate self-interest in the process and create a document which would stand the test of time.

The stance taken by the government, especially the barring of the traditional chiefs from participating in active politics, was worrying to many Zambians.[803] The action was immoral not because it was bent on guarantying a safe passage of the MMD and late president Chiluba to power; it lacked taste because it was meant to undermine the contributions made by traditional rulers to the liberation struggles of Zambia.

It has been mentioned earlier that it was largely due to the intervention of the traditional rulers in 1935 that the establishment of the first Tribal Elders' Advisory Council was

---

elections. Kaunda's father, David Kaunda, was one of the first missionaries to Zambia. He hurled from, and was born in Malawi!

[802] Fackson Banda, "The Presidency and the Media," *The Post*, (September 30th, 2009)

[803] The August 1995 Government White Paper added Article 34 (3)(b), rejected the participation of traditional leaders in active politics, and rejected the adoption of the constitution through a Constituency Assembly and a referendum, among other things.

made possible in Northern Rhodesia.[804] This acted like the first local court for the Africans. This was the foundation of both political and legal Zambian set-ups as we know them today. Traditional rulers are an integral part of the Zambian social mosaic. Their contribution to freedom, development and social justice is indisputable.

The Chiluba government had nothing to lose if it had allowed the will of the people to prevail, *viz*, the adoption of the constitution through a Constituency Assembly and the allowance of traditional chiefs to take active stage in national politics. Both the Mung'omba Commission and the assumption of office of Senior Chief Inyambo Yeta as UNIP president, prove that both these demands were workable in Zambia with relatively little political capital expended.[805] In this regard, Mwanawasa has a much more venerated legacy than Chiluba with regards to the constitution reform process in Zambia. It is strongly accepted that if Mwanawasa did not die, the NCC could have passed into law.

§11.12 In Search of a Democrat

The Rule of Law is how popular legislatures are controlled and limited. It acts as a shield that protects citizens against the abuse of powers because it lays down a set of procedures which govern the use and misuse of coercive power. However, Chanda and Ng'andu charge that the thread of self-censorship and general cowardice runs through the history of the Judiciary in Zambia. Since independence the traditional conduct of the Zambian Judiciary in political cases has generally been one of leaning towards the Executive.[806]

---

[804] See §5.15

[805] In 1996, Senior Chief Inyambo Yeta was UNIP vice-president when Kaunda was UNIP president. After the 1996 presidential elections, which Kaunda boycotted, Inyambo Yeta succeeded Kaunda as UNIP president.

[806] The duo postulate that in political matters between an ordinary citizen and the state, or between an opposition party and the state, the courts have almost

Chanda and Ng'andu conceive that the Rule of Law has dilly-dallied because Zambia "has never been ruled by a democrat."[807] By a "democrat," Chanda and Ng'andu do not imply someone who identifies with the centrist-to-left wing ideals of the US Democratic Party.[808] They, rather, use the word democrat in the ordinary sense to denote a supporter of democracy.

To the duo, neither Kaunda nor Chiluba was a democrat. For most analysts, Kaunda's regime was repressive and autocratic: "The elections [of 1991] were celebrated not only as a return to democracy, but also as a victory for the people of Zambia in their struggle against an oppressive and autocratic regime."[809] Although regular presidential and parliamentary elections were held in the Second Republic, "the elections had not been considered free and fair."[810] Not only was the Second Republic a dictatorial and repressive regime, but it was "no longer observing human rights and the Rule of Law."[811]

The arguments made in Volume Two on the *Chiluba Matrix* are enough to suggest, by implication, that some critics considered Chiluba to have been paying mere lip service to democracy. For many analysts, however, Chiluba began on a democratic path especially in his first term of presidential office. Things began to change when he opted for constitutional amendment in 1996 to eliminate Kaunda and Chief Inyambo Yeta as potential opponents in that year's presidential elections.

---

invariably, decided in favor of the state, even in cases where evidence clearly showed that the private citizen or the private organization deserved justice.
[807] Phiri, *supra.*
[808] In US politics, the two major political organizations are the Democratic Party and the Republican Party. The Republicans identify with the centrist-to-right wing ideals of the American political specturm.
[809] Bizeck J. Phiri, "Democratization and Security Sector Reform in Zambia," < www.iiss.org.uk/EasySiteWeb/GatewayLink.aspx?alId=20024> (Retrieved: August 2nd, 2010)
[810] *Ibid.*
[811] *Ibid.*

§11.13 Rule of Law - Legacies

Politicians in Zambia should think of the legacy they would leave after their tenure of office. There are very few examples of leaders who have left a lasting impact on politics in Africa. However, this statement does not mean that such leaders who turned out to be autocratic did not begin on the path of democracy. Exemplary leaders are important because they tend to leave behind a legacy which future generations would emulate. In Africa, like in many nations worldwide, political leaders do not achieve ascendancy in their own times. History is usually the judge. Notwithstanding, everyone would wish to be associated with some of Africa's first leaders because of their fearlessness in the face of danger and even death. Some of them are Nelson Mandela, Kwame Nkrumah, Julius Nyerere, Walter Sisulo, Ketumire Masire, Kenneth Kaunda, and so many more.

In democracy, it is not enough to only have a heart for the people. It is even more important to respect the good laws of the land and to rule per those laws. Political leaders, like leaders in general, will be judged per their works. Few are idolized because of a speech they made, but the majority is weighed on the performance scale.

In Zambia, the Rule of Law will always be tied to development. What is the Rule of Law if the majority cannot make enough money to care for those they love? What is the Rule of Law when the majority does not have enough food to feed their families? What is the Rule of Law if over 50 percent of the productive force cannot find employment? What is the Rule of Law if freedom means debt, foreign aid and perpetual insubordination to conditional shackles prescribed by the international monetary agencies?

The Rule of Law is necessary in laying down a foundation upon which development may rest. It is even more, it creates an environment in which freedom and human rights thrive. Future Zambian democrats should insist that law rules above men and that the rights and freedoms of the citizens are granted an unalienable recognition.

§11.14 Incentive for Posterity

Mwanawasa, although credited for a militant combat against corruption and a crusade for good governance and the Rule of Law, the former lawyer could easily be known as the leader who never finished what he began. In 1991, he began as Zambia's Vice-president. He resigned in 1994. In 2001, he was given the presidency of Zambia by Chiluba. He died in 2008 before finishing his term.

It is ironic that Malupenga chose *An Incentive for Posterity* as title to Mwanawasa's biography. It is, however, important to note that Levy Patrick Mwanawasa will go into history books as the president who advanced the ideals of democracy and gave credence to the movement that triggered plural politics in 1991. Upcoming Zambian leaders have a challenge to ensuring that they do not take Zambia back to a one-man rule, while making sure that the young democracy founded by Chiluba and enhanced by Mwanawasa does not frail and wither away. However, and more importantly, that the efforts of the Chiluba administration in reintroducing plural politics and the hard work of the New Deal Administration in fostering the ideals of good governance should be surreptitiously guarded to realize the dream of the Zambian fathers and mothers, of a free, prosperous and democratic nation. Future generations have both a duty and responsibility to ensuring that Zambian democracy survives and thrives.

12| The Case of Human Rights

Why, why, why the entire cosmos quivers?
Why all rights continue to turn to wrongs?
Receivers get more blessings than givers?
To sheer dins, we dance, and not to songs?

Chapter Focus

At the end of reading this chapter, you should be able to:

- Understand the importance of human and people's rights in Africa
- Recognize that issues of human rights in Africa can adequately be assessed in the context of historical disparities
- Understand the role of the African Union in safeguarding Africa's peace
- Review foreign-injected regime changes in Africa with regards to the Libyan case

BRIEF INTRODUCTION

In this chapter, human rights are briefly discussed from the perspective of Africa. The chapter reminisces on the failure of the African Union to protect the continent from human rights abuses, especially those abuses perpetuated in the pretext of promoting democracy by foreign entities.

Charles Mwewa

§12.1 Respect and Dignity

❝ All humans need to be treated with respect and dignity.
Even the servant in your house deserves respect. Even those
who differ with you in opinion or view deserve respect.
Even those who commit offences big or small have human
rights. Torture is a human travesty, whatever the excuse!"[812]

Humans are not the same as other higher primates; they have
quality to their life and that is priceless. No other human being
should have the audacity to vituperate the inherent human dignity
to satisfy some political or personal *agenda*.

There is no place or region where the human rights of the
people have not been recognized. Conventions, resolutions,
declarations and recommendations all attest to this unalienable
human capacity. From the Universal Declaration of Human
Rights[813] to documents detailing the worthy of women, children,
the gay and lesbians and even animals' rights, the dignity of
human life has been articulated.

In its preamble, the *African Charter on Human and People's
Rights* stated, "Freedom, equality, justice and dignity are
essential objectives for the achievement of the legitimate
aspirations of the African people."[814] The *Law of Lagos*[815] took
this further to encompass human rights abuses in the exercise of
Emergency Powers, thus, "The proclamation of a State of
Emergency is a matter of serious concern as it directly affects and

---

[812] Charles Mwewa, Facebook, June 3rd, 2010.
[813] The Universal Declaration of Human Rights was adopted in the UN's
General Assembly in 1948.
[814] *The African Charter on Human and People's Rights* was adopted by the
18th Assembly of the Heads of States and Government of the Organization of
African Unity (OAU) on June 27th, 1981 in Nairobi, Kenya. This was itself
an adoption of the Charter of the OAU signed at Addis Ababa on May 25th,
1963 and which came into force on September 13th, 1963.
[815] The *Law of Lagos* was a resolution reached on January 7th, 1961 at the
conference organized to discuss the Rule of Law by the International
Commission of Justice in Lagos, Nigeria.

may infringe upon human rights."[816] The efforts made by local, regional and international bodies, such the UN, in advocacy and education on human rights is accompanied by rigorous campaigns to end torture and unlawful arrests and detentions. The *Conference of the African Jurists on African Legal Process and the Individual* affirmed the resolution of the Lagos Conference. It deplored and condemned any legislation which permitted detention without trial. It emphasized the importance of respecting the provisions regarding the conditions of arrest and detention contained in various criminal codes. It also urged that respect for those provisions should be extended as far as possible to all kinds of arrest and detention.[817]

§12.2 Human Rights Advocacy

There is plenty of literature and documentation in regards to human rights advocacy. The following instruments and documents all innumerate on the need to safeguard against human rights abuses: *Convention on the Prevention and Punishment of the Crime of Genocide* (1951); *International Convention on the Suppression and Punishment of the Crime of Apartheid* (1976); *Optional Protocol to the International Covenant on Civil and Political Rights* (1976); *OAU Plan of Action* (1980); *Recommendations of the Gaborone Seminar on Human Rights and Development in Africa* (1982); *Convention Against Torture and Other Cruel, Inhuman or Degrading Treatment or Punishment* (1984); and many others dealing with women, labor, refugee, prisoners, the environment and other rights.

Zambia is a signatory to all regional conventions and protocols that protect and safeguard human rights. In April 1969, thirteen governments from regional nations signed at Lusaka

---

[816] Hamalengwa M, Flinterman C. & Dankwa E.V.O, (eds.) *The International Law of Human Rights in Africa*, p. 39
[817] *Ibid.*, p. 56

315

what came to be known as the *Lusaka Manifesto on Southern Africa*. The Manifesto declared, "We wish to make it clear, beyond all shadow of doubt, our acceptance of the belief that all men are equal, and have equal rights to human dignity and respect, regardless of color, race, religion, or sex. We believe that all men have the equal right and the duty to participate, as equal members of society, in their own government."[818] In this declaration, the mention of men also refers to women.

§12.3 Zambia and the African Union

The African Union (AU), which is the predecessor of the Organization of African Unity (OAU), perpetuates the original mandate of the OAU, *viz*, "To accelerate the process of integration in the continent to enable it play its rightful role in the global economy while addressing multifaceted social, economic and political problems compounded as they are by certain negative aspects of globalization."[819] One of the roles the AU plays in global affairs is the promotion and the protection of fundamental human and people's rights.

The process of the creation of the AU began with the Sirte Extraordinary Session in 1999, which decided to establish an African Union. This was followed up by the Lome Summit in 2000, which adopted the *Constitutive Act of the Union*. The Lusaka Summit of 2001 drew the roadmap for the implementation of the AU, and the Durban Summit in 2002, launched the AU and convened the first Assembly of the Heads of States of the AU. From the organization's inception, Zambia has been a key player in the AU affairs.

On December 11th, 2003, the AU decided "To continue, in concert with the Commission of the African Union, to enhance

---

[818] Hamalengwa M, Flinterman C. & Dankwa E.V.O, (eds.) *The International Law of Human Rights in Africa*, p. 104
[819] "African Union in a Nutshell" <http://www.africa union.org/About_AU/au_in_a_nutshell.htm> (Retrieved: June 3rd, 2010)

interaction and coordination with the different organs of the African Union in order to strengthen the African Mechanism for the Promotion and Protection of Human and Peoples' Rights."[820] Thus, the issue of human rights is an important aspect, with both local and international connotations. Within the *Zambian Constitution* itself is embedded a Bill of Rights,[821] which solidifies the essence of the protection of human rights.

Even though Zambia is a signatory to major regional and international human rights' bodies, human rights abuses continue to be a problem.[822] To the extent to which these abuses and disregards are allowed by government or bodies mandated with this task, to the same extend Zambia's democracy suffers irreparable damage. In Zambia, the issue of arrest and detention impinges upon the very basis of human rights and freedoms, and has been rampant not only in the First and Second Republics, but in post-Third Republic as well.

§12.4 "A History of Failure"

To the West, the AU is a toothless organization whose, "History of failure is not a secret."[823] This thesis was retooled when the AU's bid to act as peace broker in the Libyan war failed because, "The organization's track record promoting democracy and preventing massacres is abysmal. The African leaders know it."[824]

---

[820] "Decision on the 16th Annual Activity Report of the African Commission on Human
and Peoples' Rights, Doc. Assembly/AU/7 (II)" <http://www.africa
union.org/official_documents/Decisions_Declarations/Assemblypercent20A
Upercent20Decpercent2011percent20II.pdf> (Retrieved: June 4th, 2010)
[821] See Bill of Rights under §11.6
[822] See Chapter 13 of this volume
[823] Peter Goodspeed, "A Peace Deal that No-One is Buying," *National Post*, (Tuesday, April 12th, 2011), p. A1
[824] *Ibid.*

The AU plan in Libya, like Resolution 1973, called for immediate ceasefire[825] and an opportunity for opened channels for humanitarian aid and talks between the Libyan government forces under Gaddafi and the rebels, mostly based in the Eastern City of Benghazi. The *Libyan Case* is an important study of how Africa continues to be used as a pawn in the international chess game. The case defies all aspects of international law, the doctrine of sovereignty and the role of the Security Council in peace-keeping missions.

But even more than that, it showcases how Western and African interests differ exponentially in value. To the West Gaddafi was a "Crazy bastard who wants to kill all his people."[826] However, to many African leaders, Gaddafi was, in fact, a "Brother Leader."

Aisha Gaddafi, the daughter of Gaddafi, slammed NATO, "You want to kill my father on the pretext of protecting civilians?"[827] Indeed, on the issue of "pretext of protecting civilians," many commentators lamented the rush with which NATO was engaged to bringing the so-called dictator down. However, even within the US itself, there was concern that NATO might be overlooking the inherent tribal factions in Libya in its quest to effect regime change. Will,[828] thus, warned that the US was intervening in a civil war in a tribal society, the dynamics of which the US did not understand. He further asserted that, the US was supporting one faction, the nature of which it did not

---

[825] Security Council Resolution 1973 demanded an immediate ceasefire in Libya, including an end to the current attacks against civilians, which it said might constitute "crimes against humanity" (UN Security Council SC/10200, "Security Council Approves 'No-Fly Zone' Over Libya, Authorizing 'All Necessary Measures' to Protect Civilians, by Vote of 10 in Favor with 5 Abstentions," Security Council 6498th Meeting (Resolution 1973), March 17th, 2011

[826] www.electrotanji.com, "Zanga Zanga," (April 20th, 2011)

[827] Sandeep, "Libya: NATO Wants the Fall of Gaddafi, Who Parade in Tripoli," *Pisqa*, (Friday, April 15th, 2011)

[828] George F. Will, "Is it America's Duty to Intervene Wherever Regime Change is Needed?" *The Washington Post*, (March 21st, 2011)

know. He added, "Many...call Gaddafi's opponents 'freedom fighters,' but no-one calling them that really knows how the insurgents regard one another, or if freedom...is their priority."[829] Clarfield[830] argues that the Libyan civil conflict was not about democracy; it was about an ancient tribal war. And the price that drove all parties involved was the "Control of Libya's immense oil wealth."[831]

Moreover, if Gaddafi had "lost the confidence of his own people and the legitimacy to lead,"[832] then that confidence and legitimacy would only go to expose Western hypocrisy. Gaddafi neither had the confidence nor the legitimacy of his people; he assumed power through a military coup. NATO was being driven by something deeper than oil, otherwise the massacre in Ivory Coast would not have happened. The warning should have been heeded; ISIS emerged strongly in the same areas the West claimed had interests and the issue of Bengazi remained a thorn in the US Democrats' flesh after 2011.

---

[829] *Ibid.*
[830] Geoffrey Clarfield, "The Tribes of Libya: A Brief History," *National Post*, (Thursday, April 21st, 2011), p. A15
[831] *Ibid.*
[832] *Ibid.*

13| Naked before Government

> Until we begin to see beyond political parties,
> and stop banking our fate in our leaders. Until we
> begin to believe that among us are rising stars,
> we may think Zambia is headed to the doom.
> Zambia is more than politics!

Chapter Focus

At the end of reading this chapter, you should be able to:

- Understand the meaning "Naked before Government"
- Identify events and peoples who fell prey to the oppressive jaws of the One-Party System
- Identify events and peoples who became victims of the Third Republic
- Review the legacy of Simon Mwansa Kapwepwe
- Outline circumstantial evidence of a political murder

BRIEF INTRODUCTION

This chapter lays bare the issue of historical repression in Zambia. Real victims can retell their ordeals and from their account lessons are learned that future Zambian leaders should take to heart in their quest to create a strong, free and democratic nation.

§13.1 Naked before Government

Centrist democrats and fiscal conservatives ardently argue against a large government for no other reason than that it runs the risk of becoming too powerful. Power is addictive. A smaller government is deemed to be more efficient and easier to manage. There is perhaps nowhere where government exercises enormous power other than in socialistic systems. There, government may be said to exist *without* the people. The Second Republic under Kaunda and UNIP was, without prejudice, a good example of a government *without* the people.

It can be appropriately said that in Kaunda's Zambia everyone existed naked before the government. Kaunda had marshaled one of the most powerful intelligent systems in Africa: "The UNIP government intelligence network was probably one of the most sophisticated and atrocious systems on the continent of Africa."[833] The reasons can only be speculated. However, it was obvious that the UNIP government did not want anyone to challenge its power. To do so, it resorted to the use of the Emergency Powers.

Per Chisala, the existence of the State of Emergency obliterated the presence of civil liberties in Zambia. He informs that institutions in Zambia were infiltrated by agents who reported people averse to Kaunda: "Every Zambian suspected of being disloyal was detained, tortured and blacklisted from employment."[834] Chisala then gives a heart-breaking narration of what victims of the Kaunda intelligence regime went through. The case of Reverend Jones Sinyangwe begs to be retold:

> Reverend Sinyangwe said he was driving his...car along the Great East Road in Lusaka on October 17th, 1977, when a Nissan Sunny car driven by Maxwell Chiyokoma overtook him and one of the passengers signalled him to stop. Sinyangwe recognized Chiyokoma and he stopped. As he approached Chiyokoma's car, the two men grabbed him and bundled him into the back seat and sped off towards Kafue. "I was kidnapped and taken to a farm in Shamabale area between Chilanga and Kafue where I was tortured," [Sinyangwe said].

[833] Beatwell Chisala, *The Fall of President Kaunda*, p. 156
[834] *Ibid.*

Sinyanzwe remained in solitary confinement under intense torture but was not charged or taken to court. He was subjected to electrical shocks, blindfolded and stripped naked while electric devices were connected to his genitals. They gave him a lot of water to drink so that he could urinate but they had tied his penis with a string to stop urine from coming out. After loosening the string, he was ordered to urinate in a bucket of sulphuric acid which splashed onto his legs and thighs and burnt him. Sometimes, they squeezed his throat and chocked him. There was no toilet and when he messed the floor, he was meant to clean with his bare hands.

After three months of this inhuman treatment, the health of Sinyangwe deteriorated and he was released on instructions from the Director General, Paul Malukutila, with a strong warning not to reveal anything. But Sinyangwe was not the same. He had lost sex potency and this condition led to the breakup of his marriage.[835]

The case of Sinyangwe is a depiction of the extent to which the UNIP regime under Kaunda went to silence suspects. In fact, Sinyangwe's case was one of personal vendetta. Prior, Sinyangwe had installed computer gargets at the Office of the President (O.P) which made the Director General very pleased. Sinyangwe was then asked to join the intelligent agency but he declined.

This infuriated the boss who in response paid Sinyangwe with dreadful tortures described above. Chisala has also implicated the secret agency in the torture of Peter Mutafungwa,[836] Justin

---

[835] *Ibid.*, p. 158
[836] Peter Mutafungwa, an astute community organizer and journalist, accused the UNIP government of plundering the wealth of Zambia in 1985. He claimed he saw dead bodies decomposing in acid, sliced razor blades and biting ants and snakes at the infamous intelligence headquarters dubbed The Red Brick. He was disgracefully tortured and only escaped from there with the help of a Special Branch Officer. That officer mysteriously died after Mutafungwa escaped!

323

Chimba,[837] Nkaka Puta,[838] and the death of Archbishop Elias
Mutale.[839] Under the notorious State of Emergency, people's
rights and freedoms barely existed. People were tortured for
voicing out the indignities of the regime, let alone made to
disappear for exercising their freedom of speech, expression or
association. Perhaps the most heart-wrecking incident involved
the death of Josephine Mundashi Kapansa. Chisala narrates how
Kapansa died in a road accident after she had confronted Kaunda
over the rental arrears incurred by the Angolan Ambassador.

> Kapansa was a wealthy landlady who owned a chain of houses
> in Lusaka and one in Middlesex, London. At the time of her death,
> she was planning to build a pleasure resort at Siavonga on the banks
> of Lake Kariba. One of her houses was rented by the Angolan
> Ambassador but he had vacated it without paying rent amounting to
> $39,000, and Kapansa is said to have made an appointment at State
> House, for April 8th, 1991, to go and complain. A month before her
> death, Kapansa had told her mother and some relatives about some
> Special Branch people who were trailing her. On the day she died,
> four men in a blue Land Cruiser went to her house but they did not
> find her. They arrived a few minutes after she had left...they talked
> to her unsuspecting nephew...who showed them the direction where
> she had gone, and they followed her. The next thing...Kapansa was
> dead. Her mother ...suspected the state.[840]

The above cited examples were suitably chosen to illustrate,

[837] Justin Chimba, Zambian nationalist and politician, was Minister of Labor
and Mines in Kaunda's government when he resigned to join Kapwepwe's
UPP party in 1972. Kaunda detained him for a few years and released
Chimba to his death.
[838] Nkaka Puta was detained and tortured under the *Preservation of Public
Security Act* for the sole reason that he was son of Robinson Puta, a UPP
member. Puta was a Ndola lawyer.
[839] Elias Mutale was the Archbishop of Kasama Diocese. He died in a road
accident along the Great East Road near the Lusaka Showgrounds on
February 11th, 1990 after advising the president to return the K4 million
which General Christon Tembo alleged Kaunda banked outside Zambia.
Tembo was a suspect in the 1986 coup plot against the Kaunda's UNIP
government. Archbishop Mutale's death is hugely blamed on Kaunda.
[840] *Ibid.*, pp. 163-4

in a nutshell, the brutality of the UNIP regime. Chisala mentions other examples like the unceremonious disappearance of Berrings Lennox Lombe "who was kidnapped and killed in October 1982. Up to now nobody including his family and relatives, knows the circumstances of his death."[841] What is devastating in Lombe's case is that the police refused to properly investigate his death and when the relatives took the matter to court in 1983, the expert witness, a pathologist said, "All the documents pertaining to the post-mortem have been sent to State House."[842] Citing insufficiency of evidence, the court dismissed the case.

The Special Branch in the Second Republic operated like the secret police in European dictatorships. In fact, they "operated like people who were above the law."[843] They interrogated and tortured people in secret places like the Red Brick without the knowledge of the regular police.

The incidents above go on to show how repression can be prevalent but at the same time be suppressed under fear of disclosure. People, who live under a repressive regime, are told not to voice out their bitterness because doing so would expose them to the risk of life itself. The result is that other freedoms, such as speech and expression, are taken away in the quest to hide the indignities of the regime.

What might have begun as an isolated incident could end up implicating others, leading to more serious abuses. To cover-up the evils of one event, several evils might be committed. Thus, to tolerate one undemocratic incident, is to open a floodgate of more abuses. When the UNIP regime silenced people, it also took away their rights and freedoms. Those who did not want to dance to the tune of the dictatorial regime were labeled dissidents and persecuted, like Fostino Lombe and Simon Mwansa Kapwepwe, to mention but two.

---

[841] *Ibid.*, p. 165
[842] *Ibid.*
[843] Former Lusaka Police Chief, Mwenda Muyunda, in the *Zambia Daily Mail* of February 3rd, 1993

§13.2 "Prisoner of Conscience"

A brief story is told here about an unsung child of the Zambian soil, one Changala Chanda Mulilabantu Lombe also known as Chinkangala Fostino Lombe, born December 25th, 1946 in the Northern Province of Zambia to Lombe Mulenga Tailoka and Chilambwe Kapaso. He and his parents are all deceased. However, before he passed away, he dictated his story he titled *Prisoner of Conscience*.

The substance of his real-life story begins with the clash of two childhood friends and political heavyweights in Zambia, Kenneth Kaunda and Simon Kapwepwe in 1971. Kaunda and Kapwepwe, then Vice-president, had sharply differed over broad-view policy and direction where the country was being driven. Kapwepwe offered to resign from government and UNIP in July 1971 and formed the UPP. Prior to the announcement of his resignation, there was intense lobbying for support in the rank and file of UNIP. Kapwepwe received promises from some UNIP devotees.

When Kapwepwe finally resigned from UNIP and government, senior Cabinet Ministers who had promised him support failed to resign because Kaunda introduced the tribal card into the resignation. Only one Cabinet Minister and three junior Ministers honored their promises: Justin Chimba, James Chapoloko, John Chisata, and Peter Chanda. Kapwepwe enjoyed a great deal of support at the grassroots level.

Soon Kapwepwe announced the National Executive Committee of UPP. Except for the two easterners, the rest of the members came from Northern Province, and fitted well into the Kaunda alleged-tribal chessboard. Kaunda capitalized on this omission as leverage. Lombe himself was introduced to Kapwepwe by Chimba Mwananshiku, and Kapwepwe asked Lombe to work for him as Administrative Secretary.

Kapwepwe imposed a very strict disciplinary code of conduct

on himself and others. He was a selfless and humble person, per Lombe. His truthfulness and punctuality endeared him even to his critics and enemies. He had many enemies because of his openness and unshakable belief in fair-play. Kapwepwe chose to defend those who were weak. He was liked and admired by millions. He was no firmer in God, yet his love for the truth and people could not be disputed. Per Lombe,

> President Kaunda and the UNIP leadership were afraid of the man and the advent of UPP. Kaunda, as a result, decided to detain the National Executive Committee of UPP in September 1971. There was no other reasonable cause for these detentions other than political. It was a black September, as the two of us [Kapwepwe and Lombe] sat in the office reflecting on what had just happened. As soon as it was known as the national leaders of UPP had been detained, ten UNZA students left school to come and help organize UPP. Boniface Kawimbe...was one of them. Kaunda condemned the students and withdrew government grants from them. His political strategy to weaken Kapwepwe and force him into surrender failed. Kapwepwe addressed them in the hall with a lot of media presence, "I promise you sweat, no sweet. If you are men enough take up this challenge. The road to freedom will be rough and tortuous and many will fall by the way side...."[844]

In October 1971, Lombe left to set up UPP branches in Northern Province with Kawimbe and Davies Mwaba. They received massive support there and this included an endorsement by Senior Chief Nkula of Chinsali. Within days the UPP had organized itself in Northern Province contesting against the likes of Willard Mung'omba.[845] UPP was expanding at an astronomical speed. This worried Kaunda a great deal; Lombe narrates how UPP was finally banned:

> Sometime in January 1972, I was transferred to Eastern Province to spearhead the campaign of establishing UPP in that province. Eastern part of Zambia was the stronghold of UNIP. It was during this time I was waiting for transportation to take me to Chipata, the

---

[844] Unpublished story as told to Munyonzwe Hamalengwa by Lombe
[845] Willard Mu'ngomba was the chairman of the Mu'ngomba Commission

provincial Capital of Eastern Province, that the UPP was banned by President Kaunda...on February 4th, 1972, alleging that he had heard the "cries of the people" and had heeded their demand to have UPP banned, because if he did not, there would be bloodshed in the country. He also announced the detention of Simon Mwansa Kapwepwe, his Executive Committee, all provincial leadership and in some cases, district leaders as well. He promised the nation at the same press conference that some of the detained would be taken to court for trial. There was no single trial.

I escaped this detention because the government knew I was in Kasama, and therefore sent my detention order there, when in fact, I was in Lusaka. After finding out that I was not in Kasama, the police did not know where to find me. The nation was crippled in a state of apprehension, frustration and anger at the turn of events. ANC, which was a very ineffective opposition party was given an ultimatum of six months in which to make a decision; to disband, join UNIP or face consequences that UPP had suffered. There were 424 men and one woman...detained.

The country's constitution was still multiparty, and the formation of other political parties was legal. A week after the detentions, all UPP members and leaders who had survived convened in Lusaka, where it was resolved that we all went underground until further instructions from Simon in prison. On March 6th, 1972, on a secluded farm house about 100 people held an election and launched a new political party called the Democratic Peoples' Party, DPP. I emerged the national president of DPP. Radio Zambia announced the formation of a new party and read out all the names of its leaders. I was very delighted, but more so Kapwepwe and other detainees as I later learned. The die was cast, we had to organize DPP, fight for the release of detainees, and support the families of the detained people where necessary. We were fortunate the law allowed the organization of the party as soon as an application for registration was filed with the registrar of societies. In practice, all ex-UPP officials became DPP officers and ex-UPP property changed to DPP and we began to function as an old established party. I was twenty-six years old.

In April 1972, Kenneth Kaunda announced that UNIP Central Committee had decided to introduce One-Party State in Zambia. He went on with a lot of useless talk justifying the introduction of One-Party State. Two days later I called a press conference and challenged him with the fact that it was out of cowardice, that he was seeking refuge in One-Party State; that it was never in the interest of Zambia to have One-Party rule. He never replied to these charges but instead went ahead and established the commission of inquiry, headed by Bishop Mutale, a Roman Catholic prelate and a personal friend.[846]

Lombe was arrested on August 15th, 1972 after the Registrar of Societies refused to register DPP saying, "It was not in the interest of Zambia to do so."[847] He was later detained at Mumbwa with "thirteen other political detainees who belonged to Adamson Mushala, leader of an armed group, which was fighting militarily to topple the Kaunda regime from power."[848]

Per Lombe, Kaunda moved very quickly to introduce a One-Party State dictatorship. By hooks and crooks, Zambia was ushered in a new era of severe repression and oppression on December 13th, 1973, and on the 30th of the same month, most of the detainees and Lombe were released from detention. The *Zambian Constitution* had been changed to absorb ANC and to allow only a single political party, UNIP, to operate. It was illegal to form other political parties.

From there Kaunda ruled Zambia with a heart of steel and a hand of iron. All former UPP and DPP members were blacklisted and could not find employment in Zambia without clearance from UNIP.[849] In 1976 Kaunda, fearing dwindling political support, decided to allow former UPP and DPP members to re-join UNIP.

The detention of Kapwepwe at Mukobeko Maximum Prison in Kabwe greatly weakened Kapwepwe's political influence. Some blame this on Kapwepwe himself believing he broke away from UNIP when he had "immense opportunity constitutionally to take over the presidency [of UNIP] on February 5th, 1968, at Chilenje Hall during a UNIP conference when Kaunda announced his resignation over tribal squabbles in the party. But

---

[846] Unpublished story, *supra.*

[847] *Ibid.*

[848] *Ibid.*

[849] Among those who were blacklisted was John Ziba who went on to becoming Senior Private Secretary to President Mwanawasa.

Kaunda rescinded his decision to resign after 24 hours. Some UNIP members accused Kapwepwe of being power-hungry."[850]

On June 27th, 1973 Kapwepwe returned to Chinsali. It is commonly believed that Kaunda continued to haunt Kapwepwe there. If Kapwepwe was alive and wielded enormous popularity among the Bembas, Kaunda was threatened. "The president sent more than 50 armed soldiers and policemen to search his [Kapwepwe's] house. All they found were two duiker skins and the state charged him for keeping government trophies without a license and pornographic photographs. The skins were gifts from Emperor Haile Sellasie of Ethiopia, but Kapwepwe was arrested and kept in the cells at Chinsali Police Station. Later he was transferred to Chinsali Prison and this was the beginning of his poor health."[851]

Kapwepwe re-joined with an aim of contesting for UNIP presidency. But when Kapwepwe announced the intention to contest the UNIP presidency, Kaunda and UNIP panicked so much that they illegally amended the party constitution to include a timeframe clause, which permitted any UNIP member to contest any party post. The new clause stipulated that only UNIP members who had been in UNIP for at least five years were eligible to hold party posts. This, of course, excluded Kapwepwe, Harry Mwaanga Nkumbula and Chiluwe,[852] who had expressed intentions to [challenge] Kaunda.[853]

It is now on record that Kaunda had intended to kill Kapwepwe. Chisenga Bunda, an MMD MP for Mambilima disclosed to Parliament on December 19th, 1991 that Kaunda had ordered the killing of Kapwepwe. The carnage was to be accomplished by drowning him in the Atlantic Ocean. At that

---

[850] Chisala, *supra*, p. 313

[851] Unpublished story, *supra*.

[852] Robert Chiluwe was a Lusaka businessman who had worked as Managing Director for National Import and Export Corporation (NIEC) and Steelbuild. Chiluwe, a Harvard University graduate, once remarked, concerning Kaunda, that "What would you expect from illiterate Chilenje boys!" This infuriated Kaunda.

[853] Unpublished story, *supra*.

time Kapwepwe was at Mukobeko Maximum Prison where he was immediately removed for the purposes of facing his demise. However, he was "brought back after the South African Broadcasting Corporation and a West Germany Radio Station broadcast the incident. [This] allegation [was] never challenged by Dr. Kaunda or UNIP."[854]

Kapwepwe died on January 26th, 1980. Before his death Kapwepwe had instructed that he be buried at Mwankole Hill in a cow's hide, in a toga, and without placing wreaths on his grave. He was buried wrapped in a reed mart, a traditional royal burial. Thousands of people attended the burial including Kaunda, whom onlookers said had shed crocodile tears. Tomb inscriptions on Kapwepwe's gravesite reads: *A Gallant Freedom Figher*! Paradoxically, Kaunda refused to grant Kapwepwe a state funeral. To many, this was unacceptable: "Although Kapwepwe made tremendous contributions to Zambia's liberation struggles and personal sacrifice, the extent of President Kaunda's hatred for him was probably demonstrated when he denied him a deserved state funeral."[855]

It is deeply ironic and saddening how Kaunda in the *Post* columns narrates a long tribute to his friend Nyerere whom he describes they were "bound together in a journey collectively involving people of Africa and the world."[856] Kaunda ends the tribute with a eulogistic lamentation that, "On October 14th, 1999, I heard that my brother Mwalimu Julius Kambarage Nyerere had passed on. I wept like a kid. After I had put him to rest, I came back to Lusaka."[857] From "crocodile tears" at Kapwepwe's funeral to weeping "like a kid" at Nyerere's burial, one wonders why the journey "involving people of Africa and the world" should not have begun at home, with a childhood friend who equally gave so much to the struggle for Zambia's independence!

---

[854] Chisala, *supra.*
[855] *Ibid.*, p. 317
[856] Kenneth Kaunda, "KK's Diary: Mwalimu, A Journey Together," *The Post* website (Retrieved: August 16th, 2005)
[857] *Ibid.*

It is important to note that in the miscellany of Zambian political trailblazers, the name of Kapwepwe has permanent significance. This honor only follows those who either die during national duty, like presidents Mwanawasa and Sata or relinquish power willingly like President Nyerere of Tanzania. A poem below tiltled *Gallant Kapwepwe*, is a tribute to Simon Kapwepwe:

> Thou art not, father of a nation
> And yet, thou art in deeds
> A father to a nation
> Thy life, this light brighteth
> Thy death, this river drieth
> "Oh, Kapwepwe, Oh but why!"
> Let these drums cry
> Gallantry wrapped in reeds
> The Mighty in toga's buried
> The Brave with no pall's carried
> By thy name, a rock
> On thy legacy, a smoke
> In this race, our nation's finder
> At this hill site of Manda
> Riseth fumes in democracy's hide
> Thy cause is our hope and pride!

Simon Mwansa Kapwepwe lived for a cause, a purpose larger than life. In his death, the birth pangs of democracy oozed. Just like the Good Lord has said, "Unless a grain of wheat falls into the earth and dies, it remains alone; but if it dies, it bears much fruit."[858] Indeed, eleven years to his death, in 1991, the seed that was planted bloomed into flowery petals of plural democracy in Zambia. The challenge for Zambia is to harness the pricey reward of the hard-fought-for democracy so that political wolves who masquerade as democrats are not given a chance!

Despite this *salaam*, it is, however, important to note that hero-worship of Kaunda on the part of Kapwepwe and many

---

[858] St. John 12:24

UNIP leaders, especially in the early days of Zambia's political independence, played a part in Kapwepwe's demise. Kaunda, a good man, was made into a tub-thumper due to the *Kapitao* Syndrome of the first Zambian political leaders.

§13.3 "Thoughts are Free"

In this section, this author has borrowed, where necessary, in full or in part, from Munyonzwe Hamalengwa's, "The Law of Detention,"[859] used by permission. In his other book, *Thoughts are Free,*[860] Hamalengwa details how he was detained in Zambia without trial by the Kaunda regime while serving as Vice-president of UNZASU in 1976. The measuring rod of Zambia's democracy now and in future will be the extent to which criminal and social justice is propagated both as means of enhancing fundamental human rights, and a sure show of political reaction. Importantly, the Zambian political system must ensure it balances the power an incumbent can exercise at any given time with the practical reality of leadership over divergent views and political concerns. As follow up, the *Zambian Constitution*, especially in regards to the Bill of Rights, criminal justice and the law on detention requires reformation.[861]

In 1976 UNZA was closed and several UNZA Student Union (UNZASU) leaders arrested, and later detained. Among them was Munyonzwe Hamalengwa, a former prominent Toronto lawyer, senior law lecturer and Acting Dean, School of Law, at the Zambian Open University. Hamalengwa narrates in *Thoughts are Free,*[862] the circumstances that led to his arrest and

---

[859] In *Class Struggles in Zambia 1889-1989 & The Fall of Kenneth Kaunda 1990-1991*, pp. 146-148
[860] *Infra*
[861] See Chapter 14
[862] Munyonzwe Hamalengwa, *Thoughts are Free: Prison Experience and Reflections on Law and Politics in General* (Toronto: Africa in Canada Press, 1991)

Charles Mwewa

subsequent detention: "It must have been Monday, February 9th, 1976 at the University of Zambia, Lusaka, Zambia. I looked up towards the balcony window-door and saw silhouettes of men carrying club-like objects. Several soldiers carrying machine guns and communication gear rushed into the room almost knocking me down."[863]

Kaunda's soldiers would later arrest Hamalengwa without a warrant; subject him to torturous conditions before detaining him at Mumbwa Detention Prison, a notorious detention center for political prisoners in the colonial days and during the Second Republic. On March 6th, 1976 Kaunda issued the reasons for the detention of Hamalengwa. The detention order stated, "That on dates unknown but in January and February, 1976, you collaborated with certain persons in plotting and indulging in subversive political agitation among the students of the University of Zambia."[864] What the regime called "subversive political agitation" were, in fact, UNZASU's refusal to support the Government of Zambia (GRZ)'s endorsement of the National Union for the Total Independence of Angola (UNITA) led by Jonas Savimbi, a party that UNZASU believed was supported by Apartheid South Africa.[865]

President Kaunda did not meander from the law to action his character. In fact, he used the *Preservation of Public Security Act*[866] to detain all whom he considered a threat to his rule. Most autocratic rulers cannot be accused of lawlessness because they operate under the shadow of the legitimate statutes of their nations. Like Kaunda, they only use the law against interests they consider averse to their continuity. In this way, they can manipulate laws to suit their *agenda*.

Similar tactics were used by the Apartheid government in South Africa. While Kaunda's actions cannot be equated to the atrocious acts of the Apartheid Era, in principle, both regimes

---

[863] *Ibid.*, p. 3.
[864] *Ibid.*, p. 25
[865] Hamalengwa, *supra.* p. 17
[866] *The Preservation of Public Security Act* (Laws, Volume II, Cap. 106)

operated under similar undemocratic tendencies. Mandela was imprisoned under the auspices of the *Suppression of Communism Act*, which was enacted solely to deal with groups opposed to the apartheid ideals. Mandela writes: "The Act outlawed the Communist Party of South Africa and made it a crime, punishable by a maximum of ten years' imprisonment, to be a member of the party or to further the aims of Communism."[867]

Just like the South Africa Apartheid Era which did not last forever, in Zambia, events shaping up within and outside of Zambia in the late 1980s forced Kaunda to submit to change. Dissatisfactions by different interests across the country put pressure on Kaunda to call for multiparty elections. In this drama, there were several contributing factors, including the university students, some academics and lawyers, the churches, private businessmen and organized labor, as well as dissatisfied politicians who had been discarded by, or had become disillusioned with, UNIP and its leadership and the One-Party State.

Hamalengwa, in his study, *Class Struggles in Zambia*, documents that, detention had been a common feature in colonial Zambia[868] and by ordinance No. 5 of 1960, the Legislative Council of Northern Rhodesia enacted the Preservation of Public Security Ordinance, s.4 of which reads as follows:

---

[867] Nelson Mandela, *Long Walk to Freedom* (London: Little, Brown and Company, 1995), p. 117.

[868] There had been a State of Emergency in Zambia almost continuously since before independence in 1964. The State of Emergency, now dormant and now activated can be said to have been a permanent feature of political experience in Zambia. The British colonial government established three sets of emergency powers in Zambia: (1) Emergency Powers Order-in-Council 1939-61; (2) Emergency Powers Ordinance, 1948; and (3) Preservation of Public Security Ordinance, 1960. The first one formed part of the constitutional framework of every British dependence in Africa and Asia" (Munyonzwe Hamalengwa and Paulsen Himwiinga, "The State of Emergency in Zambia in International Law: A Historic, Political and Legal Analysis" Unpublished, 1990)

(1) If at any time the Governor is satisfied that the situation in the Territory is so grave that the exercise of the powers conferred by section three of the Ordinance is inadequate to ensure the preservation of public security, he may by Proclamation declare that the provisions of sub-section (2) of this section shall come into operation accordingly; and they shall continue in operation until the Governor by a further Proclamation directs that they shall cease to have effect as respects things previously done or omitted to be done.

(2) The Governor may, for the preservation of public security, make regulations to provide, so far as appears to him to be strictly required by the exigencies of the situation in the Territory, for – (a) detention of persons; (b) requiring persons to do work and render services.

Hamalengwa further documents that on July 28th, 1964, the Governor, by Notice 376, issued Proclamation No. 5 under which he declared and proclaimed the coming into force on that date of the provisions of s.4(2) of the Preservation of Public Security Ordinance. On that same day, the Governor, by Government Notice No. 377, amended the Preservation of Public Security Regulations by the introduction, among other things, of Regulation 31A in these terms:

31A(1) Whenever the Governor is satisfied that for the purpose of preserving public security it is necessary to exercise control over any person, directing that such person be detained and thereupon such person shall be arrested and detained.

Hamalengwa notes that, it is a notorious fact that the immediate purpose of the measures taken then was to deal with the disturbances brought about in the parts of the Northern and Eastern provinces by members of the Lumpa Church. When Northern Rhodesia became the Republic of Zambia on October 24th, 1964, s. 2(1) of the *Zambian Independence Act* of that year provided:

2(1) Subject to the following provisions of this Act, on and after the appointed day all law or provision of an Act of Parliament or of any enactment or instrument whatsoever, is in force on that day or has been passed or made before that day and comes into force thereafter, shall, unless and until provision to the contrary is made by Parliament or some other authority having power in that behalf, have the same operation in relation to Zambia, and persons and things belonging to or connected with Zambia, as it would have apart from this subsection if on the appointed day Northern Rhodesia had been renamed Zambia but there had been no change in its status.

It was stipulated further:

4(1) Subject to the provisions of this section, the existing laws shall, notwithstanding the revocation of the existing orders or the establishment of a Republic of Zambia, continue in force after the commencement of those Orders as if they had been made in pursuance of this Order.
(6) For the purposes of this section, the expression "the existing laws' means all ordinances, laws or statutory instruments having effect as part of the law of Northern Rhodesia....

Per Hamalengwa, the emergency declaration of July 28th, 1964 continued after independence. It was for duration of six months and by a resolution passed on April 24th, 1965, the National Assembly extended the life of the declaration for a further period of six months.

Hamalengwa shows that, this extension was followed by six-monthly renewals of the declaration until s.8 of the *Constitution (Amendment) (No.5) Act*, 1969, made the six-monthly renewal unnecessary. Because of the amendment, the declaration continued in force for an indefinite period unless and until it was revoked by either the president or the National Assembly. Upon the coming into power of the MMD government in 1991, the declaration was revoked. However, democratic reforms to Emergency Powers have been slow in coming to Zambia.

Per Hamalengwa, "While the state was organizing the Zambians under the One-Party system, an undercurrent of state repressive apparatus was also being enshrined. The institution of One-Party system was a trend towards authoritarianism and so was the institutionalization of the Emergency Powers."[869] After more than five decades of Zambia's independence, the Zambian justice system was still begging for serious reforms.[870]

§13.4 Circumstantial Evidence

This segment is reproduced in full from Munyonzwe Hamalengwa's unpublished article titled, "Circumstantial Evidence of a Political Murder."[871] Between 1991 and 2002, there were a spate of suspicious deaths and murders of high profile political figures in Zambia. All cases remain politically, and to some extent, legally, unsolved. The Zambian Government under the MMD was accused of committing these murders, if not directly, at least indirectly through surrogates, criminal elements or the underworld figures.

Many governments, including the apartheid government of long ago South Africa, when they kill, do not leave a trail of murder. The killings in Zambia in the Third Republic have included the deaths of Wezi Kaunda, the son of former president Kaunda, and at the time of his murder, a political leader in the opposition UNIP;[872] Ronald Penza, a dismissed Minister of Finance in the MMD government;[873] the death of Baldwin Nkumbula, the son of Harry Mwaanga Nkumbula - a founding politician of modern Zambia - and a member of an opposition party until just before his murder when he had re-joined the ruling

---

[869] Hamalengwa, *supra.*

[870] See Chapter 14

[871] July 16th, 2001

[872] Kaunda was killed on November 3rd, 1999 by Moses Mulenga and Amon Banda. "Mulenga told the Supreme Court sitting in Ndola that he robbed and murdered Major Kaunda and that he...did it out of banditry." See *Lusaka Times,* "Wezi Kaunda's Killer Confesses," Wednesday, September 8th, 2010.

[873] Penza was gunned down on November 6th, 1998. See Anthony Kunda, "Penza's Slaying: Was it Murder?" *New African,* February 1999; and Fred M'membe, "Speculation Follows Penza's Death," *The Post,* (November 9th, 1998)

MMD;[874] the murder of Ben Ngenda, a young prominent lawyer, who defended high profile cases of the people of Zambia in and out of court; and on July 6th, 2001, the murder of Paul Tembo, who resigned from the MMD where he was the Deputy National Secretary and then joined a new and powerfully threatening (to the ruling party) party called Forum for Democracy and Development (FDD).[875]

Penza, Kaunda, and Tembo died under similar circumstances: armed men went to their homes at night and killed them in the presence of their wives. In each of the cases, if the wife was somewhere in the house, the husband was forced to the area where the spouse could witness the killing. Hamalengwa wonders the odds were the chance that these killings were done by different people! Ngenda was killed at night by armed men. Nkumbula died in a suspicious car accident. President Mwanawasa, then serving as Vice-president of Zambia, survived a suspicious car accident.

Hamalengwa observes, "If you name any democratic country where a disproportionate number of high profile politicians are killed, the suspicions will be blamed on political assassins. This does not matter whether it is in Kenya, Apartheid South Africa, segregated US, or elsewhere, politics will be blamed in such circumstances. It should not be different in Zambia."

Some media outlets called for further police investigations. In a volatile political assassination environment, it is not foreseeable that the police could be an independent force. Only an independent commission of inquiry composed of a mixture of

---

[874] Nkumbula resigned his cabinet post as Minister of Sports citing rampant corruption. He died in a car accident in August 1994. Chiluba's son, Castro, was a passenger in the vehicle and survived the crash with injuries.

[875] In an article titled, "State behind Murder, Says Opposition," the *CNN* on July 7th, 2001, reported that, "Opposition leaders in Zambia are alleging that the murder of President Frederick Chiluba's former campaign manager was a state-sponsored assassination. Paul Tembo, 41, who had joined the opposition in a bid to unseat his former boss, was shot dead at his home. He was murdered, in front of his family, hours before he was to testify against three Cabinet Ministers in a court case."

the Judiciary, scholars, trade unions, the civil society and other entities are likely to come up with a credible report. Zambia should have moved this way.

§13.5 "The Other Society"

Vernon Mwaanga who served under the Kaunda regime as Ambassador to the USSR, Permanent Secretary in the Office of the President (O.P), Permanent Ambassador to the United Nations, Editor-in-Chief of the *Times of Zambia* and the *Sunday Times of Zambia*, and as Minister of Foreign Affairs, narrates in his book, *The Other Society*, how the criminal justice, which he helped create, turned against him.

Mwaanga observes, "The prison was designed to take a maximum of 200 people, but at that time there were 437 of us; somehow we had to live together and share very limited facilities...there was one dirty kitchen and two taps for all our water requirements."[876]

Without question, the prison conditions of any nation at any given time, is a direct reflection of the criminal justice regime of the ruling government. If one wants to know how unjust or negligent a government is, the best place to begin from is the prison. Prison conditions say vociferously what regimes do not say out loudly.

Father Mutinta called Mwanawasa a tyrant with regards to prison conditions in Zambia: "I am wondering what has gone wrong with us to accept the inhuman prison conditions in our country as normal. I can assure you that under the tyrannical leadership of President Mwanawasa prisons are places of keeping under lock and key all those opposed to his dictatorial rule."[877] The Monze Catholic priest believed that the cruel way with

---

[876] Mwaanga, *The Other Society*, p. 39
[877] Given Mutinta, "Prison Conditions," *The Post,* (Saturday, August 6th, 2005)

which people were treated in the Zambian prisons did not equal to the gravity of their offences.[878]

Mwaanga further writes, "As I toured the kitchen and outside toilets, I felt revulsion and extreme indignation. The pigs at my farm eat and live better than those overcrowded souls. The conditions have to be seen to be believed."[879] In Zambia, as in most governments, politicians usually pay lip-service to the justice system. This lip-service ought to end if meaningful change must take root in Zambia.

"To be seen to be believed" is where politicians and governments have failed their people. Officers and administrators, in their quest to flatter their bosses so as to keep their political positions, have not disclosed the real conditions of the prisons. This has led to an illusion that all is well when serious inefficiencies exist. It is not a question of funding as it is one of prioritization.

Not only did the Kaunda regime neglect prison conditions, no attempts were made at changing old colonial oppressive laws. Mwaanga notes, "The more I looked at the facts, the more convinced I became that the *Preservation of Public Security Act* was being grossly abused; it had become a punitive weapon for dealing with suspects accused of committing small offences which fell within the jurisdiction of lower courts of law."[880]

In Zambia, law has become a "punitive weapon" and not a solace for justice seekers. The rich and powerful, who in most cases belong to the ruling aristocracy, do use the law to maintain their positional influence while the poor majority languish in filthy prisons banking only on the mercies of God. In a perfectly working democratic arrangement, the Judiciary, guaranteed by the Separation of Powers, is the last resort for those seeking justice to be done.

The Executive branch of government compromises the autonomy of the Judiciary by exerting pressure on judges and

---

[878] *Ibid.*
[879] Mwaanga, *supra.*, p. 44
[880] *Ibid.*, p. 68

thereby dictating who and when justice should be done. In many cases, justice never sees the light of day! Political interference on the interpreter of law, the Judiciary, means that prisoners do not receive fair trials. This also means that judgments for the detained is unfairly delayed and even denied to deserving prisoners and detainees. If Zambia must move from the rhetoric of democracy to a true democratic maturity in which the people are the true masters, the independence of the Judiciary must be guaranteed in practical terms.[881]

Mwaanga had opposed the imposition of the One-Party State, seen by many as the beginning of Zambia's democratic malaise. Per Mwaanga, the creation of a One-Party State excessively gave the president excessive executive powers which have made it impossible for the Judiciary to be freely independent: "When the One-Party constitution was drawn up in 1973, I was one of the very few people who presented controversial testimony advocating a party-time Central Committee and placing a limit of two terms of five years each on the holder of the Office of President of the Republic."[882]

There are two reasons why insistence has been made on the legacy of the Second Republic in Zambia. First, Kaunda was the longest serving president in Zambia. Of the more than five decades Zambia has been in existence, Kaunda's legacy spanned more than half of that. For over 27 years, every system and process in Zambia had the name of Kaunda written all over it. Second, all the present leaders, now or in the near past, have dealt with the Kaunda regime, in one way or the other. For example, all the presidents of Zambia after Kaunda have been influenced, for better or for worse, by the UNIP ideology or Kaunda personally. Michael Sata was so endeared to Kaunda that the late president renamed the Lusaka International Airport in 2011 after Kaunda, even though many other things are already named after Kaunda. There are many valiant sons and daughters of the soil

---

[881] See §11.8
[882] Mwaanga, p. 311

wasting in graves whose names should salute the Zambian streets, public infrastructure and national monuments.

Second Republican President Chiluba led an underground unofficial opposition revolution against Kaunda via the Zambia Congress of Trade Unions (ZCTU) and was imprisoned in 1980. Third Republican President Mwanawasa, served as Solicitor-General in the Kaunda administration, and represented several opponents of UNIP as a private attorney. Fourth Republican President Banda directly served in the Kaunda administration as ambassador to the US and as Minister of Foreign Affairs. Fifth Republican President Sata served under Kaunda in several ministerial positions. Only the sixth Republican President Lungu has no direct link to Kaunda, except perhaps that growing up he could have been influenced greatly by Kaunda's policies and politics.

Kaunda's predecessors appointed former Kaunda sympathizers to ministerial and ancillary positions. In practice, it was the same recycled leaders Zambia had entertained for almost over forty years, except of course, for a few new breeds from time to time.[883]

Mwaanga contends that he originally advised against the State of Emergency which provided for detention without trial, and he saw it as an "affront to our professed democratic principles and incompatible with our national philosophy of Humanism." Mwaanga meant well although powerful forces blew in the opposite direction.

For many people, it must take bitter experiences to change their thinking about something. Mwaanga did, but his was justifiable. He argued against Kaunda's life presidency, as noted above, and by his prison time in 1985, he still did. He castigated "Third world leaders who think that they were ordained by God to rule till death."[884]

---

[883] Such as Nevers Mumba, George Kunda, Hakainde Hichilema, Edgar Lungu, to mention but a few.

[884] Mwaanga, *supra*.

For Africa, it serves worse to hold on to power indefinitely;[885] for Zambia, the price has been too grave already. Indeed, only by the Rule of Law, and only in the hands of just men and women can the *other* society become *this* society! And only by guarding with diligence democratic ideals, can true justice be found, just as Plato offers, "No-one is just willingly but under compulsion."[886]

§13.6 "A Mockery of Justice"

The above phrase is the title of Richard Sakala's book published by Sentor Publishers in 2009 in Lusaka. Like Vernon Mwaanga's *The Other Society*, this book, *A Mockery of Justice*, is Sakala's attempt at explaining the circumstances that led to his arrest, detention and acquittal by the Zambian justice system under the watch of late President Mwanawasa.

The Mwanawasa administration accused Sakala, former State House Press Aide in the Chiluba administration, of the theft of motor vehicle. However, Sakala, who also was the Presidential Housing Initiative (PHI) chairman, disputes the allegation, noting that people do not steal their own vehicles: "I was sent to prison for stealing my own car. This was a car I ordered from Japan in my own name, a car I cleared at the border in my own name, a car I cleared with Zambia Revenue Authority in my own name, a car I registered with the registrar of motor vehicles in my own name, and indeed a car I used on official business for two years without any difficulties."[887]

---

[885] Despite economic troubles, the African geopolitical parity is increasingly leaning towards democracy and the Rule of Law. For example, one of the last longest reigning leaders in Africa, Hosni Mubarak, during the *March of a Million* on February 1st, 2011, bowed out and announced he would be stepping down at the end of his tenure. He eventually stepped down before his tenure due to heightened protests.

[886] Plato, *The Republic*, as quoted in Jene M. Porter, ed., *Classics in Political Philosophy* (Prentice Hall Canada Ltd., Scarborough, 2000), p. 20

[887] Sakala, *A Mockery of Justice*, p. 257

Sakala further argues that his second-hand car was one of the three PHI ordered in order to improve the efficiency of the project. Sakala adds that the purchase of the cars was necessitated by work demands and they were only bought after intense debate with the PHI administrative team.

Per Sakala, the allegation of motor theft was a calculated move to put him in prison. He reveals that the real motive why he was arrested was because of President Mwanawasa's desperate attempt to settle a personal score against him. The grudge against him, he argues, was not "punishment ostensibly for the charge of motor vehicle theft but in reality, the president was intent on punishing me for my alleged remarks about his health. There was no doubt that the president was behind my going to prison."[888]

Sakala had a difference with Mwanawasa. Sakala had advised late president Chiluba against adopting Mwanawasa as MMD's presidential candidate for the 2001 elections. Somehow Mwanawasa had gotten wind of it. Mwanawasa is then alleged to have calculated that accusations bordering on slander were bailable. His option was to accuse Sakala of a motor vehicle theft which is not bailable in Zambia. "I knew from experience the finality of a presidential detention. Nobody would believe the president was behind my arrest and incarceration, least the Judiciary. I knew from experience that, as a presidential detainee, you lost all rights including the protection of law."[889]

Sakala was eventually acquitted after serving three years and four months in detention. The reason why this section has been designed is not so much as to vindicate Sakala's position as it is to drive a point regarding the state of Zambia's justice system in the Third Republic. If Sakala's acquittal and release from detention, and by extension President Chiluba's acquittal in the plunder case, symbolize a change in the delivery of justice in Zambia, such a shift would yield little on the scale of justice. For even in the Second Republic, as repressive as it was, from time

---

[888] *Ibid.*, p. 134
[889] *Ibid.*, p. 135

to time, Kaunda pardoned, and even engineered, the acquittals of detainees.

What should be the standard, by which a shift in scope and administration of justice in Zambia should be measured, is the level of political interference and the extent to which the Executive branch of government is far removed from interfering with the independence of the Judiciary. Until Zambia reaches a point when the president's whims would not dictate justice, political detainees would not receive fair treatment under the law.

Critical analysis and the episodic review of the *Sakala* case will reveal that the Zambian justice system is still wanting. For all clear conscience, the allegations of corruption and theft of motor vehicle are serious offences which no democratic system should tolerate. However, in accordance with the fundamental principles of democracy, and of the Rule of Law, every person is, and remains, entitled to fair and due process.

The rules of natural justice[890] stipulate that every individual must be heard before a decision or judgment is passed on them. In this regard, too, such an individual is entitled to an impartial hearing without any biases. As far as Sakala was concerned, he was guilty of abuse of office, and not theft of motor vehicles as the Mwanawasa regime alleged.

Per *The Post* edition of August 2nd, 2002, "President Mwanawasa…told Parliament that…Sakala bought the vehicles at K2 million each, three months after government had bought them at K120 million each."[891] But, even if as Sakala claims that, in fact, government bought the vehicles at K70 million and that he only bought them at K12 million each, that would still

---

[890] The Rule of Natural Justice stands on two legs: the first leg is contained in the Latin maxim, *"nemo iudex in causa sua*: no man is permitted to be judge in his own cause" and the second leg is *"audi alteram partem:* let the other side be heard." Thus, justice is deemed to be done only where there is absence of bias and the opportunity is granted to all parties to be heard before judgment is entered.

[891] *Post* (August 2nd, 2002) as quoted in Richard Sakala, *A Mockery of Justice*, p. 174

constitute abuse of office. There is, thus, no argument against the fact that Sakala abused office.

A Mockery of Justice is germane to this debate for another important reason. It enables us to gauge the level of power abuse in Zambia. Indeed, we have established that Sakala abused his office while serving in the Chiluba administration. Naturally, we may be forced to think that since the New Deal administration began the daunting task of prosecuting former public office abusers, it should itself be not guilty of the same allegations.

However, that is not the case. In *A Mockery of Justice*, Sakala quotes Professor Paul Mwaipaya as follows: "Democracy and free expression are a threat to a mediocre leadership which thrives on ignorance and fear."[892] In other words, democracy will threaten any government that is sleazy in implementing the ideals that freedom enthrones. Because in democracy people are free to exercise their democratic rights and freedoms, it impinges on those who lead that they operate in a spirit of accountability and responsibility.

Mwaipaya further urges, "What generally happens in such a nation [where leaders thrive on ignorance and fear] is the abuse of human dignity and human rights; the practice of political intimidation. Such leadership is notorious for practicing nepotism, favoritism, suppression of liberty, equality, freedom of expression and freedom of choice."[893]

Is it a familiar experience for those in power to always transfer blame to someone else when they are themselves culpable? Indeed, both the Chiluba and New Deal administrations were at fault for the abuse of office. *A Mockery of Justice* only serves to reveal events and issues bordering on abuse of office which the common Zambian would not have been aware of. In that sense, Sakala's *A Mockery of Justice* lives by its title.

---

[892] Sakala, *supra.*, p. 73
[893] *Ibid.*

14| Criminal Reforms

*It is neither senseless snobbishness nor willful
blindness to accord criminals a second chance.
After all, to some extent, the degree of
punishment emitted to the convict is a measure
of the law's discernment on their eligibility into
the school of second chances.*

Chapter Focus

At the end of reading this chapter, you should be able to:

- Identify critical reform priorities of the Zambian
  criminal justice system
- Assess the state of Zambian prisons
- Trace the legacy of repression from the Colonial Era

BRIEF INTRODUCTION

This chapter is a follow-up to Chapter 13 and discusses
criminal justice in Zambia and the state and conditions of
Zambian prisons. It proffers a yardstick of how stable or
insane the politics of the nation are at any given point in time.

§14.1 The State of Zambian Prisons

It is rare to read anything about Zambia in the Canadian press.
When something is finally reported about Zambia, it must be
significant. The state of Zambian prisons is very significant. The
following article appeared in the Canadian *Metro* newspaper:

> Prisons in Zambia are so overcrowded that inmates are sometimes
> forced to sleep seated or in shifts, and children behind bars are

vulnerable to rape by adult prisoners, aids organizations said. A report released by the Prisons Care and Counselling Association (PRICCA), AIDS and Rights Alliance for Southern Africa (ARASA), and Human Rights Watch Tuesday said that some prisoners are detained for years enduring such conditions before they are even brought to trial.

"Zambian prisoners are starved, packed into cells unfit for human habitation, and face beatings at the hands of certain guards or fellow inmates. Children, pregnant women, pre-trial detainees, and convicted criminals are condemned to brutal treatment and are at serious risk of drug-resistant TB and HIV infection," said Kenneth Roth, Executive Director of Human Rights Watch. The groups are calling on the Zambian Government and its partners to make immediate improvements in prison conditions and medical care.[894]

This article paints a sad picture of precious men, women and children in the Zambian prisons. It is obvious that the old concept of imprisonment, which equated inmates as ruthless criminals and a danger to the community, does not always stand. Some people like Richard Sakala who have served terms in the Zambian prisons are described as "learned and knowledgeable people, gentlemen among their peers."[895]

Zambia has 53 prisons. All of them were built before independence for a total of 5,500 prisoners. By 2011, the prisons were housing more than 15,000 prisoners.[896] 1,000 prisoners were released on parole in 2011 "to address overcrowding in prisons."[897]

Prisons should not be considered as punishment chambers anymore. In contemporary times, prisons have been chambers of knowledge and ideas. Some of great Zambian books have been conceived behind bars. These books include Sakala's *A Mockery*

[894] *Metro*, "Zambian Prisons Unfit for Human Habitation," (Thursday, April 29th, 2010)

[895] Zarina Zarina Geloo, "Time to Break Out of Old Prison Ideas," *The Guardian Weekly*, December 3rd – 9th, 2005

[896] See *Zambia Weekly*, "1000 Prisoners on Parole in 2011," Week 1, Vol. 2, Issue 1, January 7th, 2011, p. 1

[897] *Ibid.*

of Justice, Mwaanga's *The Other Society* or Hamalengwa's *Thoughts are Free*.

Geloo charges that, "It is no longer the insane or social misfits that inhabit the cells. People in other countries have been known to acquire degrees and other forms of education while in cells – this means they access books and write and their minds are kept alive."[898] Prisons, therefore, can be centers for reformation and knowledge enhancement.

As reported in the *Metro*, Zambian prisons are in dire need of a make-over. It is travesty that "prisoners are starved, packed into cells unfit for human habitation, and face beatings at the hands of certain guards or fellow inmates." It is even felonious that "children behind bars are vulnerable to rape by adult prisoners."

There are two factors that make it difficult to know exactly what obtains inside the prison walls. First, it is the design of prisons themselves. They are meant to "lock" up people and their secrets. In other words, what happens inside the prisons is meant to remain, and even die, within the prisons.

Second, because of the sensitive nature of such exposure, most governments, and justifiably for the governments in developing countries, are reluctant to devour information on the state of their prisons. Thus, it is only through the eyes of prison survivors that society at large can know more of what happens inside the prison bars. Sata "thanked President Levy Mwanawasa for taking him to prison two times because he now knows that which he did not know from outside the prison."[899]

Most political prisoners are usually high profile figures who are well-known by the international community. As such, they are treated relatively "better' than common criminals and less known victims. Ironically, most of what is known about prisons is narrated through the testimony of former political prisoners.[900]

---

[898] Zarina, *supra.*
[899] Amos Malupenga, "They Only Allowed Me Two Minutes with My Wife, Reveals Sata," *The Post*, (August 14th, 2005)
[900] In Zambia, for example, both Vernon J. Mwaanga and Richard Sakala were very important persons and high profile politicians. Through their

Charles Mwewa

A thorough analysis of Mwaanga's *The Other Society* and Sakala's *A Mockery of Justice* reveal that Zambian prisons have moved from bad to worse. The events of the two books are over two decades apart. And yet in all angles they regurgitate the same prison ordeal.

In 1985, Mwaanga re-told the sad story of the Zambian prisons then. It was a pathetic sight and grave disservice to human rights. Everything from ventilation to capacity to sanitation left much to be desired. The conditions were inhuman:

> There were 17 of us in the cell and at night it became very warm. A cell of similar size next door (cell eight) had had 57 inmates the previous night and I wondered how they had managed. I inspected the kitchen, laundry, toilets, showers, penal block and library. All these places were filthy and unfit for human habitation. I was surprised that no one had died, at least since I had been there, from food poisoning. The inmates received their food on old newspapers, those who were lucky, that is – because there were no plates of any kind. The conditions had to be seen to be believed. *These are the painful realities of prison life in Zambia today* (Emphasis added).[901]

In fact, Mwaanga hints that the situation had been like that for a long time. Implicitly, Zambian prison conditions had been in a poor state of affairs for the better part of the 1970s and 1980s. When Mwaanga writes, "These are the painful realities of prison life in Zambia today," he is alluding to the 1980s. However, even after two decades, prison conditions in Zambia have not improved.

Writing in *A Mockery of Justice*, Sakala laments, "Every single day in prison is punishment without measure."[902] This is

---

books, *The Other Society* or *A Prisoner's Diary* and *A Mockery of Justice*, respectively, we have come to know about the state of the Zambian prisons. However, because their treatment in prison was one of privilege, it is difficult to gauge how the other not-so-important, and they are in the majority, are treated. It could be assumed that their situations are worse than imagined.
[901] Mwaanga, *The Other Society,* p. 170
[902] Sakala, *supra.*, p. 55

about 24 years after the Mwaanga detention ordeal. And by April 2010 that situation had only worsened, for "Children, pregnant women, pre-trial detainees, and convicted criminals are condemned to brutal treatment and are at serious risk of drug-resistant TB and HIV infection."

§14.2 Reformation or Punishment

The critical question to ask is: Are Zambian prisons systems of reform and reintegration or torture chambers? Since the Second Republic, Zambian prisons have become popular as places where detainees are tortured or are given "numerous threats of impending torture."[903] The ushering in of the MMD government in 1991 promised so much in terms of the protection of the rights of the detainees. It was expected to be more humane to the plight of the prisoners than in the Second Republic, which Mwanakatwe captures unchalantly:

> Yet over the whole period of twenty-seven years of Kaunda's rule the power of detention of people was used more against political opponents than the detention of spies or saboteurs from Rhodesia or South Africa. Even long after the independence of Zimbabwe and the beginning of negotiations for peaceful political change in South Africa, Kaunda never entertained the idea of lifting the State of Emergency. It was his most powerful weapon for use against his political opponents. The police have been beneficiaries of the additional powers they are given when State of Emergency is in force.[904]

There is a very important lesson to be learned from this experience. In the interest of democracy, it is imperative that Emerging Zambian Leaders take stock of the immorality of a prolonged State of Emergency. President Kaunda used it as

---

[903] Hamalengwa, *Thoughts are Free*, p. 19
[904] John M. Mwanakatwe, *End of Kaunda Era* (Lusaka: Multimedia Publication, 1994), pp. 146-7

"powerful weapon...against his political opponents" long after the purpose for which it had been imposed had elapsed.

Admittedly, the insecurity of the Unilateral Declaration of Independence (UDI) of Ian Douglas Smith in Rhodesia was real. In that sense alone the State of Emergency was justified, but only in so far as it went to curb the hostility of the clandestine acts of sabotage the neighbors were engaged in intending to destabilize Zambia. President Kaunda himself has admitted that the UDI was "extremely difficult times. Happening just a year after our independence, UDI made Zambia, a promising young nation, pass through great hardships and challenges."[905]

But the president turned the weapon for his external enemies against his own people, albeit, his political opponents. From being a noble instrument aimed at suppressing external rebellion, the State of Emergency became a lethal injection in the veins of Zambia's democratic free voice. With it, Kaunda had murdered freedom of speech and expression; with it he had solidified his position as the supreme leader of the "young and promising nation."

With the State of Emergency, the prisons had become abodes of punishment, places where the promising brains of Zambia went to waste. Following the electoral victory of the MMD government in 1991, President Kaunda escaped with impunity, "Yet so as through fire."[906]

If anything, that was a sign that the new government would adopt a new style of political rubrics. There was a real promise that a police officer above the rank of Superintendent would not have the power to arrest any person in respect of whom he or she had reason to believe that there were grounds justifying the arrest. There was a real promise that detainees would not be unlawfully tortured. There was hope that there would be change from subjecting detainees and prisoners to cruelty where their "physical strength and well-being was impaired after release

---

[905] Kenneth D. Kaunda, "KK's Diary: UDI, 40 Years Ago," *Post Lifestyle*, (December 4th, 2005)
[906] I Corinthians 3:15b

because of the severity of their torture and ill-treatment."[907]
That promise has not been fulfilled. The MMD government, like the UNIP government in the Second Republic, did not respect the rights of prisoners in Zambia. However, not all hope is lost. Emerging Zambian Leaders have a mandate to articulate democratic ideals that favor respect for life, dignity and the right to detention with trial without being subjected to inhuman treatment or torture.

§14.3 Criminal Justice

The Zambian criminal justice system continues to be a big worry both in terms of access to justice and justice delivery. This is not to imply that the Zambian Government is not taking steps to curb the situation. "Since the re-introduction of multiparty democracy in Zambia in 1991, some progress has been registered in the governance system of the country, including its criminal justice system. However, many challenges remain across Zambia's criminal justice institutions, and these inhibit the efficient and effective delivery of justice to its citizens."[908]
A lot has been said previously about the abuses of power and office prevalent in the Second Republic. There is undeniable evidence that the Kaunda regime had set a bitter precedent of rampant mistreatment of prisoners and abuse of their democratic and other rights.

§14.4 Sons unlike Their Fathers

The thematic argument in this book is that historical corollaries impact greatly on Zambia's contemporary challenges.

[907] Mwanakatwe, *supra.* p. 147
[908] The Criminal Justice System in Zambia: Enhancing the Delivery of Security in Africa (Policy Brief of July 6th, 2009) <http://www.issafrica.org>

Imprisonment and the treatment of prisoners are not exceptions. While in many respects we should emulate President Kaunda, in one cardinal respect, however, we should not. The Kaunda regime maintained a bitter and oppressive colonial apparatus by perpetuating the same oppressive laws and tactics that victimized and dehumanized the Africans in the Colonial Era.

At the height of the colonial rule, and during a boycott, the colonial administration police ambushed the Northern Rhodesian women. It was during one of these episodes that Kaunda witnessed women with babies' straddle on their backs outside the butcher-shops in Lusaka being whipped by the police. It is widely believed that because of this episode, Kaunda vowed not to eat meat. He remained a vegetarian.

Kaunda and Nkumbula were arrested in November 1953 for what the colonial regime called unlawful publications. ANC had been publishing a newspaper called the *Congress News*. The authorities later learned that the publication was authorized. The duo was released.

On January 6th, 1955, Kaunda, Nkumbula and Sikalumbi were arrested. Prior to the arrest, their houses were thoroughly searched. The trio was accused of being found in possession of prohibited publications. Sikalumbi was acquitted, but Kaunda and Nkumbula were found guilty by a Lusaka Resident Magistrate court which sentenced them to two months in prison with hard labor. The duo was later released a day earlier.

In March 1959, Kaunda, Kapwepwe and other freedom fighters were arrested. In May 1959, Kaunda appeared before Senior Resident Magistrate, Thomas Pickett, in Lusaka, and was charged with convening an unlawful assembly. In June 1959, Kaunda was sentenced to nine months in prison with hard labor. He was sent to Lusaka Central Prison where he cleaned "communal lavatory [toilet] buckets."[909] Kaunda was moved to Salisbury Central Prison in Southern Rhodesia by bus handcuffed to Wilson Chakulya. In 1962, then as National Secretary of

---

[909] Chisala, *The Fall of President Kaunda*, p. 13

UNIP, Chona was charged and convicted with "publishing a seditious publication contrary to section 53D (i)(d) of the *Penal Code*."[910]

Notwithstanding the above, Kaunda would use the same tactics, if not worse, to punish his fellow Zambians in the Second Republic. For example, on January 9th, 1981, Kaunda and UNIP suspended seventeen union leaders from ZCTU and MUZ including the man that would ten years later replace Kaunda as president, Frederick Chiluba.

The deemed cause for the arrest of the seventeen was "for causing the country 205,681 man-days of lost work because of wild cat strikes aimed at overthrowing the government."[911] Kaunda's undemocratic tendencies were based on fear, fear that any agitation by the people amounted to treasonous activities. Subsequently, on July 27th, 1981, UNIP amended the constitution to "abolish primary elections; candidates for National Assembly elections must be approved by the Central Committee of UNIP."[912] And by November 1981, this was practically a norm.

Second Republic politics was based on justified blame. As propounded in this book, this, too, was a bequeathed attitude from the colonial masters. Even now, former colonial forces do not admit that they plundered and destroyed Africa. They would, rather, accuse lack of Africa's economic underdevelopment on Africa's poor leadership, corruption or bad policies and their attendant untimely implementation.

Justified blame was a political tactic aimed at entrenching dictatorial tendencies without tracing the blame to the incumbency. Therefore, the president or his or her political party would have decided to subvert justice or introduce unpopular policies but then look for a scapegoat. That scapegoat would usually be an omission or revolting activity seen to have

---

[910] See *R. v. Chona* (High Court of Northern Rhodesia, 1962); John Hatchard and Muna Ndulo *A Case Book on Criminal Law* (Lusaka: Government Printer, 1983), pp. 306-307
[911] Grotpeter et. al., *Historical Dictionary of Zambia*, p. xxv
[912] *Ibid.*

originated from the opposition parties or the ruling party's hardliner nemesis.

Thus, Kaunda did not only punish his fellow countrymen and women, but he never bothered to improve prison conditions, let alone repealing or amending the repressive laws inherited from the colonial government. Clarence Darrow said, "True patriotism hates injustices in its own land more than anywhere else."[913]

[913] Famous Quotes and Authors, "Patriotism and Nationalism Quotes and Quotations," <www.famousquotesandauthors.com> (Retrieved: February 6th, 2011)

SELECTED BIBLIOGRAPHY

Abidde, O. Sabella   "Of Rumored, Attempted &
                            Successful Coups," (2004)

Acemoglu, Daron &
  James Robinson   *Economic Origins of Dictatorship
                            and Democracy* (Cambridge:
                            Cambridge University Press,
                            2009)

Achebe, Chinua   *Things Fall Apart* (New York:
                            Knopf Doubleday Publishing
                            Group, 1958)

Achola, Paul Pius Waw   *Implementing Educational
                            Policies in Zambia* (Washington,
                            D.C.: World Bank, 1990)

Actionaid-Denmark   "Facts about Corruption," June,
                            2005

Adar, Korwa G. & Isaac
  M. Munyae   "Human Rights Abuses in Kenya
                            under Daniel Arap Moi, 1978-
                            2001," (2001) *African Studies
                            Quarterly*, Vol. 5, No. 1

Africa Image   "Sharp-dressing Ex-Zambian
                            President Stole £23m," (Monday,
                            June 29th, 2009)

African News   "Zambia: Levy's Order to Arrest
                            Sata was Improper – Prof.
                            Chanda," (Thursday, July 28th,
                            2005)

Africa Today   Volume 46, Number 2, 53

Agazzi, Isolda   "Africa: Climate Change
                            Assistance So Near and Yet So
                            Far," Thomson Reuters
                            Foundation-*AlertNet*, July 24th,

	2010
Ahmad, Tahir Mirza	*Christianity: A Journey from Fact to Fiction* (Surrey, UK: Islam International Publications, 2006)
Aihe, D.O	"Neo-Nigerian Human Rights in Zambia: A Comparative Study with Some Countries in Africa and West Indies," *Zambia Law Journal*, Vols. 3 & 4 Nos. 1&2
Aihe, D.O	*The Constitution of Zambia: A Historic and Comparative Study*, Ph.D. Thesis, University of London (Unpublished, 1968)
Alden, C	*China in Africa* (London: Zed Books, 2007)
Aldridge, Sally	*The Peoples of Zambia* (London: Heinemann Education Books, 1978)
AllAboutLove.com	"Homosexuals are Born that Way," <allaboutlove.com> (Retrieved: November 26th, 2010)
Allan, W.	*Land Holding and Land Usage among the Plateau Tonga of Mazabuka District, A Reconnaissance Survey, 1945* (Westport, Conn.: Negro Universities Press, 1970)
Amoako, K.Y.	"Governance and Development in Africa: The Critical Nexus," Economic Community for Africa, February 18th, 2004
Anglin, Douglas G.	"Political Scene in Zambia," (1975) *Canadian Journal of African Studies*, IX, 2, pp. 337-340
Anglin, Douglas G.	*Zambian Crisis Behavior* (Montreal & Kingston: McGill-

Anglin, Douglas & Timothy Shaw

Queen's University Press, 1994)

Zambia's Foreign policy: Studies in Diplomacy and Dependence (Boulder: Westview Press, 1971/72)

Asare, Charles

New Testament Ministers' Manual (Accra: Heritage Graphix and Communications, 1998)

Ashcroft, Bill; Griffiths Gareth; & Helen Tiffin

Key Concepts in Post-Colonial Studies (London and New York: Routledge, 1998)

Ashley, Mike

The Mammoth Book of British Kings and Queens (London: Robinson, 1998)

Associated Press

"Wal-Mart Bids $4.25B to Buy S. African Retailer," *Toronto Star*, (Tuesday, September 28th, 2010)

Babu, Mohamed

African Socialism or Socialist Africa (London: Zed Press, 1981)

Bagambiire, Davies

Canadian Immigration and Refugee Law (Aurora: Canada Law Book Inc., 1996)

Banda, Fackson

"The Presidency and the Media," *The Post*, (September 30th, 2009)

Banda, Gabriella

Adjusting to Adjustment in Zambia: Women's and Young People's Responses to a Changing Economy (Oxford: Oxfam, 1991)

Bank of Zambia

Issues in Zambian Economy (Lusaka: Bank of Zambia, 2003)

Barker, Anne

"Holyland Corruption Scandal Grips Israel," *ABC News*, (April 29th, 2010)

Barnes, Carolyn

"Microfinance Program Clients

and Impact: An Assessment of Zambuko Trust, Zimbabwe," (2001)

Bates, Robert H.   *Patterns of Uneven Development: Causes and Consequences in Zambia* (Denver: University of Denver, 1974)

Bates, Robert H   *Rural Responses to Industrialization: A Study of Village Zambia* (New Haven: Yale University Press, 1976)

Bates, Robert H.   *Unions, Parties and Political Development: A Study of Mineworkers in Zambia* (New Haven and London: Yale University Press, 1971)

Bayart, Jean-François   *The State in Africa: The Politics of the Belly* (London and New York: Longman, 1997)

Baylies, Carolyn & Morris Szeftel   "Elections in One-Party State in Zambia" in Cherry Gertzel (ed.) *The Dynamics of the One-Party State in Zambia* (Manchester: Manchester University Press, 1984)

BBC   December 14th, 2006

BBC   September 27th, 2000

BBC   June 24th, 2004

BBC   April 6th, 2009

BBC   March 22nd, 2006

BBC   March 11th, 2002

BBC   February 18th, 2009

BBC   January 21st, 2004

Behrent, Megan   "Immigration, Emigration and Exile: The Figure of the 'Been-to' in African Literature," (1997),

	Postimperial and Postcolonial Literature in English,
Belloc, Hilaire	*The Servile State* (London & Edinburg: T.N. Foulis, 1912)
Berger, E	*Labor, Race and Colonial Rule: The Copperbelt from 1924 to Independence* (London: Oxford University Press, 1974)
Berton, Pierre	*The Smug Minority* (Toronto: McClelland and Stewart, 1968)
Betz, R	*Assessment of Human and Institutional Resources Development Project – Zambia* (Washington: USAID and Academy for Educational Development, 1990)
Beveridge, Andrew A. & Anthony R. Oberschall	*African Businessmen and Development in Zambia* (Princeton, N.J.: Princeton University Press, 1979)
Bhagavan, M. R.	*Zambia: Impact of Industrial Strategy on Regional Imbalance and Social Inequality* (Uppsala: Scandinavian Inst. of African Studies, 1978)
Bhengu, M. J.	*Ubuntu: The Essence of Democracy* (Cape Town: Novalis Press, 1996)
Bigelow, Poultney	*White Man's Africa* (New York & London: Harper & Brothers Publishers, 1898)
Bjerremand, T.	*Proposals to Strengthen Small Scale Sector in Zambia* (Copenhagen: World Band and Frigo Consult, 1990)
Black, Ian &	

Michael White

"EU Accounting Worse than Enron, Says Whistleblower," (August 2nd, 2002)

Blackmon, Douglas A. *Slavery by Another Name* (New York: Anchor Books, 2008)

Blackstone, William (1765) *Commentaries on the Laws of England*, 259-60, 1

Bliss, Anne M. &
J. A. Rigg

Zambia (Oxford: Clio Press, 1984)

Blomström, M &
A. Kokko

"The Economics of Foreign Direct Investment Incentives," Foreign Direct Investment in Real and Financial Sector of Industrial Countries, 2003

Bloom, Paul &
Frank C. Keil

Thinking Through Language (Yale University: Blackwell Publishers Ltd., 2001)

Bonnick, Gladstone G. *Zambia Country Assistance Review: Turning an Economy Around* (Washington, D.C.: World Bank, 1997)

Bostock, Mark &
Charles Harvey

Zambian Copper: A Case Study of Foreign Investment (New York: Praeger Publishers, 1972)

Boyle, Christina "Britain's Sexy Spy Scandal: Parliament Aide Katia Zatuliveter Accused as Russian Agent, Denies Claim," *Daily News*, (December 5th, 2010)

Bratton, Michael "Zambia Starts Over," (1992)

Bratton, M. & N. Van De Walle

Journal of Democracy, Vol. 3: 81-94

Democratic Experiments in Africa: Regime Transitions in Comparative Perspectives (Cambridge: Cambridge University Press, 1997)

Brockman, Norbert C.

"Lenshina Mulenga Mubita, Alice c.1924 to 1978: Lumpa Church, Zambia," (1994) *An African Biographical Dictionary*

Broodryk, J.

Ubuntu: Life Lessons from Africa (Pretoria: Ubuntu School of Philosophy, 2002)

Brown, Karima

"Zuma Calls for G-20 to Initiate IMF Reforms," (Toronto, June 29th, 2010)

Burawoy, Michael

"Consciousness and Contradiction: A Study of Protests in Zambia," (1976) *British Journal of Sociology*, 27 (1): pp. 78-98

Burawoy, Michael

The Color of Class on the Copper Mines: From African Advancement to Zambianization (Manchester: Published on behalf of the Institute for African Studies, University of Zambia, by Manchester University Press, 1973)

Burdette, M. Marcia

Zambia: Between Two Worlds (Boulder, Colo.: Westview Press, 1988)

Burnell, Peter

"Zambia at the Crossroads," (Summer, 1994) *World Affairs*, Vol. 157, No. 1: pp. 19-28

Business Day "Poverty Alleviation and Micro Finance: Can Nigeria Learn From India?" 2008, from www.businessday.org (Retrieved: February 8th, 2011)

BusinessWeek April 3rd, 2000

Bwalya, Obine *Let Us Play AIDS* (Lusaka: Sweeza, 2002)

Bwalya, Obine *Let Us Play HIV* (Lusaka: Sweeza, 2002)

Caplan, Gerald L. "Barotseland's Scramble for Protection," (1969) *Journal of African History,* x, 2, 277

Caplan, Gerald L. *The Elites of Barotseland 1878-1969* (C. Hurst & Co., 1970)

Carmody, Patrick *Education in Zambia* (Lusaka: Bookworld, 1999)

Carson, Ben *Think Big: Unleashing Your Potential for Excellence* (Grand Rapids: Zondervan Publishing House)

Carter, Hazel *An Outline of Chitonga Grammar* (Lusaka: Bookworld, 2001)

Castro, Joseph "How a Mother's Love Changes a Child's Brain," *Live Science,* January 30th, 2012

Central Statistical Office *Formal Sector – Employment and Earnings Inquiry Report 2006* (Lusaka: Central Statistical Office, 2006)

Central Statistical Office *HIV /AIDS Service Provision Assessment Survey* (Lusaka: Central Statistical Office, 2005)

Central Statistical Office *HIV / AIDS Service Provision Assessment Survey 2005 –Key Findings* (Lusaka: Central Statistical Office, 2005)

Central Statistical Office *Strategic Plan* (2003-2007)

Chabal, P. and J. P. Daloz *Africa Works: Disorder as Political Instrument* (Oxford: James Currey, 1999)

Chanda, Casmir *Teaching and Learning of English in Secondary Schools: A Zambian Case Study in Improving Quality* (London: Commonwealth Secretariat, 2008)

Chao, Loretta "Something Borrowed," (November 16th, 2009) *The Wall Street Journal*

Cheeseman, Nic & Marja Hinfelaar "Parties, Platforms, and Political Mobilization: The Zambian Presidential Election of 2008," (2009) *African Affairs*, 109/434, 51–76

Chêne, Marie "U4 Helpdesk," Transparency International, October 20th, 2008

Chifwambwa, Sambwa Gabriel "Mwanakatwe," *The Post*, (December 29th, 2009)

Chikulo, Bornwell "Elections in One-Party Participatory Democracy," in Ben Turok, *Development in Zambia* (London: Zed Press, 1979)

Chiluba, Frederick *Democracy: The Challenge of Change* (Lusaka: Multimedia Publications, 1995)

Chimpinde, Kombe & Abigail Chaponda "PACT, Nation Can't be Led by an Under-Five, Says Sata," *The Post*, (Thursday, September 30th, 2010)

Chisangano, David *The Enraged Vulture* (Lusaka: ZEPH, 2004)

Chisala, Beatwell S.   *The Downfall of former president
                           Kaunda* (Lusaka: Co-op Printing,
                           1994)
Chisala, Chanda   "How Black Pride Produces
                           Black Poverty – Part 3," at
                           www.chandachisala.com (Posted
                           and retrieved: September 6th,
                           2010)
Chisembele, Sophena   "General Comments on the
                           Treatment of Zambian Freedom
                           Fighters Today," (2004)
Chisembele, Sophena   *Zambia, The Struggle and
                           Aftermath* (London: Sylsop
                           Books, 2016)
Chishimba, C. P.   *Perspectives for Teachers of
                           English as a Second Language*
                           (Lusaka: UNZA Press, 2009)
Chona M. Mainza   *Kabuca Uleta Tunji* (London:
                           University of London Press,
                           1971/2010)
Chondoka, Yizenge &
   Frackson F. Bota   *A History of the Tumbuka from
                           1400 to 1900* (Lusaka: Academic
                           Press, 2007)
Christian Aid   June 28th, 2004
Christie, Roy   *For the President's Eyes Only*
                           (Johannesburg: Hugh and
                           Keartland Publishers, 1971)
CIA   "Zambia: Economy Overview,"
                           The World Factbook, (December
                           8th, 2010)
Clark, Desmond   *The Stone Age Cultures of
                           Northern Rhodesia, with
                           Particular Reference to the
                           Cultural and Climatic Succession
                           in the Upper Zambezi Valley and*

Clark, Kerr; John Dunlop;
Frederick Harbison;
and Charles Myers

Clausen, Lars

Cole, David G. & E. Cyril
Greenall

Coleman, F.L.

Collett, Peter

Colson, Elizabeth

Corcoran, Terrence

Cornell, Drucilla and
Karin van Marle

its Tributaries (Westport, Conn.:
Negro Universities Press, 1970)

Industrialism and Industrial Man
(New York: Oxford University
Press, 1960) as quoted in John
Myles and Jill Quadagno,
"Political Theories of the Welfare
State," (March 2002) *Social
Service Review*
*Industrialisierung in
Schwarzafrika: Eine
Soziologische Lotstudie şweier
Grossbetriebe in Sambia*
(Bielefeld: Bertelsmann
Universitatsverlag, 1968)

Kaunda's Gaoler (London:
Radcliffe Press, 2003)
*The Northern Rhodesia
Copperbelt 1889-1962* available
online at
http://www.pulfordmedia.co.uk.
(Retrieved: December 19th, 2010)
"Zambia Boldly Goes," *New
Statesman*, August 3rd, 2009
*Tonga Religious Life in the
Twentieth Century* (Lusaka:
Bookworld, 2006)
"When Big Business Goes Bad,"
Financial Post Magazine
(October 2010)

"Exploring Ubuntu: Tentative
Reflections," (2005) *African
Human Rights Law Journal*: 195

369

CounterPunch

Cross, Sholto

Cunningham, Simon

Daily Telegraph

Damachi, U. G.

Davis, John Merle
& Robert I. Rotberg

Defence Act

Dickerson, Mark O. &
Thomas Flanagan

Discover Zambia

Djokotoe, E &
P. K. Chama

September 20th, 2005

"Politics and Criticism in Zambia:
A Review Article," (1974/6)
*Journal of Southern African
Studies* 1, No.1, pp. 109-115

*The Copper Industry in Zambia:
Foreign Mining Companies in a
Developing Country* (New York,
N.Y.: Praeger, 1981)

February 7th, 2010

"Kenneth Kaunda: Humanism in
Zambia," in U. G. Damachi (ed.)
*Leadership Ideology in Africa:
Attitudes towards Socio-economic
Development* (New York: New
York University Press, 1976)

*Modern Industry and the African:
An Enquiry into the Effect of the
Copper Mines of Central Africa
upon Native Society and the Work
of the Christian Missions*
(London: Cass, 1967)

Cap. 106 of the Laws of Zambia
(preamble)

*An Introduction to Government
and Politics: A Conceptual
Approach* (Toronto: Nelson,
2006)

"The Diaspora in the Economic
Development of Zambia,"
Volume 5, 2010/2011

"Show Me the Money! How
Government Spends and
Accounts for Public Money in

	Zambia," Transparency International, Primus Media, 2007
Dorfman, Ariel	"Now, America, You Know How Chileans Felt," *New York Times*, December 16th, 2016
Dorman, T. E.	*African Experience: An Education Officer in Northern Rhodesia (Zambia)* (London; New York: New York: Radcliffe Press; in the United States of America and Canada, distributed by St. Martin's Press, 1993)
Dresang, Dennis	"Ethnic Politics, Representative Bureaucracy and Development Administration: The Zambian Case," (1974) *American Science Review* 68 (4)
Dresang, Dennis	"The Political Economy of Zambia," in Richard Harries (ed.) *The Political Economy in Africa* (Cambridge, Mass.: Schenkan Publishing Co., 1975)
Dugger, Celia W.	"Former President of Zambia is Acquitted," *The New York Times*, (August 17th, 2009)
Dyzenhaus, D.; R. S Moreau; & A. Ripstein, (eds.)	*Law and Morality* (Toronto: University of Toronto Press, 2007)
Ebow, Bodzi-Simpson, (ed.)	*The Law and Economic Development in the Third World* (New York: Praeger Publishers, 1992)
Elliot, Charles	*Constraints on the Economic Development of Zambia* (Nairobi: Oxford University Press, 1971)
Emergency Act	Repealed by 5 of 1960

Emergency Powers Act	Cap 108 of the Laws of Zambia
Englebert, Pierre	*State Legitimacy and Development in Africa* (London: Lynne Rienner Publisher, 2002)
Englebert, Pierre	"The Contemporary African State: Neither African Nor State," (1997) *Third World Quarterly,* Vol. 18, No. 4: 767-775
Epstein, A. L.	*The Administration of Justice and the Urban African: A Study of Urban Native Courts in Northern Rhodesia* (London: H. M. Stationery Office, 1953)
Erikson, Karen	"Zambia: Class Formation and D'etente," (May-August 1978) *Review of African Political Economy,* 9, pp. 4-26
Esping-Andersen, Gosta	*The Three Worlds of Welfare Capitalism* (Princeton, N.J: Princeton University Press, 1990) as quoted in John Myles and Jill Quadagno, "Political Theories of the Welfare State," (March 2002) *Social Service Review*
Evans, Rob	*Guardian*, January 14th, 2005
Evans, Timothy G.; Alayne M. Adams; Rafi Mohammed & Alison H. Norris	"Demystifying Nonparticipation in Microcredit: A Population-Based Analysis," (February 1999) *World Development,* Volume 27, Issue 2, pp. 419-430
Fagan, Brian M.	*A Short History of Zambia: From the Earliest Times until A. D. 1900* (Nairobi; Lusaka; London: Oxford U.P., 1966)

Fallachi, Oriana — *A Man* (New York: Simon and Schuster, 1979/80)

Farlex — "Microcredit," *Farlex Financial Dictionary,* 2009

Fashoyin, Tayo — *Policy Reforms and Employment Relations in Zambia* (Harare: ILO Sub-Regional Office for Southern Africa, 2008)

Fawcett, J. E. S. — *The Application of the European Convention on Human Rights* (Oxford: Clarendon Press, 1969)

Feulner, Edwin J. — "Saluting a 'Great Charter' of Liberty," Heritage.org, June 17th, 2015

Finance Corporation — "Doing Business 2011: Making a Difference for Entrepreneurs," November 5th, 2010

Financial Times — February 6th, 2005

Fincham, R & G. Zulu — "Labor and Participation in Zambia," in B. Turok (ed.) *Development in Zambia* (London: Zed Press, 1979)

Find Law — January 10th, 2003

Firstbrook, Peter — *The Obamas* (New York: Crown Publishers, 2010)

Foreign Judgments (Reciprocal Reinforcement) Act — Cap. 76 of the Laws of Zambia

Foucault, Michel — *Society Must be Defended: Lectures at the Collêge de France, 1975-1976* (New York: Picador, 2003)

Frank, T.M — *Race and Nationalism: Struggle for Power in Rhodesia-Nyasaland* (London: George Allen & Unwin Ltd., 1960)

F.W., E. Hoch — *Bemba Pocket Dictionary – (Bemba-English & English-Bemba)* (Lusaka: The Society of the Missionary of Africa, 2008)

Gann, L. H. — *A History of Northern Rhodesia: Early Days to 1953* (London: Chatto and Windus, 1964)

Gann, L. H. — *The Birth of a Plural Society* (Manchester: Manchester University Press, 1958)

Gann, L. H. & Peter Duignan, (eds.) — *Colonialism in Africa: 1870-1960* (Cambridge: University Printing House, 1969)

Gardiner, Nile & James Phillips — *The Heritage Foundation.* April 21st, 2004

Gelfand, Michael — *Northern Rhodesia: In the Days of the Charter* (Oxford: Basil Blackwell, 1961)

Geloo, Zarina — "Time to Break Out of Old Prison Ideas," *The Guardian Weekly*, (December 3rd – 9th, 2005)

Gertzel, Cherry — "Dissent and Authority in the Zambian One-Party State," in Gertzel, Cherry (ed.) *The Dynamics of the One-Party State in Zambia* (Manchester: Manchester University Press, 1984)

Gertzel, Cherry — "Introduction: The Making of One-Party State," in Gertzel, Cherry (ed.) *The Dynamics of the One-Party State in Zambia* (Manchester: Manchester University Press, 1984)

Gertzel, Cherry	"Labor and the State: The Case of Zambia's Mineworkers Union – A Review Article," (1975) *Journal of Commonwealth and Comparative Politics,* 13, 3: 290-304
Gertzel, Cherry (ed.)	*The Political Process in Zambia: Documents and Readings, 2 Volumes* (Lusaka: University of Zambia Press, 1974)
Gewald, Jan-Bart; Marja Hinfelaar; & Giacomo Macola	*One Zambia, Many Histories: Towards a History of Post-colonial Zambia* (Leiden, Boston: Brill, 2008)
Ghazvinian, John	*Untapped: The Scramble for Africa's Oil* (Orlando: Harcourt Inc., 2007)
Giamanco, Kristin	"Homosexuality: Born or Made?" *Serendip* (Spring 2005)
Gifford, Paul	*African Christianity: Its Public Role* (Kampala: Fountain Publishers, 1999)
Gifford, Paul	*African Christianity: Its Public Role* (London: Hurst & Company, 1998)
Glover, Paul	"Grassroots Economics," from http://www.context.org/ICLIB/IC 41/Glover.htm, (Retrieved: February 10th, 2011)
Goal, Carol	"Stark Warning Out of Africa for Western Economies," *Toronto Star*, (Wednesday, March 2nd, 2011)
Goldberg, Nathanael	"Measuring the Impact of Microfinance: Taking Stock of

	What We Know," Grameen Foundation USA Publication Series, 2005
Goldsworthy, David	"Civilian Control of the Military in Black Africa," (January, 1981) *African Affairs*, Vol. 80, No. 318: 49-66
Gonzalez, Adrian	"Sacrificing Microcredit for Unrealistic Goals," Microfinance Information Exchange, January 2011
Good, Kenneth	"Debt and One-Party State in Zambia," (1989) *The Journal of Modern African Studies*, Vol. 27: 297-314
Good, Kenneth	"Zambia: Back into the Future," (1988) *Third World Quarterly*, Vol. 10: 37-54
Grant, William D	*Zambia, Then and Now – Colonial Rulers and their African Successors* (London: Routledge Taylor & Francis Group, 2009)
Grotpeter, John J.; Brian V. Siegel; & James R. Pletcher	*Historical Dictionary of Zambia, Second Edition* (London: The Scarecrow Press, Inc., 1998)
GRZ	*Interim Report of the Constitution Review Commission*, June 29th, 2005
Guardian	May 5th, 2004
Guardian	March 6th, 2007
Guardian	February 6th, 2010
Guevara, Ernesto "Che"	*The African Dream: The Diaries of the Revolutionary War in the Congo* (New York: Grove Press, 1999)

Guled, Abdi	"The Big Man Syndrome in Africa: A Major Policy Challenge for Obama's Administration," WardheerNews.com, (May 24th, 2009)
Gulhati, Ravi	*Impasse in Zambia: The Economics and Politics of Reform* (Washington, D.C.: World Bank, 1989)
Gupta, K. K. Das	*In Search of the Central Africa Past* (Lusaka: Times Printpak, 2004)
Haantobolo, G.	"The Role of the Zambian Legislature in the Transformation of the Zambian Defence Force 1964-2000: A Paper Submitted to the Civil-Military Relations SADC Project," June 2000
Haar, Gerrie Ter	*Spirit of Africa: The Healing Ministry of Archbishop Milingo of Zambia* (London: Hurst, 1992)
Haggard, H. Rider	*King Solomon's Mines* (London: Cassalle and Company, 1885)
Haglund, D	"Policy Effectiveness in the Zambian Mining Sector," SAIIA Policy Briefing, No. 19, July 2010
Hall, Richard	*Kaunda: Founder of Zambia* (London: Longman and Company Ltd., 1964)
Hall, Richard	*The High Price of Principles: Kaunda and the White South* (Harmondsworth: Penguin, 1973)
Hall, Richard	*Zambia* (New York: Frederick A. Praeger, 1965)
Hall, Richard	*Zambia, 1890-1964: The Colonial Period* (London: Longman Group Ltd., 1976)

Hamalengwa, Munyonzwe	*African-Canadians under Legal, Judicial, Political and Media Attack* (Africa in Canada Press: Toronto, 2016)
Hamalengwa, Munyonzwe	*Class Struggles in Zambia 1889-1989 & The Fall of Kenneth Kaunda 1990-1991* (New York: University Press of America, 1992)
Hamalengwa, Munyonzwe	*Getting Away with Impunity: International Criminal Law and the Prosecution of Apartheid Criminals* (Africa in Canada Press: Toronto, 2015)
Hamalengwa, Munyonzwe	*Political Halley's Comet: The Death Penalty in Global Comparative Perspective* (Diamondbooks: Toronto, 2017)
Munyonzwe Hamalengwa	"Rumors of an election coup in the United States," *The Zambian Observer*, December 13th, 2016
Hamalengwa, Munyonzwe	*The Book on Judges* (Toronto, (Diamondbooks: Toronto, 2017)
Hamalengwa, Munyonzwe, (Ed.)	*The Case against Tribalism in Zambia* (Africa in Canada Press: Toronto, 2016)
Hamalengwa, Munyonzwe	"The Political Economy of Human Rights in Africa," (1983) *Philosophy and Social Action* Vol. IX, No. 3 reprinted in *Journal of African Marxists,* No. 7, 1985
Hamalengwa, Munyonzwe	*The Politics of Judicial Diversity and Transformation: Canada; USA; UK, Australia; South Africa; Israel; Colonial and Post-*

378

	Colonial World and International Tribunals (Africa in Canada Press: Toronto, 2012)
Hamalengwa, Munyonzwe	*Thoughts are Free: Prison Experience and Reflections on Law and Politics in General* (Toronto: Africa in Canada Press, 1991)
Hamalengwa, Munyonzwe & Himwiinga, P. A.	*The State of Emergency in Zambia in International Law: A Historic, Political and Legal Analysis* (Toronto: Munyonzwe Hamalengwa and P.A Himwiinga, 1990)
Hamalengwa, M; C. Flinterman & E.V.O. Dankwa, (eds.)	*The International Law of Human Rights in Africa* (Dordrecht: Martinus Nijhoff Publishers, 1988)
Hamilton, Alissa	"The Construction and Destruction of National Identities through Language in the Narrative of Ngugi wa Thiong'o's *A Grain of Wheat* and Joseph Conrad's *Under Western Eyes*," (1995) *African Languages and Culture* 8, 2: 137-151
Hannum, Hurst (ed.)	*Guide to International Human Rights Practice* (Philadelphia: University of Pennsylvania Press, 1984)
Hansen, Karen Tranberg	*Distant Companions: Servants and Employers in Zambia, 1900-1985* (Ithaca: Cornell University Press, 1989)

379

Harding, Col. Colin	*In Remotest Barotseland* (London: Hurst & Blackett, 1905)
Harrington, H. T.	"The Taming of North-Eastern Rhodesia," (1954) *Northern Rhodesia Journal,* Vol. 2, No. 3: 3-20
Harris, John; Janet Hunter; & Colin M. Lewis, (eds.)	*The New Institutional Economics and Third World Development* (London: Routledge, 1995)
Hartman, J.	"Derogations from Human Rights Treaties in Public Emergencies," (Winter 1981) *Harvard International Law Journal,* Vol. 22, No. 1
Hauben, Ronda	"Lobbyist Jack Abramoff Pleads Guilty and Washington Trembles," (January 10th, 2006)
Haugen, Gary & Victor Boutros	"And Justice for All Subtitle: Enforcing Human Rights for the World's Poor," (May 2010 - June 2010), *Foreign Affairs,* Vol. 89 No. 3
Hayek, F.A.	*The Road to Serfdom* (London: G. Routledge, 1944)
Henderson, Ian	"Early African Leadership: The Copperbelt Disturbances of 1935 and 1940," (1975) *Southern African Studies* 2(1), pp. 83-97
Henderson, Ian	"The Limits of Colonial Power: Race and Labor Problems in Colonial Zambia, 1900-1953," (1974) *Journal of Imperial Commonwealth History,* 2(3), pp. 297-307

Henderson, Ian — "The Origins of Nationalism in East and Central Africa: The Zambian Case," (1970) *Journal of African History,* 11(4), pp. 591-603

Henderson, Ian — "Wage Earners and Political Protest in Colonial Africa," (1973) *African Affairs,* 72, pp. 288-299

Henderson, Ian — "Workers and the State in Colonial Zambia: The Evolving Structure of the Zambian Society," (1980) *Southern African Studies,* University of Edinburg, pp. 23-43

Henriot, Peter — "Being a Christian in a Christian Nation," Jesuit Center for Theological Reflection, December 2nd, 1998

Herman, Arthur — "China's Debt Bomb," *New York Post,* (February 8th, 2010)

Hill, Catharine & Malcolm F. McPherson — *Promoting and Sustaining Economic Reform in Zambia* (Cambridge, Mass.: John F. Kennedy School of Government, Harvard University: Distributed by Harvard University Press, 2004)

Hill, Lawrence — *The Book of Negroes* (Scarborough: Harper Collins, 2007)

Himwiinga, P. A. — *Emergency Powers in Zambia,* LLM Thesis, University of Zambia, 1984

Hinfelaar, Hugo F.   *History of the Catholic Church in Zambia* (Lusaka: Bookworld, 2004)

Hinfelaar, Marja A.   *First Guide to Non-Governmental Archives in Zambia* (Lusaka: National Archives of Zambia, 2004)

Hinfelaar Marja A.   "Remembering Bishop Joseph Dupont (1850-1930) in Present-Day Zambia," (2003) *Journal of Religion in Africa*, Vol. 33, Fasc. 4, pp. 365-376

Holleman, J. F.   *White Mine Workers in Northern Rhodesia, 1959-60* (Leiden: Afrika-Studiecentrum, 1973)

Houston Chronicle News Services   January 26th, 1997

Howell and Others v. Lees-Millais and Ors   (2007) EWCA Civ 720 (July 4th, 2007)

Huntington, Samuel   *The Third Wave: Democratization in the Late C 20th* (Norman, OK: Oklahoma University Press, 1993)

Hyman, Eric L.; Robert Strauss; and Richard Crayne   "An Enterprise-Development Strategy for Zambia," (1993) *Development in Practice*, Vol. 3, No. 2, pp. 103-115

Ihonvbere, Julius O.   *Economic Crisis, Civil Society and Democratization: The Case of Zambia* (Trenton & Asmara: Africa World Press, Inc., 1996)

Ihonvbere, Julius O.   *The Politics of Adjustment and Democracy* (New Brunswick,

Ihonvbere, Julius O.

Imakando, Joe

Institute for Security
Studies - Africa

Internet World Stats

Jabani, Patrick
JCTR

Johns, Sheridan

Johnson, Walton R.

Kalusika, Simon E.

Kangende, Kenneth

NJ.: Transaction Publishers,
1994)
"The 'Zero Option' Controversy
in Zambia: Western Double
Standards vis-à-vis Safeguarding
Security?" (1995) *Afrika
Spectrum,* Vol. 30, No. 1: 93-104
Prayer Our Secret Weapon
(Lusaka: Bread of Life Church
International, 2005)

"The Criminal Justice System in
Zambia: Enhancing the Delivery
of Security in Africa," Policy
Brief of July 6th, 2009
"Facebook Users in the World,"
(October 14th, 2010)
"Dual Citizenship," 2009
"Whose Interests is Zambian
Politics Serving?" Political Ethics
Release of November 11th, 2009
"State Capitalism in Zambia: The
Evolution of the Parastatal
Sector," (October 1975) Annual
Meeting of the African Studies
Association, San Francisco
*Worship and Freedom: A Black
American Church in Zambia*
(London: International African
Institute, 1977)
*South Sudan Right of Self –
Determination and Establishing
of New Sovereign State: A Legal
Analysis* (Lusaka: UNZA Press,
2004)
Female Superstitions of Sex
(Lusaka: Minta Publishers, 2004)

Kangende, Kenneth	*Male Superstitions of Sex* (Lusaka: Minta Publishers, 2003)
Kangende, Kenneth	*Zambian Myths and Legends of the Wild* (Lusaka: Minta Publishers, 2001)
Kanja, M. George	*Intellectual Property Law* (Lusaka: UNZA Press, 2006)
Kanyama, Chibamba	*The Post* editorial of May 10th, 2009
Kapalaula, Mwamba	"Constitutional Impasse," *The Post,* (May 10th, 2008)
Kapatamoyo, Meluse	"Is the *Redundancy Act* Working in Zambia?" Women.WageIndicator.com, (2009)
Kashoki, Mubanga E.	*Loanwords in Silozi, Cinyanja and Citonga* (Lusaka: UNZA Press, 1999)
Kasoma, Francis P.	*Community Radio: Its Management and Organization in Zambia* (Lusaka: MISA, 2002)
Kasoma, Francis P.	"Press Freedom in Zambia," in Festus Eribe and William Jong-Ebot, (ed.), *Press Freedom and Communication in Africa* (Trenton, NJ.: Africa World Press Inc., 1997)
Kasonde, Joseph M. & John D. Martin	*Experiences with Primary Health Care in Zambia* (Geneva: World Health Organization, 1994)
Kasonde-Ng'andu, Sophie	*Gender and Primary Schooling in Zambia* (Brighton, England: Institute of Development Studies, 2000)

Kaunda, Danstan
"Corruption: Two Steps Forward, Two Steps Back." *Inter Press Services*, January 15th, 2008

Kaunda, Kenneth D.
"African Development and Foreign Aid Speech," *Modern History Sourcebook*, March 18th, 1966

Kaunda, Kenneth D.
Humanism in Zambia: And a Guide to Its Implementation (Lusaka: Kenneth Kaunda Foundation, 1974/87)

Kaunda, Kenneth D.
Kaunda on Violence (London: Collins, 1980)

Kaunda, Kenneth D.
"KK's Diary: UDI, 40 Years Ago," *Post Lifestyle*, (December 4th, 2005)

Kaunda, Kenneth D.
"The Function of the Lawyer in Zambia Today," (1971& 1972) *Zambia Law Journal*, Vols. 3 & 4, Nos. 1 & 2, pp.1-5

Kaunda, Kenneth D.
The Riddle of Violence (San Francisco: Harper & Row, 1981)

Kaunda, Kenneth D.
Zambia Shall Be Free (London: Heinemann, 1962)

Keller, Wolfgang
"Absorptive Capacity: On the Creation and Acquisition of Technology in Development," (April 1996) *Journal of Development Economics,* 49, 199

Kelly, Robert E.
National Debt: From FDR (1941) to Clinton (1996) (Jefferson, NC: McFarland and Company Ltd., 2000)

Khanna, Parag
How to Run the World: Charting a Course to the Next Renaissance (New York: Random House Publishing Group, 2011)

Kirk, Russell

The Conservative Mind, 7ᵗʰ Edn. (Chicago: Henry Regnery, 1986)

Kocieniewski, David

"House Panel Finds Rangel Guilty," *The New York Times,* (November 16ᵗʰ, 2010)

Kosack, S &
J. Tobin

"Finding Self-Sustaining Development: The Role of Aid, FDI and Government in Economic Success," (2006) *International Organization,* 60: 205-243

Kozlowski, Mark

The Myth of the Imperial Judiciary (New York: New York University Press, 2003)

Krasner, Stephen D.

Defending the National Interest: Raw Materials Investments and US Foreign Policy (Princeton, NJ: Princeton University Press. 1978)

Kyambalesa, Henry

"MMD's Quest for Statutory Media Regulation," *Zambia News Features,* (August 29ᵗʰ, 2010)

Lamarche, Lucie

"The 'Made in Quebec' Act to Combat Poverty and Social Exclusion: The Complex Relationship between Poverty and Human Rights," in Margot Young; Susan B. Boyd; Gwen Brodsky; & Shelagh Day, (eds.) *Poverty: Rights, Social Citizenship, and Legal Activism* (Vancouver, BC: UBC Press, 2007)

Langworthy, Harry W.

Zambia before 1890: Aspects of Pre-colonial History (London: Longman, 1972)

Larmer, Miles and

Alastair Fraser

"Of Cabbages and King Cobra: The Populist Politics and Zambia's 2006 Elections," *African Affairs*, 106/425: 611-637

Lascelles, David and Sam Mendelson

"Microfinance Banana Skins 2011," CSFI, 2011

Legum, Colin

Zambia, Independence and Beyond: The Speeches of Kenneth Kaunda (London: Thomas Nelson Ltd., 1966)

Lester, N. Rodah

Cassava is the Root (Toronto: Rodah Lester, 2010)

Ligi, Amanda

"The Pros and Cons of Globalization," (April 28th, 2006)

Liswaniso, Mufalo

Voices of Zambia: Short Stories (Lusaka: Neczam, 1971)

Liswaniso, Mufalo & Alfred W. Chanda

Handbook of Media Laws in Zambia (Lusaka: Zambia Independent Media Association, 1999)

Lockhart, Kirbey

Zambia Shall Be Saved (Lethbridge: Paramount Printers Ltd., 2001)

Lombard, C. Stephen

The Growth of Co-operatives in Zambia 1914-71 (Manchester: Manchester University Press [for] University of Zambia, Institute for African Studies, 1971)

Lombe, Fostino

Prisoner of Conscience (Unpublished Manuscript)

Longwe, Sara H.

Legalized Discrimination against Women in Zambia (East Lansing, Mich.: Office of Women in International Development, Michigan State University, 1985)

Louw, D. J.	"*Ubuntu*: An African Assessment of the Religious Other," (1998) *Proceedings of the Twentieth World Congress of Philosophy*
Low, Susan	"Borrow, Blend, Adapt," available online at www.pictureyourmeeting.com (2009)
Lukuku, Whitney	"A Culture of Entitlement," Saturday, March 26th, 2011
Lusaka Times	"Kachimba Warns Shoprite on Casualization," (September 10th, 2010)
Lusaka Times	"Zambia: M'membe Granted Bail," (June 7th, 2010)
Lusaka Times	"Zambia: State House Launches Diaspora Survey," (June 29th, 2010)
Machona, Goodson	"A Harvest of Treason Trials" Conciliation Resources website (Retrieved: April 11th, 2010)
Macintosh, Stewart Kenneth	*The State, Structural Adjustment and the Prospects for Democratization: The Case of Zambia*, Thesis (M.A.), Dalhousie University, 1991
Madison, James	*The Federalist,* Clinton Rossiter, (ed.), (Mentor 1961) 48
Mainichi Daily News	January 24th, 2001
Majula, R. R.	*The Impact of Corruption on Public Administration in Zambia* (Lusaka: Litovia Ltd, 2008)
Makasa, K	*Zambia's March to Political Freedom* (Nairobi: Heinemann Educational Books, 1985)

Makai, Kozhi Sidney	*Born Beating the Odds* (Independence, TX.: Scrolls & Scribes, 2008)
Makai, Kozhi Sidney	*Culture & Leadership* (Saarbrücken, Germany: VDM Verlag, 2008)
Makai, Kozhi Sidney	*How Can I Come Up?* (Bloomington, IN.: Authorhouse, 2005)
Makai, Kozhi Sidney	*Our 'I Dos' Were...Different* (Independence, TX.: Scrolls & Scribes, 2013)
Makai, Kozhi Sidney	*Puzzle Pieces* (Independence, TX.: Scrolls & Scribes, 2008)
Makgetla, Neva Seidman	"Theoretical and Practical Implications of IMF Conditionality in Zambia," (Sep., 1986) *The Journal of Modern African Studies*, Vol. 24, No. 3, pp. 395-422
Makungu, M. Kenny	*The State of the Media in Zambia: From the Colonial Era to 2003* (Lusaka: MISA, 2004)
Malila, Mumba	*Commercial Law in Zambia: Cases and Materials* (Lusaka: UNZA Press, 2006)
Malila, Mumba	*Commercial Law in Zambia: Essential Texts* (Lusaka: UNZA Press, 2005)
Malupenga, Amos	*Levy Patrick Mwanawasa: An Incentive for Posterity* (Grahamstown: NISC (Pty) Ltd., 2009)
Mamdani, Mahmood	"Africa: Democratic Theory and Democratic Struggles," (October 10th, 1992) *Economic and Political Weekly*, Vol. 27, No. 41:

2228-2232

Mandela, Nelson — *Long Walk to Freedom* (London: Little, Brown and Company, 1995)

Mann, Michael — *An Outline of Icibemba Grammar* (Lusaka: Bookworld, 1993)

Manow, Phillip — "Comparative Institutional Advantages of Welfare State Regimes and New Coalitions in Welfare State Reforms," pp. 146–64 in *The New Politics of the Welfare State,* edited by Paul Pierson (Oxford: Oxford University Press, 2001)

Mansfield, C — *Via Rhodesia* (London: Stanley and Paul, 1911)

Marcive - York University & Millennium Challenge Corporation (US) — *Zambia and Millennium Challenge Corporation: Combating Corruption and Improving Government Service* (Washington, D.C.: Millennium Challenge Corporation, 2006)

Marx, Karl & Frederick Engels — *The Individual and Society*, (Moscow: Progress Publishers, 1984)

Marwick, Harold Williams — *The Mining Law of Northern Rhodesia* (London: British South Africa Co., 1964)

Matheson, Ishbel — "Chiluba's Legacy to Zambia" BBC, (May 4th, 2007)

Matibini, Patrick — *The Struggle for Media Law Reforms in Zambia* (Lusaka: MISA, 2006)

Mazrui, Ali — "Pan-Africanism and the

Intellectuals: Rise, Decline and Revival," in Thandika Mkandawire (ed.) *African Intellectual* (Dakar: Codesria, 2005)

McCulloch, Neil

Poverty, Inequality and Growth in Zambia during the 1990s (Brighton, England: Institute of Development Studies, University of Sussex, 2000)

Medad, Jean Francois

"Corruption in the Neo-Patrimonial of Sub-Saharan Africa," in Arnold J. Heindenheimer and Michael Johnston (eds.), *Political Corruption: Concepts and Context* (New Brunswick: Transaction Publishers, 2002)

Meebelo, Henry S.

Main Currents of Zambian Humanism Thought (Lusaka: Oxford University Press, 1973)

Metro

"Zambian Prisons Unfit for Human Habitation," (Thursday, April 29th, 2010)

Miller v. Minister of Pensions

(1947) 2 All E.R. 372

Mills, Greg; Jeffrey Herbst & Stuart Duran

"Mobilizing Zambia: A Strategy Report on Accelerating Economic Growth," The Brenthurst Foundation, Discussion Paper 2010/02

Ministry of Finance

Zambia Poverty Reduction Strategy Paper, 2002-2004

Ministry of Finance and National Planning

2006 Annual Report – Fifth National Development Plan

391

Ministry of Finance and
National Planning

Progress Report (Lusaka:
Ministry of Finance and National
Planning, 2008)

*Fifth National Development Plan
2006-2010* (Lusaka: Ministry of
Finance and National Planning,
2006)

Minter, William

*King Solomon's Mines Revisited:
Western Interests and the
Burdened History* (New York:
Basic Books, Inc., 1986)

Misgeld, Klaus; Karl Molin;
& Klas Åmark

*Creating Social Democracy: A
Century of the Social Democratic
Labor Party in Sweden*
(Stockholm: Tiben, 1988)

Modern History Sourcebook

"President Kenneth Kaunda of
Zambia: African Development
and Foreign Aid," March 18th,
1966

Molteno, Robert

"Cleaverage and Conflict in
Zambian Politics: A Study in
Sectionalism," in William Tordoff
(ed.), *Politics in Zambia*
(Manchester: Manchester
University Press, 1974)

Molteno, Robert

"Conclusion – Independent
Zambia: Achievements and
Prospects," in William Tordoff
(ed.), *Politics in Zambia*
(Berkeley: University of
California Press, 1974)

Molteno, Robert

"Zambia and the One-Party
State," (1972) *East African
Journal*, 9(2), pp. 6-18

Molteno, Robert · "Zambian Humanism: The Way Ahead," (1973) *The African Review*, III, 4, pp. 541-557

Momba, J · *The State, Peasant Differentiation and Rural Class Formation in Zambia: Case Study of Mazabuka and Monze Districts*, Ph.D. Dissertation, University of Toronto, 1982

Monbiot, George · *The Guardian*, February 8th, 2005

Montesquieu · (Hafner, 1949), *The Spirit of the Laws*, 152

Moore, Robert C. · *The Political Reality of Freedom of the Press in Zambia* (Lanham: University Press of America, 1992)

Moyo, Dambisa · *Dead Aid: Why Aid is Not Working and How There is a Better Way for Africa* (New York: Farrar, Straus and Giroux, 2010)

Moyo, Dambisa · *How the West was Lost* (Vancouver/Toronto: D & M Publishers Inc., 2011)

Mphaisha, Chisepo J. J., (ed.) · *The State of the Nation Volume I: Politics and Governance* (Lusaka: Kenneth Kaunda Foundation, 1988)

Mtshali, B.V. · "South Africa and Zambia's 1968 Election," (1970) *Kroniek Van Africa*, 2

Mudimbe, D. Y. · "*African Gnosis* Philosophy and the Order of Knowledge: An Introduction," (1985) *African Studies Review*, Vol. 28, No. 2/3: 149

Mufalo, Mbiji	"Fencing the ACC Bill of September 2010 – Part II," *Times of Zambia* <www.times.co.zm> (Retrieved: January 25th, 2011)
Mukanga, Chola	"Zambia Media As Agents of Poverty," *Zambian Economist* (February 1st, 2011)
Mulenga, Kaela	"Memorial for Zambian Heroes," (Toronto, November 1st, 2009)
Mulford, David	*The Northern Rhodesia General Election* (Oxford: Oxford University Press, 1964)
Mulford, David	*Zambia: The Politics of Independence* (Oxford: Oxford University Press, 1982)
Mulford, David	*Zambia: The Politics of Independence 1957-1964* (Oxford: Oxford University Press, 1967)
Mulenga, N. Sefelino,	"Humanism and the Logic of Self-Sufficiency," *Zambian Daily Mail*, January 30th & 31st, 1974
Munroe, Myles	*The Burden of Freedom* (Lake Mary, Florida: Creation House, 2000)
Mutale, Emmanuel	*The Management of Urban Development in Zambia* (Aldershot, Hants, England; Burlington, VT: Ashgate, 2004)
Mwaanga, Vernon J.	*Looking Back: An Extraordinary Life* (Lusaka: Fleetfoot Publishing Company, 2000)
Mwaanga, Vernon J.	*The Long Sunset* (Lusaka: Fleetfoot Publishing Company, 2008)

Mwaanga, Vernon J.   *The Other Society* (Lusaka:
                      Fleetfoot Publishing Company,
                      1986)
Mwale, Simson   "Constitutional Hiccup," *The
                      Post*, (August 30th, 2005)
Mwamba, Emmanuel   "The Musakanya Papers: Rare
                      Insight into 1980 Coup," *Zambian
                      Watchdog*, (July 6th, 2010)
Mwanakatwe, John M.   *End of Kaunda Era* (Lusaka:
                      Multimedia Publication, 1994)
Mwanakatwe, John M.   *Teacher, Politician, Lawyer: My
                      Autobiography* (Lusaka:
                      Bookworld Publishers, 2003)
Mwanakatwe, John M   *The Growth of Education in
                      Zambia since Independence*
                      (Lusaka: Oxford University Press,
                      1968)
Mwanawina, Inyambo   *Deepening Integration in SADC
                      Perceptions of Businesses and
                      Non-State Actors Survey Report
                      for Zambia* (Lusaka: Institute of
                      Economic and Social Research,
                      2006)
Mwangilwa, Goodwin   *Harry Mwaanga Nkumbula: A
                      Biography of the 'Old Lion' of
                      Zambia* (Lusaka: Multimedia
                      Publications, 1983)
Mwenda, Kenneth Kaoma *Anti-Money Laundering Law and
                      Practice: Lessons from Zambia*
                      (Lusaka: UNZA Press, 2007)
Mwenda, Kenneth Kaoma "Presumption of Innocence
                      Doctrine: Relevant in Corruption
                      Fight?" *The Post Newspapers
                      Zambia*, (November 4th, 2009)
Mwenda, Kenneth Kaoma *Public Intellectualism and
                      Sociopolitical Inquiry through
                      Metaphor and Musing*, Vol. 3

	(Toronto, Canada: Africa in Canada Press, 2016).
Mwenda, Kenneth Kaoma	*Anthology in Law and the Social Sciences*, (Toronto, Canada: Africa in Canada Press, 2016).
Mwenda, Kenneth Kaoma	*Public Intellectualism and Sociopolitical Inquiry through Metaphor and Musing*, Vol. 2 (Toronto, Canada: Africa in Canada Press, 2016).
Mwenda, Kenneth Kaoma	*Public Intellectualism and Sociopolitical Inquiry through Metaphor and Musing* (Toronto, Canada: Africa in Canada Press, 2015).
Mwenda, Kenneth Kaoma	*Public International Law and the Regulation of Diplomatic Immunity in the Fight against Corruption* (Pretoria, South Africa: Pretoria University Law Press (PULP), 2011).
Mwenda, Kenneth Kaoma	*Contemporary Issues in Zambian and English Company Law: A Comparative Study* (Amherst, NY: Teneo Press, 2011).
Mwenda, Kenneth Kaoma	*Legal Aspects of Banking Regulation: Common Law Perspectives from Zambia* (Pretoria, South Africa: Pretoria University Law Press (PULP), 2010)
Mwenda, Kenneth Kaoma	*Comparing American and British Legal Education Systems: Lessons for Commonwealth African Law Schools* (Amherst, NY: Cambria Press, 2007)

Mwenda, Kenneth Kaoma   *Legal Aspects of Combating Corruption: The Case of Zambia* (Amherst, NY: Cambria Press, 2007)

Mwenda, Kenneth Kaoma   *Legal Aspects of Financial Services Regulation and the Concept of a Unified Regulator* (Washington DC: The World Bank, 2006)

Mwenda, Kenneth Kaoma   *Combating Financial Crime: Legal, Regulatory and Institutional Frameworks* (Lewiston, NY: The Edwin Mellen Press, 2006)

Mwenda, Kenneth Kaoma   *The Legal Administration of Financial Services in Common Law Jurisdictions: with special attention to the dual regula-tion system in Zambia* (Lewiston, NY: The Edwin Mellen Press, 2006)

K.K. Mwenda and V. Mosoti (eds), Contemporary Issues in International Economic Law, (Cologne, Germany: Josef EulVerlag, 2006).

Mwenda, Kenneth Kaoma   *Anti-Money Laundering Law and Practice: Lessons from Zambia* (Lusaka, Zambia: University of Zambia (UNZA) Press, 2005)

Mwenda, Kenneth Kaoma   *Zambia's Stock Exchange and Privatization Pro-gram: Corporate Finance Law in Emerging Markets* (Lewiston, NY: The Edwin Mellen Press, 2001)

Mwewa, Charles   *Allergic to Corruption: The Legacy of President Michael Sata*

397

	of Zambia (Africa in Canada Press, 2015)
Mwewa, Charles	*A Spy in Hell* (USA: Tate Publishers Enterprises, 2015)
Mwewa, Charles	*Residential Tenancies Law: Business & Practice Companion* (Toronto: CM Publishers, 2017)
Mwewa, Charles	*King Cobra Has Struck: My Letter to President Michael Sata of Zambia* (Toronto: Africa in Canada Press, 2012)
Mwewa, Charles	*The Seven Laws of Love* (Victoria: Bookmark Publishers, 2007)
Mwewa, Charles	*Song of an Alien* (New York: iUniverse, 2009)
Mwewa, Charles	*The Burden of Zambia* (Toronto: Charles Mwewa, 2008)
Mwewa, Charles	*The Seven Laws of Influence* (Baltimore: PublishAmerica, 2010)
Mwewa, Charles	*Zambia, Struggles of My People: Western Contribution to Corruption in Africa* (Lusaka: Maiden Publishing House, 2011)
Mwibawa, Nicholas Sii	"Black Poverty as Seen by Chanda Chisala on His Blog," *Facebook*, (September 6th, 2010)
Mwiinga, Mazuba	"Chiluba the Scared Man," *The Post*, (Wednesday, June 2nd, 2010)
Mwitumwa, Nawa	*The Last Supper* (Lusaka: Nawa Mwitumwa, 2007)
Nagangula, Silas M.	*Dreams within Dreams* (Lusaka: Multimedia, 2003)
Namibia Online	

Community

Nasong'o, Shadrack
Wanjala

Nawa, Mubita C.

Ndhlovu, Gershom

Ndulo, Muna &
John Hatchard

Ndulo, Muna &
John Hatchard

Ndulo, Muna & T. Turner

New African
New York Times

Ngilazi, Henry

Nkhuwa, Daniel;
Jonathan Mwanza &

"South Africa: Kenneth Kaunda
Honored for his Humanism,"
(October 21st, 2007)

*Contending Political Paradigms
in Africa: Rationality and the
Politics of Democratization in
Kenya and Zambia* (New York:
Routledge, 2005)
The Roadmap to True Leadership
(Grand Prairie: Why Not!
Motivational Speakers USA,
2007)
"Zambia: State House Launches
Diaspora Survey," (June 29th,
2010)

A Case Book on Criminal Law
(Lusaka: Government Printer,
1983)

*The Law of Evidence in Zambia:
Cases and Materials* (Lusaka:
Multimedia Publications, 1991)
Civil Liberties Cases in Zambia
(Oxford: Oxford University Press,
1984)
No. 469 (January 2008)
"Zambia Detains Nine as
Rumours of Coup Plot Fill the
Capital," (October 9th, 1988)
"Zambia Ex-president Chiluba
Acquitted of Graft," *Reuters,*
(August 17th, 2009)

Kangwa Chama	*The Sustainable Cities Program in Zambia, 1994-2007: Addressing Challenges of Rapid Urbanization* (Nairobi: UN-HABITAT: UNEP, 2009)
Nkrumah, Kwame	*Neo-Colonialism: The Last Stage of Imperialism* (London: Thomas Nelson and Sons, 1965)
Nweke, Collins	"Diaspora Bill: The Joy and Regrets of Lawmaking," *Nigerians Abroad Magazine* (October 2010)
Nyerere, Mwalimu Julius	"Is Africa Responsible?" Address by the President, Mwalimu Julius K. Nyerere at the Institute of Social Studies, The Hague – Netherlands, March 13th, 1985
Obama, Barack	*Dreams from My Father* (New York: Three Rivers Press, 1995)
Obama, Barack	*The Audacity of Hope* (New York: Three Rivers Press, 2006)
Obidegwu, Chukwuma F.	*Copper and Zambia: An Econometric Analysis* (Lexington, Mass.: Lexington Books, 1981)
Observer	June 29th, 2008
Ochetim, Silvest	*Pig Farming in Zambia* (Lusaka: ZEPH, 1995)
O'Donnell, Guillermo, & Philippe Schmitter (eds.)	*Transitions from Authoritarian Rule: Tentative Conclusions about Uncertain Democracies* (Baltimore: The Johns Hopkins University Press, 1986)
Office for Judicial Complaints	"Statement from the Office for Judicial Complaints – Mr. Justice Peter Smith," (April, 2008)

Ogot, Bethwell A.	*A History of the Luo-Speaking Peoples of Eastern Africa* (Nairobi: Anyangwe Press, 2009)
Okumu, Wafula	"The Travails and Antics of Africa's 'Big Men' - How Power Has Corrupted African Leaders," *The Perspectives*, (April 11th, 2002)
Ollawa, Patrick	*Participatory Democracy in Zambia: The Political Economy of National Development* (Ilfracombe: Arthur H. Stockwell Ltd., 1979)
Onstad, Eric	"First Quantum May Sue ENRC over Congo's Kolwezi Site," *Financial Post*, (Tuesday, September 7th, 2010
Otieno, Nicholas	*Journey of Hope* (Geneva, Switzerland: WCC Publications, 2005)
OZAFO Zambia	"The Avoidance of Civil War in Zambia has been Helped by the Presence of Zambian Credible Political Leaders. Do you agree?" *Facebook*, September 19th, 2010
Padmore, George	*How Britain Rules Africa* (London: Wishart Books Ltd., 1936)
Palmer, Robin (ed.)	*A House in Zambia: Recollections of the ANC and Oxfam at 250 Zambezi Road, 1967-97* (Lusaka: Bookworld Publishers, 2008)
Pape, Gordon	"The Four Deadly Investor Sins," *Toronto Star*, (Monday, October 4th, 2010)
Parker, C	"Control of Executive Discretion under Preventive Detention Law

	in Zambia," (1980) *The Comparative and International Law Journal of Southern Africa,* Vol. 3, No. 2
Paust, Jordan	"Political Oppression in the Name of National Security: Authority, Participation, and Necessity within Democratic Limits Test," (1982) *Yale J. of World Pub. Ord.,* Vol. 9, pp. 179-88
Peters, D. U.	*Land Usage in Serenje District: A Survey of Land Usage and the Agricultural System of the Lala of the Serenje Plateau, Being a Report Submitted to the Director of Agriculture, Mazabuka, N.R. in 1946* (Manchester: Manchester University Press, 1951)
Petersen, Kol	"A New Moment of Promise in Africa," Speech by President Barack Obama in Accra, Ghana (July 11th, 2009)
Pettman, Jan	"Zambia's Second Republic: The Creation of One-Party State," (1974) *Journal of Modern African Studies,* 12, No. 2, pp. 231-44
Pettman, Jan	*Zambia: Security and Conflict* (New York: St. Martin's Press, 1974)
PFhub.com	"Top Six Political Scandals in Russia," (Retrieved: January 23rd, 2011)
Phillips, James	*The Heritage Foundation,* April 21st, 2004
Phiri, Bizeck J.	"Colonial Legacy and the Role of Society in the Creation and Demise of Autocracy in Zambia,

Phiri, Bizeck J. 1964-1991," (2001) *Nordic Journal of African Studies* 10 (2), pp. 224-244

Phiri, Bizeck J. "Democratization and Security Sector Reform in Zambia," (2007)

Phiri, Bizeck J. *A Political History of Zambia: From Colonial Rule to the Third Republic, 1890-2001* (Trenton, NJ: Africa World Press, 2006)

Phiri, Isaac "Media in 'Democratic' Zambia: Problems and Prospects," (Spring 1999)

Phiri, Isaac "Why African Churches Preach Politics: The Case of Zambia," (1999) *Journal of Church and State*, Vol. 41/2, 323

Phiri, Isabel Apawo "President Frederick J.T. Chiluba of Zambia: The Christian Nation and Democracy," (November 2003) *Journal of Religion in Africa,* Vol. 33, Fasc. 4: 401-428

Phiri, Reuben "'Judiciary in Zambia has Never been Independent,' says Judge Chanda," *The Post*, (Wednesday, June 5th, 2002)

Pierson, Paul "Coping with Permanent Austerity: Welfare State Restructuring in Affluent Democracies," pp. 410–56 in *The New Politics of the Welfare State*, edited by Paul Pierson (Oxford: Oxford University Press, 2001)

Poewe, Karla O. *Religion, Kinship, and Economy in Luapula, Zambia* (Lewiston, NY: E. Mellen Press, 1989)

Porter, Jene M., (ed.)   *Classics in Political Philosophy*
                              (Scarborough: Prentice Hall
                              Canada Inc., 2000)
*Preservation of Public
 Security Act*   Cap. 112 of the Laws of Zambia
Preservation of Public
 Security Ordinance   Of Northern Rhodesia
Public Order Act   Cap. 113 of the Laws of Zambia
Rakner, Lise   *Political and Economic
                              Liberalization in Zambia 1991-
                              2001* (Uppsala: Nordic Africa
                              Institute, 2003)
Ranger, Terrence O.   "Making Northern Rhodesia
                              Imperial: Variations on Royal
                              Theme," (1924–1938) *African
                              Affairs*, 349
Ranger, Terrence O.   *Themes in Christian History of
                              Central Africa* (Los Angeles:
                              University of California Press,
                              1975)
Republic of Zambia   *Report of the National
                              Commission on the Establishment
                              of a One-Party Participatory
                              Democracy in Zambia* (Lusaka:
                              Government Printer, 1972)
Republic of Zambia   *Report of the National
                              Commission on the Establishment
                              of a One-Party Participatory
                              Democracy in Zambia: Summary
                              of Recommendations Accepted by
                              the Government* (Lusaka:
                              Government Printer, 1972)
Republic of Zambia   *Vision 2030* (Lusaka: Republic of
                              Zambia, 2006)
Reuben, Peter   "On Political Corruption,"
                              (Winter, 1978) *JSTOR: The*

Antioch Review, Vol. 36, No.1, 103

Reuters   September 6th, 2005

Reuters   February 9th, 2001

Robert, Andrew   "Chronology of the Bemba (N.E. Zambia)" (1970), *The Journal of African History*, Vol. 11, No. 2: 221-240

Robert, Andrew   "The Lumpa Church of Alice Lenshina" in R.I Rotberg and A. A. Mazrui (eds.), *Protest and Power in Black Africa* (London: Heinemann, 1970)

Robert, Andrew   *The Lumpa Church of Alice Lenshina* (Oxford: Oxford University Press, 1972)

Robinson, M.   "The Microfinance Revolution: Sustainable Finance for the Poor," June 2001

Robinson, Randal   *The Debt: What America Owes to Blacks* (New York: A Button Book, 2000)

Rotberg, Robert I.   *Black Heart: Gore-Browne and the Politics of Multiracial Zambia* (Berkeley: University of California Press, 1977)

Rotberg, Robert I.   *The Rise of Nationalism in Central Africa: The Making of Malawi and Zambia, 1873-1964* (Cambridge, Mass.: Harvard University Press, 1965)

Rothschild, Donald   "Rural-Urban Inequalities and Resource Allocation in Zambia," (November 1972) *Journal of Commonwealth Political Studies*, X, 3, pp. 222-242

Roy, Clarke

The Worst of Kalaki and the Best of Yuss (Lusaka: Bookworld, 2004)

Sachs, Jeffrey &
  MacArthur, John W.

"Moyo's Confused Attack on Aid for Africa," *The Huffington Post*, (May 27th, 2009)

Sakala, Richard

A Mockery of Justice (Lusaka: Sentor Publishers, 2009)

Samungole, Ray

"History of the Bemba People," (Unpublished, 2010)

Samungole, Ray

"History of the Lozi People," (Unpublished, 2010)

Scarritt, James R.

Racial and Ethnic Conflict in Zambia (Denver: University of Denver, 1970)

Schurmann, Anna T. and
  Heidi Bart Johnston

"The Group-lending Model and Social Closure: Microcredit, Exclusion, and Health in Bangladesh," (2009) *Journal of Health, Population and Nutrition,* Vol. 27, No. 4

Scott, Ian

"Middle Class Politics in Zambia," (1978) *African Affairs* 77, No. 308, pp. 321-334

Scott, Shirley V.

International Law in World Politics (New Delhi: Viva Books Private Limited, 2005)

Secretary of State for
  Commonwealth Relations
  by Command of
  Her Majesty

Northern Rhodesia: Report of the Northern Rhodesia Independence Conference, 1964 (London: H.M. Stationery Off., 1964)

Seshamani, Venkatesh

"A Hindu View of the Declaration of Zambia as a Christian Nation," (2000) *JCTR* 46

Sharife, Khadija

"Copper in Zambia: Charity for Multinationals," *Features*, Issue 532, June 2nd, 2011

Shaw, Timothy M.

"The Foreign Policy System of Zambia," (April 1976) *African Studies Review,* Vol. 19, No. 1, pp. 31-66

Shaw, Timothy M.

"The Foreign Policy of Zambian Interests and Ideology," (1976) *Journal of Modern African Studies,* 13(1)

Shaw, Timothy M.

"Zambia After Twenty Years: Recession and Repression Without Revolution," (1982) *Issue: Journal of Opinion,* Vol. XII, Nos. 1/2, pp. 53-58

Shaw, Timothy M.

"Zambia: Dependence and Underdevelopment," (1976) *Canadian Journal of African Studies*, Vol. 10, No. 1, pp. 3-25

Shipolo, Sylvester Musonda

Evil Wrapped in Gold – My Side of the Story (Lusaka: Shipload Publishers, 2008)

Shutte, A.

Philosophy for Africa (Rondebosch, South Africa: UCT Press, 1993)

Shutte, A.

Ubuntu: An Ethic for a New South Africa (Pietermaritzburg: Cluster Publications, 2001)

Sililo, Maliya Mzyece

Picking Up the Pieces (Lusaka: Maliya Mzyece Sililo, 2003)

Silwamba, Chibaula   "Donors Reduce Grants to 2011 Budget," *The Post*, (October 8th, 2010)

Simatele, Munacinga   *Food Production in Zambia: The Impact of Selected Structural Adjustment Policies* (Nairobi: African Economic Research Consortium, 2006)

Simmons, Beth   "The Internationalization of Capital," pp. 36–69 in *Continuity and Change in Contemporary Capitalism*, edited by Herbert Kitschelt, Peter Lange, Gary Marks and John Stephens (Cambridge: Cambridge University Press, 1999)

Simutanyi, Neo   "The Politics of Structural Adjustment in Zambia," (1996) *Third World Quarterly*, Vol. 17, No. 4, pp. 825-839

Sinyangwe, Chiwoyu   "Magande Advises on World Bank Loans," *The Post*, (February 9th, 2010)

Sithole, Ndabaningi   *African Nationalism, 2nd Edn.* (Oxford: Oxford University Press, 1991)

Sklar, Richard L.   *Corporate Power in an African State: The Political Impact of Multinational Mining Companies in Zambia* (Berkley: University of California University Press, 1975)

Sklar, Richard L.   "Zambia's Response to the Rhodesian Unilateral Declaration of Independence," in Tordoff (ed.), *Politics in Zambia* (Berkley: University of California University Press, 1974)

Smith, Ian Douglas	*Terrorist Incursions from Zambia: A Statement* (Salisbury [Rhodesia]: Ministry of Information, Immigration and Tourism, 1967)
Smith, Patrick	"New Trade Winds," (July 2007) *The African Report*, No. 7
Smith, R.D	"Missionaries, Church Movements, and Shifting Religious Significance in the State of Zambia," (1991) *Journal of Church and State*, Vol. 41/3, 537
Smyth, Josaleen	"War Propaganda during the Second World War in Northern Rhodesia," (July 1984) *JSTOR: African Affairs*, Vol. 83, No. 332
Sobania, Neil	*Culture and Customs of Kenya* (Santa Barbara, CA: CBC/CLIO Greenwood Press, 2003)
Sontag, Susan	"An Argument About Beauty," *Dædalus*, Fall 2002
Southhall, T	"Zambia: Class Formation and Government Policies in the 1970s," (1980) *J. of Southern African Studies*, 7, 1:19-108
Sprigg, Peter & Timothy Dailey, (eds.)	"Getting it Straight: What the Research Shows about Homosexuality," Family Research Council, Washington, D.C., 2004
State House	"The President's Office," at http://www.statehouse.gov.zm (Retrieved: June 2nd, 2010)

Stein, Nicci	"Don't Cut AIDS Cash, Rich Nations Warned," *Metro*, (Friday, July 23rd, 2010)
Stengel, Geri	"11 Reasons 2014 Will Be a Breakout Year for Women Entrepreneurs," *Forbes*, January 8th, 2014
Stevenson, Angus, (ed.)	*Oxford English Dictionary, Second Edition* (Oxford: Oxford University Press, 2002)
Stobbe, Mike	"In US Cities, HIV Linked More to Poverty than Race," Associated Press, (Monday, July 19th, 2010)
Stubbs, Aelred	*I write What I Like* (New York: C. R. HarperCollins Publisher, 1978)
Supreme Court of Zambia	"Presidential Election Petition," Judgment, 2002
Szeftel, Morris	"Political Graft and the Spoils System in Zambia – The State as a Resource in Itself," (1982) *Review of African Political Economy*, 9, 24, 5
Szeftel, Morris	"The Political Process in Post-Colonial Zambia: The Structural Basis of Factional Conflict," (1980) *The Evolving Structure of Zambian Society* (Center of African Studies, University of Edinburg), pp. 64-96
Tator, Carol & Frances Henry	*Racial Profiling: Challenging the Myth of a "Few Bad Apples,"* (Toronto: University of Toronto Press, 2006)

Tembo, S. Mwizenge   *Afrikaanse Mythen en Lengenden*
                       (New York: Michael Friedman
                       Publishing Group, Inc., 1996)

Tembo, S. Mwizenge   *Legends of Africa* (New York:
                       Michael Friedman Publishing
                       Group, Inc., 1996)

Tembo, S. Mwizenge   *Satisfying Zambian Hunger for
                       Culture: Social Change in the
                       Global World* (Indiana: Xlibris
                       Corporation, 2012)

Tembo, S. Mwizenge   *The Bridge (*New York: Linus
                       Publications, 2013)

Tembo, S. Mwizenge   *Titbits for the Curious* (Lusaka:
                       Multimedia Publications, 1989)

Tembo, S. Mwizenge   *Zambian Traditional Names: The
                       Meaning of Tumbuka, Chewa,
                       Ngoni, Nsenga, and Tonga Names*
                       (Lusaka: Julubbi Enterprises
                       Limited, 2006)

Temfwe, Lawrence   "The Relevancy and Credibility
                       of the Declaration of Zambia as a
                       Christian Nation," *Monday Issue*
                       (January 4th, 2010)

Toller, Carol   "New Research Shows Women
                       Execs Really Do Think
                       Differently—that's why we need
                       more," *Canadian Business*, May
                       7th, 2013

The Academic Office
of the Seventh IACC

411

Secretariat

Anti-Corruption for Social Stability and Development (Beijing: Hong Qi Publishing House, 1996)

The Canadian Press

"Jewish, Evangelical Groups Urge Feds to Keep Long Census," *Metro*, (Weekend, July 16th – 18th, 2010)

The Canadian Press

"Clement Ready to Testify over Census," *Metro*, (Weekend, July 16th – 18th, 2010)

The Constitution (Amendment) (No. 5) Act

Of 1969, s. (8)

The Daily Telegraph

August 30th, 2009

The Daily Telegraph

March 4th, 2010

The Economist

"It's Looking Up a Bit; Zambia," June 17th, 2006

The Economist

"Less Poor, Less Free; Hope and Worry in Zambia," (November, 2009)

The Economist

"U-Turn on the Long Walk to Freedom," (December 2010)

The Environmental Council of Zambia

Strategic and Business Plan 2007-2011 (Lusaka: Environmental Council, 2006)

The Guardian

December 14th, 2001

The Guardian

April 25th, 2003

The Guardian

August 8th, 2003

The Guardian

February 1st, 2007

The Independent

October 17th, 2000

The Independent

May 27th, 2002

The Independent

March 4th, 2008

The Inquiries Act

Cap. 41 of the Laws of Zambia

The New York Times

"Frederick Chiluba" (August 17th, 2009)

The Post	"ZAMTEL Should Have Been Sold To Zambians," (June 29th, 2010)
The Theodora.com	"Countries of the World: Zambia Economy 2010," (January 15th, 2010)
The Washington Post	November 1st, 2001
The World Bank	"Country Classifications," (August 22nd, 2010)
The World Bank	"Private Sector," (2010)
Time Asia	May 30th, 2000
Times	February 17th, 2008
Times of Zambia	"Ignore Lies – Kaunda," (Monday, November 18th, 1985)
Times of Zambia	"Country's Done Well – IMF," (March 12th, 2010)
Timothy, Holmes	*Dawn is Coming: The History of a Family Told from Information Collected* (Lusaka: Bookworld, 1997)
Tordoff, William, (ed.)	*Administration in Zambia* (Berkeley, University of California Press, 1979)
Tordoff, William, (ed.)	*Politics in Zambia* (Manchester, Manchester University Press, 1980)
Tourism Council of Zambia	*Destination Zambia 2007-8* (Lusaka: Tourism Council of Zambia, 2007)
Touwen, Anne	*Gender and Development in Zambia: Empowerment of Women through Local Non-Governmental Organizations* (Delft, Netherlands: Eburon Publishers, 1996)

Transparent International	Corruption Perception Index of June 30th, 2009
Turner, K	*Technical Report: Legal Constraints on Small-Scale Industrial Development and Proposals for Reform* (Vienna: Government of Zambia and UNIDO, 1987)
Turok, Ben	*Mixed Economy in Focus: Zambia* (London: Institute for African Alternatives, 1989)
Turok, Ben	"Zambia's System of State Capitalism," (1980) *Development and Change,* Vol. 11, pp. 455-478
Turok, Ben, (ed.)	*Development in Zambia: A Reader* (London: Zed Press, 1981)
Udombana, Nsongurua I.	"Interpreting Rights Globally: Courts and Constitutional Rights in Emerging Democracies," (2005) *African Human Rights Law Journal,* Vol. 5, No. 47, pp. 48-69
UN	The Universal Declaration of Human Rights (1948)
UNDP	*2007 Zambia Human Development Report -Enhancing Household Capacity to Respond to HIV and AIDS* (Lusaka: UNDP, 2007)
UNDP	*Economic Policies for Growth, Employment and Poverty Reduction – Case Study of Zambia* (Lusaka: UNDP, 2007)
UNDP	*Making it Possible-How the UN is Helping Zambia towards the*

	Millennium Development Goals (Lusaka: UNDP, 2005)
UNDP	*Millennium Development Goals-Progress Report 2003* (Lusaka: UNDP, 2003)
UNDP	*Millennium Development Goals-Progress Report 2005* (Lusaka: UNDP, 2005)
UNDP	*Millennium Development Goals-Progress Report 2008* (Lusaka: UNDP, 2008)
UNDP	*Zambia: Debt Strategies to Meet the Millennium Development Goals* (Lusaka: UNDP, 2007)
UNDP	*Zambia Human Development Report 2003* (Lusaka: UNDP, 2003)
UNICEF	"Introduction to the Convention on the Rights of the Child - Definition of Key Terms," (June 26th, 2010)
United Nations	*Human Rights: A Compilation of International Instruments* (Geneva: United Nations E. 78. VIV. 2, 1978)
United Nations	"The Domestic Application of the Covenant," December 3rd, 1998
United Nations Conference on Trade and Development	*Investment Policy Review: Zambia* (New York: United Nations, 2006)
United Nations Offices on Drugs and Crime (UNODC)	"Anti-Corruption Strategies: Comparative Cases from

415

	Indonesia, Pakistan and Zambia," (Vienna, 2010)
University of Zambia, School of Law	*Zambia Law Journal* (Lusaka, Zambia: University of Zambia, 1970s series)
Van-Donge, Jan Kees	"Reflections on Donors, Opposition Parties and Political Will in the 1996 Zambian General Elections," (1998) *Journal of Modern African Studies* 38, 1: 71–99
Van-Donge, Jan Kees	"The Plundering of Zambian Resources by Frederick Chiluba and His Friends: A Case Study of the Interaction between National Politics and the International Drive towards Good Governance," (2008) *African Affairs*, 108/430
Van-Donge, Jan Kees	*Zambia* (Oxford: CLIO, 2000)
Van-Donge, J. & G. Harries-Jenkens, (eds.)	*The Military and the Problem of Legitimacy* (London and California: SAGE Publications, 1976)
Venter, Al J.	*Barrel of a Gun: A Correspondent's Misspent Moments in Combat* (Havertown, PA: Casemate Publishers, 2010)
Vine, W. E.	*Vine's Expository Dictionary of New Testament Words*, unabridged edition, (Iowa Falls: Riverside Book and Bible House)
Virmani, K. K.	*Zambia: The Dawn of Freedom* (Delhi: Kalinga Publications, 1989)

Vogel, Steven Kent

Freer Markets, More Rules: Regulatory Reform in Advanced Industrial Countries (New York: Cornwell University Press, 1998)

VonDoepp, Peter

"Political Transition and Civil Society: The Cases of Kenya and Zambia," (Spring 1996) *Studies in Comparative and International Development*, Vol. 31, No. 1: 25-47

Wa Thiong'o, Ngugi

"Europhone or African Memory: The Challenge of Pan-Africanist Intellectual in the Era of Globalization," in Thandika Mkandawire (ed.), *African Intellectual* (Dakar: Codesria, 2005)

Weekly Angel

"S.M. Chisembele: Death of a Hero," (March 13th – 19th, 2006)

Weeks, John

Kwacha Appreciation 2005-2006 – Implications for the Zambian Economy (Lusaka: UNDP, 2007)

Weeks, John

"The Reduction of Fiscal Space in Zambia – Dutch Disease and Tight-Money Conditionalities," International Poverty Center, Country Study, January 14th, 2008

Weir, Alison

Britain's Royal Families: The Complete Genealogy, Revised Edition (London: Pimlico, 1996/2002)

Welch, Jr., Claude E.

"Civilian Control of the Military: Myth and Reality," in Claude E. Welch, Jr. (ed.), *Civilian Control of the Military: Theory and Cases from Developing Countries*

Welch, C & R. Meltzer

Wele, Patrick Motondo

Welensky, Sir Roy

Westhead, Rick

Williams, Basil

Williams, Geoffrey

Wills, A. J.

Woldring, Klaas

Woldring, Klaas &
Chibwe Chibaye

Wood, Goldon

Woolmington v. DPP

(Albany: State University of New York Press, 1976)
Human Rights and Development in Africa (Albany: State University of New York Press, 1984)
Zambia's Most Famous Dissidents (Solwezi: PMW, 1995)
4000 Days (London: Collin, 1964)
"Fighting a Culture of Corruption," *Toronto Star*, (Tuesday, November 23rd, 2010)
Cecil Rhodes (New York: Henry Holt & Company, 1921)
Independent Zambia: A Bibliography of the Social Sciences, 1964-1979 (Boston, Mass.: G.K. Hall, 1984)
Introduction to the History of Central Africa: Zambia, Malawi and Zimbabwe, 4th Edn. (Oxford: Oxford University Press, 1985)
"Corruption and Inefficiency in Zambia: A Survey of Recent Inquiries," (1983) *Africa Today*, Vol. 30: 51-74

Beyond Political Independence: Zambia's Development Predicament in the 1980s (Berlin; New York: Mouton, 1984)
"Comments" in Amy Gutmann, (ed.), (1997) *A Matter of Interpretation*, 50, 51
[1935] AC 462

World Bank

Zambia: Public Expenditure Management and Financial Accountability Review (Washington, D.C.: World Bank, 2004)

Wright, Eriklin

Class, Crisis and the State (London, Verso, 1978)

Writes, Morgan

"How Welfare Began in the United States," (February 2nd, 2008)

Wrong, Michela

"A Crisis of Leadership: G8: Africa - Where Exactly is the Acclaimed 'New Breed' of Progressive African Politicians? Without it, Aid is like Petrol on a Fire," *New Statesman*, July 4th, 2005

Yamba, Dauti

Ificholeko ne Nyimbo (Ndola: African Literature Committee, 1947)

Yamba, Dauti

English-Bemba Phrase Book (London: Macmillan, 1948)

Yamba, Dauti

Inshila Ya Chupo (London: Macmillan, 1958)

Yapwantha, Edward Radford

The Constitution of the Republic of Zambia [microform]: Judicial Interpretation of Some Basic Fundamental Rights (Ottawa: National Library of Canada, 1981)

Yeko, Balamn

"Exile Politics and Resistance to Dictatorship: The Ugandan Anti-Amin Organizations in Zambia, 1972-79," (1996) *African Affairs*, 96: pp. 95-108

Yergin, Daniel and

Joseph Stanislaw's | *The Commanding Heights: The Battle for the World Economy* (New York: Simon & Schuster, 1998)

Yogis, John A.; Randall R. Duplak; & Royden Trainor | *Sexual Orientation and Canadian Law* (Emond Montgomery Publications Limited, 1996)

Yorkshire Post | "Ex-MP David Chaytor Pleads Guilty to Expenses Fraud," (December 3rd, 2010)

Young, Alistair | *Industrial Diversification in Zambia* (New York: Praeger, 1973)

Young, Robert | *Post-Colonialism: An Historical Introduction* (Oxford: Blackwell Publishers, 2001)

Yunus, Muhammad | *Creating a World without Poverty* (New York: PublicAffairs, 2007)

Zambia Development Agency | "Chinese Investments in Zambia," available online at http://www.zda.org.zm/246-chinese-investments-zambia (Retrieved: November 7th, 2010)

Zambia Development Agency Act | Laws of Zambia, No. 11 of 2006

Zambia Independence Act | Of 1964, ss. 2(1) and 4(1)

Zambia Information Services | *Mulungushi Conference: Proceedings of the Annual Conference of the United National Independence Party* held at Mulungushi, 14th-20th August, 1967

Zambia National Gazette   Gazette Notice Numbers 629 of
                              2004 and 640 of 2004
Zambia Weekly   "Agricultural Subsidies are
                              Increasing," Week 32, Vol. 1,
                              Issue 18, (August 13th, 2010)
Zambia Weekly   "China – According to China,"
                              Week 30, Vol.1, Issue 16, (July
                              30th, 2010)
Zambian Watchdog   "Global Fund Freezes Zambia
                              Aid Due to Corruption," (June
                              15th, 2010)
Zimba, Lawrence   "The Constitution of Zambia
                              (Amendment) Act, No. 18 of
                              1974," *Zambia Law Journal,* Vol.
                              10, pp. 86-89
Zukas, Simon   *Into Exile and Back* (Lusaka:
                              Bookworld, 1993)
Zulu, Alexander Grey   *Memoirs of Alexander Grey Zulu*
                              (Ndola: Times Printpak Zambia
                              Ltd., 2007)

INDEX

C

D

E

F

M

NOTES

www.ingramcontent.com/pod-product-compliance
Lightning Source LLC
Chambersburg PA
CBHW062150270326
41930CB00009B/1488